AFRICA TODAY

Edited by C. Grove Haines

BALTIMORE: THE JOHNS HOPKINS PRESS

Copyright 1955, The Johns Hopkins Press
Second printing, 1956

Distributed in Great Britain by
Geoffrey Cumberlege: Oxford University Press, London

Printed in U.S.A. by Reese Press,
Baltimore, Maryland

Library of Congress Catalog Card No. 55–6220

On the title page: dance headpiece from the French Sudan,
in the Wurtzburger Collection of African Sculpture,
Baltimore Museum of Art

foreword

There is in process a significant and hopeful awakening of American interest in Africa. Little more than a decade ago it had scarcely entered the stream of public consciousness; yet now, in the mid-nineteen-fifties, the discontents, the agitations, and the aspirations of native African peoples are frequently spread across the public press, and terms such as *Mau Mau* and *apartheid* are widely known even if not understood. This is, in a sense, a measure of growing public awareness both of the strategic importance of Africa to the security of the Western World and of the fundamental international obligations which the United States has come to assume.

The recent global war and the nature of international politics since its conclusion have been largely instrumental in developing a broad public interest in Africa. But, as always in such matters, higher education and scholarship have brought their influence to bear and continue to do so in ever-increasing measure. There has been in recent years a notable development of university teaching programs in the African field, a growing trend among graduate students to single out that field for their concentration, and a consequent increase in the product of scholarship relating to Africa. If this movement in intellectual circles is, like the popular awakening, at least partly in response to the political preoccupations of our time, it is also one which will develop its own momentum and, by its very nature, broaden and deepen the general understanding of Africa.

This volume is in itself evidence of the seriousness of current intellectual interest in Africa, for it grew out of the Conference on Contemporary Africa which The Johns Hopkins University School of Advanced International Studies sponsored in Washington, in August, 1954, as part of a special graduate summer program devoted exclusively to African affairs. The fact that more than four hundred individuals—academicians, business men, government specialists—were willing to brave the sweltering heat of Washington in August in order to attend and participate in this conference is eloquent testimony to the size and enthusiasm of the group of scholars and professional people in the United States who are focusing their attention upon Africa.

The subjects to which the Conference addressed itself were those represented in this book, but the book is in no sense a transcription of the Conference. It is composed of a series of essays written by the men and women of special knowledge and competence in their fields of activity who guided the discussions at the Conference.

The responsibility for organizing the Conference as well as for planning the book was mine, but I could have fulfilled neither of these without the generous and competent assistance of my friends and colleagues at the School. Above all, I wish to record my heavy debt of gratitude to Dr. Vernon McKay for his counsel, and to Miss Priscilla Mason, Administrative Assistant at the School, who managed the Conference, and quite literally guided this book through all the stages of its development from manuscript to printed page.

December 1954   *C. Grove Haines*
                                                          WASHINGTON, D. C.

contents

VIII

introduction

LORD HAILEY OF SHAHPUR, P.C., G.C.S.I.

It is perhaps unnecessary to enquire now into the reason for the great increase during recent years of the interest shown in Africa by the American public. I am in any case less concerned here with this general interest than with that more particular interest which has induced the members of discussion groups or of academic institutions to undertake specific studies on Africa's problems. In a modern democracy it is public opinion which ultimately controls policy, whether in external or internal affairs, but there is a wide gap between the expression given to public opinion and the definite formulation of policy. The processes by which policy is actually formulated are often obscure; but there is one point on which all students of politics are agreed—the debates of study groups or the discussions organized by academic thinkers have a definite function in assisting to canalize the issues which will eventually emerge as a determination of national policy. It is this fact which adds significance to the extension of the system of Area Studies and to the organization of group discussions in which the American universities have lately taken so prominent a part, often with the assistance of one or other of the great foundations in the United States.

In addressing the Conference last August, Dr. de Kiewiet observed that there were some African questions in which the interest of Americans greatly exceeded their knowledge. That might be said with equal truth of most of the countries of Western Europe. But for some years American interest in Africa has been distinguished by one feature in particular which is not always so prominent in European countries. The more dynamic quality of American interest seems to have had its roots in the deep seated feeling of Americans that it is their duty to give support to those African communities who are seeking to achieve political independence. I am not quarrelling with the instinct which has inspired that feeling. I could, it is true, wish that the school of thought which draws its inspiration largely from its dislike of "colonialism" could find a more appropriate term to express its antipathy to the manifestation of an undesirable attitude toward weaker peoples, or it may be toward minorities. It is, of course, obvious that such an attitude is not by any means confined to the nations which hold colonies. But that is after all only a subsidiary point. At the moment, the most essential point is to convey to those interested in this movement some understanding of the implications of African nationalism, as shown in the campaign for self-rule now being conducted by a number of more progressive Africans.

That these constitute at present a minority section in their own countries is obvious, but that is not an abnormal feature in similar conditions, and it is not in any sense a decisive consideration. The essential fact is that the movement for self-rule has for its object more than the attainment of an independent political status. The objective is to achieve at the same time some parity with the peoples of the more fully developed countries. The leaders in the movement are modernists, and they take their stand as such among a population whose lives have in the past been ruled to a unique degree by tradition. Not for nothing do the anthropologists remind us that for the great mass of Africans the spirits of the past still fulfill as active a part in their daily lives as do the living folk around them. That the modernist urge has led many African leaders to discard some of the most typical institutions of traditional origin, such as the chiefdom or the rule of tribal elders, is today a matter of no great importance; even where these institutions had been employed as part of the machinery of rule, as in the British territories, they are already being replaced in the natural order of things by newer organs of local government. Nor will any great difficulty be caused by the expansion of a regime of cash economy among people who have till recently lived in a regime of barter; even the more primitive of African communities have now adjusted themselves to a change in this direction.

The real difficulty for the new leaders lies elsewhere. It lies in conveying the lessons of political responsibility and social order to people whose rule of conduct has hitherto been determined solely by the ties of personal relationships. It lies again in finding the incentives which will create a competent body of labor out of a people whose lives have hitherto been geared to the simple demands of a subsistence economy. It lies in raising the standard of health in large areas where an exceptional poverty of soil has provided only an inadequate and unbalanced diet. It lies in bringing into the world of technology a population which cannot at present furnish even the operatives, to say nothing of the higher agencies which technology demands. It lies in so conducting the administrative and political life of the country that foreign investors can feel secure in risking the capital required for its development.

These are problems which arise in the main from the constitution of African society. But there is another range of problems which have their origin not so much in the constitution of African society as in the consequences flowing from the relation of various African countries with the European powers which have controlled them. Throughout the course of history, the control exercised over a relatively undeveloped country by one more fully organized has invariably left its imprint on the political institutions of the subject people. To what pattern of rule therefore will the new self-governing countries of Africa seek to conform? Will the French dependencies, where the leading men have shown themselves to be deeply attracted by French culture, seek to mould their political institutions in conformity with those of the *Union Française?* Will the British dependencies seek to reproduce the characteristic pattern of parliamentary rule and of British local government institutions, with their roots deep in Britain's past? Will the political institutions of independent Africa, in short, follow the diverse patterns of those of the European colonial powers, or will its leaders seek to evolve patterns of their own which will reflect the social structure of the African peoples and their characteristic outlook on life?

We are here in a region of speculation, attractive enough in itself, though debate on its problems must necessarily be of a somewhat academic character. But Africa's connection with Europe has left another range of problems which are of more practical urgency; it is indeed these problems which stand right in the forefront of our thinking about Africa today. It is not to be assumed that an independent Africa would comprise only countries in which Africans would exercise unchallenged control of the whole field of politics and administration, and would therefore be at liberty to mould their institutions into the form felt to be best suited to African conditions or the African outlook on life. Far from it. The Union of South Africa stands in a special category, not only because it is already a sovereign country, free of any external control, but because of the complete authority exercised by the European community over its political and economic life. It is to be hoped that the non-Europeans in the Union, so largely predominant in numbers, may in time succeed in gaining an adequate share of political liberties, but it would be unrealistic to assume that they will in any foreseeable future gain political control of the government of the country. Though Algeria, at the other end of Africa, differs from the Union in so far that it is not a sovereign state, there is equal difficulty in assuming that the African community, greatly predominant in numbers though it may be, is likely to gain complete political control of the country, unless indeed some upheaval occurs which will radically alter the present position.

Lying between these two countries there are others, such as the Rhodesias, Kenya, or the Belgian Congo (the list is not of course exhaustive) where a settled European community claims the right to protect itself from being politically submerged by the predominant African population. Time or the influence of international opinion may bring changes in the philosophy of the European nations which now exercise control of these countries, and may modify their desire or their ability to assist the local European communities to maintain their position. But there is in every case the likelihood, and in some cases the certainty, that whatever the attitude of the metropolitan power in regard to the extension of self-rule to its dependencies, the local European population would be prepared to go to great lengths to retain an effective share in the government of the country. It is also obvious that the political submergence of the European community might, if it seriously prejudiced its economic activity, affect very gravely the life of the country as a whole.

These are facts which have to be faced, putting aside for the moment any question of the moral considerations involved. That some aspects of the past history of the European connection with Africa make such considerations relevant is unquestionable. But the present conflict of interest between Europeans and Africans in the countries referred to will be decided by the balance of the forces deployed, and moral issues will only carry weight insofar as they are permitted to affect the balance on one side or the other. There is a real danger that this conflict of interest may result in creating all the acerbity of communal alienation. On the one side, there will be the upsurge of African nationalism; on the other, the strong reaction of Europeans against the potential menace to their material and social life. The ideal solution might be for the existing colonial powers to retain so much of their authority as would permit them to adjust the shares to be taken in the government by the communities concerned, as judged by the position which they may from time to time occupy in the life of the country. But the difficulty of securing acquiescence in an arbitrament of this kind is obvious. Nor can one imagine that any other form of "third-party" judgment in such a matter would prove effective; there are some sections of opinion in Africa which (as we already know) will show no respect for the judgment of any Court that is not empowered to enforce its decisions.

Our hopes must accordingly rest on the development of a spirit of accommodation between the communities; each has a contribution to make, and in the long run they must decide between themselves how far this shall be reflected in the part to be taken by each in the government of the country. But it is not possible to foresee now how far our hopes of this development are likely to be realized. The settlement of such an issue can never be easy even between communities which are by nature homogeneous; it will be doubly difficult in view of the background against which settlement has to be secured in Africa. I have intentionally spoken here of some measure of accommodation regarding the respective shares to be taken in the government of the country. I hesitate to join with those who now look forward to a phase of what is described as "integration." That seems to have implications in the social sphere which it would be premature to discuss. We shall have moved a stage forward if we can secure in Africa the political decencies of "coexistence."

At the moment the political barometer marks singular territorial variations in the atmosphere of accommodation between the communities. The government of the Union of South Africa is persistent in its attachment to the faith that it is possible to sustain two entirely separate types of civilization in the same state, with the corollary that the superior of the two must remain in political control of the whole. That negates the conception of accommodation. We cannot now foresee the sequel; but we might come nearer to doing so if we knew the answer to the question whether it is really possible for a modern industrial state to maintain a rigid line of political and social demarcation between communities whose work is jointly essential to its economic survival. There is a stronger ray of hope to be seen in the emergence of the doctrine of "partnership" in the Rhodesias. If the formula itself is, as has been suggested, too abstruse to commend itself to Africans, success will after all depend not on the shape of the doctrine but on the temper in which it is interpreted.

It is at this point that our vision begins to reach beyond the limits of Africa. The success of the effort to find some means of accommodation between the claims of the communities has an interest which is not confined to its results in the areas immediately concerned. It is one more item in the great problem which our generation has set itself to solve, the problem of building one world out of the many separate worlds our fathers knew, differing so widely in civilization and in culture, in standards of living and in political status.

one   **THE POSITION OF AFRICA
IN WORLD AFFAIRS**

Africa and the West
in historical perspective

SIR PHILIP MITCHELL, G.C.M.G., M.C.

Former Governor of Kenya

"Africa and the West in Historical Perspective" is a wide enough subject, in all conscience, for me to discuss, even if, for our purpose here, I exclude Mediterranean Africa. The forty-two years I have spent in Africa—forty of them in public service—cover a large part of the history of sub-Saharan Africa, for it can hardly be said to extend much further back than about 1870. However, a knowledge of Mediterranean Africa—Egypt, the Islamic Sudan, Libya, Tunisia, Algeria, and Morocco—is essential in any study of Africa south of the Sahara, for it includes the colonizations of Phoenicians, Greeks, and Romans, very early examples of the influence—strategic and mercantile—of sea transport, the institution of slavery in relatively settled conditions, the Roman conception of law as applied to conquests and colonies, and both the Greek and the Roman practice of colonial government. It includes, too, much of early Christian history and the rise of Islam and its great dynamic invasion of the West and so, the earliest contacts and conflicts between the two religions which seem destined to have the field to themselves in Africa, unless of course it is to be engulfed by the wave of materialistic pagan nationalism which is affecting so much of the contemporary world.

There are, too, some modern points of contact between Mediterranean and sub-Saharan Africa, divided as they are by the deserts of sand. The Nile flows from the heart of Central Africa to create

3

one of the important political and economic problems of our day; in northern Nigeria, the Emirates are an outpost of Islam south of the Sahara, and they are apt to talk in Nigerian controversies about "resuming their interrupted march to the coast"; Cairo is a great center of modern air transport, and that has strongly reinforced its contacts, dating from the days when the Caliphs ruled there, with Arab settlements all down the east coast.

Nevertheless, in a broad, general way, it is true to say that Mediterranean Africa has counted for little in the history of the rest of Africa, and for still less in the historical processes which have created contemporary continental Africa and the spiritual, social, economic, cultural, political, and strategic problems which it is our purpose to study. But it is a curious little coincidence of history that a series of events, which led directly to the development of the relations of the West with Africa, should also have been part of the final expulsion of Mediterranean Africa from Europe. It was to the camp of Ferdinand and Isabella, in the Vega of Granada, where they were conducting its final siege, which led to the expulsion of Boabdil II and the end of the Moorish kingdoms in Spain, that Christopher Columbus repaired to solicit support for the voyage which led to his tremendous discovery that the west coast of Portugal was not the end of the known world; that there was land across the limitless ocean—a land destined to become the massive bastion of the Christian civilization of the West and the leader in its vast developments of science, technology, invention, and industrial production; a land, too, which imported in its early days great numbers of Africans as slaves and, with them, an intimate share of the vast complex of problems which confront that remarkable people today.

Columbus had, of course, no thought of Africa: his course lay westwards. But he was one of that astonishing band of sailors, mainly Portuguese, who, inspired and directed by Prince Henry the Navigator, began, towards the end of the fifteenth century, the quest for some way to India, the Spice Islands, and the China Seas; to the immense riches which Europe had been able to reach only by the costly and hazardous caravan routes of Arabia and Central Asia.

One way to those riches was thought to be down the west coast of Africa, and many intrepid men set out in the little ships of the day to explore it, notably Bartolomeu Dias and Vasco da Gama, who at last succeeded and in 1488 and 1497 rounded the Cape of Good Hope. Da Gama sailed on up the east coast to Sofala, Kilwa, Zanzibar, Mombasa, and Malindi, to find that the voyage to the Indies was a common-place to the sailors of those parts; to find that he could even get pilots to take his ships there. He was followed by many others, of other nations, in spite of the trade and navigation monopoly of Portugal.

The West African coast was a part of the west coast of the known world when the first Portuguese seamen started to feel their way along it. Bartolomeu Dias had no reason to suppose that either land or trade were to be found upon his starboard hand; and what he and his successors saw of the African coast raised, in their minds, no desire to know more. Their wish was only to get to the end of the seemingly endless land to port, to put their ships about and have the sun rise on their starboard side.

But the east coast, north of about the latitude of Lourenço Marques, was the western limit of a region of ancient trade and navigation, made possible by the monsoon winds, the venturesome spirit of seamen from Oman, the Gulf States, and the northwest coast of India, and the skill of the men who built the dhows. Along that coast the Arabs, mainly from Oman, had built important towns at the main ship anchorages — Sofala, Kilwa, Zanzibar, Mombasa, and Malindi, the chief of them—where the surprised Portuguese found people living much as they lived in Marrakesh, Dar el Baida, Algiers, and Tunis. As far as Natal, Vasco da Gama was an explorer; thereafter, hundreds of dhow captains could show him the way as far into the Indian seas as he might be willing to go — if they would. He did get pilots from Malindi, but with difficulty, for commercial rivalry in those days was apt to be aggressive. The Arabs and others in the region had no wish to see the ships of the West cutting into their trade. The attempt to trade, indeed, led to a war of conquest, in which the Portuguese at first carried the day but were later driven out of all their strongholds north of the Zambesi.

The Arab power was, when first it met the West, in the form of a succession of cities or settlements, each more or less independent, but all owing a loose allegiance to the ruler of Oman who had his capital at Muscat. In the early part of the nineteenth century,

Seyyid Said (1806–56) gradually extended his authority over the coast and, after experimenting with Zanzibar as a place of residence, moved his capital to it in 1832. He then began the extension of his claims to dominion on the mainland which led, among other important consequences, not only to the spread and intensification of the slave-trade but to the responsibility for it falling inevitably, in the eyes of the world, upon him and his successors.

In a sense the principality of Zanzibar, together with its dependent cities and settlements, can be said to be the northeastern limit of the Africa we are discussing or the southwestern boundary of Arabia. It had been trading with the East, and settled from it, certainly since before the Christian era. From the seventh century B.C. there seems to have been a close connection with southern Arabia. One of the islands is described in the Periplus, in the first century, under the name of Menuthias. Traces of Greek colonization are said to have been found.

It was, then, part of a region of the world in which merchants had traded and voyaged since the dawn of history. The economic foundation of its society was slavery. It is a reasonable deduction—but not, I think, a historically known fact—that slaves from Africa were an important part of its commerce from the earliest days.

During the long years that followed the first Portuguese voyages, until the opening of the Suez Canal in 1869 provided an alternative route, the trade to the East by the route around Africa expanded to a remarkable extent and attracted all the seafaring nations of the West. As ship-design and knowledge of the ocean winds improved, and ships became able to keep the sea for longer periods, the anchorages on the west coast of Africa declined at first in importance; and such interest as there was on the part of the West in Africa declined too, until the trade in men and women revived it. But Africa retained for the great Eastern trade its first character as no more than an obstacle—an inconveniently large obstacle—which sailors had, with great labor, to get around on their way to the Indies. What little they saw of its climate gave them no encouragement to linger. Its population was dense, ferocious, and reputed to be cannibal, and if settlements were attempted at all, they were usually in the form of forts and castles where ships could be repaired, fresh food obtained, and sick mariners given a chance of rest and recovery. That was all that interested the great East Indies galleons.

But when the Dutch, in their turn and on the same quest for the trade of the East, established their victualing and ship-repair station on the shores of Table Bay in 1652, they made another dis-covery — that the malaria-ridden land had become healthy in that latitude, had a climate indeed as good as the best of Europe and a soil of exceptional fertility. It was to be two centuries before they found out, as a consequence of the great trek, the extent of the agricultural and mineral riches of the healthy districts. But when Simon van der Stel established his settlement, he established all unknowingly a colony of white people, not differing in principle from the colonies of the New World. In the temper of the day, colonization—be it in America or Africa—was held to include the undoubted right to take possession of the land by force and to expel, enslave, or exterminate any previous occupiers who resisted. No one then paused to consider what the consequences might be if the previous occupants remained and did not continue to resist.

In 1814, the Cape Colony was ceded by treaty to Britain, and, about the same time, the Abolition movement began to gain increased influence and authority. In Africa, it set off a decisive series of events.

The Dutch settlers at the Cape, especially the hardy frontiers-men, had, no doubt, little liking for their new English masters in any case. When these began to enforce the English law against those who broke it at the expense of kaffirs, and Dr. Philip and the other great missionaries of the day made it quite clear that they would not be content until they had forced the government to abolish slavery, abolition became a present reality. So the frontiers-men pulled up their roots and trekked off in their tented wagons to the north, where they expected good hunting and freedom from all governments. But what they found were the Griquas, the Zulus, Basutos, and Swazis, fierce and brave men ready to do battle, not hopelessly at a disadvantage in weapons against men armed with muzzle-loaders, and incomparably more numerous.

At first it seemed as if the issue might have been left to be decided by the musket and the assagai, as in the New World. It was by no means certain that the Trek Boers would be the victors, for, how-ever simple the life they led, they must have money with which to replace worn-out firearms and to buy ammunition or the materials to make it for themselves. But as the elephants and other game animals were shot out in the accessible places, to earn the indispensable, if small, sums they needed became ever more difficult.

Then came another dramatic, indeed decisive event. In 1877 diamonds were discovered in Kimberley and its neighborhood in quantities exceeding the dreams of avarice, and a few years later, in 1884, the great gold fields of the Rand. The possibility that the settlements in the interior might collapse from economic weakness was removed forever, and immigration from Europe and America soon established a population which was able to pacify the country and lay the foundations of a modern state. That state has become, since those days, sadly divided against itself, but I must leave it to others to tell that tangled story.

When, later, indentured labor was brought to Natal from India for the sugar plantations, a third party was added to the problem. Indeed, not content with that, a determined effort was made by the mining interest to add indentured Chinese labor to the witch's cauldron that was being mixed in Africa. It was frustrated by an organized campaign of considerable virulence, in which the issues were described as "Chinese slavery."

When, early in the nineteenth century, the awakening humanitarian conscience of the West came to see that the slave-trade was a vile and intolerable thing, and slavery itself incompatible with contemporary society, the problem was essentially different on the west coast from the east. In the West, slavery was, it is true, an economic factor of importance to the sugar colonies and the United States of America and to Brazil, which absorbed large numbers of slaves from Angola; but it was a relatively new thing, and it existed within the jurisdiction of governments whose outraged people became determined that it must cease. The sea-borne traffic, the worst part of the abomination, could be suppressed, and was, by naval action from reasonably accessible bases. When the time came to abolish slavery itself, although the price included the agony of the Civil War in America, and the temporary ruin of some of the colonies, it could be done by act of Congress or Parliament.

But in the East the matter was very different. With a willing and collaborating reception in Arabia and the Gulf, Arab settlements all along the coast and, at some places, in the interior, determined to continue the slave-trade; and at some points where there were very short sea passages, naval squadrons (even when steam had succeeded sail) were not by themselves sufficient to suppress it. Only the destruction of the trade at its sources, by then on the Great Lakes of Africa, would really be effective. That was the reason for the first ventures to the interior by governments, after Livingstone and the other early explorers had forced upon the notice of the West the full horrors and miseries endured by the suffering people of those regions.

But those explorations and ventures led to two decisive things: first, the realization by the West that, with local exceptions, the indigenous peoples, from the Atlantic to the Indian Ocean, were at that time to an extraordinary extent outside the broad stream of human knowledge and achievement; and secondly, the expectation of valuable trade and substantial profits, provided, however, that stable and humane governments were established, a task which had defeated the peoples of the region almost completely, with the doubtful exceptions of Ashanti, Benin, Buganda, and a few other principalities, almost all of them under the capricious tyrannies of rulers as ignorant as their people.

At that time, Great Britain, then unquestionably the most powerful nation in the world, was strongly opposed as a matter of official policy to any colonial adventures or increases in territory. When reluctant ministers found themselves obliged to ask Parliament for funds for the military operations in which the government was continuously being involved by their adventurous fellow-countrymen or the militant abolitionists, they usually had a rough passage. Nevertheless, leaving out of account India (where only a transfer of responsibility from one form of British government to another was involved), vast territories did in fact come under British control in that period, including the whole of the dependencies in Africa. The abolitionist crusade and considersations of naval strategy were the two most powerful causes. Commercial considerations had little appeal for governments and parliaments then strongly under the influence of the Manchester School of Free Trade, although ship-owners and manufacturers often encouraged and financed colonial adventures.

France had embarked on a new policy of colonial expansion after the Napoleonic Wars: a policy conceived in its beginnings as a

Latin recolonization of the Mediterranean littoral, but which later expanded further into Africa and to Madagascar and elsewhere, and had for one of its motives the acquisition of closed markets.

Toward the end of the century, the new Germany of Bismarck's making began, hesitatingly at first, to seek trade outlets in Africa, in the Pacific, and elsewhere, influenced no doubt by the need for markets but also by the realization that its new navy would need a network of coaling stations.

The Portuguese, who probably understood what was developing better than anyone else, became alarmed for their own very extensive possessions in Africa.

As the fantastic wealth of the mineral discoveries in the South began to have its effects, they aroused great expectations; expectations which led Cecil Rhodes to despatch his Pioneer Column and to annex, for the chartered company that was soon formed, vast, very sparsely populated stretches of forest and bush between the Limpopo and the southern limits of German claims—stretches of bush which have in latter years been found to contain great quantities of valuable minerals; expectations which led King Leopold of Belgium and a group of friends to form a company and acquire the immense territory of the Congo, also found later to possess mineral wealth of many kinds and to an unknown extent. At the end of last century, indeed, it was an almost casual business to acquire by private enterprise a Central African possession as large as many of the larger countries of Europe.

It is a measure of the unwillingness of governments to become embroiled in these adventures that so many of them did take the form of private, largely mercantile, enterprises to develop later into chartered companies, the first of which was the Sierra Leone Company of 1800, created to manage a settlement for the 14,000 slaves set free in England. It is proof of the weakness and confusion in Africa that the internal obstacles were almost entirely the mosquito and the tsetse fly, the lack of communications, the vast distances, and the hazards of flood or drought rather than any desire or capacity to oppose or resist these ventures on the part of the people. There were exceptions involving military operations, as for example in Ashanti, Benin, Matabeleland, and a few other places, but they really only serve to highlight the extraordinary story.

Allowance must be made for the fact that, over the greater part of the area, the first occupations came in the form of delivery from the horrors and miseries of the slave-trade and brought also the means of alleviating or checking famine and epidemics, especially smallpox and sleeping sickness, which even in my young days used to rage through densely populated areas like bush fires and were indeed only arrested by the vast empty stretches of country their virulence created. In three or four years at the beginning of this century sleeping sickness killed 100,000 people in Uganda.

But making all allowances, it was an extraordinary business. Here are two small personal examples of it near its end. In mid-1917, I arrived at a remote, unadministered part of the southeast of German East Africa (now Tanganyika), seconded from my regiment with orders to set up at least a rudimentary civil authority. I had my servants, an African sergeant, porters for my goods, and some twenty police uniforms and rifles and a little ammunition for them. Arrived at the chosen place — a mission station, in itself typical of the sequence so frequent in those days—I summoned the local chiefs, explained that I was the government and would they please provide me with twenty young men to be policemen? Would they also please note that from now on people must not kill their wives or children whose teeth appeared in the ill-omened order; nor must chiefs make war on their neighbors without consulting me. In fact, a whole lot of customary and often agreeable things must be given up. They were courteous and affable, provided my police recruits, and assured me that they understood all I had said and would obey the new laws. No doubt they did nothing of the sort; but why did they not just knock me on the head, help themselves to the rifles, and have nothing to do with this self-appointed government?

On the second occasion, in 1920, when taking over territory in the far west of Tanganyika that the Belgians had evacuated, I found that general disorder had started. I had as my army half a dozen African police constables, and I must have been 200 miles from the nearest government post in any direction. But the news of my presence spread by the bush telegraph, and in a week or two inter-tribe and-village fights had ceased, and I was received everywhere rather like the successful candidate touring the constituency after winning the election, although I and my party were completely at the mercy of the people, who shot or speared each other without compunction, but who regarded us as ineligible for such treatment.

And so, at the end of the last century, within the vast region enclosed by the coast of Africa, with its widely spaced forts, towns, and settlements of people from other countries, bounded on the north by the Nigerian Emirates, the Sahara, the Nile Sudd, and the Abyssinian massif, the West found itself in control of millions of people who had never invented or adopted an alphabet or even any form of hieroglyphic writing. They had no numerals, no almanac or calendar, no notation of time or measurements of length, capacity, or weight, no currency, no external trade except slaves and ivory (and on the west coast palm oil and mahogany, made accessible by the navigable rivers), no plough, no wheel, and no means of transportation except human head porterage on land and dugout canoes on rivers and lakes. These people had built nothing, nothing of any kind, in any material more durable than mud, poles, and thatch. The spade of the archaeologist might unearth the skeleton of primitive man a million years old, or stone implements alleged to date from 30,000 years back, but after that—nothing: nothing at all before the rubbish dumps of modern colonial towns. With a few notable exceptions, there were no units of government throughout the area larger than the tribe, and the tribe might amount only to a few thousand people and have half-a-dozen contending chiefs. Except in the west-coast region there were no towns, and even villages usually consisted of a very few families. There was no common language, although on the west coast there were languages spoken by some millions of people and in the East and center the slave-traders were spreading Swahili. Great numbers wore no clothes at all; others wore bark cloth or hides and skins; woven textiles were known in the accessible places, but the accessible places were not many. Their languages were unwritten, but in the case of the great Bantu group—the only one I know—when reduced to writing by the early missionaries, were found to have a systematic and well-developed grammar and to be adequate for the expression of a surprisingly wide range of thought. Even so, it came as a shock to me as a young man—a young man who spoke French and Spanish as fluently as English—to find myself learning a language that had no words for a whole range of familiar things: "fork," for example, or "tin," or "bottle," or "pound," or "yard," or "pint." "Half-past two on Friday, 25th January, 1914" or its equivalent could not be said at all in Chinyanya, Yao, and the many hundreds of other dialects. Nobody had ever had to say things like that, and there were just no words for them. And yet, the languages were very far from being any sort of "pidgin," and men of standing took a pride in speaking them correctly.

I could extend the catalogue of these surprising things almost indefinitely; but I hope I have said enough to give an idea of the point from which the modern contacts of the West with Africa started, after the historical events I have tried to summarize intelligibly had reached the climax which led to the colonial occupation of Africa. The "occupation," not the colonization, for that was only attempted in South Africa, in Southern Rhodesia, and in Angola, with a small and very limited outpost in Kenya. It has nowhere been wholly achieved, in the sense that America, North and South, Australia, and New Zealand have been colonized and have in the process created reasonably homogeneous nations.

In Africa, everywhere where colonization has been attempted, there have been the native African people, in proportions to the colonists varying from three to one, to hundreds to one. The African people and the colonists have not yet reached a durable accommodation between them, such as must be found if stable civilized states are to result from their association. But they have only been consciously trying to find it for a generation or less, and if such an accommodation is the hard core of the problems of the Africa of today, it is far too early to start talking about failure.

The occupations, and the whole process of the creation — for that I believe to be the proper word—of the Africa we are discussing may be said, with little exaggeration, to have taken place in my lifetime; and I hope I may not appear to be a very ancient man! In many respects, both occupation and development in West Africa preceded East and Central Africa, and much of the west coast had an altogther more advanced society and economy; some reservations have to be made on that account.

In the process of occupation and development, two vastly important new forces made their first appearance in the continent: one material, and the other spiritual. Mechanical transportation appeared in the form of railways and steamers at first, followed during the war of 1914–18 by the internal combustion engine, driving automobiles and trucks, and, a few years later, the aeroplane, and the Bible.

The latter I believe to have been the decisive force in the whole business and I shall return to it. The former, in a few years, transformed life and production in Africa.   Millions of men whose young eyes had never seen a wheel — even a small cart wheel — whose childish ills were treated with magic spells and incantations, have lived to ride in trains, trucks, and aircraft, to be treated in modern hospitals with the latest discoveries of twentieth century medical science. Millions who had never even imagined writing and figuring have lived to see their children graduate in teaching, medicine, engineering, law, and so on.   I know a man whose father roamed the Masai plains dressed only in a cow skin, whose mother came from the forests of Mt. Kenya totally illiterate, who has performed difficult surgical operations in a leading London hospital to the admiration of the most distinguished surgeons.   He is, in himself, the epitome of this extraordinary change.

For extraordinary it was and is, by any standards. That there should have existed for so long, so vast an expanse of Africa in which the people remained, down to my lifetime, down to today in the case of great numbers, so totally ignorant, so isolated from the broad rivers of human knowledge and achievement, is astonishing. That the Amharic alphabet should have been halted abruptly along the hills overlooking Lake Rudolph and the northern frontier province of Kenya, the Arabic at the south and west borders of the Nigerian Emirates and the town ramparts of Mombasa, Malindi, and Kilwa, is hardly credible. But both are fact.

I recall a vivid picture of a day in 1951 when I was driving in the outskirts of Malindi, in sight of its solid double-storied masonry Arab houses, among carefully tended coconut and orange groves, when a string of Giriama women came walking gracefully in to the road from a little side path, naked to the waist, clad waist to knee in kilts made of palm leaves, barefoot and balancing on their heads, heavy loads of produce for the market. Even so, their forebears, perhaps for nine or ten centuries, must have walked in to the Arab towns from Guardafui to Sofala; and here they were, in 1951, totally unchanged, uninterested and unconcerned, as my saloon car and traders' trucks and carts stirred up the dust beside them. They were by that date, it is true, survivals; but there they were, walking along in the twentieth century straight out of the tenth.

What magic was it, then, that suddenly, in a few years, roused so many of these placid, incurious people to the restless energy and ambitions of today? What spell stimulated their curiosity and aroused their enthusiasm? What caused people who could not— or would not—learn to read and write in the interval from their creation down to 1890 to crowd into schools and colleges, so that thousands have graduated in many professions, hundreds of thousands have reached high school, and millions junior school?

Millions still remain untaught, it is true. Many are still apathetic, many more, eager but unable to get a place in school. There are 100 millions or more in the continent, south of the sand, and even if schools could be built, teachers just cannot be trained at a rate that would keep pace with demand; and the cost is an immense obstacle, when the general level of wealth — or rather poverty—is still what it is.

Was it just desire for material things?   For money, clothes, blankets, bicycles, for sugar, tea, coffee, cigarettes, gramophones? In part, maybe; but goods, if not quite so many or varied, must have been available to them at points of contact with the outside world on both coasts for centuries. Was it the excitement of new things? Manufactured new things which the Arabs and the Portuguese brought have caused no such awakening before. Then what was it?

Well, I believe that, fundamentally, it was the Bible, the Bible and the brave, determined, merciful men and women who carried it and its message of hope—hope of the end of the slave-trade, of prevention of epidemics and relief of famine, of protection from the savage whims of tyrants or the obscene orgies of sorcerers—to a people who were living in a brutish lethargy induced by continuous danger, horrors, and sufferings. Maybe a generation has grown up which has forgotten these things, both in Africa and Europe, but I served in Africa forty-two years ago when they were still very recent, still actively operative in many places, still decisive of the attitudes of the mass of the people toward me and my fellows as agents of a power that had come to deliver them from the terrors and miseries of their lives, from the great man-hunt which was life in Central Africa. My eyes have seen it and my ears heard, and I take leave to say that it is not necessary to seek further for the prime mover.

No doubt the tribespeople oversimplified the matter, and so did we. Anyone who has been hurt severely knows that the mere cessation of pain is in itself a release, but can be far short of the end of trouble.

From this developed the eager acceptance of the West and of the Christian faith, the willingness to adapt life to the new ways, the wondering beginnings of education, of learning to read and write and do simple sums. Later came an awakening to the fact that the West was not all benevolence and friendliness, Christian kindness and disinterestedness; that there were harshnesses and compulsions, cruelties, and injustices. But they were mild things compared with the very recent past, when few men and women could roll themselves in their sleeping hides or mats in their smoky huts at night with any certainty that tribal enemies, slave-raiders, maurauding elephants or lurking lions or leopards would not strike them down in the night, that sorcerers or evil spirits would not slip through between the eaves and the walls in the dangerous darkness and destroy them by magic, that smallpox or sleeping sickness would not break out among them, or drought, locusts, or flood wipe out the crops so that famine, which could not be relieved, would destroy maybe half a tribe.

So the stage was set for the great awakening, which continues to this day—an awakening which has brought with it the vast range of problems which confronts us in contemporary Africa, problems which are to be discussed by many distinguished experts.

Two world wars and the continuously increasing speed and range of communications, mineral discoveries, and rising prices for nearly all that Africa produces have combined to stimulate and accelerate the speed of the immense developments which have followed the missionary and exploring journeys of Livingstone, Speke, Krapf, Rebmann, and many others. The sudden impact of the West brought with it a few—surprisingly few—wars of conquest, some local rebellions against the new authorities, and periodical outbreaks of violence, magic, sorcery, and necromancy which are, I believe, in essence, atavistic movements back into the horrors and darknesses of the past. Mau Mau, which afflicts Kenya today, is one of many such outbreaks, a septic growth in the body of society which has attracted to itself the underworld of places like Nairobi and the scum of the colony.[1] Ritual murders in Basutoland, the West African countries and elsewhere, leopard men, python cults and other disorders of the hearts and minds of people in violent transition, whose world is whirling along at a dizzy speed, whose way of living has been turned upside down in a generation—these things break out from time to time and cause great suffering and disturbances.   I have no time here to do more than note them in passing, with the observation that they are, unhappily, often seized on by tendentious writers and speakers in the West and misrepresented as political revolts, liberation movements, and resistance to tyranny.

I have said that it was not the whole population which embraced the Christian faith and became inspired with energy and enthusiastic for education. But a great many tens of thousands did. From that, there has developed the present situation, in which the contrast between the civilized, often highly educated, Christian and Moslem thousands, and the still near primitive millions is a striking feature and, politically, socially, and economically, a complicating factor of great importance.

I do not think the world has ever before been confronted with a situation in which a totally illiterate and untaught people, in great masses, suddenly embraced a new faith and culture, woke up to the value of written education, and demanded it, although lacking even knowledge of the alphabet. This happened, moreover, just at the time when, in the West, there was an equal enthusiasm for the extension of primary education to the masses, and, in consequence, two essentially different situations were confused one with the other. For in England, in spite of its great seats of learning, great achievements in scholarship and technology, and a remarkable standard of craftsmanship, the masses were illiterate to an extraordinary degree; and a great campaign to remedy that condition was set afoot. It aspired at first to little more than that, for economic needs in industrial England required that the masses should go to work at about the age of 13 or 14. It achieved more of course, vastly more, for there were the seats of learning and many other agencies to carry on the work and to give opportunity for

1 See Appendix, interview with Sir Philip Mitchell on the Mau Mau.

more advanced studies for those with the will and the determination to seek them.

It seemed natural enough to apply the same methods to Africa; and applied they were, as far as resources permitted. Few people saw then—or see now, for that matter—the fundamental differences in this matter between Africa and England, or France, or America, or the West in general.

There was little understanding that elementary education in itself, in countries having no middle or higher education, might be an indispensable stage in a much longer process as yet hardly begun, but was precious little use for anything else, so that its first fruits might well be disillusion and resentment.

Indeed, few people realized that they were teaching a continent to read, while there was at that time very little within its comprehension for it to read. I remember twenty-five years ago asking an African hospital dresser in a remote part of Tanganyika if he had anything to read. "Oh yes," he said, "I have the Bible and another book." He produced it; it was a novel which had had some vogue a few years before, *The Green Hat* by Michael Arlen. He said he did not really understand what it was about, but it was at least in English. Not unnaturally, there were many thousands of people educated to the point my dresser friend had reached who, in the early stages, had very little idea "what it was all about" and who assumed that to be able to read and write and do simple arithmetic was to be educated and would confer great advantages. Disillusion was an inevitable consequence of a situation which only more, better, and more advanced education can remedy; and there is much disillusion today.

Few of those concerned, moreover, realized the implications of introducing Western culture and knowledge in French, English, Portuguese, and Spanish, so that Africa had to develop its new civilization not only in a foreign language but in four foreign languages.

Nor was it understood how rapidly Africans in African colonial territories would advance in culture, learning and technology, wealth and political awareness, nor how soon the question would be asked "Where do we go from here?" and have to be answered in practical terms.

There did not appear to Europeans of the nineteenth and early twentieth centuries to be anything peculiar or difficult or dangerous about the process of establishing and developing each colony as a separate unit, and for three reasons. First, Europe itself was a patchwork quilt of national states of all shapes and sizes, some very small. Secondly, those were the days of great political and economic stability in the West; the perpetuity of the existing state of society seemed as unchallengeable as the gold standard; and if the long-range political problems of developing colonies received a thought, the conclusion must have been that they would just tag along with the metropolitan country.

Thirdly, the occupation of Africa occurred when the first glimpses of what joint international action might achieve were being perceived. The Abolition movement was, no doubt, the most spectacular; but there were also other examples: the International Postal Union for one, an almost miraculously competent piece of international co-operation which we now take for granted, so quietly efficient is it, and many others.

It is a reasonable deduction, in spite of 1914 and 1939, that insofar as the West was conscious of its international colonial problems, it assumed that they could be met by agreements and conventions, as occasions arose, within the framework of the balance of power as it then existed.

It is some justification for such an attitude that, today, the agencies of the United Nations and the national policies of some countries, notably the United States, show a determination to give general support, financial and technical assistance, and, indeed, collaboration in any way that they are able, without political tags, to help the colonial powers carry their heavy burden.

The collapse of the balance of power and the intensifying nationalism of the West in the first quarter of the twentieth century soon made it abundantly clear in Africa that all white men were not subjects of one government but of many—British, Portuguese, French, Belgian, German; that all Christians were not of one kind, but differed fiercely among themselves; that "love thy neighbor as thyself" had a proviso—that he belonged to your particular variety of Christianity. The late nineteenth and early twentieth century was a time when denominational differences in the West were markedly pronounced, active, and uncompromising. One consequence in Africa today is that as the movement for Christian unity spreads among the people of the West, clerical and lay, it often encounters a rigid and unyielding denominationalism among Africans. Nor was this matter of denominationalism the only confusing factor. It soon became apparent that not all the institutions of the new religion were easily adaptable to the old society and that conversion brought consequences seldom perceptible to uneducated catechumens. Take marriage for instance: the missionary societies insisted rigidly that a man could only have one wife; most Africans, in fact did, but many were polygamous, often as a result of tribal custom. This is a vast subject I must leave to others, contenting myself with observing that it is, for large numbers of Africans, a real dilemma how to be both a Christian and married in terms of contemporary Church rules and old tribal customs.

In the political field, simple people must have been confused by the compulsory changes of allegiance resulting from wars and conquests. In any case the boundaries of territories were, and are, no more than the result of conference and negotiation by statesmen in Europe, by whom, 40 and 50 years ago, African human geography was unknown and economics little understood. Frontiers were drawn with a ruler on a blank map, or by give and take about the unknown, in Western foreign ministries. The Gold Coast, Nigeria, Tanganyika, Uganda, Kenya, the Congo Belge (or Free State) meant nothing at all in terms of Africa, fifty or so years ago. Apart from differences deriving from the differences between metropolitan countries, half a century or more of colonial government has now given a certain identity and personality to each territory, which local divergencies in law and administrative practices have often accentuated, even when there is a common metropolitan country.

In fact, colonial policies and the variety of nations concerned have resulted in Africa's having developed in a series of units roughly comparable to the States of the Union but with no central government or common language.

It is the declared object of British policy and, whether declared or not, the most probable outcome of the policies pursued by other nations, that each of these territories will develop toward responsible government and independence.

In the British case, we certainly hope that that independence will be accompanied by a desire to remain associated with the Commonwealth, for we believe their own interests, ours, and those of the world in general will be served thereby. There may be local federations — Dr. Nkrumah makes no secret of his perfectly reasonable aspiration to organize an extensive one. A United States of Africa between the Limpopo and the deserts of the North is not, in itself, inherently impossible, but a lot of water will have to flow down the Nile, the Congo, and the Zambesi before there is a sufficient sense of unity for anything of the kind to happen. It may not be irrelevant to observe that these rivers flow in different directions to different oceans.

It may perhaps suffice today to note that currently British Togoland appears to be strongly opposed to union with the Gold Coast; the three regions of Nigeria are, to put it mildly, not enthusiastic about their federation; Buganda would certainly not willingly be merged in any larger unit, nor would any one of the three East African territories agree to an admitted federation with the other two. I say "admitted," because the East Africa High Commission is of course a federal authority, but there is an agreeably human understanding in all these countries not to say so aloud.

Manifestly, the West has a duty, in political terms, so to order affairs—if it is able to do so—that Africa, as the outcome of colonial developments is not Balkanized—or perhaps I should say "Guatemala'ed"! This in itself has a significance for the modern approach to colonial problems which I am sure we all should see developed more fully by other writers in this book; for, if it raises difficult issues of the gravest importance for the future, it does not alter the fact that the present requires the continuance of territorial divisions of manageable size, with a political and even an emerging national consciousness of their own to give them meaning and individuality, and a common heritage of culture, law and language to give them coherence. As a Briton, I beg leave to add, a common loyalty, which I see in the Queen and the Commonwealth. It is, in the North American continent especially, useful to remember that nearly all these conditions, except the last, existed when the successor states to the original colonizing or ruling nations of Europe were born.

I am well aware that "colonialism" has in our day become a term of reproach, even of abuse; but as a "colonialist" for forty years (for seventeen of them even that arch-sinner, a colonial governor), I am unrepentant and undismayed, although at times fearful lest the current mood of the West should result in "colonialism" being prematurely abandoned. The processes now called "colonialism" have been, beyond question, the most beneficent, disinterested, and effective force which has ever been brought to bear on Africa in all its history. That it might have been better, that it has its blemishes and faults, does not alter that plain statement of fact.

If the suffering people were to be rescued from their blood-stained misery, their hopeless poverty, and their brutish pagan life, and set upon the hopeful road of progress, the situation that confronted the West when the African colonies were occupied was one which required, above all, the establishment of strong, just and liberal authorities which would impose order and the rule of law, make the lives of the poor and weak safe from violence, protected by transport from famine and by medical knowledge from epidemics, and create the conditions in which the seeds of Christian civilization brought by the missionaries could grow and bear their fruit.

Education, for example, beginning with the teaching of the alphabet, could only then start from modest beginnings toward the university, colleges and technical institutions of today. Production and trade, without which nothing effective could be achieved, could only thus be created to provide the means whereby the striking progress which has been made could become possible.

May I just give you a few statistics? In, say, 1890 the total annual trade of the regions of East and Central Africa, from the North Transvaal border to Abyssinia, from the Great Lakes to the Indian Ocean, amounted to some hundreds of thousands of pounds—maybe a million; in 1952 it was £507 million. In 1890, neither cotton nor coffee were grown in Uganda for sale; cotton was indeed unknown and coffee known only as a low-grade wild berry. In 1953, the growers (almost wholly African) netted from their crops £30 million. In 1890 there was not a railway north of the Limpopo. In 1951 there were 3,500 miles of open track which carried 9 million passengers and close on 12 million tons of goods. In 1890 mineral production was nil; in 1952 it was £102 million.

These startling figures would, I have no doubt, be greatly surpassed by those, for example, from Nigeria, the Congo, or the Gold Coast, where cocoa alone is a vast source of wealth. They are, with law and order, security, education to the highest level, public health services and many others, and the opportunities for the African people today, the direct achievement of "colonialism"; that is to say, of stable, just, and competent tutelary government, which undertook what the mandates used to call the sacred trust of civilization, and have honored it.

There have resulted many problems inherent in the relationship of colonial power and dependent territory. Trustees do not always agree with wards about the particular stage when the ward has become an adult. When wards are numbered in tens of millions of individuals they do not all grow up at the same rate. In Kenya, where I now live, there are one African minister and two junior ministers in the government; African doctors and surgeons and lawyers and so on; thousands of people for whom the only appropriate description is civilized, but still tens of thousands for whom it is skin-clad primitives. There are African men who drive heavy locomotives and great numbers who can never have seen a train.

In West Africa where natural wealth, navigable rivers and the numbers, enterprise, and abilities of the people have profoundly affected and stimulated progress, there are still many hundreds of thousands of very primitive people.

In East and Central Africa, partly because of a healthy climate, partly because of lack of indigenous populations and great wealth in minerals requiring deep level mining, partly because of monsoon-wind navigation in the Indian ocean, there are large settled populations of Arabs and Europeans and Indians, vastly outnumbered by Africans, but hitherto having a near monopoly of enterprise, knowledge, and skill, of capital and understanding of how to use it. Apart from any metaphysical question of right to their place in these countries that may be raised—and they have a very strong claim of right—they have been, and are still, indispensable to the development and progress of all the people of all races. In any case, it is surely not going to be said of Africans that they are unable to associate in friendly co-operation with people of other races? It is true that that could be said of some Europeans in some places; of some Hindus and Moslems in other places; maybe the tolerant African, with his ready laugh and naturally friendly nature will be able to teach others a lesson the world sadly needs to learn. Be that as it may, East and Central Africa have become, by the inevitable consequences of their history, a region where a multiracial form of society, of government, and of economic and cultural development must be achieved, for the price of failure is ruin—for all alike —and the return of the jungle.

It is when all is said and done an achievement to be earnestly desired on its merits alone. If Africa and the West are looked at with humanity and understanding, in the historical perspective of their relations in the past and the glare of contemporary day, it must surely be seen that the great, overwhelmingly great, problem overshadowing all else is the human problem, on the major aspects of which others, more competent scholars than I, have written in this book. The problem, that is, of African man and woman, their present hopes and fears, wants and anxieties, their spiritual and material needs in the context of the modern world of the West, their political relations with and place in that great, unknown world which suddenly, fifty or sixty years ago, fell upon them and insisted that they must become a part of it, however unwilling and without understanding they might have been in the beginnings.

If I may venture to quote as my conclusion from a recently published book of mine: "What we have had to do since (the occupations of fifty and sixty years ago) and have to do still, is to help them to believe in that world, to feel at home in it and to look with hope and happiness to their future in it; that, at least, is my conception of 'colonialism'." [2]

The task it undertook was necessary; the first phase has been carried to its logical conclusion with competence and devotion; the second confronts us, with all its menace and uncertainties, for that is how some see it; with all its hope and promise, its call to service and to steadfast faith; its challenge to the West to see and seize the tremendous opportunity it offers to extend the brotherhood of man and the universal call of the Christian religion, until war and tyranny are forever excluded from a continent that knew no peace, had no hope and saw no future, as recently as sixty or seventy years ago, a continent that holds out its hands to the West, not as a mendicant, but as a young man still needing help and support.

[2] *African Afterthoughts* (London: Hutchinson, 1954).

commentary

DAVID EDWARD OWEN

Harvard University

Certainly I cannot venture critical comments on an article which is the result of a lifetime of experience and study, and I shall only attempt to underline some of Sir Philip Mitchell's observations and restate some of them as questions for thought—for no doubt there will be at least minor differences in point of view and interpretation. I do this reminding you that these remarks come from one whose amateur standing in the African field is unimpeachable.

Yet one question may be legitimately raised by the non-specialist. Among historians one of the favorite forms of sowing an intellectual wild oat is looking for historical analogies. But, being historians, they are usually too cautions to mention such apparent uniformities in print, except in the safe obscurity of footnotes. As I read Sir Philip Mitchell's essay, I found myself doing a little analogy-hunting, wondering whether history offered anything quite comparable to the changes occurring in Africa. Obviously the Romanization of Western Europe is hardly analogous. The extension of the Roman political system and the diffusion of Roman culture in Europe west of the Rhine would provide as many contrasts as points of similarity. And the more recent revolution in Asia is different in both character and tempo from what is taking place in Africa. The Asian cultures that were undermined and altered by Western influences were anything but primitive societies; they were ancient, complex civilizations, which were lacking chiefly in the industrial and military power necessary to meet the West on equal terms. It was hardly more than a historical accident that India fell into Western hands. At almost no other time in the history of both West and East would the conquest of India by a handful of Europeans have been conceivable.

The penetration of Africa has been a vastly different process, as Sir Philip has implied, from that which revolutionized Asia. In the main, these African societies were admittedly primitive, and the time-span has been incredibly brief. This is not a matter of the gradual erosion of an old civilization and the slow creation of a new synthesis (though I don't mean to imply that all of the old will be suddenly obliterated or that much of it will not carry over). This is cultural revolution, in the most literal sense of the term. In one decade it was the Stone Age; in the next it is not only the motor and airplane age—but with the motor and the plane and elementary education have come all those confusing abstractions that even the West, where they originated, has never been able to sort out and assimilate—natural-rights ideas, nationalism, the Ten Commandments, socialism and social justice, and the rest. These, I gather, are making a pretty heady dose for young Africans, as they did for the young intellectuals of Russia in the 1870's and '80's and, more recently, for those of India. Small wonder that in the head of the African such alien ideas should mingle uncomfortably with his inherited notions, that tensions should be created and intolerable frustration sometimes result. No doubt old Africa hands would discover plenty of defects in Joyce Cary's *Mr. Johnson* as an attempt to analyze in literary terms a phase of this process, but at least one relatively ignorant reader found it an unforgettable picture of one African caught between two cultures.

This is the kind of conflict that products of cultures more advanced than the African have failed to resolve satisfactorily. The Chinese in all conscience have had enough difficulty in making the transition, say, from the seventeenth or eighteenth century to the twentieth and in adapting their traditional civilization to new requirements. But this was just a step compared with the leap that we are asking the Africans to take (and, as Sir Keith Hancock notes somewhere, "we" includes not only imperial developers and other Westerners but African leaders themselves). What the African is being called upon to do is to dash from the Dark Ages, or perhaps more accurately in Western chronology, from the fourth or fifth millenium B.C. into the twentieth century. All this, of course, is commonplace enough to most students of Africa. I merely venture to suggest that, in the perspective of history, this African **revolution** may well be unique.

In that connection, as a student of history, 1 found especially challenging Sir Philip's speculations about the precise nature of the leaven that has affected the African lump. He suggested that two forces in particular had been decisive in the awakening of Africa—one, mechanical transportation, and the other, the Bible. And of these two he regards the latter as the primary force, not, I take it, in a restricted sense but perhaps as the totality of Western humanitarian and welfare ideas, as embodied chiefly in the missionary movement.

We have here, if you like, a problem in historical interpretation —whether, to put it plainly, one is to regard the material or the spiritual factor as primary, whether, without the ideas and attitudes implanted by the missionaries and without the social advances promoted by them, we should have the present ferment in Africa. Sir Philip has unhesitatingly aligned himself on the side of ideas. Plainly, in the fields of health and education, the original impetus came from missionairies rather than from government or, still less, from traders and concession-hunters. Until recently, indeed, governments have shown relatively little interest in such matters. This was, after all, a world of individual initiative and free enterprise, and it was the missionaries who in some measure helped to bridge the gap between Western *laissez-faire* theories and African realities.

In speaking in this fashion I realize that I am over-simplifying an extraordinarily complex process and one of which anthropologists and other investigators have so far been able to give us hardly more than a series of worm's-eye views. The kind of synoptic picture that we must assume in a discussion such as this no doubt encourages too easy generalization. I suspect that Sir Philip might agree that the process of change varies substantially from locality to locality, that in some instances the material factor may have been the decisive influence, in others, the spiritual; sometimes the older culture patterns faded and then were erased rather quickly, while in others they proved amazingly persistent and are likely to survive indefinitely. Yet, with all the local variations, it is still a not unprofitable query to ask what tropical Africa would have been like today without the elements of Western culture introduced by missionaries.

A final comment which a historian may properly make on Sir Philip's essay has to do with the role of the West in tropical Africa.

Somehow it all seems much less simple and clear than it did two or three decades ago. We used to talk easily (and loosely) about "imperialism" and "anti-imperialism," and in our teaching we unhesitatingly analyzed the partition of Africa in terms of a theory of economic imperialism that most of us would now regard as at best incomplete, if not largely false. As with many other things in the 1920's, we thought we knew the questions even if we weren't entirely sure about the answers. And with it all went the implication that the penetration of Africa by the West was "a bad thing," that African ways were better for Africans, and that the continent would have been in a happier situation if the Westerners had only stayed at home.

Some of this was a kind of sentimental reparation for the treatment Africans had received at the hands of the West; some of it may have reflected the idealized view of African society that was fashionable some years ago. It even found expression in a popular hit tune. As students of Africa, you may recall "Bongo! Bongo! Bongo! I don't want to leave the Congo!" One was given to understand that, what with the atomic bomb and other doubtful benefits of Western civilization, life was better and more secure in Central Africa.

Today these classic controversies between imperialists and anti-imperialists seem curiously irrelevant to the facts of life in tropical Africa. Indeed, the Communists have unwittingly done us a service in making the word "imperialism" synonymous with the foreign policy of any noncommunist state and thus disqualifying it for ordinary use. Even "colonialism," which has moved into the place once occupied by "imperialism" (though with a somewhat different connotation), gives little clue to the essential problems of contemporary Africa. Some of us would be inclined to doubt whether Western occupation is by definition a good or a bad thing but are content to judge it by its fruits. And we are, I think, a little less fearful of being called ethnocentric, culturally arrogant, or whatnot, if among the desirable fruits we count some of the things that the West ordinarily regards as products—an improvement in health, an advance in literacy, and at least a minimal standard of life.

This is not to imply any lack of sympathy with African aspirations for self-government nor lack of admiration for the amazing steps that have been taken in some areas. Still less can one be other than indignant over the sufferings that have been inflicted on Africans by Westerners. All that I am trying to do here is to underscore the point already made more effectively by Sir Philip Mitchell. The task in tropical Africa, literally that of building a civilization, is too stupendous to be accomplished simply by a negative anticolonialism. One dares to hope that we can shed those attitudes and assumptions, if we have not already done so, that have brought colonialism into bad repute, and that Africa and the West can be brought into a genuine and effective partnership.

the African cultural background in the modern scene

MELVILLE J. HERSKOVITS

*Director, Program of African Studies,
Northwestern University*

The *Congo Mission News* for April, 1953, reprints from the *Baptist Times* Dr. C. C. Chesterman's impressions of a tour in tropical Africa, wherein he tells of a sermon he was wont to preach to Africans on the subject of interracial partnership. "I talked to them about the hammer, the hammer with a black head and a white handle. The black head, long buried and lost from view, which had to be dug up and beaten into shape until it became a useful tool. The white handle, once a lordly tree of the forest, looking down on the others, which had to be cut down, seasoned and trimmed, and knocked into the black head." Both head and handle are necessary to make the hammer, but even so it will not be a useful tool unless properly employed. "When men use it carelessly for their own selfish ends they are apt to knock nails into the hands and feet of the best people. . . . Why not offer it as a tool for God for the remaking of Africa—the continent which God held in reserve? The best generals keep the best troops in reserve. That might be true of Africa."

Dr. Chesterman, "thought it was a good sermon, but they did not applaud it! They said, 'The head takes all the knocks'; I replied, 'Yes, but that strong black head can be reshaped by the Blacksmith if it is battered whereas the white handle, when it becomes old and dry and cracked, is thrown away without even saying "thank you."

30

Some call that ingratitude.' 'Could we have a *black* handle?' asked some. 'Well,' I replied, 'it has been tried in Abyssinia and other places, and it does not seem to work very well. It jars.' But they wanted it nevertheless. 'Any of you can use my sermon,' I said, 'if you like. It is not patented. There are no royalties on it.' 'Perhaps we shan't use it,' one replied." [1]

This parable points a series of assumptions concerning modern Africa that are of fundamental importance for Africa today. Since they tend to be obscured by the many different approaches to the questions that confront those who deal with African affairs, and by the differing ways in which conclusions that flow from these approaches are implemented in terms of practical policy, it will be profitable for us at the outset to give them explicit statement. These assumptions hold that the model for an Africa that is to function in a world society must be what is loosely termed the civilizations of the Western world; that this model must be followed as closely as possible in all its aspects, if the desired end is to be achieved; and that Africans cannot attain this end without being under the continuous direction of Euroamericans.

On broadest lines of policy, we find this point of view expressed in the "civilizing mission" of France in Africa. This conception is implicit in the statement made by M. Pierre Ryckmans, Belgian representative on the Trusteeship Council, in an article prepared by him for *Le Courrier d' Afrique* to explain the negative vote he cast for Belgium on the proposition to create a committee to study participation of native peoples in the government of the trust territories inhabited by them. "When one speaks of participation of natives in the administration of a territory, what is meant is not the progressive initiation of natives in the management of public affairs. If that was desired, we would be fully in accord; it is our publicly proclaimed policy. But no; what is desired is *to substitute the ward for the guardian* in the exercise of trusteeship; and we, who take trusteeship and our mission as trustee seriously, consider this as a contradiction in terms." [2]

1 C. C. Chesterman, "Tropical Africa Today, a Seething Cauldron," *Congo Mission News,* Leopoldville, Belgian Congo, No. 162 (April, 1953) , pp. 5–6.

2 P. Ryckmans, "Les territoires africains sous tutelle," *Le Courrier d' Afrique* (Leopoldville) (August 9, 1953) , pp. 1, 5. Italics as in the original.

Many expressions of this same point of view might be cited, but a few will suffice. Thus General Norton de Matos, ex-Governor of the Portuguese territory of Angola, phrases the matter as follows: "The resolution which we Portuguese have taken, since the earliest times when we came into contact with men of color, of religion, of habits and customs entirely different from our own, was determined by our Christian morals, our beliefs, our determination to evangelize and convert, all this intimatly related to the desire to construct a great nation, bound by a complete National unity. . . . In Africa our objective has been to convert the blacks, to lift them from the moral and material misery they were in when we encountered them, to instruct them, to clothe them, to give them human habitations, to make them rural proprietors or to transform them into artisans. . . ." [3] Again, as regards British East and Central Africa, the Secretary of State for Colonies, speaking in the House of Commons on 12 July, 1950, stated, "It has been said many times, but cannot be repeated too often, that our policy is to help Africans to develop politically, socially, and economically, so that they can play their full part in the central government and in the local administration of their territories." [4] Finally, we may cite a letter reproduced by the South African Bureau of Racial Affairs, giving a South African view of race relations, in which we read that, "The native economic question is . . . how best the native population can be led onward step by step in an orderly march to civilization." [5]

In essence, then, if we except certain parts of British West Africa, we may say that these citations provide examples of this constellation of ideas, so widely held among non-Africans in Africa, that change in the African's way of life is inevitable and essential, and that these changes must be directed—certainly on the level of policy-making and supervision—by non-Africans who understand the demands of the contemporary period. It is scarcely necessary to point out the far-reaching implications of these propositions. In

[3] Norton de Matos, *África Nossa. O que queremos e o que não queremos nas nossas terras de África* (Lisbon, 1953) , p. 15.

[4] *Central African Territories: Comparative Survey of Native Policy* (Cmd. 8235) . (London, His Majesty's Stationery Office, 1951.)

[5] South African Bureau of Racial Affairs, letter from Dr. J. E. Holloway, Secretary for Finance, to "Antonin." Mimeographed; not dated, p. 3.

human terms alone, they involve inducing controlled changes in the modes of life of millions of individuals, who make up hundreds of different societies. It is not too much to say that the task is of an order of magnitude and complexity seldom, if ever, faced during the course of recorded human history.

The approach taken toward the solution of the problems that arise from these basic assumptions has, however, changed considerably during the past decade or two. The earlier point of view, still heard among old Africa hands in all parts of the sub-Saharan continent, is phrased in terms that, on a more sophisticated level, would ascribe an assumed inability to attain the technological, political, social, and moral standards of Euroamerica to innate, biological, racial causes. A variant of this, more frequently encountered, is that the African is a child when compared to those who have developed the industrialized civilizations of Europe and America, and must be treated as such.

Recently, however, the argument has tended typically to take the form of assertions that, since Europe needed a thousand years to perfect its present civilization, it is unreasonable to expect the Africans to master its complexities in a generation. That is, the assumption, while it still holds to the inevitability of the nature of change to be anticipated and the direction essential to the process, is rapidly shifting from a racial explanation based on ascription of inherent capacity, to one based on the time-span involved in learning a more complex way of life. This becomes very clear as one listens to Europeans of many years residence in the continent, who are not convinced of the worth of the changes that have occurred, nostalgically speculate whether it was not a mistake to have given the Africans the schooling they have received. It is more sharply phrased by de Matos when he says, "Many centuries of civilization are required to train a scholar, a statesman, a true artist touched by the call of genius." [6]

Still more recently, a further question has been raised. In the early days, the possibility that the African could himself be a factor in deciding the direction of change was rarely entertained. The great human mass of Africa was regarded as lying inert, to be shaped as those of greater knowledge and wiser understanding

[6] *Op. cit.*, p. 58.

might deem best. Events in the Gold Coast, Nigeria, French West Africa, the Sudan, Kenya, Uganda, and elsewhere have demonstrated the precariousness of this conclusion, while happenings in India, Indonesia, and other parts of the Far East have impressed on those concerned with African affairs the need to correct their time-perspective in the light of these historic facts. As the European head of one educational institution in Africa phrased it, "We are all working under the pressure brought by the realization that we have only a decade at most to prepare another Kwame Nkrumah."

Expressed in somewhat different terms, it is slowly coming to be recognized that the proposals that are advanced, the plans that are laid to achieve the underlying aim of guiding the African to ends held desirable for him, face the imponderable of the African himself. As the African has come to have a more adequate knowledge of European ways, he has also come to have a more effective basis for evaluating and reacting to proposals which will affect his future. The African, that is, is desirous of making his own choices, of weighing the alternatives on the basis of values too seldom taken into account by those who plan for him. Where he is a partner in the planning, this makes for reactions to which a European colleague must adjust. Moreover, the rapidity with which the African is urging his right to make his own choices has repeatedly thrown out of line various time-tables that have been drawn in planning a wide range of developments in Africa. Four years ago a senior French official is reported as having estimated that it would take fifty years for the people of French Equatorial Africa to attain self-government; today the estimate has been lowered to twenty years. The reply of a speaker, long experienced in African affairs, when pressed for a prediction by a student in the Northwestern Seminar on Contemporary Africa, was, "As things stand I would hesitate to predict events in any part of Africa more than two months ahead," a reply that would meet with the approval of many who have seen their time-tables of change abridged under the pressure of historic developments.

It thus becomes apparent that a basic problem in seeking understanding of contemporary Africa is to assess change in terms of the pre-existing patterns of life, patterns that must figure prominently in the study of any aspect of present-day Africa. For the manner in which innovations impinge on pre-established custom must be fully analyzed, and the mode of their integration understood and predicated on the basis of probabilities, if the effectiveness of any kind of program or policy is to be adequately assessed, or its consequences for future developments realistically calculated.

Having thus posed the problem, we may turn to an examination of certain scientific principles that bear on the questions raised by an analysis of the day-to-day adjustments of the present African scene.

2

The concept of culture is one of the principal instruments for the study of human behavior. Its far-reaching significance has only begun to be grasped, but what we already know of its potentialities make it certain that it will stand as one of the great scientific contributions of our time.

In general, the nature and functioning of culture are familiar enough, and so is its definition as the totality of the way of life of a people. Of special relevance for our discussion here are the facts that cultural behavior is learned behavior, that culture is dynamic, and that it is permissive.

The fact that culture is learned at once clears away the fallacy of postulates based on racial endowment as an explanation of the differences found in the bodies of custom of different peoples. This represents an important step toward clarification of the problem, which will otherwise be clouded by uncertainty as to the innate ability of a particular group to take over new techniques, ideas, and institutions of those with whom they have come into contact. The difficulties of the problem when posed in racial terms are exemplified if we look back to the period following the First World War, when the question of racial intelligence was being debated in the United States and Europe; and the point is especially pertinent when we consider the implications of this debate for the African scene.

But the matter is now almost academic. Scientific inquiry has established beyond serious dispute that whatever may be the nature of inborn differences of a psychological order associated with differences in physical type, the range of ability in any human group is such that no item of behavior invented in any society is beyond the capacity of the members of any other to learn it, given adequate motivation and opportunity. We have seen how this fact has been impressed on Europeans in contact with Africans by the teachings of the hard school of experience, and how, as a result, explanations of the differences between Europeans and Africans today tend much more to lie on the level of history than of biology. And this, it should be noted, is no inconsiderable gain, whether for objective analysis or practical planning. It rules out one variable in a situation even otherwise sufficiently complicated, at the same time permitting a degree of flexibility in approach that cannot be attained if governed by a philosophy of genetic determinism.

Thus, initially, the proposition that culture is learned clears the way for a better understanding of the positive contribution of our approach. In the present context, this contribution has a dual significance. It both explains the ability of a people to take over from others elements of foreign cultures, and accounts for the tenaciousness of pre-existing custom, the second an aspect that is too frequently overlooked, and that, because of its relevance, it is useful to consider here.

Individuals, we know, begin to acquire the accepted modes of behavior of the societies into which they are born from the moment of birth. They learn these ways so well that much of their behavior becomes automatic. That is, they come to respond promptly and with a minimum of conscious thought to the demands made on them by their manner of living. What is more important, this automatic component in cultural behavior frees them to think in those situations where choices must be made and decisions reached. What we have, then, is the phenomenon of cultural learning that permits human beings to achieve a maximum of efficiency in meeting the requirements of the daily round. This does not mean, however, that man is a cultural automaton, for behind the immediacy of every reaction is the reserve of conviction. A man, and only a man, can give reasons why he behaves as he does; man alone can bring alternate choices to the bar of verbal debate.

This aspect of cultural learning, or enculturation, as the process is called, provides a powerful mechanism making for cultural stability. There is little difference whether we are concerned with the details of motor behavior, with institutions of broad compass, or with an entire body of beliefs and values that give meaning to life. All equally make sense to the man or woman raised in a given cultural environment. Take a simple instance from the area of motor habits. In many parts of Africa certain tools are manipulated away from the holder. In sewing, for example, the needle moves from the body instead of toward it, as is the European custom. When the saw is introduced into such a culture, the same pattern takes over, so that one sees African sawyers moving the saw with the edge away from them instead of toward them, pushing it instead of pulling it. In neither case does any loss of effectiveness in the use of the instrument seem to result, the difference between African and European habit patterns thus being merely a manifestation of different modes of cultural conditioning.

The subtlety and pervasiveness of the process of cultural learning explain why so many implications of the concept of culture remain as yet unexplored. This subtlety may be illustrated by another African example. In eastern and southern Africa the most prevalent unit of form is the circle. Houses, kraals, utensils of all sorts are keyed to this pattern. The reconciliation between the fundamentally different aspects of perception that must take place when Africans conditioned to such conventions come into contact with European custom, where the dominant design elements are the straight line and the rectangle, is at once apparent. Hence it has been found that the African from much of the western and central parts of the continent, where houses are rectangular and walls go in straight lines, adapt their building practices to the European model with far more facility than those whose habits of thought and action are framed in terms of a conditioning to circular patterns.

From simple examples of this kind we can move into situations that run the gamut of human experience, ranging from agricultural practices to religious beliefs, from artistic modes to political and economic and social institutions, for almost endless exemplifications of the principles of continuity and stability that are operative in all human cultures. The problems of earlier political adjustment in African societies, where the institution of chieftainship was imposed on groupings not organized in terms of such structured political forms, are matched by the questions that arise in the societies having a well-organized hierarchical system that are adapting themselves to European democratic parliamentary practices. Or we may take the instances where economic obligations assumed in societies marked by wide kinship affiliations of extended family and clan, in which resources and income are shared or pooled in situations traditionally calling for large expenditures, must be tempered to conform to the requirements of a free enterprise system. In such situations, Africans who are successful in trade or the professions frequently accept a burden, heavy beyond the comprehension of those whose lives are ordered in terms of the values of societies where individualism is dominant. Yet this is no different, insofar as the basic psycho-cultural elements involved are concerned, from the tenaciousness with which the European who lives in Africa holds to his pre-accustomed ways—his reluctance to adopt new foods, to change pre-established house types, to accept the forms of etiquette of the Africans among whom he lives.

What is learned, however, can be un-learned, and re-learned. If cultural learning affords a mechanism which allows societies to achieve stability in their ways of life, the same fact—and this is of the utmost significance—explains why peoples, to some degree, continuously change their habits of living. The institution of traditional chieftainship is not so strong as to prevent new governmental forms from being adopted by Africans to meet the requirements of new political orientations. The demands of broad kinship obligations are not so fixed that they have inhibited Africans from seeking and finding ways which permit them to function economically in terms of the demands of a world system that stresses large-scale production through capital investment. Europeans in Africa, in actuality, do adapt themselves to their new cultural milieu, often more than they realize.

Cultural change may be initiated from within a society, or the impulses may come from outside. This latter is by far the more frequent, though it must be made clear that no society has a patent on either process, and that human groups, all of which have contributed to the sum-total of human knowledge, dip into the common pool when historic opportunity affords and add to their own particular cultural store. If the technology and political order of Africa are being influenced toward Euroamerican norms, Euroamerican patterns of art and music and the dance reflect the influence of contact of Africans and Europeans. What is important is that this process of change through the impact on peoples of new techniques, new ideas, and even of entire blocks of institutions, when considered in the light of world history, is nothing unique, nothing even especially novel. It is, rather, a phenomenon which students of culture recognize as universal in human experience. The problem is to determine how, in a particular instance, this process has worked out, and the historical and psychological reasons why a particular line of development has occurred.

Here a complex series of factors must be taken into account. The elements of motivation and prestige will have a dominant role. The degree to which the differences between pre-existing cultures in a given aspect of life are broad or narrow will be significant, as for example, the differential adaptation of the Africans to European currency in the western part of the continent, where money in the form of cowrie shells existed prior to contact, and in the eastern part, where least common denominators of value did not exist. The nature of the contact, whether friendly or hostile, and the resulting situation, whether of dominance and coercion or of permissive choice, will similarly figure. To what degree factors of utility will enter is a more difficult problem, especially in the field of technology. Why, for example, have Africans in southern Mozambique accepted the plow, while elsewhere, despite the availability of the necessary draught animals, have they refused to substitute it for the less efficient hoe? Is the idea of efficiency, even when applied to so basic an aspect of life as the food quest, a denomination of cultural currency whose value is not necessarily transferable from one society to another?

Let us return to the phenomenon of enculturation and see how it provides a mechanism for both change and stability. We have seen how, in the early years of childhood, the enculturative experience equips the child to live in accordance with the accepted modes of behavior of the group into which he is born. We have seen how this learning process sets up reaction-patterns that function throughout the life of the individual, shaping for him the nature of the world in which he lives, and giving to the values that sanction his behavior an emotional component that pervades his responses to the situations he meets.

In early enculturation, the individual is relatively a passive element. At birth, the human organism is, in a psychocultural sense,

a clean slate, on which his culture writes the tale of its demands
and its rewards. Yet learning does not end with the attainment of
maturity, but continues with each new question that must be
answered, each new problem that calls for solution. Later enculturation, however, differs from the earlier span, in that the adult,
unlike the child, can and often does make conscious choices concerning what is newly presented to him; and this occurs even in the
smallest, the most isolated, the most homogeneous and conservative
societies. There is, in consequence, no human aggregate of which we
have knowledge that lacks some persons who, in making the choices
of their adult years, do not extend the limits of sanctioned custom.

The individual who is presented with an innovation reacts to
this new experience in terms of a pre-existing psychological base.
When we multiply these individual instances and move to the level
of a total culture, it follows equally that what is newly introduced
into a way of life is influenced by the prevailing patterns of the
culture into which it comes, inasmuch as these patterns have been
learned during the common early enculturative training of the
individual members of a given society.

In short, there is no such thing as a cultural vacuum. Since no
human society is without its culture, any innovation, whether taken
over voluntarily or imposed by force will, in some manner and to
some degree, be reconciled with the pre-existing cultural mass.
A non-controversial example of this is to be had in modern African
wood-carving. This is a direct response to Euroamerican interest
in earlier African art-forms in this medium. In many areas of
Africa where wood-carving was done in accord with long established requirements of the social and religious order, the initial
contact with European culture seriously affected the quality and
reduced the quantity of artistic production. Yet the basic patterns
have persisted, and in such a center as the Benin Native Administration School, carvings of high artistic merit are being made,
patterned along the lines of the earlier tradition, but not necessarily copying the earlier pieces. Such carvings, however, have no
ritual significance. They are made to be sold, in quite the same
manner as the works of any artist or sculptor in Euroamerican
society.

On the other hand, when an innovation is not in consonance
with earlier patterns, it will be rejected if the people are free

agents, or resisted as much as possible if they are not. The indif-
ference of the nomadic Masai of Tanganyika and Kenya to what,
in most of Africa and in terms of European thinking, is held to
be an opportunity, the attainment of literacy through schooling,
can be explained by its lack of meaning for them in terms of their
culturally sanctioned goals. There are some instances where this
resistance is so strong that all innovation is rejected, even at the
threat of social extinction, as with the Bushmen of southern Africa.
These examples, however, are not typical of African societies in
general, since African peoples traditionally tend to be receptive to
innovation.

When we examine the propositions stated at the outset of our
discussion on the nature of African cultures and their future, in
the light of the principles governing the mechanisms that make
for cultural stability and change, it is evident that we have in these
principles a corrective factor of importance. From this it follows
that this factor must receive full consideration if peaceful and
equable modes of working out the historic impulses that have
played on Africa during the past three-quarters of a century are
to be achieved. We may, therefore, next proceed to explore some
of the instrumentalities through which this end may be attained.

3

The story is told of a young district officer in East Africa
who, after judging the case of a tribesman, imposed on him a fine
consisting of the best beast in his herd of cattle. The officer was
implored by the Africans to accept another animal, or even two,
as a substitute; but he would not listen. As he turned to leave, a
spear, thrown by the man whose animal he had demanded, pierced
him, and he died. "A good man," said an elder colleague. "What
a pity he didn't know some anthropology. He would have realized
that he was asking this man to give up the bullock that was his
blood-brother, and shared his soul."

The comment on this unfortunate incident might stand as an
epitaph for all those Europeans who have lost their lives because
of ignorance of African traditional ways; for us, as students of
African affairs, it has a wider significance. The incident can almost

be said to epitomize the function that anthropology can fulfil in all parts of the world where the dominant problem is adjustment to situations deriving from contact between peoples whose cultures differ. In these areas, anthropology provides those concerned with practical affairs a scientific frame of reference within which they can order the complex elements of the problems whose solutions they seek. In addition, the anthropological approach incorporates an indispensable body of concepts and methods for the student of any aspect of human behavior, whose problem requires that he deal with cross-cultural materials.

It is thus no accident that anthropology has taken, and must continue to take, a leading part in all programs of area study. As the science of culture, it is equipped to give those in other disciplines the means of arriving at an understanding of the cultural matrix in which their problems are set. As a matter of fact, it may be said that without the theoretical and methodological resources of the cross-cultural approach, research, no less than practical programs, operates under a serious handicap. The application of these theories and these methods provides the cultural base-line which scholarly investigation must employ in all studies of cultural change. Once a base-line is established, continuing reference to these theories and use of these methods in studying the changing scene is essential if the emergent new forms are to be assessed in proper perspective. Experience has taught that where full weight is not given to the cross-cultural factor, research findings are skewed by ethnocentric preconception, and practical projects based on such findings go awry.

Let us consider some instances from Africa that document the need fully to take pre-existing cultural patterns into account. The Gonja Resettlement scheme in the Northern Territories of the Gold Coast provides us with one such example. Here there was no lack of technical planning or competence in management such as marked the far more famous groundnut scheme of East Africa, nor have the results of this planning been without some measure of return. Yet it has been seriously questioned whether the return has been of an order to justify the outlay that went into the project; and one important reason for this has to do with the labor force. Workers come from other parts of the Northern Territories, where the pressure of numbers on available resources poses familiar problems of over-population and its concomitant erosion of land with a resulting lessened economic productivity.

At Gonja, land is made available to workers for farms, which benefit from mechanized modes of preparation and cultivation. Only a few of those who have come there, however, have wished to take up land—only one, a Talengi, had in 1953 established himself permanently, despite the advantageous conditions under which this can be done. Most workers prefer to leave their families at home, where they live as members of the extended kinship groupings that afford them the security of the social collectivity to which they belong.

Even should they bring their families, the obligations they owe their broader kinship groups militate against their settling permanently. This holds particularly for the obligations a man must discharge toward his ancestors. A European, chief farmer of a section, told of how he encouraged his African workers to save a part of their wages in accordance with the European ideal of providing for future needs. One of these workers, of whom he was particularly proud, had saved £30, a substantial sum in view of the going rate of wages. However, when a death occurred in his kin group, all this was withdrawn to meet the costs of the funeral rites; while the worker likewise left to perform his duties to the dead. It is little wonder that an official in charge of a project elsewhere exclaimed, "My only hope is to resettle the old men with the rest of the families. If when they die they can be buried in their new homes, then we will have the necessary roots. But the question even then is whether they will be willing to be buried there!" This degree of anthropological realism is not unlike that of the educated East African who, when the groundnut scheme was under discussion, remarked, "We can grow all the groundnuts they need on our farms, if they will only help us to do so."

Instances of this kind could be cited from every sphere of life, and all parts of the continent. In some phases of culture, such as literacy and schooling, the advantages of mastering these new techniques have become so apparent to Africans that they are continuously pressing for extension of the opportunity to learn them. Here, however, it may be noted, we are dealing with additions to pre-existing cultural resources of peoples who had not developed the techniques of reading and writing, rather than substitutions for previously established conventions. In the field of religion, closely related to the acquisition of literacy because of the fact that most European-type schools in Africa are in missionary hands, the tale is quite different. Sundkler, the only scholar who has thus far reported on the nature of the differential adaptation of Africans to Christianity, has shown how, when Christian Africans are free to control their own churches, there is a carry-over of the pre-Christian belief system, and, to an even greater extent, of ritual.[7] Sundkler's research was restricted to the Union of South Africa, but it needs no extended investigation in other parts of Africa to discover that the same phenomena mark the independent African churches elsewhere. Where independent Christian organizations are not permitted, we find sects such as the Kibangi and Kitawala in the Belgian Congo, or the Matsuists of French Equatorial Africa, as examples of the same process. Despite the strictest missionary control over African converts, we find that beliefs in the power of magic and the use of magic charms and prescriptions persist with full conviction.

When we ask what anthropology has contributed to the understanding of modern Africa, it is difficult to point to any aspect that has not been illuminated by the results of anthropological research. Even those whose fields lie outside the sciences of man—biology, geology, agriculture—have profited from the findings of anthropology when the human factor has entered into the problem of utilizing the results of their investigations.

Many instances could be given of the growing recognition, on the most practical level, of how in Africa anthropology can aid those in other fields to obtain their objectives. Anthropologists are included in governmental, inter-governmental and other research teams which study such varied questions as diet, land-use, local government, education and urbanization. The inclusion by the World Health Organization of an anthropologist as a member of its staff working in Africa affords another example. It is rapidly becoming apparent that the fullest possible information must be on hand concerning the social structure of a people, their systems of value and belief, the nature of the economic and political goals

---

[7] Bengt G. M. Sundkler, *Bantu Prophets in South Africa* (London, 1948).

they hold desirable, and the interrelation of all these, when working with them.

A few of the cases in which misunderstanding is to be and, in some cases, has been corrected through the utilization of the results of anthropological research can be indicated briefly. Not until detailed studies of the place of cattle in the cultures of eastern Africa were made was it realized that these herds constituted the means whereby wealth was redistributed and, through this, the social fabric held taut and stable. The importance of the secret society in Africa has long been recognized, but only careful research can ferret out the role of such associations, and that of the equally important ones where secrecy does not obtain, in the changes that are occurring in political patterns. The concept of time and the time-cycle, as these enter into the sanctions underlying African institutions, lie so far beneath the level of consciousness that only the trained investigator thinks to look for them. Yet their significance for an understanding of economic motivations in a changing social order is obvious, once the point is made. Other researches are bringing to light the highly important relationships that underlie patterns of mobility making for new types of leadership in Africa; or the role of polygyny in the economics of African households.

It must be stressed that only those who have the necessary training in theory and method are equipped to obtain the data which seem so simple and are actually so difficult to sift out of the day-to-day life of any people. The mere realization of the importance of the cultural background, and the most earnest desire to take it into account, are not enough. Every science has built its achievement on the foundation of its conceptual system and its methodology, and the science of man is no exception. The requests with which all Africanists are familiar, for "a book that will tell me how to do anthropology" in connection with research in another field, or on the part of an administrator or engineer or business man, are on the level of a request to a bacteriologist to "give me a book that will tell me how to study the diseases caused by parasites" in the districts where the same persons may be living. In neither case is there any magic to such studies; but there must be method, and a disciplined knowledge of problem and theoretical resource. The contributions of bacteriology have been made by bacteriologists;

in the same way, the contributions of anthropology must be made by anthropologists.

In other words, the enlightenment on African matters anthropologists can give is contained in the works on Africa they have published, and in their more general discussions of the nature of culture and the processes of cultural change. It is to such works that students in other disciplines and those concerned with practical matters are turning, and must continue to turn. For it is from them that they can obtain solid knowledge of the cultural patterns of the people with whom they deal; information as to how these ways are changing, both as regards intensity and direction, and orientation as to the general principles that must be kept in mind in addressing themselves to the particular problems of their concern.

It is important at this point that we make explicit the role of anthropological research and the use of anthropological concepts and methods in analyzing the cultures of African societies, in terms of the objectives of such studies, the motivations that underlie them, and the uses to which they may be put. This is necessary because of misunderstanding regarding those who investigate the pre-contact cultures of Africa. Such students, it is sometimes said, stress what is past. In doing so, they are held to portray their subjects as "primitives," and hence to imply that the African is incapable of grasping the techniques needed to allow him to take his place in the modern world. Other anthropologists are said to be romantically concentrating on these cultures of earlier days so that the clock of history can be turned back, and the peoples they study maintained in a kind of Rousseauesque Golden Age in which they envisage them as having lived.

The history of anthropology shows that traditionally the subject of anthropological investigation has been the nonliterate peoples of the world, to which the word "primitive," now being progressively discarded, was applied. This, however, was a part of a total stream of intellectual history, legacies of which are found in the economists' vocabulary when they speak without any qualifying word of "underdeveloped" areas, or in the term used by the political scientists when they discuss the political development of "backward" peoples. The reasons anthropologists have devoted themselves to the study of cultures other than those of historic peoples have perhaps not been explicitly stated often enough. In actuality, such studies make it possible for them to explore the range of resources of human culture in its totality. It has been in learning to do this, moreover, that they have developed the methods that permit them to step across cultural boundaries and perceive the values of all ways of life.

There is no implication in the work of anthropologists that the peoples they study are "primitives," incapable of learning other ways than those evolved by themselves. In point of fact, it is the anthropologists who have most vigorously combatted this view, and it is due to the descriptions and analyses of their complexities that anthropologists have given that the worth of such cultures has steadily gained recognition. As far as the actual objectives of most anthropologists are concerned, indeed, questions of this kind are irrelevant. The societies whose diverse ways furnish the materials and the scientific controls for the anthropologist's investigations of the nature and functioning of cultures are his laboratory, not models for the future of the societies he studies. Nor do anthropologists today restrict their researches to the old, the remote, the "primitive." Literate, machine cultures are as much the product of human capacity as any other, and in recent years many anthropologists have worked in Europe and America. In addition, with the development of acculturation studies, most of those who today study peoples in Africa and other parts of the world are as interested in the cultural present as in the cultural past.

The principles concerning the nature of culture and of cultural change that come into play when peoples of different cultural backgrounds are in contact, were hammered out on the anvil of cross-cultural research of this kind. These principles were discovered because anthropologists were interested, as scientists, in performing the primary task of the scientist of pushing outward the boundaries of knowledge. Because these principles are pertinent to situations anywhere in the world, they are relevant to study of culture anywhere. In Africa, they should be a part of the intellectual equipment of all those who are concerned with problems of adjustment to changing conditions. And, it should be stressed, they are as important to the African as they are to the European. The results of planning and implementation will be facilitated by their use in the same way and to the same degree, whether at the instance of Europeans who administer non-self-governing Africans, or by Africans in control of their own affairs. To be sure, the cross-cultural factor does not enter for the African where his own people are concerned. But to the extent that he must work with, and understand peoples from other parts of Africa, or Europeans, or Americans, or Asians, then the better his cognizance of the scientific principles that apply to situations of cross-cultural contact, the surer will be his grasp of the problems with which, as a man of affairs, he must deal.

This leads us to the question of the use to which scientific anthropological findings are to be put. Let us briefly consider this point in terms of what we know about the adjustment of men to their cultural milieu. There is little doubt that, as one looks at the degree of integration of many pre-contact cultures, realizes the adjustment of the peoples who lived in terms of them, and compares this with the difficulties that arise as a result of the need to adjust to changing conditions, one cannot but wonder at the value placed on the new as against the old. But to recognize this is not to advocate a return to the old. A people whose culture is historically integrated, and which is attuned to the natural environment in which it is found, avoids many of the complications that arise under rapid cultural change. There is reason to believe, also, that such an undisturbed state makes for a greater psychological ease, and facilitates individual adjustment to a greater degree than where well-established habit patterns must be altered to conform to new circumstances. Yet once a process of change has begun, its course must be run. The situation can never be what it was before, no matter how a people may try to recover the past.

In the light of these propositions we can see the fallacy in policies which envisage returning African peoples to a previous tribal status, when such policies are purportedly based on a presumption of greater adjustment in the earlier state than can be achieved under present conditions. In insisting on this rationale, the grain of truth is more than counterbalanced by the other element in the equation, that the processes of history are irreversible. The misuse of a valid proposition in no way lessens its scientific validity; the contribution of the study of man can only be made if its lessons are learned by those who would make use of them.

4

We have discussed, in brief statement, some of the findings of the science of culture that should aid us in placing the rapid march of events in Africa in proper perspective, and in anticipating the future working out of present-day developments. As minimal in this we must recognize that in the long run it will be the African who, in terms of his own cultural history, will be the determining factor in shaping the African cultures of the future. By the same token, we realize that these African cultures will be different from those of the past. Already we see how selective the African can be. After the manner of all cultural change, this will without doubt continue, with Africans taking what they want of the ideas and institutions of other peoples with whom they have had contact, and building them into the continuities of their own past.

Granting the development of closer lines of affiliation between all parts of the world, then the role of Africa in this world society will follow the lines laid down by the opportunities afforded the peoples of Africa to master the resources of the larger world, and the responsibilities this participation will lay on them. In the process, however, all those concerned, whether Africans or others, will profit by drawing policy and organizing procedure in consonance with findings of the scientific study of human culture. Otherwise, with the lessons of world history unheeded, the way will be one beset by the continuation of those tensions that have marked the striving of men everywhere for security and self-realization.

commentary

ROBERT T. PARSONS

Dean, The Kennedy School of Missions,
The Hartford Seminary Foundation

The problem for all of us who would work with Africans in Africa today has been well stated: in striving to understand contemporary Africa one of the first things to be done is to understand the African way of life and the processes of culture change. The many factors involved in this undertaking which have been discussed in Dr. Herskovits' essay, provide basic considerations for this book. They will enable us to have a clearer view of the other facets of the contemporary scene in Africa as they are brought under the scrutiny of the participants in this book.

I find myself in substantial agreement with the essential argument put forward; therefore, my remarks will consist of selecting a few statements which seem to need clarification and additional emphasis. The most important of the factors mentioned above, in my opinion, is this: that the African people are playing the decisive role in the drama of culture change now being staged; that in this role they command our full respect as they respond to the rapid and extensive changes, and in doing so retain such a high degree of sanity. The need for full respect is indicated in several sections of the essay. Reference is made to the approach of the social scientist as one that is without any implications of superiority or inferiority, without any attempt to place a ceiling upon the possibilities of growth and wholesome adjustment. This seems to me to be but another way of emphasizing the importance of recognizing the African people as real people, and that the positive attitudes which this recognition prompts will greatly affect the outcome of cultural change for good.

In the first section of Dr. Herskovits' essay our attention was

called to the aims of the administering powers as they induce controlled changes throughout Africa. These aims were referred to,
it seems, simply to indicate "that change in the African's way of
life is inevitable and essential" and, in the minds of the agents of
change, must be directed by non-Africans. However, an understanding of the nature of culture change will require us to know
to what extent these purposes have been implemented; in what
ways the attitudes and interests of the governing powers, as influenced by policies and programs in the homelands of these governments, have affected the processes of change. These questions likewise should be raised with reference to other agents of change, chiefly
religious and economic. Further complications in the processes of
change are those in which two or more agents of change have
related activities. Also, there are other situations in which there
are interactions of the several agents of change, and the African
finds himself in the midst of these forces with severe conflicts in
his loyalties. For example, in areas of West Africa, Africans are
torn between loyalties to a new religion, loyalties to the pre-existing
tradition and customs, and loyalties to a new government. All this
is mentioned to show that only as we endeavor to grasp the significance of the totality of the dynamic forces operating in Africa
will we understand contemporary Africa.

In considering the partnership in planning that is developing in
a number of African areas, Dr. Herskovits made this observation:
"There are special reactions to which a European colleague must
adjust if the African is a partner in the planning." This is true,
but one would inquire if the reverse is not also true, namely, that
the African must learn to adjust himself to a situation in which he
is to be a partner of the European. Moreover, in some areas of Africa
the dominant minority (the Europeans) have treated the majority
members (the Africans) as Western societies have treated their
minorities, by requiring them to meet a higher set of qualifications
and standards of conduct than was asked of their European counterparts, before they were considered fit for the partnership.

It has been noted, and rightly so, that the African desires to make
his own choices. One might add at this point that there are instances
in which the choice of some Africans was to request the continued
assistance of the European in helping to plan and organize programs
of change. Not only have some of the African people sought assist-

ance from European groups but they have insisted that non-Africans who have a sympathetic understanding of their culture are in a better position to help them select elements in their culture that can be used in new social situations.

Three additional comments concerning the agents of change are these:

Firstly, the agents of change often use considerable pressure to cause people to accept a new practice, only to find out later that, because of their lack of an accurate understanding of the culture, they have introduced the wrong practice. Then to their dismay they find that the leaders of the people who first accepted the new practice and have reconciled it with the pre-existing practices resist very strongly any attempt to return to a former course of action.

Secondly, agents of change have taken a negative attitude toward certain cultural practices and have urged the people to eliminate them, without recognizing the need for a substitution. Even though they have not thereby created a vacuum, they have certainly left the people poorer in their expressional life, and have required them in some instances to seek destructive forms of expression. A case in point is the removal of the drum and the dance from the recreational life of the people because there seemed no way to separate these forms of recreation from their religious associations, which were incompatible with the new religion. Some of the violence in Kenya today is thought to stem from this cultural change.

Thirdly, the agents of change may gain new insights into the processes of acculturation as they study the techniques used by a subject people to accommodate themselves to the dominant group. The outward reactions of the people may not be the accurate ones. One such technique is that of ready agreement of the African with a European as a means to personal advancement while, at the same time, he may hold radically different ideas about the methods and goals of the innovator as his culture is changed. Often the European has not established sufficient rapport to know what Africans are thinking or to evoke their frank opinions. Instead, there is the practice of silence on the part of the African when, to be true to his convictions, an African would likely have to contradict a European, but to do so might place his employment in jeopardy.

At another point in the essay under discussion, the statement was made that "the cross-cultural factor does not enter in for the African where his own people are concerned." This statement it seems to me needs some qualification. Would it not be better to say that the cross-cultural factor does not enter in except when the African who is concerned with his people has had no continuous contact with the impinging culture? If he has had this contact then he is no longer a person within the culture, but a person to some extent between the two cultures. He is one step removed from his people with problems of adjustment to each of the cultures in contact. His own people have difficulty understanding him, and new tensions and conflicts arise. On the other hand, his way may be blocked as he tries to enter into the life of the impinging culture. A common example is that of persons returning from school life to find that they are to some extent misfits in their own communities. To assist these persons educators might well seek an understanding of these cross-cultural problems through the help of the anthropologist.

In dealing with the relative merits of an older cultural pattern, as over against a new pattern, this statement was made: "Once a process of change has begun, its course must be run." It does not seem quite accurate to apply this to all situations of change, for at times the process of change seems to be halted, temporarily at least, and sometimes it seems to have been directed along different lines from the course it first took. For example, there are rural situations in Africa that have been improved to the point that the movement of the African men away from their families to the towns and cities has ended. The rural area now meets the needs of the entire family better than the commuting to the city had ever done. Again, some Africans who at an earlier time turned away from their cultural ways, are now turning back to them, seeing in them values and adjustments denied them in the areas of rapid change. It is agreed, however, that even in the return to a former pattern, the pattern was not the same as before.

Near the close of the essay, emphasis was laid upon the important contribution of anthropology to an understanding of Africa, the need for trained anthropologists, and the need for a better use of anthropological findings. Great credit must be given to all of those who have made investigations, for they have endeavored to properly record the culture they were studying; yet today it is very significant to learn of the corrections which African scholars are making of earlier studies. Not only are the African scientists pointing out the inaccuracies but they are revealing the biases and the prejudices that lie back of some of the Western scientists' conclusions. Is it not fair to say that it is likely that the best accounts of the culture of African peoples will be written by trained Africans?

In the concluding portion of Dr. Herskovits' article a prediction was made of the likelihood of the development of closer lines of affiliation between all parts of the world in which Africans will play their unique and helpful role. It seems to follow that in this affiliation there will be need for genuine association, friendship, and partnership. In this task too, as well as in so many others, the Africans seem extremely well fitted, for students of Africa have discovered that there is a large capacity for friendship among African people everywhere, or as E. W. Smith put it in *The Golden Stool*— "a genius for friendship." And he continues, "No people perhaps are more capable of a deep and constant fidelity to those whom they love—for their sakes they will go through fire and water and brave a thousand deaths. A people characterized by such fine faithfulness have in them the making of good citizens," and may one add, citizens of the world.

Africa's strategic significance

ADMIRAL RICHARD L. CONOLLY, U.S.N. (Ret.)

President, Long Island University

I will refrain from the usual disclaimers of responsibility because, being in a retired status, obviously all my opinions are my own. It would not be difficult to disassociate my ideas from the strategic concepts which have prevailed and received official acceptance since the end of World War II.

Let me say at the start that the strategic appreciation which I will advance is based upon a belief that decisive action in the really important strategic areas in a large-scale war will result from the movement by sea or land of relatively massive land forces into such areas in order to establish effective control thereof, and not by bombardment *alone,* whether massive or otherwise.

The significance of any given area from the strategic point of view depends on various factors inherent in it. These might be enumerated as: geographical position favoring exerting substantial effect upon enemy positions or forces; material resources usable for waging war; trained fighting forces and sources of fighting men; harbors, airfield sites, and transportation facilities; defensible and adequate lines of communications; defensible and adequate military bases or sites which could be developed as such; and governments and peoples favorably disposed toward us and our cause, preferably for reasons of self-interest or self-preservation.

Strategically, on a large continent like Africa there are many areas separated and isolated by distance, by mountains, by deserts, and by jungles. These separate areas may be considered strategically, in a limited sense, as islands or island base areas accessible, however, to sea lines of communications. They potentially provide bases at which resources can be collected and stored and from which can be mounted and projected ground, air, and sea operations or amphibious or triphibious offensive operations including, but not confined to, bombardment. The continent may be considered in one sense as an aggregate of separate base areas and in another, in its entirety, as a vast defense complex.

In both a political sense and in a military strategic sense, Africa requires a defense in depth. In both, its defense begins in Turkey, Iran, and Pakistan. I would define the essential elements of a defense in depth as: first, successive lines of defense, one behind the other, becoming progressively stronger; second, an adequate base of operations under the defender's control; third, lines of communication connecting the first with the second; and fourth, the forces and resources available for use in the area. The best base of military operations in the Middle East would constitute the best and probably the only protection for Africa from invasion by the Soviet Union operating through Iran and across the Mesopotamian Valley or through Turkey. Loss of the outer ramparts would entail defense within the African continent itself.

The most important lines of communication are the sea routes in the Atlantic connecting all strategic areas with the home bases of the Atlantic powers, the sea routes into and traversing the Mediterranean, the sea routes around the Cape of Good Hope, and the air routes across the African continent.

The defense of the Mediterranean sea routes requires defense of the entrances into it and would, undoubtedly, precipitate a continuous battle by air and by sea to keep them operating. Such a battle would be largely an air-sea contest waged from air bases afloat (carriers) and fighter and bomber bases ashore, on the North African littoral, the islands of Sicily, Malta, Crete, and Cyprus. Although the effort required would be large on both sides, the results would be worth it from the point of view of the over-all defense of the continent.

Defense of the Atlantic and Indian Ocean sea-routes would be largely an antisubmarine effort and therefore an extension of the "Battle of the Atlantic."

The effective use of African base areas depends upon several factors. Few, if any, provide adequate indigenous material resources for direct use in the strategic action to be projected from them. By this statement, I do not mean to discount the importance of certain "strategic" products of the African continent such as wheat, minerals, timber, and so on. They are vast. It is assumed that the value of the material resources of the continent to our peace-time economy and to our over-all war potential will be assessed under the economic treatment of the subject.

The asset available in these base areas and most useful on the spot is the local human resource of indigenous labor — in most cases unskilled labor. Another, perhaps more important human resource, is troops drawn from local sources. In the use of such a base area, the good will and support of the local population and the local governments (wherever they are representative of the population) is of the utmost importance. It has double effect whether or not the local populace is for you or against you. To use an area as a base in the face of a hostile local population would impose great strains on the military forces of anyone making the attempt. Such an operation would require the employment of large forces to maintain order, to control guerrilla activities, and even to prevent pilferage, sabotage, and depredation of military stores on a large and perhaps even crippling scale. If the population feels that the military forces are fighting in its cause, all these factors are reversed.

The strategic value of North Africa to the French has always included as one of its principal elements the availability of man-power for military purposes. The fighting men drawn from North Africa in both world wars have served France well. Traditionally, those from Morocco have been by far the best, next, those from Algeria and, of least value, those from Tunisia. The reason for this is the same as everywhere — whatever it is that constitutes good fighting men—tradition, spirit, and physique.

During the postwar period prior to the formation of the mutual defense pacts of Western union and then NATO, according to the press of that era, both France and Britain had formulated rather nebulous strategic concepts on a purely unilateral national-strategy basis, which probably had, however, an implicit reliance on help from prospective allies. These tentative strategies were inadequate and completely unrealistic, but they were based on one sound principle: namely, defense in depth. The fatal defect lay in the fact that in order to have a defense in depth you have to have something up front. But, in both of these concepts, there was practically nothing up front.

In the case of the British, the defense in depth extended from Palestine, where they did have a considerable number of troops (although in a politically precarious position), thence back through the Suez Canal, Egypt, and the Sudan. It was finally to be based on British East Africa, where a new Britain overseas was envisaged. This development apparently was to include new military- and naval-base facilities that would provide for the possible loss of Suez.

French strategy in both world wars employed French North Africa as a base, a source of military manpower; and, in days when the defense of metropolitan France became critical, it was considered as a position into which the French armies would retire for continued defense with the expectation of ultimate return for the recapture of the homeland. Such a retirement was not necessary in World War I and in World War II was prevented by the Petain-Laval government. Actually, however, possession of French North Africa by the Vichy French government did serve to keep France alive. French North Africa was later used as a base by the allied forces to mount the reinvasion of Europe in Sicily, Italy, and southern France, and it did thereby assist materially in the recapture of metropolitan France. The concept, born of desperation, of falling back into Africa for the eventual regaining of France from that base was accomplished.

I will consider in turn the strategic areas believed to be important either as bases of offensive operations by us or in the defense in depth of successive elements of resistance to attack.

Tangiers and Gibraltar bestride the Straits of Gibraltar and control the approaches to the Straits and the western entrance into the Mediterranean by the important Atlantic powers. Possession of this position is essential to the success of any military operations in the Mediterranean against a possible Russian thrust. During World War II, operations inside the Mediterranean against the German enemy were considered by some to be in jeopardy due to the threat that the German armies might operate over and around the Pyrenees, down through Spain to Gibraltar. Actually, I believe a reserve striking force was prepared in case such a threat developed into reality during the invasion of Sicily. The Tangiers position is flanked on the southwest by Morocco, on the east by Algiers and Tunisia.

Morocco has become a great base for our strategic air forces. It has every natural advantage for such. Politically, it is somewhat unsettled but its troubles may not be insoluble by some means or other. In case of war, a solution would surely have to be found. It is of prime importance not only because it provides a superb site for this indispensable air-base complex but also because it flanks the Tangiers position, the sea approaches to the Straits of Gibraltar, and the routes from Northern Europe around the Cape of Good Hope. Casablanca could be used as a base for naval operations in the antisubmarine war of the Atlantic, as it was in World War II. Morocco could be made defensible from attack by any means from any quarter. This is an area of great strategic value and of prime importance to the Western powers in case of war with the Soviet Union.

The next strategic area which I will consider is the Northwest African bastion comprised of and including Spanish Morocco, Algiers, and Tunisia. This area obviously could control the western Mediterranean. If occupied in force it provides a springboard and a mounting area for a massive invasion or threat thereof of the whole Western European continent; control of Tunisia at the eastern end comprises an immediate threat against the occupation and use of Sicily and challenges the control of the Straits of Sicily. This area, too, provides a training area removed from the immediate threat of the active operations on the Western European front, wherever that might be established at the time. It provides sites for naval and air bases, good harbors at Mers el-Kabir, Oran, and the Gulf of Arzue in one single complex and to the eastward —Algiers, a complex of great strength at Bizerte and Tunis.

Libya, in World War II, was the battleground over which was fought for several years a seemingly never-ending contest for the control of Egypt and the whole North African coast. It has two sea ports of real importance, Tripoli and Tobruk. A number of airdromes were established in the area to support the ground action. It offers sites for many more if needed to contest control of the eastern Mediterranean and for the defense of Northwest Africa from attack from Egypt.

Now we will consider Egypt. This nation has within its grasp the control of the Suez Canal and perhaps ultimately the decision as to whether or not the Middle East is friendly or hostile. Fortunately, this picture is considerably brightened by the friendly attitude and the military potency of Turkey which would sit on the flank of any enemy operations directed into the Near East and against the Suez Canal. But Egypt is more than the mere guardian of the canal. It could serve as it has in the past as a base of offensive operations against an enemy attack on the canal itself or against the threat of the invasion of Africa through the Isthmus of Suez. The use of Egypt by the Western powers as a base of large-scale operations would be dependent upon keeping the sea routes open around the Cape of Good Hope, as a minimum. It would probably require that the Mediterranean in its entirety be kept usable for sea traffic. In case Egypt were lost, our operations from the Northwest African base against enemy forces operating to the westward would be dependent upon control of the eastern Mediterranean, and particularly the coastal waters along the southern shores. Loss of such control for a period deprived Britain of countless opportunities for operating against Rommel's lines of communication across the Libyan desert and finally brought about the Battle of El Alamein when he had reached the end of his tether. Rommel's failure here was without doubt due to his lack of control of the same sea area and his inability to use it to support his attack.

The recent loss by Britain of its long-held Egypt base is a heavy blow to hopes of successfully defending the Middle East from eventual Soviet domination by political action or, in war, by early and rapid conquest, occupation, and exploitation. British rationalizations of this loss on the grounds of a need for defensive dispersion do not sound convincing. The allied powers are now dependent on Egypt for the best possible base for the defense of the Middle East and thus of the outer works for the defense of Africa. Suez is both a land bridge from Asia to Africa and the connecting link in the water routes through the Mediterranean and the Indian Ocean. This position has long been recognized as one of the vital strategic focal points in the world. It still is. Its permanent loss to allied use in war would be a political-strategic debacle of stunning proportions. Although the present situation seems inevitable in the light of the developments of the last few years, a more favorable result might have been anticipated if the United States, Egypt, and Britain, in concert, had prosecuted a more enlightened, more consistent, and more farsighted policy beginning fifteen or even ten years ago. The fiction that Britain alone and without aid could assume political and strategic responsibility for the entire Middle East and the assumption on our part that our interests were not involved, that we could remain aloof from the scene and delegate the responsibility, has precipitated the present situation. The offer of a Middle East command including the Arab states, in November, 1951, was too little, and it came too late.

What is the significance of Eritrea, Ethiopia, the Somalilands and Somalia from the allied defense point of view? These are of principal importance for possible use of the ports for minor naval operations in control of the western Indian Ocean. The ports are Masawa, Djibouti, and Mogadiscio. The area lies across the path of a thrust out of Egypt to the southward. Although not vital to us, it would be essential to keep it from Communist subversion or Soviet control.

Sometimes referred to as Capricorn Africa, British Southeast Africa, Kenya, and Uganda and Tanganyika, are very rich. The British during World War II and in the postwar period had high hopes of building a great naval base at Mombasa and of developing a new great port at Mikandani. This was to substitute for a possible loss of Suez and was part and parcel of the exaggerated depth to be provided to defenses. I doubt that it will be developed for a main base of large-scale long-range operations to equal the British Egypt base; and, to my mind, it is too far in the rear for such use in the initial stages of a war.

Madagascar, with its great anchorage of Diego Suarez, is of prime importance in protecting the sea lanes in the Indian Ocean, particularly those that pass around the Cape of Good Hope. The British, in World War II, considered it of sufficient importance to capture it from the Vichy French and establish a Free French régime there.

South Africa occupies the key position in the control and protection of the around-the-Cape sea traffic. These routes were much used in World War II. Recently, the South African government has asked for defense talks with the United Kingdom concerning the use of Simonstown naval base, for some time (since the twenties) held by the Royal Navy under an agreement between the two countries within the Commonwealth. However, the South African government seems to be adopting simultaneously a much more co-operative attitude toward participating or at least collaborating in the defense of the free world.

Dakar is another strategic position which, in World War II, the British considered of sufficient importance for an attempt to wrest it from the control of Vichy France. It guards the sea lanes passing around the Cape from the North to the South Atlantic.

So far, I have been considering the strategic use the Western allies could make of these base areas in operations against an enemy, a land-bound enemy, who would be attacking Western Europe or who would attack down through the Middle East. Let us now consider what effective use such an enemy might make of these areas against the Western hemisphere provided his thrusts were successful and he had penetrated finally clear to Gibraltar, across North Africa, and down the east coast of Africa and perhaps ultimately seized positions in Dakar and Morocco. I will take these possibilities under consideration in order that we may see the importance of denying the strategic areas of Africa to our probable enemy in another war and the vital necessity of preventing this penetration and exploitation by our enemy.

The loss of the Middle East would, if it included Egypt, give the enemy access to the African continent by land. The way then would lie open to thrusts westward along the North African coast and southward into the Sudan and through Ethiopia. The prize along the latter route would be British East Africa and South Africa. Along the former route it would be control of the Mediterranean, severance of our lines of communications through that sea, and pre-empting the Northwest African bastion which guards the southern flank of Western Europe or, conversely, provides the springboard for assault on Western Europe. From there to Morocco is a short step (though a tough one) and ultimately the seizure of Dakar would naturally follow. We would then have the Soviet Union at our own doorstep, the control of the Atlantic challenged and South America threatened. Nor have I mentioned the loss of the tremendous material resources of the continent. Again, whatever their value, loss to the enemy has double effect. Our loss is his gain. The balance in many of the basic commodities essential either to a dominant economic position or a pre-eminent war potential, would swing in his favor. This is the nightmare that, in the years to come, we must prevent, either in whole or in part, ever becoming reality.

Wherever and whenever my voice could properly be raised, I have advocated consistently, persistently, and even pertinaciously a bolder and more aggressive foreign policy for the United States and its allies, together with provision of the means to back it up. We need, also, to give more heed to long-range major considerations and to make fewer concessions to the easement of the localized tensions of the moment. Since our statesmen, with the help of the military and our allies at times, began to formulate our postwar policies and to execute our ill-devised peace settlements of World War II, divided councils and compromise of issues have well-nigh been our undoing. Our action, in both political and military spheres, has been usually several years late and either confined to the defensive or, at best, the counter-offensive.

We have desperately needed better understanding, on the part of many of our statesmen, of the basic elements of military strategy and of what has come to be called geopolitics. Many of our military leaders have lacked both a broad strategic appreciation of the world of today and a realization that our military strategy must be formulated to support a national policy, that our military establishment must be so constituted as to give effect to our diplomacy in "peace" (cold war) or to implement our military strategy in "real war." Between the two, policy and strategy, there is an interplay of action and reaction. While national policy and our national military strategy must be mutually supporting, policy plays the key role. Upon its soundness and our determination in its execution depends the welfare and future of our nation and probably the fate of the free world.

Let us hope that our statesmen and military leaders of the future can prevent the loss to Communism and domination by the Soviet Union of the second largest continent—Africa.

commentary

PAUL H. NITZE

President, Foreign Service Educational Foundation;
Former Director, Policy Planning Staff,
Department of State

I propose to deal with two sets of points raised by Admiral Conolly. The first set concerns certain geopolitical considerations respecting Africa. The second set concerns the relationship between military-strategic considerations on the one hand and political considerations on the other.

As to the first set, Admiral Conolly emphasized the lack of internal communications in Africa, and suggested that Africa could be viewed as an aggregation of islands.

This brings to my mind the changing relations of sea power, land power, and air power over the years. I think one can say that at one time sea power possessed very great strategic advantages. Nations holding command of the sea could concentrate at selected points much more rapidly and effectively than nations relying primarily upon land power. With the development of railroads and the proliferations of roads and other means of internal communications, this advantage was somewhat reduced.

In our Civil War the position of the North, with its control of the sea, would have been clearly and readily predominant had it not been for the railroads which had been built in the South. Similarly, in World War I the German railroad net enabled her to keep the issue in doubt for some years.

In World War II the situation was further complicated by the rise of air power. Today in an atomic age, dispersal and potential defense in depth become of even greater significance.

If this is true, then Africa, a continent of immense size, characterized by the most difficult internal communications bearing upon the southern approaches to Europe and to the Middle East and linking the Atlantic and the Indian oceans, may have a particular and unique strategic significance.

Admiral Conolly also emphasized the necessity for co-operative relations between governments and peoples of an area and those who are endeavoring to defend it. In an age when sea power was in the clear ascendancy it was possible to maintain bases such as Gibraltar and Suez, irrespective of the political relations of the naval power with the government and peoples of the surrounding area. Under today's conditions this is no longer possible. Today there must be a correspondence of interest and viewpoint between the defending power or powers and the governments and peoples of the area to be defended.

It is this factor which constitutes the basic challenge of the military and political problem of Africa. The West, being strong in both sea and air power, has great potential advantages in the defense of an area such as Africa, provided the political problems can be worked out. My former colleague, C. B. Marshall, has emphasized the point that the test of a nation's greatness is whether it can adjust from a position where it once disposed to a position where it must deal with problems. The Spaniards were not able to make that transition successfully and suffered the consequences. At one time the West disposed with respect to Africa. Today it is necessary to deal with Africa. The basic challenge is whether the West can do this constructively and imaginatively.

This leads me to the further point of the interrelation of strategic and political considerations. The potentialities of what might happen in the event of a hot and general war do have a bearing on what happens in time of peace or of cold war. And, by the same token, the constructive adjustments and developments in the economic and political spheres during peace or cold war bear importantly upon the prospects of successful general defense in the event of a hot war.

Admiral Conolly referred to the necessity for collaboration between our statesmen and our military men if these problems are to be resolved and progress is to be made down both lines simultaneously. I would suggest that this is not just a problem for the United States but one for the West generally. Furthermore, much of the difficulty has seemed to me to inhere not in lack of collaboration between statesmen and the military but in the real dilemmas and issues which must be faced in action. Sometimes it has been as difficult for the military to grasp the real nature of the political problems faced by the statesmen as vice versa.

Part of the problem which has had to be faced both by statesmen and military men in the past, has been the allocation of resources, not just material, but also of attention and thought to be given Africa as against other geographical areas. It would seem to me that a trend toward increased emphasis upon Africa and African affairs, of which this book is an example, is already discernible.

two | **THE HERITAGE OF AFRICA**

native cultural and social patterns in contemporary Africa

ELIZABETH COLSON

Goucher College

To generalize about the cultural and social patterns of the
natives of Africa makes as little sense as it would if one attempted
to generalize for all the peoples of the South American continent
without regard to the differing ecological, economic, social, and
political conditions under which these people live. Africa, even
south of Sahara, is a vast continent, with widely different ecological
zones, varying from deserts through tropical rain-forests to the high
plateaus where proximity to the equator is tempered by altitude.
Before the peoples of Asia and Europe began their penetration of
the continent, it was inhabited by native peoples who varied in
every conceivable way—in physical type, in the languages they
spoke, in subsistence activities, in economic and political organization, in religion, and in artistic traditions. Within the continent
there were Bushmen hunters in the far south, nomadic pastoral
peoples in the north and east, people who combined a mixed
economy based on farming and the possession of livestock, and
purely agricultural groups. There were areas in which each small
group, sometimes each family, was practically self-subsistent with
little or no tradition of trade or techniques of marketing. In other
areas, and especially over much of West Africa, craft specialization
was well advanced and there existed a highly developed system of
internal trade with organized markets and specialized traders.
Within the continent could be found powerful centralized states
such as the kingdoms of Dahomey, Ashanti, and Nupe in the West,

69

or the kingdoms of Buganda, the Lunda, and the Lozi in Central Africa. Elsewhere there were large tribal aggregates completely lacking in specialized political institutions or recognizable political authorities. Finally, many peoples were organized in tiny autonomous bodies in which the largest group recognizing a common allegiance might consist of no more than a hundred souls.

The natives of Africa, varying as they originally did from one another, have met the incomers from Asia and Europe at different times and under differing conditions. In East, Central, and South Africa, they have known Europeans and Asiatics as settlers and contenders for political domination. In the West African areas of Nigeria, the Gold Coast, and French Equatorial Africa, they have known whites largely as traders, missionaries, administrative officers, or as the upper echelons of commercial and industrial developments. The social and cultural patterns of Africans today are the result of the past centuries of contact with peoples stemming from Europe and Asia, and of the present conditions within the territories where these people are associated. If one wants to understand the life of native Africa today, it is the interacting society of black and white which is important, not some attempt to reconstruct the cultural and social patterns of the past.

Having said this, is there any generalization which one can make about African native cultures? Probably it is safe to say that over much of Africa, even today, life is conditioned by certain attitudes toward property and persons which are characteristic of a nonindustrial stable society, in which opportunities and power depend upon status within social groups rather than upon control of investments; where, indeed, the safest form of investment, and often the only one, is still to be found in the building up of claims against persons. This is true whether one speaks of the West African areas—whose people are rapidly moving toward political independence and an economy tied largely to foreign markets—or of the hinterlands far from direct contact with markets and industries; or of Central Africa, where today most of the people are caught in a web of labor migration which draws them out of the rural areas for a part of their working lives; or of South Africa, whose native peoples have been overwhelmed by the inability to make a living in the overpopulated and eroding reserves while at the same time they are not encouraged to settle permanently in the industrial centers where they earn their livelihood. It is true whether the Africans turn to a subsistence economy or to a more complex economy based on craft specialization and the existence of markets. Even in the towns—ancient to West Africa but newly introduced by the Europeans over much of the rest of Africa—the old pattern continues, though with varying chances of satisfying the needs of those who turn to it to find security and status.

One can argue that this dependence upon personal relationships, institutionalized in various fashions, is the result of a long indigenous development within Africa. It is maintained by the hard facts of existence in present day Africa. The African natives are faced with the same problems that beset all people—security of life and property, provision for the nurture and maintenance of their children, assistance in sickness and old age, the mobilization of assistance for economic activities beyond the scope of the individual, and provisions for assistance to handle unforeseen accidents such as entanglement with the law, the necessity to meet a civil claim, or the payment of medical and funeral expenses. In the old days, over much of Africa, men depended for the safety of their lives and property, as they did for meeting their other needs, upon the obligation of kinsmen, or of other associates, to come to their assistance if the need arose. Men were therefore primarily concerned with associating themselves with those who had some diffuse obligation to assist and protect them, and the maintenance of these social ties was a matter which took precedence over other interests. The ambitious counted their wealth in terms of followers and used such wealth as came their way to increase the number of followers and to bind these more firmly to them. Today the various central governments have assumed the obligation of guaranteeing the safety of persons and property throughout the territories over which their mandates run. In general, therefore, throughout Africa the larger groupings such as clans, large lineages, age-sets, guilds, and other bodies which had such political functions are disintegrating and disappearing under the new conditions of public peace. But the central governments have not assumed obligations to provide for the other needs catered to by the old system, and here the African must continue to rely upon the willingness of his fellows to assist and protect him.

The introduction of a money economy, the opportunities for

employment, and the development of capital resources have made it possible for the exceptional individual to provide for his own needs without reliance upon the assistance of others. But by and large, the new economic developments have not provided for the development of new institutions to meet the old needs, which are still present. The African continues to meet them in the same fashion, through a reliance upon personal obligations to him of those who stand to him in certain social relationships. What one of my colleagues has written of the Yao of Nyasaland applies generally to Africans in the rural areas everywhere.

> . . . it should not be forgotten that the people are still bound most rigidly by their kinship obligations which they may not easily forego. If a man does neglect his duty to his kinsfolk they will soon criticize him and finally desert him. Their desertion means that he loses security socially and economically. He has no one to help him in infirmity, in illness and old age, and he cannot be assured of a proper burial. Furthermore, he will believe that he will be a target for his relatives' witchcraft. Men who become wealthy have done so usually by neglecting their kinship obligations and frequently by living too far away for kinsfolk to get at them. If they are accessible to their kinsfolk their obligations often prove too much and keep them down to a common economic level.[1]

With the presence of trading stores and the increase of foreign goods, the native is often faced with the problem of whether he shall spend his wages for immediate personal consumption or perhaps use his income to build up an independent enterprise, or whether he shall use it at least in part to build up that store of good will among his fellows upon which he is well aware he may be dependent in the near future. He may also have to decide whether he will devote his time to his job or his profession at the cost of loss of status in the social system which promises him ultimate security, or whether he will take time off to meet the social obligations which are incumbent upon him. To take time off from his job to attend a funeral may anger his employer with whom he is in a short-term contractual relationship. To fail to attend will embroil him with his fellows upon whom he relies for long-term status and security. What to Western eyes may seem the foolish

[1] J. C. Mitchell, "An Outline of the Social Structure of Malemia Area," *The Nyasaland Journal*, Vol. 4 (1951), 45–46.

dissipation of wealth through casual gifts or the unthinking waste of time, may to the African be a calculated investment against the future and a method of obtaining immediate social status which in turn will lead to an increase either in followers or in potential assistance.

Wealth, moreover, is often still interpreted not in terms of obvious ownership of resources or a higher standard of living, but in terms of the number of people against whom one has a claim. Wealth is therefore likely to be more widely dispersed than it is in Western society, and the form of investment—in social relationships rather than in capital goods—has slowed the emergence of wide differentials based on wealth and standards of living. Even in West Africa, where perhaps the new standards have been most widely accepted with the development of an educated professional and commercial group, this is still a characteristic of African society in the towns as in the country. For instance, among the Yoruba of Nigeria a wealthy man is expected to give generously to his friends and relatives.

> A person spends money "so that people will know him" and so as to attract a large number of followers. One of the important measures of social position is the number and rank of the individuals who associate with him, and particularly who accompany him when he goes about town. No man of high rank would be seen in the streets alone, while an ordinary individual invites the members of his club . . . to his house for food and drink at the time of a religious ceremony, funeral, wedding, or any other event, so that he may have a large crowd dressed in fine clothes following him when he goes in the streets. This is one of the principal reasons for joining a club, and it is also related to the great interest of the Yoruba in children and large families.[2]

The willingness of the wealthy man to disburse his funds upon a following does not mean that in Africa the lazy man who depends upon others for his subsistence is either admired or encouraged. Typical of African society is the assumption that all members of the society who are able-bodied should be productive in some fashion. This is reflected in the rules of land-tenure enshrined in society after society. The basic living was wrung from the land,

[2] W. Bascom, "Social Status, Wealth and Individual Differences Among the Yoruba," *American Anthropologist*, Vol. 53 (1951), 497.

and every person was assured of access to land though his individual rights of ownership might be limited. What G. I. Jones has to say of land ownership among the Ibo of Nigeria applies, with various qualifications, to most African societies with which I am familiar.

> The Ibo system of land tenure is based on three cardinal prin-
> ciples: that the land ultimately belongs to the community and
> cannot be alienated from it without its consent; that within the
> community the individual shall have security of tenure for the
> land he requires for his compounds, his gardens, and his farms;
> and that no member of the community shall be without land.[3]

This basic land law is only now disappearing in certain areas where land has acquired high value either because of population densities or because of obvious differential values produced by the new opportunities for the disposal of surplus produce.[4] Elsewhere it is still assumed that every adult has the right of access to land and, usually, that he has this access because of his membership in the community, which in this regard may be considered a land-holding corporation. Ownership of the land is vested in this corporation. The individual cultivator has only customary rights of use. These may be very extensive insofar as they apply to the produce of the land which he cultivates, but his rights to dispose of the land are usually minimal.[5] The individual cultivator obtains his rights through membership in the community which "owns" the land, and this also usually guarantees him other rights against persons, which may include rights to assistance in agricultural

[3] G. I. Jones, "Ibo Land Tenure," *Africa*, Vol. XIX (1949), 313.

[4] See Siegfried F. Nadel, *A Black Byzantium* (London: Oxford University Press, 1942), 181, for an instance of this among the Nupe of Nigeria. See also, L. Mair, "Native Rights in Land in the British African Territories," in *Land Tenure Symposium, Amsterdam, 1950* (Leiden: 1951), 58, who refers to the development of land sales and changes of rules governing tenure in certain areas of the Gold Coast.

[5] See Isaac Schapera, *A Handbook of Tswana Law and Custom* (London: Oxford University Press, 1938), 195–207; and Isaac Schapera, *Native Land Tenure in the Bechuanaland Protectorate* (The Lovedale Press, 1943), Chap. VIII (Twsana); Hilda Kuper, *An African Aristocracy* (London: Oxford University Press, 1947), 44 (Swazi); Hugh Ashton, *The Basuto* (London: Oxford University Press, 1952), 145–157 (Suto); Max Gluckman, "The Lozi of Barotseland in North-Western Rhodesia," in, E. Colson and M. Gluckman (eds.), *Seven Tribes of British Central Africa* (London: Oxford University Press, 1951), 61–68 (Lozi); John F.

activities. If he is expelled from the community, he loses at the same time all rights to the land which he cultivated or in some other way exploited. He may be compensated for the loss of a crop but not for the loss of the land itself. But so long as he remains a member of the community, it is in the common interest to ensure that he has sufficient land to maintain himself and his family. On the other hand, it is, or was, in general easy for someone who moves from his original home to obtain land elsewhere if he is prepared to accept the authority of the community into which he moves. If there is unused land, the members of the community are agreeable to its use by a newcomer, for unused land has no value. By allotting it to a newcomer, they gain a new member and thus strengthen their body politic. Allowing it to lie idle benefits no one. The newcomer may pay a small token rent, which in most cases simply acknowledges the ultimate rights of the community from which he holds his land. The real increase in wealth which the community gains is in additional manpower, not in produce.

This attitude toward land is probably common to societies which are not oriented toward constant change and which do not indeed conceive of change as an element to be used in calculating future advantages. Many tribes considered the future to the extent of allowing for long fallow periods for the regeneration of exhausted soil or even maintained unused blocks of land to provide for the further expansion of the population of the tribe. But the value of land was assumed to be a constant factor, since it was viewed in

Holleman, *Shona Customary Law* (Capetown: Oxford University Press, 1952), 7 (Shona); Phyllis Kaberry, *Women of the Grassfields* (London: Her Majesty's Stationery Office, 1952), 30 (Bamenda); Daryll C. Forde and G. I. Jones, *Ibo and Ibibio-Speaking Peoples of South-Eastern Nigeria* (London: Oxford University Press, 1950), 21–23 (Ibo); Charles K. Meek, *Law and Authority in a Nigerian Tribe* (London: Oxford University Press, 1937), 100–104 (Ibo); S. F. Nadel, *op. cit.*, 181–201 (Nupe); W. H. Beckett, *Akokoaso* (London: School of Economics Monographs on Social Anthropology, No. 10, 1944), 56–58 (Akan); Kofi A. Busia, *The Position of the Chief in the Modern Political System of Ashanti* (London: Oxford University Press, 1951), 42–48 (Ashanti); Siegfried F. Nadel, *The Nuba* (London: Oxford University Press, 1947), 22–39 (Nuba); John Middleton, *The Kikuyu and Kamba of Kenya* (London: International African Institute, 1953), 52–57 (Kikuyu), 85–86 (Kamba); H. E. Lambert, *The Systems of Land Tenure in the Kikuyu Land Unit;* Part I, "History of the Tribal Occupation of the Land" (Communication, No. 22), (Capetown: School of African Studies, 1950), (Kikuyu).

terms of its subsistence potential under the existing land-usage system. There was no reason to expect that future changes would increase the value of any piece of land. To hold land unused against this problematical rise in value or to attempt to build up a large estate for speculative purposes was outside their area of calculation. They preferred to invest unused land to attract additional members who would strengthen the existing community.

Today, in many parts of Africa, the population is pushing hard on the available productive land, and it may already have increased well beyond the number that the land can carry. In some areas, this has been met by attempts to limit rigidly the amount of land that a man may cultivate in order to ensure that all members of the community still have access to some land. A man who ceases to cultivate must cede his land back to the group from which he holds it for reallocation to another member of the community. Here the old standards are still strong, and the numerical strength of the community holding the land is maintained at the expense of the land itself. Elsewhere, new systems of land-holding are coming into existence which provide for individual ownership and the sale of land to the highest bidder. This strikes at the root of societies based on the principle that wealth lies in people and the maximizing of personal bonds between them.

This same concept lies behind another aspect of African life which has puzzled administrators in many parts of Africa. In those areas in which natives are able to maintain large herds of cattle, the herds tend to increase at a rate which destroys the available pasturage. In many cases, to the Westerner it appears that the natives make no obvious practical use of their herds. They are not raised primarily for meat or for hides; their milk may be an incidental matter; they may not be used in agriculture or for transport. Yet men are anxious to invest in cattle. Those who go away to work in outside labor centers may invest part of their earnings in cattle on their return, or, while they are gone, they may send home money for the building up of herds. In some areas, natives have begun to use oxen for plowing or transport, but even so they are still intent on building up large herds rather than on improving the quality of their draft animals. At one time it was fashionable to talk about the mystical and ritual value which Africans attached to their cattle and to assume that this explained their eagerness to possess herds and their reluctance to dispose of surplus stock when urged by well-meaning advisors in the administration. The mystical and ritual values are certainly important, but this is only part of the story.[6] Over much of Africa, cattle are a form of wealth invested primarily in the building up of a varied range of social relationships which give the cattle-owner rights over persons. In some areas, the chief form that these take are in a series of marriage payments, which bind together the families of husband and wife in a system of mutual obligations. Through these payments, cattle are dispersed widely throughout the community. Elsewhere, cattle-owners have some variation on the South African *mafisa* system.[7] The man who owns cattle does not keep them all in his own hands where they would be in danger of being destroyed at a single stroke in a cattle epidemic or where they would be too plainly visible to his creditors or others who might have some claim against him. In former days, moreover, when cattle raiding was a common sport among many tribes, it was good sense not to have all one's assets in a single location. Instead the wealthy owner loans many of his cattle out

[6] In part, reluctance to part with cattle may be due to the fact that there is no satisfactory alternative form of investment. S. F. Nadel, *A Black Byzantium*, 201, reports that the Nupe apparently disposed of their cattle fairly rapidly as new forms of investment through trade opened to them, and they saw the utility of keeping their capital fluid for trading purposes. Among the Tonga of Northern Rhodesia, I met a keen appreciation of the investment value of cattle, and I had to agree with them that under the present interest rates, money invested in cattle gave a much higher return than if it were placed in a bank or a postal savings account.

[7] Such examination of material from East Africa and the Sudan as I have been able to make suggests that marriage payments loom large here and that cattle loans are not important. But this may simply mean that the loaning system has not been worked out for the various tribes of these regions. At least some of the East African tribes had a system of loans. See Isaac Schapera (ed.), *The Bantu-Speaking Tribes of South Africa* (London: Routledge & Kegan Paul, 1937), 201, (South African natives generally); Isaac Schapera, *A Handbook of Tswana Law and Custom*, 246–48 (Tswana); H. Ashton, *op. cit.*, 181, 213 (Suto); H. Kuper, *op. cit.*, 155 (Swazi); Elizabeth Colson, "The Role of Cattle Among the Plateau Tonga of Mazabuka District," *Rhodes-Livingstone Journal*, Vol. 11 (1951), 17–24 (Tonga); J. F. Holleman, *op. cit.*, 319 (Shona); Jean G. Peristiany, *The Social Institutions of the Kipsigis* (London: Routledge & Kegan Paul, 1939), 150–52 (Kipsigis); J. Middleton, *op. cit.*, 76 (Kamba); Edward E. Evans-Pritchard, *Kinship and Marriage Among the Nuer* (London: Oxford University Press, 1951), 27 (Nuer).

to other men. These have full rights to use the animals for work, if it is customary to hitch them to plow or sledge, and to use the milk and butter. If an animal dies a natural death, they may have the use of meat and hide. They have no right to kill an animal and must satisfy the owner that they are not responsible for the death of any animals in their care. The herder thus gets many benefits from his acceptance of the responsibility for the care of the cattle of another, but ownership does not pass to him either of the original animals or of their increase. But by accepting the cattle, the herder becomes in many respects a client of the owner and bound to support his interests. In some cases, as the cattle increase, the herder may transfer some of the increase on to other people who agree to herd for him, and they thus become his clients, while he still remains responsible to the original owner for the cattle's safety. Loan and acceptance of an animal creates a bond between herder and owner which has utility for both on occasions in which the cattle are not directly involved. This is so well recognized by some tribes that it is not customary for them to loan cattle to kinsmen, for they argue this is wasted effort: kinsmen already have obligations to you, and you use your wealth in cattle to build up obligations against other people.

The herding system gives the poor man access to cattle. It permits the owner to diversify the risks to his cattle and, at the same time, to use it for establishing those claims upon people which assure him of assistance and a following on a wide variety of occasions. In these circumstances, it is not surprising that African cattle people are often more concerned with the quantity than with the quality of their herds. If they reduced their herds and concentrated on raising a few superior animals, as advised by their administrators, they would also have to curtail their herding associations. The owner gets no direct benefit from the majority of his cattle, for these are being used by other men, and so the quality of the animals is of little direct importance to him. The benefit he derives comes from the set of ties which they enable him to create or reinforce with other people. At the same time, wealth in the form of cattle is widely disseminated amongst the people of an area, though ownership may be more concentrated. Wealth differentials are thus obscured. Wealthy men have more clients than other men; they may not be obviously better off in terms of their standard of living.

In general, therefore, the African natives have been concerned to invest their capital, land, and cattle and their personal time in building up the system of mutual obligations incorporated in their social systems; and, in turn, in times of emergency they play upon this system to meet their needs. It is not surprising that they cling to this system and prefer to invest their wealth in maintaining it, for they have yet to develop the necessary legal mechanisms to ensure that direct contractual claims for the carrying out of specific obligations are enforced. As far as I know, under the various systems of native law still in force to govern relationships among Africans, there are few provisions which attach a penalty for the nonfulfillment of an executory contract.[8] Those who attempt to provide for their needs on an impersonal contractual basis may therefore be left in the lurch with no redress, either under customary law or in the European courts which recognize customary law as governing civil cases in which natives alone are concerned. In many areas of Africa today, men who are away at work may send back money to wives or to elderly parents to enable them to obtain labor for clearing fields or for some other essential agricultural work. If a woman hires someone to perform a specified piece of work at a given time for an agreed upon sum, the hired person may not fulfill his contract. If he does not, and she has already paid him for the work, she can sue and recover the original payment. She cannot recover the value of the crop which she has lost owing to his failure to work as agreed. She will have to fall back upon her relatives for food until the next harvest. A man may give a sum of money to another on the understanding that it will be used for the immediate purchase of cattle. The middleman may allow a number of years to pass without producing the promised animals. He may then be sued for recovery of the original sum; and today a small interest may be added to this amount, but the plaintiff cannot recover the loss he has suffered from the failure to deliver the cattle at the agreed upon time. In a fishing area, a man may pay a net-maker against the making of a net. If the maker does not supply a net within a reasonable time, again the original sum may be recovered, but the plaintiff can collect no damages to cover the loss he suffers because he cannot fish. Nor in these cases, where the relationship between the two involved is an impersonal one, does the delinquent

8 I owe this point to my colleague Dr. H. M. Gluckman of Manchester University.

suffer any loss in his status with respect to other people. Obligations which arise through the social system are still enforced by public opinion and informal pressure even where there is no redress in the courts; obligations arising under specific impersonal contracts are immune to such controls.

It is not only the African native himself who continues to depend upon the existence of the tissue of social relationships for security and assistance. The administrator and the foreign employer may decry many of the effects of the system where these impinge upon their interests, but they too rely upon it and benefit from it. Perhaps this is not true of all of Africa, but certainly in many areas it is only because the system of obligations built up on social ties continues to operate that the present industrial and administrative systems can function.

Through much of South and Central Africa, industries rely upon the labor of natives who are considered to have their roots in the reserves or rural areas. For at least a portion of their working lives, most native men are resident in the urban areas where they contribute their labor to the growing industries. Eventually, it is assumed that they will return to the tribal areas from whence they came. By this time they may have lost the skills basic to agricultural or pastoral production. They may no longer have the strength necessary to be fully productive members of the rural community. They must still be supported. Wages earned while they are employed in industry or while they are employed in other capacities, such as personal servants or farm laborers, are not based on the assumption that these are men who must provide financially for their old age, nor do old age pensions exist for them when they can work no more. Instead they become dependent upon their relatives or other members of their communities for food, clothing, and shelter. While they are still at work, their wives and children must in many cases still be cared for through the working of the old system of personal obligations. In some cases, the men of a community will have an informal arrangement so that not all are absent at the same time. Instead they go out in rotation, so that there will always be men to help in the activities upon which women, children, and the aged depend for their food. Those who are away must provide tax money and the other essential cash for those who remain at home. Men who become sick or disabled during their time in the urban areas again usually find themselves forced to rely upon their claims against relatives or neighbors in the rural areas for their future care. The initial return may be eased by a small disability payment, but when this is exhausted the men become completely dependent upon the good will of their fellows. In the reserves of Northern Rhodesia it is possible to encounter old men who have become blind while away at work outside the Territory. They may have been gone for thirty or forty years, continuously employed in the service of whites. Now blind and useless, they have been brought back by the police to be handed over to the people in the villages where they originated years before. It is assumed by employers and by the government that these people have an obligation to look after them. More or less graciously, they do so, though any immediate kinsmen of the migrants may be dead, and only the most tenuous claim—by Western standards—gives them a right to expect assistance.

The administration, at least in British territories, depends as firmly upon the continuing strength of this network of obligations as does industry. The administrative system uses a program of legal penalties for a large number of offenses in order to maintain its control and ensure public order. It also provides for the payment of damages in civil suits arising between Africans. Today the number of offenses for which Africans are liable to legal action is constantly increasing as the administration presses for more and more regulations in line with its efforts to improve African standards of living. These regulations work toward improvement of health, the development of agriculture, and the increase in educational standards. Meantime those who offend against the regulations or otherwise embroil themselves in minor misdemeanors are liable to be hauled into court and fined. The administration probably has no wish to introduce a large scale program of corporal punishment or of jail sentences in lieu of fines. Neither alternative would compensate those who claim civil damages. Yet under the present conditions, it is often impossible for an individual to pay even a moderate fine or meet a minor suit for damages from his private means. Where he can pay, it may be only at the expense of his capital equipment upon which he relies for his subsistence activities. Yet the existence of the general system of social obligations which require people to help each other in emergencies allows the courts to continue to assess fines and damages, and even to see that these are collected in a fair number of cases, thus upholding the legal rules and impressing the people with the power of the authorities. For when a man is fined, he can count upon his kinsmen, or associates bound to him by some other tie, to contribute at least a portion of his assessment. He in turn expects to add his portion when they too run foul of the law, but he does this only in small amounts and as he is in funds.

At the same time, public pressure is brought to bear against the man who might involve himself too frequently in difficulties with the authorities or with other people, for he constitutes a continual drain on the funds and property of his kinsmen and others who are under some pressure to assist him to pay for his misdeeds. That this is a powerful force in deterring potential troublemakers has been reported for many tribes. Among the Nandi, "A man is not expected to produce all the cattle for compensation from his own herd: his relatives and clansmen must help; they hate having to part with their animals, and as a result, express their disapproval and show their displeasure by avoiding the offender, which is a form of punishment that the Nandi find hard to bear." [9] The Nandi are a Kenya tribe, pastoralists and convinced cattle-thieves. But C. K. Meek has much the same to say of the Ibo of Nigeria, when he points out that collective responsibility, especially within a kinship unit, is an important aspect of native law.

> . . . the members are so closely bound together that the conduct of one may affect them all. But the sense of collective responsibility, being founded ultimately on the principle that union is strength, extends also to the local group composed of many kindreds. It is a powerful factor, therefore, in promoting social cohesion, and when it is allowed full play, in matters of law and authority is of immense value as a means of imposing a high standard of conduct on the members of the group. Numerous instances have been given to show how the heads of kindreds and local groups constantly warned the younger men to exercise self-restraint, lest the ill-advised conduct of one of their number should implicate them all. [10]

[9] George W. B. Huntingford, *The Nandi of Kenya* (London: Routledge & Kegan Paul, 1953), 102. See also, G. Wagner, "The Changing Family Among the Bantu Kavirondo," *International Institute of African Languages and Cultures, Memorandum XVIII* (1939), 29, with reference to the Bantu Kavirondo.

[10] *Op. cit.,* 338–39.

As a last resort, if a man proves not to be amenable to the general pressure of his associates, they may refuse to help him to pay a fine or to settle a damage suit, and then abandoned by his fellows he becomes a charge upon the prisons for maintenance until his release. In the old days the withdrawal of support was still more serious, for it meant that they were no longer prepared to consider him a member of their body, and being outcaste he was fair game to the next comer. Even today, the trouble-maker who has been abandoned by his kin may have to seek refuge in some other area.

Are there signs of the development of new mechanisms which will take over the function of providing for the needs which the old system satisfied in some measure, but which today are jeopardized by the clash between the new individual opportunities and the old communal responsibility? Here there seems to be a difference between developments in South and Central Africa and those in West Africa. In the former areas, where the urban centers attract Africans in increasing numbers, permanent settled community life is not encouraged, and the attempt to build up new forms of organization or to expand the old system of personal ties breaks before the constant shift of population. Boris Gussman, writing on the basis of his work in urban areas of Southern Rhodesia, speaks probably for most of the urban natives of East, Central, and South Africa, when he says:

> The average urban African is unhealthy, badly housed, uneducated, and he lacks any security in town even if he happens to have been born there. These are his greatest and his constant worries. . . . Neither money nor the work that he performs can release him from any of his real troubles. He cannot obtain better health, a better education for himself or for his children, or a better or more permanent home in the urban areas however much he may earn or save. These amenities, although provided free or at subsidized rates, are all in short supply and whenever the African requires any of them, whatever his station, his income, or his background, he must take his turn in the queue.
>
> Men of all races work only to achieve some end. If that end is unobtainable, or not valued very highly, they either work lightheartedly or not at all. The African in town is in just this position. His expenditure is limited almost entirely to consumable goods, the kind of bric-a-brac that a traveller picks up on his travels. With none of the tribal sanctions capable of operation, with few kinsmen in town to remind the worker of his obligations, and with no urban public opinion, there is nothing,

either in his own social system or in that of the West, to inspire him to greater effort. He does not, therefore, respond to offers of more money in return for harder work with the same readiness as a European and he becomes a bad kinsman and a bad worker.[11]

In West Africa, where the natives have a greater stake in the life of the towns, observers strike a less pessimistic note, and here apparently from the towns new forms of organization are spreading generally throughout the West African region. These in part at least are built on an extension of the old traditional loyalties, or at least embody some of the same functions. This development has been described by Kenneth L. Little, who says:

> Social relationships are still organized to a large extent on the basis of traditional institutions over a large part of the West African region. But there is a growing area of social life in which the substitution of monetary motives and of a monetary exchange has led to a modification of customary rights and obligations, making them less continuous and comprehensive. The fact that many kinship groups are no longer economically self-sufficient impairs their solidarity for other social purposes, and the result is that occupational and other associations which cut across tribal and kinship lines have taken over many of the activities previously performed by the extended family, the lineage, and similar traditional organizations. Consequently, there is increased specialization not only of economic activities, but of all the principal activities of community life, including the training and care of children, provision of mutual aid and protection, religion, leisure, and government. From the point of view of individual participation, it means that a person tends to belong to a far larger number of social groups, including many groups with whom his social relations are of a contractual rather than a personal kind.[12]

The old stable African societies with their basic assumption that wealth and security rested upon a system of close personal obligations is disappearing, and the Africans are seeking new institutions which will provide them with the same sense of security. The great problem today is to ensure that the new institutions as they emerge shall reflect the common interest of black and white in developing the potentialities of Africa for the benefit of all elements in the new society.

11 Boris Gussman, "Industrial Efficiency and the Urban African," *Africa,* Vol. XXIII (1953), 141–42.

12 Kenneth L. Little, "The Study of 'Social Change' in British West Africa," *Africa,* Vol. XXIII (1953), 279–80.

commentary

ROBERT A. LYSTAD

Tulane University

Professor Colson, in synthesizing materials on cultural and social patterns from large and varied regions of Africa, has offered a generalization which aptly describes the patterns of social relationships throughout the areas of our interest. ". . . Over much of Africa, even today, life is conditioned by certain attitudes toward property and persons . . . in which opportunities and power depend upon status within social groups rather than upon control of investments." While these attitudes remain pervasive, however, the conditions which permit them to exist are gradually changing. Thus, another similarity between African societies can be found in the ubiquitous clash between the pre-European social systems, based upon communal and family networks of rights and obligations, and the growing contemporary systems, which are based more and more upon individual opportunities and associational relationships. There is a further similarity, she believes, in the pattern of solution to this growing conflict: "The old stable African societies with their basic assumption that wealth and security rested upon a system of close personal obligations are disappearing, and the Africans are seeking new institutions which will provide them with the same sense of security."

With greater or less rapidity, Negro societies are relinquishing their former definition of wealth and power in terms of status within the family and communal groups and in terms of claims upon persons. Control of property is more and more becoming the standard by which the individual achieves status. Furthermore, the group within which status is achieved is a group no longer defined largely in terms of community and family but in terms of associations which are secondary groups by nature. In certain

phases of social organization, this shift in emphasis is more pronounced than in others. Those phases most affected involve political
and economic relationships, particularly the control of large numbers of people in large territories and the control of large aggregates
of capital goods. Finally, Professor Colson indicates that in West
Africa, the area in which Europeans have not developed permanent,
resident interests or assumed a position of continual political dominance, certain institutional mechanisms for orderly change to the
new patterns are emerging. In South and Central Africa, however,
disorganization of the native culture without immediate prospect
of reintegration is the predominant characteristic.

Because the symptoms of social disorganization are recognizable
throughout Negro Africa, it is necessary to discuss African cultures
from the standpoint of this concept. Elements of disorganization
are to be found in all societies, and the prevalence of dispute and
conflict, ranging from nonviolent litigation and the segmentation
of political groups to violent raiding and warfare, attests to its
presence in pre-European Africa. Indeed, the imposition of peace
upon African societies by the Europeans "cured" certain symptoms
of indigenous disorganization. Paradoxically, however, the forcible
prohibition of such manifestations of disorganization closed the
avenues to statuses and abolished many of the statuses which were
in fact integral parts of the native social organizations. The present
progressive, though usually peaceable, breakdown is in large part
a result of this imposition; and, at the present stage of African
social change, it is difficult to judge which is the less desirable.
Which is the less desirable: to lose one's life striving for status;
or to have no status toward which to aspire? The answer depends
upon the effectiveness with which new institutions are able to
provide statuses and acceptable ways of achieving them.

Social disorganization may be defined as the condition of a society
in which there is contradiction and conflict between the norms of
the society. There is in the disorganized society, furthermore, uncertainty about the rules of behavior by which the goals may be
achieved, an uncertainty which may proceed to such an extent that
the behavior of the individual becomes completely unpredictable.
The process of disorganization has not continued to the extreme
in any of the societies discussed by Professor Colson. It is still
possible to identify the culture and social organization of func-

tioning tribes by name and location, and even in the mixed populations of the cities of South Africa these identities have not been completely obscured. But contradiction in cultural and social goals and in the means to these goals most certainly is to be found. The African cannot simultaneously aspire to wealth defined as control of personal relationships and to wealth defined as property; nor can he simultaneously achieve status through the distribution of property in order to build claims against persons and through the acquisition and possession of large amounts of property. Adoption of the new goals and modes of achievement means increasing lack of participation in the old society; and a society composed of individuals some of whom participate, some of whom do not participate, is disorganized.

A question must be raised, however, about the standard by which a society is judged to be disorganized. Goals and modes of achievement which appear to an observer to be contradictory may not be so considered by the members of the society. Or goals and modes of achievement may appear contradictory to certain segments of a society but not to others. In either case, the verdict of "disorganized" must be withheld until the consensus of the members of the society can be determined. It takes no special acumen to determine whether or not behavior is predictable, to know whether or not one's kin can be depended upon to supply help in a crisis or to attend a funeral. If it is the consensus of the members of a society that the behavior of the other members is unpredictable, that one can no longer depend upon commitments previously considered binding, *and if that situation is deemed deplorable and reprehensible by the consensus,* then that society is disorganized in fact as well as in principle.

By this test, it is difficult, if not impossible, to characterize African societies as disorganized in fact—although it may well be said affirmatively with more assurance of Central and South Africa than of West Africa. The general lack of assurance stems from the difficulty of establishing a consensus for almost any African society which has been in intensive contact with the West. In a pre-European African society, this consensus could be determined with considerable accuracy, because the societies were relatively homogeneous, the statuses and the modes of achieving them were known and universally accepted. Now, however, the very disorganization of the old society is accompanied by the organization of new associational groups—students, trade unions, political parties, tribal associations, churches—which render the determination of a consensus difficult. These emerging segments of African societies may agree that the old, acknowledged rules of behavior do not apply with the same force as before, but they do not consider this condition to be immoral or pathological. They are in process of establishing new rules, and, as Professor Colson has indicated, these are the rules of a more individualistic and associational type of society rather than those of the communal society.

Africans and Africanists alike may well agree that the old societies are now disorganized. But the emerging societies are only transitionally disorganized; they are as yet too young to be tightly organized; they do not now control the processes of organization. It is likely, too, that they will never achieve the degree of organization of the old societies. Certainly it is to be doubted that the introducers of modern change, the Europeans, have presented a culture void of contradiction and conflict between norms. But a new social organization is emerging, and it is toward the bases of such organization that attention must now be directed.

Professor Colson has noted the trend in African cultures away from the communal, familistic patterns of a former era and toward what may be called a complex communal society.[1] The dominant characteristics of such a society are already evident in certain of the complex states of West, East, and Central Africa in which the unifying principle has long been a political organization, the centralized state. These characteristics are: (1) increasingly greater division of labor, as well as labor based upon contractual obligations rather than upon community or family obligations; (2) greater class differentiation based upon qualifications of schooling and wealth rather than upon birth; (3) increasing importance of associations such as professional groups, trade unions, student organizations, co-operatives, churches, and the state; (4) increasing impersonality in community relationships, especially in the urban areas, but extending even into rural communities where familiarity rather

---

[1] The term, to my knowledge, first appears in Wilson, Logan, and Kolb, William, *Sociological Analysis* (New York: Harcourt Brace, 1949). It developed out of a recognition of the limitations of the folk-urban, sacred-secular dichotomy.

than intimacy or customary obligation becomes the dominant characteristic of social relationships; (5) increasing dependence for the control of behavior upon codified law and the state rather than upon custom and public censure; (6) diminishing economic self-sufficiency and greater participation in national and even world markets; (7) a strong sense of unity binding the total society together.

It is difficult to conceive of essentially agricultural economies in Africa supporting the extreme specialization, differentiation of associations, and individualistic impersonality which is characteristic of Euroamerican culture. Hence the strong sense of local unity, still to be found in the African communal type of society, is not likely to be dissipated quickly; and parochialism—though expanded to include the larger community or state—is foreseeable as a characteristic of African societies for some time to come. Two factors reinforce this prediction. First, there is the abundant evidence that the institution of kinship in the communal society has remarkable powers to resist rapid change. Charged as it still is with crucial functions in the socialization process and in providing for social welfare in those large areas as yet untouched by state functions, kinship remains a strong unifying force in African society and will continue to do so. Second, most African societies are more or less unified internally by common resistance to European domination. While in itself this is a weak principle of organization, it nevertheless provides the basis on which numerous associations can unite with a common goal and similar modes of achieving that goal. In doing so, it strengthens the sense of unity binding local communities to each other and contributes to the solidarity of the whole complex communal society.

Disorganization of the old cultural and social patterns is evident in Africa. But there are signs of hope for a new and different Africa in the acceptance of new goals and the modes of achieving them by many segments of the societies—the generation of students, the urban dwellers, those who work under contract, and those who have long and intensively been in contact with the West. It is these groups which are forming the new associations, writing the new rules of behavior, forging the new systems of rights and obligations which provide the bases for a less cohesive but nonetheless dynamic and effective social organization.

the role of Christianity and Islam in contemporary Africa

GEORGE W. CARPENTER

Executive Secretary, Africa Committee, Division of Foreign Missions, National Council of the Churches of Christ in the United States of America

It may not be out of place to comment on the fact that Christianity and Islam are placed, for this discussion, among the elements which constitute the *heritage* of contemporary Africa. Neither religion originated in Africa; both entered the continent from abroad. Neither is professed by more than a minority of the population. Yet both are indeed forces to be reckoned with and no discussion of contemporary Africa can fail to take account of them. It might indeed be asked whether they should not rather be included among the "elements of political and social upheaval" to be considered later. Christianity in particular is very often— and quite unjustly—charged with the whole responsibility for that breakdown of traditional African life-pattern which is everywhere in evidence. The role of economic development, industrialization, urbanization, communications, European law and administration, a money economy, and a whole wide range of contacts with the outside world tends to be overlooked; and it is rashly assumed that the Christian missionary has been the principal agent of change. Hence it is interesting to note that the contents of this book also include colonialism (or its effects) and Western education and culture within the elements covered by the term "heritage." Thus we are up-dating our conception of what is contemporary. All of these factors and forces *are* part of the current actuality which confronts us. They are all there even if in parts of Africa they arrived

90

only yesterday and are still moving in. Realistic appraisal must take account of them. But they are there in a dual role: on the one hand they already represent accepted facts—even vested interests; on the other they are forces of change of which the full effects are yet to be felt. Only with full recognition of their vitality is it appropriate to speak of them as part of Africa's heritage.

It is not practicable to bracket Islam and Christianity together in this discussion, because they differ greatly in nature, influence, and geographical distribution. Neither is it possible to describe specific situations in detail. Only broad generalizations can be attempted in the space available, generalizations to which many exceptions must be admitted. Attention must also be focused more particularly on the role of these religions as forces progressively modifying the rate and direction of social change than as constituents of current behavior patterns. To this end historical depth is essential for even a brief presentation. This is important too because both religions—but especially Christianity—influence Africa from without as well as from within. They are components of African life and help shape its future. And they are factors in the life of the nations which have relations with Africa, and they influence the attitudes and policies of those nations toward Africa. Both these modes of action must be taken into account.

It is only fair to add that the author claims no competence whatever in respect to Islam. Twenty-seven years of missionary experience in Belgian Congo and a little knowledge of other areas have afforded him first-hand acquaintance with African Christianity. But Islam was not a living force in those parts, so the present discussion is based on books, documents, and discussion with colleagues.

Islam: historical perspective

Islam arose in the Arabian Desert and soon spread across Egypt and North Africa, submerging or surrounding the Christian churches in its path. Arab traders carried it to the east coast of Africa where it also took root. But after the first tide of expansion its further spread was slow and uneven. The Ethiopic Church resisted successfully and has maintained itself through the centuries in the isolation of the highlands. The Coptic Church in Egypt has maintained a bare existence under continual pressure and attrition. On the upper Nile the Kingdom of Donqola, in which Christianity was the state religion with at least a nominal hold over the people, remained a barrier to Mohammedan advance until the early fourteenth century. When it was finally conquered, Arab migrants advanced into the upper Nile Valley in search of living space rather than as missionaries. But they intermarried freely with the Negroes and Hamites who inhabited the country, and Islam thus became the dominant cultural force of the northern Sudan. Their relations with the people farther south were often predatory—they raided them for slaves, women, and cattle. The resistance thus aroused set a limit to the advance of Islam which has at many points persisted to this day.

Largely through trading-relations with tribes farther west, Islam gradually spread across the sub-Sahara regions to the west coast of Africa. The pattern of its advance and of its progressive adaptations to local cultures is complex and irregular. It has been studied carefully by J. Spencer Trimingham, whose writings present the matter in full detail.[1]

As a result of this process, extending over many centuries, Islam is found in various degrees of cultural purity from the Mediterranean coast of Africa across the vast wilderness of the Sahara and throughout most of the grass and scrub country south of the desert. At some places it extends to the Atlantic and Guinea coasts; at others, tribes of forest-dwelling peoples or of agriculturists have remained pagan or have in recent times chosen Christianity in preference to Islam. Farther to the east the Azande and the south Sudan peoples have resisted Islam and have been relatively receptive to Christianity. For Kenya and Tanganyika the slave-trading activities of the "Arabs" (who were of predominantly African descent with perhaps not more than 1 per cent Arab blood) engendered a general hostility to Islam throughout the nineteenth century, except in the coastal regions where the Moslem faith had long been established.

[1] *Islam in Ethiopia* (London, Oxford University Press, 1952); *Islam in the Sudan* (London, Oxford University Press, 1949); *The Christian Approach to Islam in the Sudan* (London, Oxford University Press, 1948); *The Christian Church in Post-War Sudan* (London: World Dominion Press, 1949); *Islam in West Africa* is in preparation, 1954.

The subjection of nearly the whole of Africa to European colonial rule during the nineteenth century had the incidental effect of strengthening and revitalizing Islam in many areas. In West Africa both French and British authorities found Islamic states whose rulers were quite willing to accept a "protected" status which guaranteed their own authority and gave them a large degree of autonomy. European intervention thus enhanced their prestige and that of the politico-religious system of Islam, which they embodied, in the eyes of neighboring tribes as well as of their own people. A rapid expansion of Islam has resulted.

In the upper Nile Basin a much more complex series of events took place. Turkish misrule in Egypt delivered the eastern Sudan to the mercy of powerful slave-traders who became, in effect, independent rulers. The country was devastated, population declined, and the people who remained sank into utter misery.

> The whole economic and social welfare of the Sudan, and to a large extent of Egypt, had come to depend upon slavery. The country was worthless to Egypt, in spite of Mohammed Ali's ambitions, except for the slave trade, therefore Egyptian rule was based on it. Such a system, based on greed and sanctioned by Islam, had no consideration for the welfare of the people. The suffering masses themselves, reared in a tradition of fatalism, passively accepted the new order. Religion alone could give the needed impulse to concentrate all this submerged feeling into active expression.[2]

In 1881 Mohammed Ahmad, the self-styled Mahdi, convinced of a special call to initiate a new world order, led a revolt which overcame the forces sent against it and, in 1883, gained complete political control of eastern Sudan.

> The British Government, now in control of Egypt which it had just saved from civil war, decided upon the abandonment of the Sudan and sent General Gordon to perform the task, impossible in its double form, of withdrawing the garrison and leaving behind a form of orderly government. . . . Khartoum was besieged and Gordon was killed when it fell on January 1885.
>
> . . . .
>
> After the fall of Khartoum the Mahdi set to work to organize his empire, but . . . he died in June of the same year.[3]

2 Trimingham, *Islam in the Sudan*, p. 93.
3 *Ibid.*, p. 95.

His successor was unable to maintain unity among the Mahdi's followers and tried to rule by tyranny and oppression. Great Britain reoccupied the Sudan (1896–98), and the condominium with Egypt, in which Great Britain was the dominant partner, was established. Egypt's "real role in the modern Sudan . . . has been that of Islamic cultural reinforcement." [4] The importance of this role has been demonstrated by the recent plebiscite, which has rejected British authority, despite the enormous material and cultural gains of the past half-century, in favor of closer politico-religious ties with Egypt.

The Mahdist movement continues as a factor—chiefly political in character—in present-day Sudan and as a strand in the fabric of Islam in territories as distant as northern Nigeria. It wins West African adherents partly by propaganda among those who go on pilgrimage to Mecca.

In East Africa, colonization has had still another result in that it has brought into Africa a large number of immigrants from South Asia, including many Moslems from what is now Pakistan. These Asiatics continue to form a distinct ethnic and cultural unit, largely unassimilated, with interests often sharply at variance with those of the African and European groups. They include many petty tradesmen and some middlemen. As yet their cultural and religious influence on the Africans has been slight, but it might become important if common interests, or even a strong common antagonism to the European, brought them together. Already they exert an indirect influence on African affairs because their countries of origin, India and Pakistan, are solicitous for their welfare and make political capital of matters affecting them. This is so far a political rather than a religious interest.

In all these countries the activity of the agencies of Islamic advance appear to vary from complete apathy to intense and successful propaganda. Fully trained professional Moslem missionaries —Africans all—are found in some places. Elsewhere holy men and teachers win personal renown and attract followers. Again itinerant traders, notably the Hausa, may be effective agents of propaganda. It is noticeable that in parts of West Africa Islam is found chiefly along the main roads rather than in sequestered communities. The

4 *Ibid.*, p. 97.

Mahdist cult especially is being spread westward by "organized propaganda through agents among peoples filled with . . . expectancy of a Messiah who will drive out the Christians." [5] Wherever Arabic is introduced it constitutes a vehicle for the spread of Islam. This is currently a matter of importance in south Sudan, where Arabic has just supplanted English as the official language of the government. Troop movements during the war were another factor —Central Africans from many areas came into contact with Islam for the first time and found it congenial.

The contemporary significance of Islam

When one attempts to characterize Central African Islam, one is tempted at first to regard it as a weakened or attenuated form as compared with that of the Near East or North Africa. Many of its adherents are racially of pure African stock, without even a fictitious descent from any Arab ancestor. Many speak not more than a few words of Arabic; they recite the Koran, if at all, by rote and without understanding. Their knowledge of the faith sometimes embraces little more than a few stories of the Prophet and some maxims or proverbs; their practice of it goes little beyond the prescribed ritual prayers and almsgiving. Observers note that different aspects of Islam appeal to different groups. Some regard it chiefly as a political system, a potential reinforcement in their struggle for autonomy, for freedom from colonial rule, or perhaps merely for supremacy over their neighbors. To others Islam is primarily a religion, appealing partly because it comes to them from within Africa, not from Europe; because it reinforces their existing sense of community with new sanctions; and because it promises salvation without imposing high ethical standards.

Yet it may be doubted whether this variety of content and appeal, this protean character, is not the very genius of Islam, working itself out now in Africa as it has done so many times before in other cultural settings.

Of the Islamic system, apart from those elements indispensable for the maintenance of its distinctiveness, each people adopted those elements which harmonized most with its national character and ways of life. Whilst all Muslim peoples learn to

[5] *Ibid.,* p. 160.

reverence the *shari'a* as the divine law and symbol of the system, their lives are ruled by their own indigenous *'āda* or customary law. This process of mutual assimilation has meant that Islam has become practically indigenous in each country into which it has spread.

These two factors—the possession of a distinct individuality and the solidarity of a vast social system, together with its power of becoming indigenous by the assimilation or resetting of elements of other cultures—explain the enormous strength of Islam and the tenacity of the grip it holds over its adherents.

An important clue to the understanding of Muslims which arises out of this is that their religious and social life forms a natural whole. Muslims place extreme emphasis on the externals of religion and make no important ethical demands. They have a unified and attainable religious-social code of behaviour. They do not live as Christians do, in a state of tension, feeling that their lives fall short of their religious standard. Therefore no strain is put upon them. Their religious life is wholly a matter of behaviour and conformity. Social customs, though pagan in origin, all alike take on religious and Islamic sanctions. Nobody is wholly conscious of what elements are distinctly religious and Muslim, and what are merely social and pagan, identified with Islam by no logical implication. The result of this is that Islam is a vast complex system but only secondarily a motive power within.[6]

What does the Islamization of an African people mean in terms of its capacity to utilize the resources of Western culture and to continue in the stream of development to which contact with the outer world opens the way? In this respect the influence of Islam seems completely negative; it places a formidable roadblock in the way of progress. This is perhaps the most serious result of the Islamic advance of the past century. There are several reasons for this:

1. Islam is intensely conservative. The creative genius of its early centuries has long since given way to a fatalism that accepts whatever is as part of God's will. This makes passive acceptance a virtue and equates a desire for change with rebellion against God. By assimilating the rites, beliefs, and traditions of African culture it gives them too the sanction of its authority and thus perpetuates them. Hence a community which has embraced Islam is more impervious to change than one which has not.

6 *Ibid.,* p. 107.

2. Islamic education is restricted in aim and content. The so-called schools in Islamic territories in Africa rarely do more than teach the pupils to recite the Koran by rote in Arabic. As a means of fitting them to live more effectively in the modern world they are usually quite valueless.

3. Islam is a man's world in which the place of women is extremely low. This means that home and family life are devoid of any liberating influence and tend only to perpetuate the stagnant and superstitious attitudes of the past.

4. The Islamic world tends to regard the West with hostility and defiance, not unmixed with envy. Thus Islam in Africa affords a rallying-point for those who, for whatever reason, oppose Western influence, activity, or control.

5. Islam reinforces and perpetuates lines of segregation, especially between religious groups, instead of working toward a larger total integration. It accepts the existence of minorities, as groups having their own religious sanctions and legal codes, politically subject to the Islamic state. It does not recognize any right of individual choice between such groups or dissidence from the group into which a man is born except the right to become Moslem. Personal religious or political freedom has no place in the Islamic system.[7].

Thus the acceptance of Islam by an African people is apt to represent, for the present at least, an irrevocable choice in favor of the old ways and against the new.

Yet even here the situation is not all dark, because Islam as a whole is confronted by Western technological and social progress and is forced to achieve a dynamic response if it is to survive.

The Islamic community is, for the Muslim, the Kingdom of God on earth. This means that the history of the community is sacred. It is not merely the record of how Muslims have lived: it is the illustration of how God intended that they should live.

Here we come upon the kernel of the modern Muslim's discomfiture—the burden of a recent history which seemed to have let them down, of a weakness in the world which did not coincide with the "truth" about Islam. . . . Peoples living in other than the Islamic way had been allowed to become more powerful and more successful. . . . The endeavor to rehabilitate its on-

7 See Wynor Wilton, "Religious Freedom among Arabs," *Christian Century* (April 14, 1954), pp. 463–65.

going history . . . is the fundamental fact of present-day Islam.
Muslims wish to re-instate Islamic history in its true, divinely-ordained function, and to do so through their own efforts. This
is . . . the theological imperative within current Islamic social
reform. . . . Islam being what it is, Muslims feel that they must
solve the problem or perish. It is not only the welfare of their
community which is at stake, but the validity of their faith.[8]

It cannot be said that this process of revitalization is evident as
yet in African Islam, apart perhaps from a few advanced thinkers
at such centers as Gordon College, in Khartoum. But that it exists
at all is encouraging, for the dilemma it reflects cannot long escape
the consciousness of those Africans who are coming more and more
into contact with Western culture and technology, and who will
perforce ask themselves whether their Islamic faith is to debar them
from advantages which their neighbors enjoy.

There is one further respect in which an internal renewal of
Islam is essential, namely in its capacity to foster nationhood in
the modern sense and in its ability to produce statesmen capable
of leading such nations. The characteristic pattern of the Islamic
state has been a personal despotism resting on mass loyalty
grounded in religion, on fear, and on military force. Such states can
rarely attain great size, long duration, or lasting internal stability.
Nor are they effective in promoting mass welfare. The pattern is
quite incompatible with the complex administrative structure and
varied technical competence required for the multiple functions of
modern nations; it cannot engender a patriotic loyalty transcending
religious and cultural differences; it does not provide scope for
potential leaders nor assure security to competent servants of the
state. Until Islam is able to develop a more adequate political philosophy, Moslem states are not apt to achieve maturity or stability.

Yet Islam has positive cultural values which must not be forgotten.

1. It intensifies the group loyalty of its members and permits no
barriers of color or race to break the universal brotherhood of all
Moslems. In respect to segregation within the group, its practice
is better than that of many Christians; as regards inter-group barriers, it is not as good.

[8] Wilfred Cantewell Smith, "Trends in Muslim Thought and Feeling," *Moslem
World,* Vol. XLII, No. 4 (October, 1952), pp. 321–22.

2. Islam is profoundly conscious of God. Its insistence on the unity, sovereignty, and power of God creates a sense of creaturely dependence which is reinforced by the ritual obligation of frequent prayer. This definiteness stands in contrast to the vagueness of much popular Christianity. But it involves weakness as well as strength in that it leads to fatalism and saps initiative and personal responsibility.

3. Its insistence on sobriety, self-control, and personal dignity is an element of strength. The temperate lives of Moslems often contrast favorably to those of other social groups—including Christians—in the same community.

4. The universality of Arabic as a means of communication throughout the Islamic world (except on the fringes) provides a focus of cultural cohesion of great importance, supported by strong religious sanctions.

Christianity in Africa: historical perspective

As noted above, the Coptic and Ethiopic churches are the only pre-Islamic Christian bodies that still exist in Africa. Of the latter, Trimingham writes:

> North-east Africa was the only African region where Islam had a rival in the presentation of a new religious conception of life to Hamites and Negroes. Consequently, had Abyssinia become Muslim . . . nothing could have stopped the spread of Islam throughout the whole of the continent. . . .
> The Abyssinians, in the security of their natural fortress, allowed their once vigorous and expanding Christianity to stagnate at a low cultural and spiritual level. . . . The shock of Islamic conquest . . . instead of stimulating the Abyssinians, led to exhausting internal struggle and a withdrawal upon their moribund Christianity as the symbol of their national independence to be guarded at all costs, so that it degenerated still further into a form of higher tribal religion isolated in a sea of Islam.[9]

The rest of Africa was largely cut off from Europe by the Sahara until the fifteenth century when Portuguese explorers advanced progressively down the west coast and eventually rounded the Cape of Good Hope. But the lack of good harbors and navigable rivers,

[9] *Islam in Ethiopia*, pp. xiv–xv.

the high coastal ranges, the hostility of the people, the insalubrious climate, tropical diseases, and the absence of commercial incentive so impeded exploration and settlement that the map of Africa remained largely blank until the nineteenth century. Western influence was confined to the coastal margins of the continent.

For three centuries, roughly 1550 to 1850, the dominant Western activity in Africa was the slave trade. It may be noted that the enslavement of Africans for transplantation to America was approved by church dignitaries as a means of bringing them under Christian influence and saving their souls! In the sixteenth century Roman Catholic missions were established at many points on the west coast, and thousands of slaves were held by them. These missions eventually stagnated and had largely disappeared before the modern period. Important permanent settlements grew up, such as those at Luanda, Cape Town, Lourenço Marques, and Mozambique, which became centers of government and formed the basis for later claims of European sovereignty over hinterlands as well as coastal zones. In the region of Cape Town successive waves of migration brought substantial numbers of Dutch, English, and French migrants who established themselves on the land, and whose descendants today number some two and one-half million. They constitute a predominantly Protestant, Calvinistic body in which religious faith is still a major influence.

The pietistic movement and evangelical revival which began in the latter part of the eighteenth century had a double influence on Africa. On the one hand they initiated the movement for the suppression of the slave trade and the emancipation of slaves; on the other they gave rise to the modern era of Christian missions, primarily in the Protestant churches, but, by indirect stimulation, in Roman Catholicism also. How far this Christian and humanitarian concern motivated the various explorers whose labors finally opened Africa to European cultural—as well as religious—penetration we may never fully know. Certainly, in the greatest of them, David Livingstone, that motive was dominant. He was a missionary turned explorer, deliberately undertaking to open the road so that others might follow, bringing "Christianity and commerce" into the heart of Africa. It is well for Africa that the era of exploration was also one of rising Christian concern. Reginald Coupland, writing on the life of Wilberforce, "sums up the labours of the great emancipators and shows how but for their passionate sense of moral values, sustained by profound religious faith, Africa would have become 'a vast slave-pen' once the explorers had finished their task." [10]

The story of the partition of Africa among the great powers, the establishment of communications and ordered government, the growth of plantations, mines, and industries (with their enormous impact on African life), and the concurrent spread of Christian missions and implantation of African churches cannot be told here. Abundant sources are available, but the student may find it difficult to keep a balanced judgment as to the relative importance of the various elements. In fact, it is too soon to know. Only in the light of history will it be possible to understand the full impact of the complex of forces now at work.

The role of the Christian mission and missionary

One important group of these forces centers around the missionary and the institutions related to his work. The missionary was usually the first and is still in many instances the only non-African whose presence among an African people was motivated more by concern for them than for himself. Of course no one can claim absolute purity of motive. Selfishness is not unknown among missionaries, and ecclesiastical or sectarian advantage has doubtless often been a factor in mission policy. Nevertheless the missionary has rarely been wanting in concern for "his people," and this concern is the common element unifying the protean variety of his activities.

The missionary had, first of all, to create bridges of understanding between the people and himself. He learned their language, inadequately perhaps by present-day standards, but far more thoroughly than any one else cared to do. (And the pioneering efforts of many missionaries in this field accumulated the materials and developed many of the tools of present-day linguistic research.) He introduced reading and writing, the basic first step in cultural intercommunication. And he produced books, most particularly

10 Quoted from Max Warren, *C.M.S. News Letter* (February, 1954); the reference is to Reginald Coupland, *Wilberforce* (London: Collins, 1954).

translations of the Scriptures, which have had untold influence on African life.

In this process the missionary began to discover what no representative of Western culture had previously suspected—that Africa had a deep, rich, varied, and complex cultural life of its own, containing many elements of positive value, and constituting a way of life in which each individual had his place in the functional social whole—clan, community, tribe, or nation. It may be well to recall that much less than a century ago the existence of this African culture was still unknown to the Western world and that even more recently nobody realized how easily the pattern could be shattered or how great the resultant upheaval might be. To the missionary must go much of the credit for discovering and exploring African culture, even though from the outset he also found himself in opposition to some of its manifestations, such as polygyny, slavery, child marriage, and ritual murder. Faced with what seemed obviously evil and revolting practices, the missionary could do no other than oppose them, but it must not be supposed that he took the negative course of mere denunciation. Rather he undertook to awaken a Christian conscience among his converts so that the church at least, as a purified society, would be free of them and would use its influence to eradicate them from the life of the community. We know now that any single custom is apt to have functional ramifications that make social change a vastly more complex process than was realized a generation or two ago; but we must also recognize that change from within as a result of an aroused social conscience is a perfectly valid process—one which operated in our own society, for instance, in the abolition of slavery and is working to overcome racial segregation. It is doubtless true also that no society is ever in complete internal adjustment; one change gives rise to others in endless succession. African societies are no exception. There is evidence that they were in flux before the current invasion of Western culture intensified the strains and enormously increased the tempo of change. In this process the missionary's influence has been mild, benign, and constructive as compared with those of industry, commerce, and often even government.

We must face the fact that the traditional African society was doomed from the moment that African productive capacity became economically vital to the Western world. It is fortunate, rather than otherwise, that the missionary was there to mitigate the shock of change and to provide bridges of understanding and intercultural communication.

One of the most important of those bridges has been the Christian school. Throughout Negro Africa, missions started schools long before governments saw any occasion for doing so, and governments have generally been more than willing to continue to entrust the bulk of educational work to the missions. Not only was it the cheapest, simplest, and most effective way of getting the work done, but there has also been a widespread realization that the most vital goals of African education must be integrity of character and unselfish devotion to the public good, qualities fostered by Christian training and motivation. Beyond question, Christian schools in Africa have made and are making a very great contribution. Tens of thousands of schools, numbering millions of pupils, are in operation. In some areas there is scarcely a village too remote for its children to have access to at least a rudimentary school. Probably 85 per cent of all elementary education in non-Moslem Africa is conducted under Christian auspices. Standards are continually advancing, and a steadily increasing number of pupils go on to secondary schools and even to universities.

Yet there is cause for concern. The sheer magnitude of the task is staggering. Missions find their personnel so deeply involved in teaching—or worse, in educational administration—that they have no reserve of time or strength for other tasks. A missionary charged with the direction of a large station school and the oversight of several hundred village and regional schools with a total enrolment of ten or even twenty thousand pupils is not able to enjoy much personal contact with any of them.[11]

The Christian motive must be mediated through a teaching staff whose own appreciation of it may be but fragmentary. So many of the pupils may be in school for purely selfish motives that the sense of vocation and responsibility is lost, and Christian teaching is received merely as factual knowledge and not as an invitation to share a vital experience. Government intervention in the form of programs, supervision, and subsidies helps make possible the fur-

[11] The figures are based on actual cases.

ther development of the system, but it also involves increased paper-work and makes the missionary more than ever an administrator. Teachers also are apt to regard themselves as civil servants rather than exponents of Christian vocation when their salaries come in large part from government. Yet the schools cannot expand fast enough to meet the popular demand for education. Thus the pro-gressive secularization of African education seems inevitably bound up with its further expansion. Missions and churches are beginning here and there to face the choice of whether to continue to spread their influence ever wider and thinner, or whether to ask govern-ment to provide a separate system of secular schools so that Chris-tian schools may work more effectively with smaller numbers.

Apart from their specifically Christian emphasis, the general cul-tural importance of these schools is very great. It is here that the new generation is becoming literate and learning a European lan-guage. Here are found the clerical and manual skills that will enable thousands of young people to take employment not at the lowest level of day labor but in higher and higher categories of skilled employment and progressively in self-employed crafts and professions in the new Africa. Here are the seminal ideas of Western culture, which, while they assuredly challenge the funda-mental assumptions of African life, do so not in a negative way but as tested insights freely available for a reintegration, on new foundations, of all that is shaken. For reintegration must and will occur, and signs of its beginning are already evident.

Another bridge of understanding provided by the missionary is the ministry of healing. Hundreds of hospitals and dispensaries scattered all over Africa treat several million patients a year. As a direct demonstration of Christian concern for others the total effect is impressive. As a challenge to African conceptions of causation and as a background for the teaching and application of science in other realms (such as agriculture) it may be even more impres-sive. Most of all this service creates a bond of personal contact in a relation of helpfulness which is greatly needed, whether between missionary and African patient or between African staff members of one group and patients of other groups. The creation of bonds of trust and fellowship across traditional barriers is a Christian contribution of fundamental importance.

Beyond all these, however, it is this writer's considered opinion that the most important function of the missionary in Africa is that of establishing ties of intimate personal friendship with a certain number—necessarily small—of Africans. The formal intercourse of church, school, hospital or other professional relationships do not provide adequate channels for the deepest levels of communication. In fact the difficulty of true communication between people of different languages and cultures is seldom fully recognized. Any idea must be expressed in words. The speaker selects words to clothe his thought or feeling, using the conceptual framework and the connotations which his own background supplies. He assumes on the part of his hearer an identical or at least a basically similar set of meanings. But if the hearer's cultural background is very different this assumption is not valid. The hearer will hear with reference to his own conceptual framework and connotations. Radical distortion of meaning may thus occur, and the probability of such distortion increases rapidly as one proceeds from simple familiar things to more abstract and general issues. The only way to overcome this barrier is such prolonged and intimate fellowship that connotation both of idea, of feeling, and of motive become shared, each one exploring deeply the other's mind and heart. If possible it should take place in the languages of both participants so that the conceptual resources of both languages may be freely utilized. It should, of course, not be merely abstract discussion but should be part of the experience of working together at whatever task is in hand. In this way alone the missionary can most truly share his own life with others, and that sharing is the highest expression of the Christian love, the *agapé*, which is at the heart of the Gospel. Unquestionably it is by such sharing that the great spiritual pioneers and leaders of Africa have most often come to their full stature.

The discovery, development and encouragement of African Christian leadership is the basic responsibility of the missionary. The linguistic and cultural barrier to complete communication will almost certainly limit his effectiveness in reaching masses of people with his message. It will certainly limit his ability to prescribe the application of Christian principles in unfamiliar cultural settings. In both these respects he can serve best by sharing himself as deeply as possible with a few African associates and trusting them to work out the expression and application of the Christian message in their own language and culture. Stagnation has doubtless often resulted from the unwillingness of missionaries to entrust this interpretative task to the leaders of the African church and from undue insistence that the African church adhere to foreign (i.e. European) standards and formulations.

Apart from these tasks within his field of service, the missionary has had an important influence as interpreter of Africa to the churches and general public in Europe and America, and sometimes as witness and advocate in securing the redress of wrongs. The gradual transformation of public sentiment from an uncritical acceptance of human exploitation in colonies to a deeply humanitarian concern for dependent peoples everywhere is largely the result of a growing awareness of them as *people,* an awareness for which missionary propaganda is partly responsible. This public sentiment is a factor which increasingly affects the formulation of policy in respect to dependent and underprivileged peoples. As advocate the missionary corps may find itself compelled to protest government policies which threaten the welfare or the rights of the people. It may be necessary also to stimulate public discussion of issues, both locally and internationally. As an instance one may cite the statement of the Archbishop of Canterbury in Convocation (October, 1953) with reference to racial discrimination in South Africa:

> It is important that the facts be known here and be faithfully evaluated: and it is part of our duty to God and to our neighbour to let our judgment be known—first because it is always a Christian duty to judge the world by the mind of our Lord; secondly because this particular question of policy in South Africa has immediate repercussions throughout the continent and closely affects parts of it for which we are responsible; thirdly because it has repercussions far beyond Africa or the Commonwealth; and fourthly because this policy will, if pursued long enough, plunge Africa into strife and bloodshed and bring ruin upon all the races within it.
>
> But it is not the duty of the Church here to interfere in any other way with affairs in South Africa; and attempts to do so are likely to injure the very cause which we have at heart. It is the business of the Church in the Province of South Africa and other Christians there to defend the application of Christian principles to political and social life there. . . . Our part is to support them . . . in the ways which they ask of us, and so to assure them of our understanding, our sympathy, and our patient prayers.[12]

[12] "Racialism in South Africa," *The Voice of the Church* (London: South African Church Institute, 1953) , p. 4.

For these and other purposes, Christian councils and other inter-group agencies have come into being and are developing into increasing usefulness. The International Missionary Council promotes inter-council relations and conducts important basic research. It is also joint sponsor with the World Council of Churches of the Commission of the Churches on International Affairs which maintains contact with the United Nations and its specialized agencies.

A more specialized but often important role of missionaries is that of contributing their knowledge and insight in the academic fields of African studies. In this relationship they also stand to receive much, since the contributions of anthropology, sociology, and political science have important bearings on the missionary task and on the functions and methods of the African church.

The role of the African church

Thus far attention has been focused on the missionary, especially in his role of intercultural interpreter or bridge. But a bridge normally has two abutments, and the missionary finds the essential fulfilment of his task in the formation and growth of an indigenous church potentially equivalent to that which sent him forth.

In point of numbers the modern evangelization of Africa has been singularly successful as compared with other major areas. The total membership of African churches numbers some 21 million, about equally divided between Roman Catholics and Protestants, or somewhat more than 10 per cent of the population. In many parts of the continent the balance between mission and church is rapidly shifting, so that, whereas the mission was until lately the dominant partner, the African church is increasingly assuming responsibility for its own affairs.

Yet the visitor to Africa is more apt to be impressed by the weakness and immaturity of these churches, and especially by their inadequate leadership, than by their strength. Thus a commission on theological education, visiting Central Africa in 1953, reported of the churches there:

They are relatively young, dating usually from the last quarter of the nineteenth century, and reaching some considerable size only in our own century. They are limited and greatly affected

by the tribal and undeveloped society of Africa. Illiteracy has
been a fetter from the start, and too often a continuing ball and
chain, not merely among ordinary members but even among
responsible workers. Most of the church and mission groups are
conscious of two major difficulties calling for large-scale efforts
at discipline, and, of course, for more adequate spiritual commitment and church teaching: inability to achieve Christian family
life, breached by polygamy and adultery; inability to win true
and full liberation from the fears and superstitions of the old
society. Some groups add a third of similar magnitude but differing in type—the new materialism of a money economy.[13]

The primary weakness of the African church is doubtless the
dearth of trained and capable leaders, the inevitable result of very
rapid growth, a widely dispersed membership living chiefly in
scattered village communities, a preliterate culture, and almost
innumerable languages. Great reliance has been placed on the
village catechist.

In the many thousands of small villages entered more or less
successfully by the missions, it is the catechist who has carried
the daily and weekly burden, with a modicum of supervision and
supplementary service from a missionary or pastor. There was
need for the multiplication of village workers, both for the maintenance of worship and for the simplest of teaching. That need
called forth the catechist and has made his humble service most
useful, even until this day in many areas. . . . He has general
responsibility for the life and care of the local congregation and
its interests—or for several small congregations. . . . He may conduct a "village school" which does not have the programme nor
the quality to be recognized as a regular school. . . . Where the
catechist is the only person with any Christian training or modern
education, however slight, he is informal counselor to the community. . . . The total burden has frequently been too great, and
he has performed only part of this wide range of responsibilities.[14]

While better-trained church leaders exist, they are everywhere in
short supply, and their training is rarely adequate, especially in
the special field of relating the universal Gospel to the social and
cultural conditions of Africa—an area naturally outside the purview of standard European works on pastoral theology! Thus
leadership is the most critical need of the African church. The

[13] M. Searle Bates, et al., Survey of the Training of the Ministry in Africa,
Part II (London: International Missionary Council, 1954), p. 31.
[14] Ibid., pp. 33–34.

commission on theological education made just one basic recommendation:

> That the training of ministers be moved to a central place in the work of missions and churches, with whatever severe readjustment that change will require.[15]

Granting this weakness, and recognizing that it must be met if the African church is to meet its responsibilities, the question may still be asked whether the widespread planting of churches, even at a low initial level of understanding and leadership, has not been sound strategy. Studies in other parts of the world seem to indicate that unless the church takes root as an accepted part of the life of the the community within the first two or three generations, it is apt to remain an uninfluential minority. In much of Africa, Christianity has won or is rapidly winning this acceptance. It remains for the seed thus planted to grow to full fruition, progressively influencing African life from within.

A second weakness of African Christianity is that it has not so far effectively met the challenge of the cities. In some of the older west-coast towns the churches have become relatively static ingrown communities reproducing the denominational pattern of the missions that began work there. In many of the newer cities a phenomenal influx of people is taking place, a migration with which the churches have been unable to cope.

> The spectacular growth of cities and large towns . . . brings a whole new set of problems and opportunities. . . . Africans dependent upon money wages, and crowded into small areas with no chance to grow food, appear as a new social species. The tribal community is broken up, though some elements of its life—not always the most helpful elements—continue in strength. The congested African quarters are a linguistic jumble, and the relationships of groups coming from various tribes and regions often present difficulties. Problems of drink, sex mores, and amusements take new and conspicuous forms. Human needs in this confusion of insecurity are even more obvious than in rural areas. The migration of varied groups of Christians into the cities is a special issue for the churches, challenging the established distribution of personnel and buildings, and also the traditional understandings of comity. It frequently appears that sects and independents emphasizing mass emotions and disregardful of existing

15 *Ibid.*, p. 94.

church connections, are most ready to act with numerical success in the cities. With certain exceptions . . . the urban record of the traditional missions and churches is the familiar one, "too little and too late." [16]

A further source of weakness and embarrassment in Protestant circles is the pattern of sectarian divisions within which mission work is conducted, and which tends to be perpetuated in the African church. As an initial move to overcome this handicap the missions in some African territories have agreed to the use of a common name for the entire African Protestant Church in the area—usually "The Church of Christ in . . . ." This has not generally been followed up as yet by the establishment of national church councils by which the nominal unity of the church would be made a functional reality nor by serious efforts to achieve a common polity. Efforts in this direction are now beginning.

There is also a strong tendency for African churches to break away from mission ties and from each other, forming an ever-increasing number of tiny sects and unrelated congregations. This is particularly true in the Union of South Africa, but the same tendency is found elsewhere—even in the United States. In Belgian Congo the government has sternly repressed separatist sects. It would appear that the church, as a type of social group, meets a vital need of uprooted Africans who have lost the social ties and religious sanctions of the past. So far these independent churches have little or no sense of responsibility beyond their own group, and there is no indication as to how they may be brought into a wider and more fruitful fellowship.

Beyond these questions affecting the life and development of the African church there is a more fundamental range of questions as to the significance of Christianity to the African and the sociological function of the church. Different aspects of Christianity are emphasized in different communions, and it would be impossible in brief compass to define its meaning to African Christians. It may be suggested that that meaning lies more in the realm of reinforcement of community life through shared trust and commitment than in individualized experience, and more in the realm of emotional and volitional response than of intellectual comprehension.

[16] *Ibid.,* pp. 39–40.

As regards the value of the church and of Christian faith in African society there are at least four such values which are of major importance:

1. Christianity provides a simple yet inexhaustible standard of personal moral conduct: *"thou shalt love."* This is within the understanding of everyone, it is the test of every relationship, it is applicable within any culture. Yet it progressively transforms personalities and social situations wherever it is applied. It demands and develops the highest personal integrity. It does not solve any moral issues directly—people may not even agree as to the solution which most nearly meets its requirements—but it creates relationships in which any social problem becomes soluble.

Of course, those who do not practice the ethic of love are not in a position to urge it on others. It is essentially a religious principle because it can only legitimately be presented as God's commandment, not man's; and as such it challenges all alike. Africans are quick to detect the hypocrisy of those who hold that "Christianity is good for the African" but who reject it for themselves.

2. The Christian church, as the fellowship of those who have committed themselves to the Christian way, is a focus of social integration of the utmost importance to Africa. Because it reaches from the individual and the local group out through the community and nation to the whole world, because it reaches back through the past and forward through the future, because it is a living fellowship involving personal commitment, group acceptance, and action together under religious sanctions, it is uniquely able to replace, for its adherents, the old tribal groupings which cannot survive changed conditions. Here, however, there is a dilemma which Western Christianity has never solved: how can the church meet the need to be *universal,* to embrace the whole community, and to be at the same time *pure*—that is, a living fellowship of those who are personally committed to Christ? It may be that African Christianity, with its strong sense of community, will help find an answer.

3. The Christian tradition, arising in Hebrew-Judaic life, which was closely akin to African cultures, affords a cosmology which meets African needs for an intelligible universe. It is becoming clear that man cannot live without myths, that he suffers frustration when his world fails to make sense. Our Western passion for

verbal exactitude has closed our eyes to great values in the Hebrew-Christian Scriptures which the imaginative African grasps without effort. He may yet help us recover our appreciation of the basic insights on which our culture is based by taking them for his own.

4. Christianity is compatible with the total Western cultural pattern which is becoming a world culture. It has already faced the issues posed by nationalism, science, and technology and does not fear to face any new issues which may arise.. Hence, adoption of Christianity imposes no limitation on the general social evolution of an African individual or group. The ethical tensions of Christianity, insofar as they influence personal and group behavior, operate as a social force within any culture whatever, Western as well as African. The permanence of Christianity is not that of a fixed unchanging system but of a creative energy, a kind of life.

The conflicts of the faiths

Many people are concerned for the outcome in those areas where Islam and Christianity are competing for the allegiance of African peoples. There are African churches that are static or retreating before a Moslem advance. There are other areas where Christianity is making relatively small gains against Islam. The issue is not simply a conflict of religious ideologies; undoubtedly political factors are involved, because just now African Islam is reinforced by nationalistic, anti-European sentiments and by fear of change.

But there are two other religions or world-views which are also competing for African allegiance on a much more universal scale: the old animism and the new secularism. Where Islam is available as a cloak for animism, many of the old concepts and practices will doubtless continue in a new guise, as pagan festivals were perpetuated within early Christianity. Only very gradually will popular religious conceptions be modified. Where Christianity is accepted, change will probably be more rapid, since Christianity brings in schools and is associated with Western secular culture. But secularism—the view that religious faith in any form is of negligible importance—is the real attitude of many representatives of Western culture and is being presented powerfully and persuasively by their own behavior. It is implicit in the priority which governments give to questions of material welfare as against human relations, in the dominance of the profit motive in industry, in the wage system that treats laborers as "hands," not as people. It dominates the dehumanized, impersonal, atomistic life of the cities and towns. This is the radical, the fundamental conflict of faiths in Africa. The African, who is basically religious, is shocked by the blatant materialism of the European. If the African follows all too many Europeans in relegating religious faith to the status of excess baggage—a nonessential luxury—then neither Islam nor Christianity has much chance of saving Africa from disaster.

commentary

DR. GLORA M. WYSNER

International Missionary Council

In considering the role of Christianity and Islam in contemporary Africa, perhaps it would be well with the background of Dr. Carpenter's essay to have in mind some facts regarding the relative strength of Christianity and Islam in Africa. The following statistics are taken from the *Atlas of Islamic History*.[1]

Percentage of Moslem Population

French Equatorial Africa	30%
French West Africa	34%
British Cameroons	50%
Gambia	84%
Liberia	20%
Nigeria	33%
Nyasaland	· 9%
Sierra Leone	11%
Tanganyika	19%

1 Philip K. Hitti, (ed.), Princeton Oriental Studies, Vol. XII (Princeton: Prince ton University Press, 1951).

One statement cannot be made which will cover all of Africa, for in some areas, such as Northern Nigeria, the British Cameroons, French Equatorial Africa, the Moslem population is high, while in other areas, such as the Congo, the Rhodesias and South Africa, the Christian church is strong and Islam is weak.

Although neither Christianity nor Islam originated in Africa, Islam has existed there for over one thousand years. The Berber Moslems first began their push outward from North Africa and into the Western Sudan. Both Christianity and Islam are missionary religions. Both have tried to win the pagans in Africa. At the present time, the Moslems in Africa south of the Sahara about equal in number the Christians.

Dr. Carpenter has mentioned the trained Africans serving as professional Moslem missionaries in Africa. It had been said that Al-Azhar in Cairo has trained and sent 2,000 Moslem missionaries into Africa since World War II. That number may be exaggerated. However, the number is no doubt large.

It is interesting to note that Islam has not spread to any extent among the Christian population in Africa. The loss of Christians to Islam in Egypt each year is comparatively large, while the loss of Christians to Islam in Negro Africa is very small. On the other hand, there have been some losses from Islam to Christianity in Africa. Wherever the Christian church is strong in Africa, Islam makes little progress. Islam in Africa differs greatly from Islam in Arab countries. It has taken on many of the African pagan characteristics. Islam has great ability to adapt itself to new situations, and in many parts of Africa where Islam is strong numerically, it has many of the features of Africa but has, as a religion, made a very superficial impact upon the people. Moslems from other parts of the Moslem world do not look upon African Moslems as being orthodox. Many of them belong to the Ahmadiya movement which originated in India. The Mahdist movement mentioned by Dr. Carpenter is an interesting one for it has sprung up in various forms in a number of places. It comes from the belief in a hidden Immam—leader—who would some day appear to lead the Moslem peoples to power. Usually these movements have turned into political movements such as in the Sudan.

To sum up and emphasize some of the points stressed by Dr. Carpenter, and perhaps adding a few, we might point out the effects of Islam in Africa and compare these to the effects of Christianity in Africa.

I. Islam, while serving as a curb to the excessive practise of polygamy, sanctions it. This question of polygamy is one with which the Christian church in Africa continues to wrestle. It insists upon monogamy. But the very fact of monogamy raises grave social and economic problems in African society.

II. Wherever Islam has gone, it has developed Koranic schools. In many places Africans have been attracted to Islam because of their great desire to learn to read and write. Africans have been attracted by the superiority of the Moslem literate who had some degree of education. Christianity, from its very early days in Africa, has been interested in an educational program much broader than that of the Moslems. In fact, about 85 per cent of the educational work carried on in Africa is in the hands of the Christian forces. One must admit that many of these schools are poor and have taught only the rudiments of reading and writing. However, the vast majority of the Koranic schools are very poor, giving some instruction in Arabic and teaching the pupils to memorize the Koran. On the other hand, Christian education has developed some excellent schools and has far surpassed the Islamic schools, in its contribution to the development of the African peoples.

III. Islam has made its contribution in building up three important written languages in Africa through its teaching of Arabic— Swahili, Hausa, and Fulani.

IV. Islam has made its appeal to the African because it has been presented to the Africans by Africans and is looked upon as an African religion, while Christianity is looked upon as a "foreign" religion. Yet Christianity at its best has stimulated research into African culture; it has encouraged the production of literature in African dialects; it has sought to emphasize the best in African life. Christianity has a greater task in becoming a truly indigenous religion than has Islam. Islam in Africa is much more tolerant than orthodox Islam in other parts of the Moslem world. However, as Islam and Christianity come into closer contact, there is no doubt that tensions will increase.

V. Islam has entered African community life without disrupting that life. Hence it has not disturbed one of the great strengths of the African—the community. Christianity with its emphasis on individual religion has frequently been an element in the disintegration of community life.

I would not agree with Dr. Carpenter that the Islamic world regards the West with hostility and defiance. In Africa the colonial powers have given every consideration to Islam, in fact they have often furthered it by their attitude toward it.

If Islam holds true to its tenets that all peoples of the world are of two groups—those belonging to "dar-el-Islam," the household of Believers, and all others outside this household—then tension cannot help but increase between Moslem areas and non-Moslem areas of Africa. As it becomes stronger will it take on more potent political aspects—will it strive to create Moslem states?

Islam appeals to the African because there is no race prejudice within the faith. No matter what the color of a man's skin, no matter what his social standing, no matter what his economic status, he is always welcome to worship at the mosque and to mingle with his fellow Moslems. Christianity cannot say so much for the practice of its faith.

So far, there have not developed among the Moslems in Africa any great Moslem leaders, as there have in other parts of the Moslem world. On the other hand, Christianity has produced some outstanding Christian leaders who have left their imprint on Africa and who are helping to shape the destinies of some parts of that great continent.

A glance at history and the Islamic areas will show that Moslem countries are not democratic countries as we know the meaning of the term "democracy." It is a real question whether Islam can produce in the political field true democracy, because Islam is not only a religion, it is a social system and a political system.

Islam is spreading in Africa because it is easier for a pagan to become a Moslem than to become a Christian. Unfortunately, the pagan who becomes a Moslem carries over many of his superstitions, his social mores, and his moral standards into his new faith. Hence, Islam has not and probably will not make significant changes in the moral, social, and economic life of the people. On the other hand, Christianity, with its thousands of schools in Africa, with its concern for social betterment, with its ministry of healing, and with its insistence on high moral standards, has done and will continue to do much for the uplift of African peoples. However, Islam and Christianity are not the only forces vying for the soul of the African. Animism, secularism, and other forces are also playing their roles in African life.

However, the African is at heart a religious man. If he accepts Islam, he needs few adjustments and few changes. On the other hand, if he accepts Christianity, profound changes must be made in his way of life. I would like to point out one important element to which Dr. Carpenter did not refer but which I believe must be given increased consideration if Christianity is to play its role. In a good many instances we need to present Christianity to the African with a theology that meets the needs of the African people. In much of the presentation of Christianity we have emphasized *sin* and the forgiveness of sin. The African needs freedom from *fear*. Christianity has that message. Islam does not.

the European heritage:
approaches to African development

PAUL HENRY

*Secretary General, Commission for Technical
Co-operation in Africa South of the Sahara, London*

It will probably be convenient for the historians of the
future to consider the year 1950 as one of the great dividing lines
of history, although 1939 would probably be more adequate. The
world of European ascendancy which was built during the latter
part of the nineteenth century and the first part of the twentieth
came to an end through the Japanese attack against Southeast Asia
in 1941, the emancipation of the Arab states in 1945, the final
departure of Italy from Africa, and the various constitutional
changes in the African territories controlled by other European
powers, which have taken place since the end of World War II.

This is not to say that Africa, or for that matter the Middle East
or Southeast Asia, should be counted out as close associates of
Europe and the Western world, but rather it is to indicate that
the basic nature of the relationship between European powers and
their former territories has changed or is changing and that important consequences are bound to arise concerning the economic
future of the African continent.

As it happens, the European continent, or at least the part of
the continent which was historically concerned with overseas development, that is, Western Europe, is undergoing at the same time
a process of economic, if not political, integration.

It would be surprising if these two long-term developments did not react one against another, especially when it is recalled that the potential protagonists of the European movement for economic and political integration are France, which considers its African territories as an integral part of the French Republic; Belgium, which controls the center of Africa; Holland, which has lost most of its overseas possessions; Germany, which was never able to recover its former African colonies.

On the other hand, the political awakening of Africa is considered by many as a part of a world-wide problem which can be interpreted either in terms of racial antagonism, or of economic conflict between economically advanced countries and underdeveloped territories, and conceived in this way it has to be placed in its proper perspective against the background of a fundamental challenge to the Western conception of freedom and dignity of the individual.

Furthermore the African continent is probably the only part of the world, excepting some parts of the South American continent and islands such as Borneo and New Guinea, where the economic potential is not yet fully assessed, and where widely divergent estimates can be put forward as postulates to divergent policies. For instance, it is practically impossible to have a satisfactory answer from competent technicians to the simple question: "Is Africa potentially rich or actually and potentially poor?"

The resulting confusion is such that, when talking about the African future, experts and politicians may be thinking of entirely different problems and still using the same words, while accepting for the sake of argument convenient generalizations.

There is, of course, an innate confusion in the social, political, and economic conditions of Africa today. It comes from the extraordinarily short period during which the African continent and its population had to go through the successive stages of the most violent impact of European colonization on hitherto isolated communities.

The colonization of North Africa dates back to 1830, when Algiers was occupied by the French troops. Tunisia and Egypt were placed under European control in the 1880's. The Zulus were finally beaten in 1877. Central Africa was placed firmly under European control in 1900 after the last slave-traders were beaten by the French, the Belgians, and the British. The Sudan passed under British domination in 1894, after the battle of Omdourman. Morocco and Tripolitania were occupied by France and Italy in 1912. Ethiopia was conquered by Italy in 1936.

This means that in the lifetime of four generations the inhabitants of Africa—Arabs, Berbers, and Negroes—have been submitted directly or indirectly to the pressure and tension of the Western world, which in the meantime went through the fundamental changes of industrialization and the throes of two world wars. The African economies were geared forcibly to a world market with wide fluctuations in prices and outlets. Hundreds and thousands of men had to serve in the armed forces of the European powers, sometimes against their own fellow Africans, sometimes against Europeans, sometimes against Asiatics. In the last twenty years thousands of students were trained in America and in Europe, even in Asia, in close contact with fellow students, representatives of European races, and others who were not concerned with the maintenance of a close connection between the colonies and their metropoles. In Africa itself the native inhabitants saw, in a short time, changes in the composition of the European population living in their midst, as well as in the role and responsibilities they assumed in relation to themselves.

All this is understood, or at least it should be, when referring to Africa today and its future. Insofar as we are concerned with the African continent as being and remaining in close association with the future of the Western world, we must keep in mind the fact that all classes and races in Africa who are in direct or indirect contact with Western administration and enterprise are in a state of flux which is likely to introduce into any analysis or forecast an unpredictable factor.

An important school of thought in the Western world, while not denying the process of change, maintains that it can be somehow kept under control and, so to speak, canalized by institutional methods, while the metropolitan countries concerned could go on imposing their own criteria. It is postulated that the economic interests of the African population necessarily coincide with those of European countries, taken separately or federated into some sort of body politic with extension overseas.

Another school is inclined to be more pragmatic and accept the fact that, for better or for worse, European views about what should be done in Africa have to take into account the views and reactions of the African population, even though the native inhabitants are not yet in a position to play their full role technically and otherwise in the European type of undertaking, in mining, industry, and agriculture. Also this school considers the process of the granting of self-government and semi-national independence as unavoidable.

In a recent lecture given by W. C. Klein, from Holland, who was formerly Adviser to the South Pacific Commission, we find the following statement, which is typical of the first school of thought:

> The unsatisfactory conditions in tropical Africa can only be remedied by long term international treaties or by European Federation . . . we must realize and admit the reasonableness of the thesis that France, Belgium and eventually Portugal, owing to their colonies, play a big role in the limited Eurafrica combination which does not include British territories. France is united with Africa and its African colonies occupy the smaller half of the area of the African tribal bloc of colonies of continental powers. Germany and Italy, which will certainly belong to a future continental European Federation, have practically lost their colonies in Africa.

The present territorial distribution of Africa is regarded as bringing

> . . . disadvantages, unpractical situations and doubling of efforts of the past and of the present day. . . . Perhaps big savings are only realisable in case a Federation of continental Europe creates the means for an efficient co-operative action in conjunction with the British Commonwealth whereby both groups of countries agree, under at least a long-term treaty, to take the required parallel decisions in mutual consultations. We could in this way obtain the maximum of results from the great expenditure that is still needed in tropical Africa.

In this moderate statement, two main ideas are made clear: Africa is a *passive* continent, which was divided up between the European powers, according to local contingencies, military and otherwise, and sometimes modified by European diplomacy. Europe is still in a position, so to speak, to make up her mind and change this territorial distribution or palliate its economic consequences through an act of will or through the projection onto Africa of the European process of economic integration.

It would be a mistake to believe that such conceptions are limited to "continental powers" and that in fact the division between the two schools of thought coincide with the well-known differences of opinion between Great Britain, on the one hand, and the potential members of the federated Europe, on the other, about the specific problem of European integration.

For entirely different reasons, the Union of South Africa, or the Federation of Rhodesia, members of the British Commonwealth, are not far from thinking that the territorial division resulting from the "scramble for Africa" has outlived its usefulness. Not so long ago Marshal Smuts pointed out that Africa south of the Sahara should be reorganized along regional lines, taking into account natural resources and communications rather than political connections. As a matter of fact, the recent creation of the Federation of Rhodesia and Nyasaland is a perfect illustration of the thesis according to which European powers or European settlers in Africa are justified in reorganizing boundaries to promote a better framework for economic development which in turn will not fail to benefit the native inhabitants. It can be argued that the views expressed by the native populations of the areas concerned were not representative; but in any case, although these views were opposed to the federation idea, they were not taken into account, and the European economic and political criteria prevailed.

This is not all. Some authoritative voices have maintained not only that there should be a rearrangement of boundaries for economic purposes, but also that a redistribution of population to constitute homogeneous entities, from the point of view of racial composition, should take place in order to avoid racial conflicts within the same areas of economic activity.

As a summary of this "revisionism" from the inside, which could be the counterpart of Dr. Klein's statement, the following might be quoted:

> Few people suppose that the frontiers of the various states and colonial territories of Africa are fixed for all time; since the "scramble for Africa" in the eighties, indeed, many big changes as well as frontier rectifications have been made. But clearly the rapid pace of change in Britain's position in the continent is the most powerful solvent of the status quo. Britain's gradual withdrawal—leaving successor governments equipped with democratic institutions behind—is matched by the rising ambitions of other African interests.[1]

[1] Unsigned article, "The Shape of Africas to Come," *New Commonwealth* (July 8, 1954).

There we have clearly, as seen through the prism of various national interests, the same conception of Africa as predominantly an undisputed empire for the European nations and races. The Anglo-Saxons may have a different approach to the problem from that of Afrikaans comembers of the Commonwealth; the European powers such as France and Belgium may be more concerned with the immediate practical problems than Germany, Italy, and Holland, who have no responsibilities in Africa; but they all seem to share this conception.

Apart from its immediate political and economic connotations, one may ask whether the old thesis of the white man's burden is not under a new cloak. The European races have got the capital, the knowledge, and the culture which shall in due course bring the African populations to the level of civilization of the European races. There is no doubt that the almost miraculous transformation of the conditions of living for the human race, black, brown, or white, in the African continent is an almost unanswerable argument in support of this contention. In less than seventy years, the total number of non-European inhabitants in Africa more than doubled while Africa was enabled to support more than four million European inhabitants on a Western standard of living.

The essence of the problem is this: while acknowledging the substantial contribution that European colonization has brought to the welfare of the African continent, we must now find methods which will take into account as facts the emergence of African political and economic consciousness and still promote a type of economic development which is indispensable from the point of view of Africa as well as from the point of view of Europe.

It is not certain that European races are still in a position to evolve in time a long-term strategy, especially when they have to face the challenge of non-African and non-European interests and conceptions.

The natural tendency is to take refuge in an oversimplified version of the problem as, for example, on the cultural plane Christian conceptions against Moslem or pagan, or on the economic plane economic progress against natural stagnation, or on the political one law and order against tribalism and conflicts.

The brutal facts seem to be that such oppositions do exist wherever European intervention has gone deeper than a loose kind of economic association in which the white races satisfy themselves with the giving of technical and economic advice, facilitating exports of local products or of products mainly resulting from native cultivation and, generally speaking, providing a minimum framework for an improved version of the traditional barter-trade between the tropical zones and the Western regions.

Direct European enterprise, such as agricultural settlement and plantations, mining and industrial activities have almost invariably started a process of mutual antagonism and competition. The shortcomings of populations whose efficiency was measured according to the criteria of the most advanced type of economy and methods of production have added to the ancient idea that Africa and its populations were just emerging from primitive conditions. There is a different and more far reaching idea that, if Africa as a continent is to be made complementary to the industrialized regions of Western Europe, then the inhabitants of Africa would be reduced to passive and inefficient agents.

This thesis is so closely interwoven with the problem and the conception of European paramountcy that it deserves to be studied more closely. The extreme view has been stated as follows by Dr. H. Schmittenhenner:

> Africa will always remain for Western Europe a tropical zone natural and complementary. . . . This continent has still great potentialities. It can be maintained that it represents the future of the West as vast regions are still to be developed and unknown wealth to be discovered; a cultural transformation of the African world depends largely on the Western support and the development of Africa is impossible without American and European markets. The West needs a tropical agricultural zone and a complementary zone which would bring it the minerals of which it is short. *The African producers should not become jealous competitors.* Joint projects could assign to the various European countries and peoples and to their industrial regions distinct complementary zones. The two continents are mutually interdependent and naturally complete one another and their destiny is to become one great economic area.

There is no need to insist on the rather primitive theory of geographic specialization which lies behind this statement. What is important is the definition of the objective of European economic policy in Africa implied in it, that is, the establishment of economic zones complementary to Western Europe as a whole, or to various European countries and peoples in particular.

That such an objective is still very much in the mind of European leaders can be found in their official pronouncements, and it would be enough to mention the names of Mr. Bevin and Mr. Schuman. The latter, when announcing the so-called Schuman Plan for coal and steel suggested that France could bring "Africa as a dowry to Europe."

The second school of thought is mainly concerned with the economic future of Africa, insofar as it affects directly the standard of living of the African populations, excluding the European elements settled in Africa who could in any case take care of themselves. This is well stated in the introductory sentence of Chapter 6 of the United Nations publication entitled "Enlargement of the Exchange Economy in Tropical Africa":

> The primary aim of economic development in Africa as elsewhere is to raise the standard of living of the populations and this implies increasing per capita production.

Its apparent pragmaticism is in fact based on another postulate which is directly opposed to the theory of the natural coincidence of the economic interests of the African populations and of those of European settlement and domination. It is assumed that, somehow, political emancipation and the obtaining of self-government is a necessary prerequisite to economic progress and that the standard of living will be raised more quickly in self-governing areas than in nonself-governing territories.

This approach has the great merit of taking into consideration as an important factor of the economic problem the increased political consciousness of the non-European races in Africa. It is abundantly clear that no economic progress can be achieved in the regions where the non-European element considers, rightly or wrongly, that every initiative, public or private, taken by the European element is directed against their long-term economic, social, and cultural interests.

On the other hand, it presupposes that somewhere in the world, if not necessarily in the metropolitan powers concerned, there are areas of economic activity which dispose of a substantial economic surplus and that these wealthier regions are willing to redistribute this economic surplus just for the sake of "raising the standard of living of the population" of other areas.

It also assumes that the populations concerned have a clear idea of what economic progress means and will naturally tend to direct their activities toward it.

It is enough to state these assumptions in simple terms to realize that the second school of thought places itself deliberately in the perspective of the well known problem, which is far from being limited to Africa: the problem of the underdeveloped territories of the world. It applies to the specific conditions of Africa a type of analysis which would apply also to Asiatic and South American conditions with the convenient qualification that the *de facto* dependence of most of Africa in relation to Western Europe is an aggravating factor.

Even if the Africans are not ready to participate fully, on terms of equality, in the type of modern economic activities which require efficiency and knowledge, they must be given an equal chance or, better still, they must be put, thanks to their political advances, in such a position that they can formulate their own terms for European enterprise taking place in their territories: taxation; nationality; rules of employment; wages; etc. The natural framework for these activities would be the territorial limits of the nation-state (like Liberia, Egypt, or Ethiopia) or of the administrative units if and when they become semi-independent through the process of responsible governments (like the Gold Coast).

The economic needs of each unit and therefore the direction of investment will be determined in each case by the usual constitutional process as accepted by the people which might be a democracy or a dictatorship, but it is assumed in any case to represent the highest possible expression of the public will.

Whatever association there should be between an Africa composed of self-governing units applying their own economic criteria, on the one hand, and Western Europe and the West in general, on the other, should be the result of bargaining on equal terms and on the basis of mutual economic interests. If the emancipated territories wish to maintain financial and technical connections with their former European metropoles, they would do so because it is profitable to them and because they recognize that it is easier in the modern world to use to the full the existing financial systems and technical resources of the big powers than to try to set up their own machinery. The same, of course, would apply to defense.

This brings up another assumption, which will by now sound a familiar note. Such territorial units as are likely to be granted or already have been endowed with responsible governments are in most cases the inheritance of a process of territorial division of Africa which had nothing to do with economic considerations. Perhaps it is enough to mention the Kingdom of Libya, the creation of which is the outcome of a purely diplomatic bargaining process, with no consideration given to the natural division of the country and to the long-term interests of the inhabitants.

It is quite possible that we should find quite unexpectedly the explosive problem of territorial redistribution of Africa underlying the problem of economic progress within the framework of existing territorial units with the postulate of the paramountcy of African interests.

This is indeed a familiar problem to European minds which are justly preoccupied by the apparent conflict between the "nation-state" and the normal and free interplay of economic forces. However, such disequilibrium as there was between the economic resources of the African territories within their present limits was compensated by the attempt to establish an economic equilibrium between the resources of the metropolitan and other colonial areas belonging to the same political and economic unit rather than between the local resources of any given territory. In other words, the protagonists of economic progress within the limits of self-governing political units should be keenly aware of the fact that they are substituting one problem of economic equilibrium for another one, and not necessarily an easier one to solve.

There is, furthermore, another assumption which should be clearly sorted out from the convenient generalizations about nationalism: i.e., that the government of the territory in question will necessarily be at the service of all the inhabitants to promote an economic policy of *internal redistribution* of the economic product, not only by imposing on the employers—usually foreigners—a policy of high wages but also through the agency of social-welfare services such as health, education, technical and scientific advice. In other words, the assumption is that, as has happened in the West, after a painful process of awakening social consciousness, the ruling class (or tribe) will be mainly preoccupied with the standard of living of the majority of the inhabitants and not with promoting its own social interests.

Otherwise, a situation could well be imagined where foreign employers of local labor would arrive at some gentlemen's agreement with the local government, not automatically furthering the cause of economic progress and improvement in the standard of living of the native inhabitants.

As to the acknowledged technical backwardness of the majority of the African populations, it is maintained that it can be corrected through a policy of technical assistance brought from the outside and applying the knowledge and techniques evolved by experts coming from more developed communities to what are considered as objective factors of this backwardness—that is, poverty of the soil, high incidence of disease, difficulty of transportation and marketing, problems of housing, etc.

In other words, while due emphasis is given to the importance of political factors in the process of economic development, it is assumed that these factors will not impede a policy of technical assistance insulated from such political problems as the domination of one racial element over another.

It remains to be seen how these various approaches can be reconciled with the facts of life in Africa today and whether they bring us any nearer to a positive policy concerning our objectives which are to keep Africa somehow associated with the Western world while promoting a dynamic policy of economic and social progress.

We have found that the territorial division of Africa was in general considered as the source of difficulties for a proper economic development of the African continent, either considered as a whole or within the framework of several natural regions.

There are, of course, important practical and legal correctives to this Balkanization of Africa which render it rather different from the division of Europe into nation-states acting as sovereign powers over the national economy and restricting the movements of persons and goods.

The first corrective lies naturally in the very vastness of Africa. Most of the territorial administrations have their hands full with the enormous territories which they have to develop and might very well be unconcerned with interterritorial co-operation. Nigeria, for instance, is completely self-sufficient for internal transportation. In any case, the capital investment in road and rail transportation came from the metropolitan countries at a time when the main economic objectives were to serve the trade between the metropole and its colonial territories. Such transcontinental connections as The Cape to Cairo Railway or the Trans-Saharian were partially built or projected to serve national and imperial schemes and not necessarily to respond to strictly economic criteria.

Incidentally, it is striking to note that the African countries which remained free from colonial connections, such as Liberia and Ethiopia, have no railways of their own.

In other words, there is very seldom a strict case of duplication, although there are of course many cases of lack of co-ordination. Duplication would mean that capital investment in Africa was so distorted as to create too many facilities for a limited amount of traffic. In fact, one example freely quoted is the French Congo-Ocean Railway running parallel to the Belgian railway from Leopold-ville to Matadi, and even this could be questioned in view of the ever-increasing production of the Belgian Congo and the potential mineral production of French Equatorial Africa.

On the other side of the picture there are many examples of concrete co-operation in surface transport. The Katanga region, in the Belgian Congo, is served by railways coming from Angola on the western side, from Rhodesia and Mozambique on the eastern side. The Federation of Rhodesia and Nyasaland is served by the railway connected with Beira and will soon have a new railway connection through Portuguese territory to Lourenço Marques. The northeastern part of the Union of South Africa is connected directly with Lourenço Marques. In Central Africa, the Chad region is in fact served by road and rail connections with Lagos in British Nigeria. The Nile Valley from Cairo to Khartoum is served by river and rail connections. The whole of French North Africa, although separated into three national or territorial entities, has railway connections from Casablanca to Tunis.

The big rivers of Africa have been internationalized since the very beginning of European penetration in Africa. Air transport has developed tremendously during the last ten years without any special difficulties due to the existing territorial division. There again the only example of possible duplication in airport facilities can be found in the Brazzaville-Leopoldville region where both the French and the Belgians have built or are building airports of international class.

We are far, therefore, from agreeing with the criticisms often expressed even by such detached observers as Dr. Klein. In 1949, when American observers were invited to participate actively in the work of the Overseas Territories Committee of the OEEC, they insisted quite rightly on the necessity of co-ordination between the respective development plans of the European powers with responsibilities overseas and in Africa in particular. One of the obvious fields of co-operation was transportation. The American government disposed then of a good stimulus in the way of dollar loans or counterpart funds within Marshall Plan aid to facilitate capital investments in roads and railways. The Lisbon Conference which was the outcome of the agreement between the European and African powers concerned, called to discuss the problem of co-ordination with the assistance of ECA, discovered that the problem was more in the nature of local co-operation within economic regions than in the nature of an all-embracing and rational plan for the whole of Africa. The resulting regional conferences at Dschang and Johannesburg were restricted to listing a series of questions which called for bilateral co-operation; for example, in Western and Central Africa the evacuation of the Chad region, or in the southern part the construction of a new railway line between Rhodesia and the Portuguese coast, etc.

In the Preliminary Report of the so-called "Strasbourg Plan" it is stated:

> The co-ordination of overseas transport within homogeneous geographic zones (of Africa) offers immense scope for practical co-operation; in technical matters in connection with railways, roads, water and airways, ports and freights, standardisation of equipment, etc. It is in this field that the effects of national and local particularism, with their resultant duplication and waste are most felt and it is here too that effective co-operation would yield the quickest and biggest dividends.

We have here, applied to a most practical and concrete problem, the approach which postulates that anything which is done within the existing territorial distribution is necessarily wasteful. We have said enough to suggest that this is not the case, except in very specific and limited circumstances.

If this were meant to indicate that a "functional" approach to these specific questions would be advantageous, there would be no difficulty. But far more is implied. In particular this approach is used as one of the main justifications for the co-ordination of "European investments," the direct participation of European powers not responsible for overseas territories, the setting up of organizations which could arbitrate between the various national and territorial claims and even of supra-national authorities. These would be competent to deal with such "reallotment schemes" as would be made necessary by a "rational" territorial distribution which in fact means redrawing the map of Africa using doubtful economic criteria.

It is not surprising that these conceptions are expressed mostly by experts of countries who have no longer any territorial interests in Africa or who never have had. Being outsiders, they want to get in. They are apt to consider the birth of political consciousness among the African populations as artificial movements fostered from the outside and therefore a political redistribution of these populations as practical.

The second corrective lies precisely in the African populations themselves. Two main reactions to the frontiers established by the European powers and superimposed upon the map of Africa can be recognized.

The politically conscious Africans tend more and more to identify themselves with the otherwise artificial entities created by the European colonizing powers. Most of them are so conditioned by their new cultural environment (including the European language they use) that they become nearly "nationals" in the Western sense of their respective territories. It is an open question whether this attitude will extend progressively to the greater number or whether the tribal connections will finally pull back Africa to its former tribalism, which was a far greater obstacle to the free interchange of goods and ideas than the so-called European type of nationalism. The Westernized Africans would certainly consider as a great step backwards the setting up by the Western powers of any supra-national agency which could have the last word in any political redistribution of territories, even though based on economic considerations of higher productivity and lower costs.

On the other hand, the great masses of the Africans prove themselves to be superbly unconcerned with the frontiers established by the European powers. They show a surprising degree of response to economic stimuli. The great lesson of the movement of African labor is that Africans are far more mobile than any other population in any other continent. Apart from the fact that they love traveling for its own sake, they are apt to cover enormous distances to be employed for a certain period of time and then come back to their villages. Most of these migrations, officially assisted or not, are of an international nature. Labor from French Africa goes to the Gold Coast, Nigeria, and the Anglo-Egyptian Sudan. Labor from Tanganyika and Rhodesia as well as from Portuguese Africa goes to South Africa. Labor from Ruanda-Urundi works in Uganda. Furthermore, apart from the officially reported interterritorial trade, a lot of it is taking place through the agency of specialized tribes, such as the Hausa or Oriental traders like the Lebanese and the Indians.

It seems almost as though Africa is using the very facilities put at its disposal by European settlement and economic penetration to build up an inter-African economy not substantially different from the one of the pre-European days. Even North Africa is connected with Africa south of the Sahara, and the shores of the Red Sea are not too far away for a good Moslem of Dakar.

Africa and the Africans are in fact very much alive. They are not the passive and undifferentiated combination of space and human masses that European economists mainly preoccupied with "efficiency" are apt to dispose of through "reallotment of territories." The progressive building up of political consciousness within the existing territorial boundaries has in practice facilitated the exchange of goods and persons. The African laborer and trader is using to the full modern facilities in transportation introduced by the Europeans. Africa and its various components are now fully alive and any "master plan" evolved by a "master race" has no chance whatsoever of being applied in practice.

Africans are people. Even in the most backward parts of Africa, that is, the parts which were in the backwaters of history, the African populations had evolved their own economic and social systems which represented for them the optimum adaptation to the existing environment. There are now few places even in darkest Africa which have been left outside the new economic and technological currents—nothing to compare in any case with the aboriginal populations of the Amazon, for instance. Great differences can be noted superficially between the aptitudes of the various populations and their reaction to changes. Obviously, Arabs and Berbers are different from Negro races. On the other hand, many Negro races are derived from a mingling of Arab, Hamitic, and Semitic blood. Nowhere is the frontier between races clearly traced. Africa is a land of bewildering variety in people as well as of massive uniformity in landscape. Very little is known of individual racial characteristics, although wild generalizations are usually formulated by Europeans about the Arab mind or the Negroes. It is often seen that serious psychologists, sociologists, and economists base their whole theories on limited geographical experience as if the common factor were such elements as the color of the skin or a common religion.

In the past, the human factor in African development was not sufficiently taken into consideration; and this has contributed greatly to the dramatic failures that have had such far-reaching economic consequences, even to the present time.

Such recognized phenomena as urbanization and disintegration of tribal life may have entirely different connotations in Algiers, Dakar, Casablanca, and Johannesburg. We say "may have" as we do not exactly know. On the aptitude of Africans to industrial work, we have widely divergent estimates. For instance, Algerian labor employed in France in certain big industrial concerns such as the Renault factory is considered as showing a good average degree of efficiency after a period of training. On the other hand, you would hear contrary views in Algeria itself, where Algerian labor is considered wasteful and inefficient. The Belgian copper mines, which are following a different policy of training and promotion, as far as African labor is concerned, have produced different results (and I would say more hopeful ones) from those of the Northern Rhodesia copper mines.

We must therefore keep in mind, before we generalize on any method adequate to develop African productivity, attract investment, and raise the standard of living—apart from benefiting Western economy as a whole—that the very basic facts are far less known than in the case of a European type of economy.

This being said, we may now place ourselves in the perspective of the second school of thought which is mainly preoccupied with the problem of raising the standard of living.

We have to note first that to raise the standard of living is a sociological proposition as well as an economic one. It is intended not only to give higher monetary wages and purchasing power to the inhabitants of Africa but also to bring them into a different kind of civilization where man is in control of nature and has to keep abreast of antagonistic factors by the constant application of technology and scientific knowledge. There is far more than a difference of degree between the natural African standard of living (and this applies to non-European types of societies in general) and Western standards; there is difference of nature and sociological content.

This explains why there is such a misunderstanding between Europeans and politically conscious Africans when they talk about economic progress. The Africans still accept the subsistence economy, taken as a total concept with all its implications, as the natural economy to which the Europeans should somehow bring, as gifts, the most practical benefits of Western technology: the bicycle, easy transportation, sewing machines, and the like. The Europeans consider what remains of the natural economy, after the impact of their own settlement and economic penetration, as a remnant of primitive barbarism from which, somehow, Africa should progressively and forcibly emerge.

Whatever the case may be, there is little doubt that it is a painful process to pass from the stage of the natural economy to the dynamic level of a modern economy, which we will not try to define as capitalistic, but rather as technological and scientific.

If we neglected the time factor and the racial factor, we could broadly apply the terms of economic analysis which applied to the industrialization process of Western communities during the nineteenth century. Indeed, such analysis is valid in specific cases where urban populations have broken all connections with the subsistence economy. But these cases are few.

Professor Frankel has drawn attention to the fact that "the factors of production cannot be assumed to be ready for recombination. They are highly specific to particular ways of life and work which had achieved equilibrium within a narrowly circumscribed ecological and human environment. . . ."

The United Nations brochure on the "Enlargement of the Exchange Economy in Tropical Africa" expressed the same idea in slightly different terms:

> . . . one aspect of the fact that a large proportion of productive resources in tropical Africa is employed within the framework of predominantly subsistence society is that responses to money incentives are still very limited in scope. Resistances to change arising from lack of familiarity with a money economy impose in effect additional hindrances to the achievement of greater mobility of resources and to the readiness to adopt new methods which economic development implies. . . .

This type of analysis leaves aside precisely the time factor and the racial factor—the time factor, because it presupposes that given sufficient financial and technical means the process can be accelerated and "deepened" in order to include the great majority of the total non-European population. The industrialization and modernization of the production and distribution structure can be brought in, so to speak, in a ready-made and neatly wrapped parcel which would avoid the great social and individual stresses which European populations had to undergo during the nineteenth and twentieth centuries.

The racial factor is omitted because this analysis assumes that, apart from any question of economic exploitation of one race by another, technology and science can be completely divorced in the mind of the African populations from the intellectual processes of Western science. It should not be forgotten, however, that advanced technology appears from the point of view of the dominated races as an instrument of white supremacy.

There have been, however, in Asia, for instance, well organized political movements which refused to have anything to do with modern economic development, and these did not arise from "resistances to change arising from lack of familiarity with a money economy." They arose from a basic refusal of the new way of life offered by Western technology which was (quite properly) regarded as part of a philosophy and a *weltanschauung* antagonistic to the Asian attitude to the visible world.

There has not been yet such a fundamental refusal on the part of native populations in Africa, although some disturbing clues could be found in the so-called return to African traditions implied in the Mau Mau movement, in the recent boycott of European goods in Uganda, and in the Ghana movement in the Gold Coast. In other words it is by no means certain that economic progress as such, meaning a better combination of the factors of production with a view to a higher standard of living, is an accepted aim either for the politically conscious or the masses in Africa.

The resistance may not come after all from backwardness, intellectual and otherwise, but from a different philosophy of life. That is a very different thing from a basic inability of the African to operate modern means of production.

The technological and scientific type of civilization characteristic of the West is a natural product of the attitude of the Western world toward its environment, which it wishes to control not only in its natural aspects, such as the soil, the subsoil, water, and mining resources, etc., but even in its proper human aspects, such as the growth of population. We must be conscious of the implications of the fact that this type of civilization is on the contrary a foreign product for the peoples of Africa as a whole.

There are at least some common assumptions in what we will call the Euro-African and the "universalist" schools of thought concerning the economic development of Africa. In the former, Africa can be integrated in an enlarged and co-ordinated European economy usually called Euro-African. In the latter, Africa can be fully integrated in the world market economy. It is recognized by both schools that the process is a difficult one. There are differences of appreciation as to the importance of the local and political factors, but it is agreed that in the end, taking account of natural resources and ecological factors, Africa should be but another part of an economically and organically integrated whole.

Both schools of thought have to face the problem of capital investment and, in particular, to acknowledge the rather discouraging fact that to build up the "infra-structure" of Africa would require enormous sums and bring practically no direct return. They both tend to assign to a relative backwardness the rather limited participation of the inhabitants of Africa in their own economic improvement in the way of productivity and capital formation.

The Euro-African school, in its most extreme form, would advocate European immigration to operate modern means of production and as limited a use as possible of African labor. The universalist school believes that through a process of gradual education the Africans will acquire the dynamic conceptions and the necessary abilities to control fully their environment and will finally turn out to be not only friendly associates with the Western world but also active participants.

It is held in common by the Euro-Africans and the universalists that the problem should be approached from a different angle when dealing on the one hand with homogeneous societies and on the other with plural societies.

Africa is indeed a continent where plural societies can be found. The whole of French North Africa, Kenya, the Federation of Rhodesia, and South Africa are usually classified as plural societies with two or three levels of civilization usually corresponding to racial divisions coexisting in one given territory. Homogeneous societies are usually those in which there is no European settlement, as in most of French West Africa, British West Africa, and of course the independent nations, Liberia, Ethiopia, and Egypt.

It is an accepted view that the political problem, and therefore the economic one, is easier to solve in homogeneous societies than in plural ones. It is time to question these basic tenets. It seems to us that the problem of economic development of Africa cannot be divorced from the much more intractable problem of the difference of outlook toward the outside world between Western society as a whole and non-Western. This fundamental cleavage does not mean any difference in individual abilities and practical intelligence. It does not imply any notion of superiority or inferiority. It simply takes into account the challenge that the Western world, in trying to export its technology and scientific attitude, has met or is meeting everywhere in Asia and Africa.

We have to face the fact that "economic development disintegrates and atomizes native society . . . in place of a whole people it creates a plural society devoid of any common social will."

And yet economic development of Africa is a must, even from the exclusive point of view of the African population just to survive. The Western impact has liberated forces which can be brought under control only by a greater and deeper measure of Western control of the whole productive process.

Another brutal fact is that, if the Western type of technology had to be withdrawn suddenly from Africa or were reduced to impotence, adjustments between population and resources would still take place; and a new equilibrium would have to be found at a tremendous cost in terms of human suffering or in terms of dollars if the Western world wanted for political reasons to attenuate the hardships.

Wherever European enterprise, industrial or agricultural, has intervened deeply, it had the effect described by Furnivall, and this applies not only to so-called plural societies but also to homogeneous societies. The real criterion is not the coexistence within one given territory of two different races, but the coexistence of two types of productive processes and the increased gap between the two due to the increased capitalization of the Western type of production.

It is often said that relations between Europeans and non-Europeans were much better in Africa fifty years ago and even twenty years ago, even in the areas like South Africa or French North Africa, where Europeans and Africans worked on the same land. The deterioration of these relations is usually attributed to an increased political consciousness or alternatively artificial agitation fostered from the outside. It seems much more likely that it is due to the enormous and increasingly hopeless difference there is between the Europeans and the Africans in their way of life, the increased reliance of the former on what are considered artificial and magic processes—in one word, the complete and final substitution of the highly artificial order of things for the "natural order of things." The natural order is showing a surprising vitality, and there is a growing conviction among the African elite that not only is there nothing about it to be ashamed of but that Africa's survival depends on a reasonable and limited use of Western technology rather than on total Westernization. The former would serve as an instrument which could be used or not, but which should not be regarded as a means of transforming the existing civilization and philosophy of life.

We are far from both the Euro-African and universalist schools of thought. Insofar as participation in the world market is concerned, in respect to their export crops, no Africans will deny that it has brought them substantial material benefits. But that is a very different proposition from a total integration in the Western type of economy and a substitution of a new type of civilization for the old one.

Perhaps a solution to the problem of economic development for Africa could be found more easily if the objectives of these developments could be reexamined in the light of recent experiences which tend to demonstrate the vitality of African civilizations. There is little doubt that these objectives should be far more limited than the ones proposed to us by the Euro-African or the universalist school. Africa cannot and does not want to be integrated in any institutionalized federation, political and economic, with Western Europe. Africa, as a whole, cannot and does not want to be fully integrated in the Western type of economy regularized and controlled by technology and science. On the other hand, Europe and America cannot afford to let Africa remain completely outside their orbit of civilization, since a ruthless domination would inevitably succeed in using Africa for its own aims.

The relative failure of the Western type of economic development in Africa is to be measured not in comparison with objectives such as the total Western civilization of its populations, which, according to us, is out of reach, but in relation to limited objectives of peaceful coexistence between two types of civilization which cannot remain isolated from one another and have to be articulated at some precise level in the economic, political, and cultural fields. This level has yet to be found. It will vary according to the density of European settlement in any given area, which in turn determines the intensity and frequency of contacts between the two types of civilization.

In the extreme case where European settlement is practically negligible, and where Western enterprise applies only to limited resources and areas, as in Liberia or Saudi Arabia outside Africa, European enterprise has no specific responsibility for the welfare of the populations except for the limited number of native workers employed and their families.

At the other extreme, as in South Africa or French North Africa, European enterprise and technology is so ramified within the natural economy and draws within its orbit so many of the local inhabitants that the responsibility for welfare and the promotion of jointly accepted rules of behavior have to be shared between the enterprise and the governmental authorities.

The temptation is strong to move as much as possible toward the Western type of enterprise with limited responsibilities in underdeveloped areas to which self-government would be granted as a convenient way to avoid responsibility for local welfare. The postwar experience with other underdeveloped areas suggests that this is too easy a way out. A Western type of enterprise cannot just be an island of high productivity and efficiency in an ocean of poverty and low standards.

It seems that the genuine failure of Western enterprise and economic development lies precisely, both from the point of view of long-term returns and "level of articulation," in the neglect of those aspects of Western technology which can be used by the African societies to reinforce and improve their own integrated social structure. We have seen that transportation, far from disintegrating African societies, has helped them to renew and revitalize the old currents of culture and civilization. We have little doubt that putting at the disposal of native agriculture cheap fertilizers and wherever possible cheap energy would reinforce and modernize the "natural economy" and give it the means to face the challenge of an increased population while not altering the philosophical and religious background to which the Africans are justly attached.

This policy leaves completely open the question of the final level at which the African type of economy will be articulated to the Western type. It depends on so many factors—positive, as the actual wealth of Africa and its unknown potential wealth; negative, as the growth of population—that it would be idle to try to fix it now. But it is based on the principle that the African population will never be Westernized in the sense of undifferentiated participation in the Western world of interchangeable factors of production and technological total control of the environment.

It is based on the assumption, which helps to explain the disturbing conflicts, latent or explosive, between the European races and the African races all over the African continent, that the non-Western type of civilization has strong roots and that any attempt to eradicate them is bound to fail at very high costs in human and economic terms.

Finally, it does not deny that the extent of contracts between the European and the African races can be broadened without involving the total substitution of one civilization for another.

even in individual cases, provided Western economic development is not conceived as the instrument of a political will to mold the future of Africa into the strait jacket of the European conception of cultural and political evolution.

commentary

HORACE MANN BOND

President, Lincoln University

Earlier in this volume we had some provocative references to the history of barbarism and its relevance to self-government. Mr. Henry's essay does much to establish the supreme irrelevance, to the question of African participation in economic and political self-determination in 1954, of whether it was your grandfather or your great-great-grandfather that believed in magic. I was reminded of an ancient great-aunt of my youth, nearly fifty years ago in the mountains of Kentucky. She had as long and as bloodcurdling an armory of superstitious beliefs and magical practices as one might ever hope to see anywhere in Africa today. She was second generation African in America, and among her great-nephews she enjoyed a fine reputation as an almost original African sorceress.

Much later in my life, it was a great blow to my ancestral pride to discover that without exception her impressive repertoire derived straight out of Yorkshire, Scotland, and Ireland; whatever African demonology our family may once have had long since had been submerged by the stubbornly dominant and still persisting beliefs of the sturdy Elizabethan mountain folk who were our only neighbors, up Cumberland Gap way. In these parts today, the faith ordeal by rattlesnakes in religious revival meetings is yet occasionally met with, and even in pleasant Pennsylvania where I now live that form of ritualistic murder known as "hexing" crops up every year or so among our rural farmers of old German extraction.

To this day it is with painful foreboding that I walk under a ladder, permit three cigarettes to be lit from one match, or refrain from expectorating when a black cat crosses my pathway. Almost regretfully I am obliged to credit my concern for taking these emimently wise precautions against the evil spirits to the cultural influences of my European, not African, social heritage.

It is from the same source that I derived that other quaint mental encumbrance, the inveterate conviction that all men are created equal; that liberty, equality, and fraternity are the natural rights and proper pursuit of all humanity; and that it is the proper natural right and political essential of every social contract, that every man— *every* man—should exercise an equal voice through an unfettered and unlimited franchise in the determination of his destiny and the destiny of the society that is to exercise controls over him.

It is for this reason that I found Mr. Henry's essay both enlightening and enlightened; it seemed to me to suggest the fine flavor of the Enlightenment, which yet stands as the very original inspiration of Western revolutionary thinking. It is quite true that even those descendants of our American revolutionaries, who take great pride in the title, are now horrified at the very idea of a contemporary "revolution"; but I take it that we agree it is nothing short of "revolution" in Africa and Asia that we must now deal with, and one of the choices to be made is whether to accommodate ourselves to a "revolution" after the style of the eighteenth-century ideology of the *Philosophes* or the mid-nineteenth-century variety set in motion by Karl Marx and Friedrich Engels. We have to deal with an ideological conflict that has been in process for at least two hundred years, and with specific reference to theories of colonialism in general and Africa in particular. That which the West now properly fears is the true "Third Force"; and I think we of the West do ourselves an injustice by not realizing that the world today is rent by a triangular conflict of forces—within itself the two "schools of thought" regarding Africa, described by Mr. Henry as "European" and "Universalist," and, from the outside, the shadow of a newer rationale that has loomed in the modern world with increasing insistence since 1848.

We now know that our Alexander Hamilton and his Federalists quite properly identified what they regarded as the political excrescences of our early post-revolutionary American direction as springing from a foreign ideology. The seeds of revolution were first cultivated in Europe and were lodged in the brains of our Benjamin Franklin and Thomas Jefferson through conversation and correspondence. The revolution was made here in America first, perhaps because this unformed culture was more susceptible to the contagion of freedom than the older nation in which those great ideas had first been propagated. I think it is of the greatest significance to realize that the revolutionary ideas of eighteenth-century France and America saw clearly the indivisibility of natural rights everywhere in the world and sought a revolution for Africa and Africans as well as for Frenchmen and Americans.

We Americans know that Benjamin Franklin, that strangely universal genius, worked unceasingly for the abolition of African slavery in the American colonies and in the youthful United States. It is less well known that he collaborated with French and English philosophers to abolish African slavery everywhere and to create self-governing, free nations in Africa. In 1772 the radical pamphleteer Pierre du Pont de Nemours published in Paris a scathing indictment of African slavery in the American colonies, French, and English; and he proposed that slavery be abolished and that Africa, particularly West Africa, be developed as free, self-governing nations, producing under democratic political institutions with free labor those tropical products before derived from African labor enslaved in the Americas. In the best physiocratic manner, de Nemours quoted at length from calculations made by Benjamin Franklin as early as 1752, and given by him to Adam Smith.

That impassioned essay of 1772 (one of the few copies in an American library is to be found at The Johns Hopkins University) bears rereading today. It is a fascinating example of how basic philosophy and economic motive can affect estimates of the readiness of Africans to assimilate Western institutions, though written nearly two hundred years ago. De Nemours wrote with passion threaded with what we should now, doubtless, call the nonsense of Rousseau and the "noble savage"; but with amazing prescience he portrayed the inevitability of the slave revolt that was to come in Santo Domingo twenty-five years later and the bitter realities of the revolt of the masses everywhere two centuries later, when men who governed "backward peoples" could not find within themselves the faith in all human beings that came so naturally to the enlightened mind of the eighteenth-century philosopher. De Nemours described African populations "as not inferior in industry, intelligence, and morality to many European peasant populations of the period, and as superior to some."

My point is that the West has already long since discovered and articulated, in its own original genius of universal emancipation, an infallible panacea for the solution of its African woes. We Africans, being incontrovertibly a simple people as Rousseau and de Nemours and Franklin thought us to be, are likely to hear with amazement a series of bold, forward-looking pronouncements that are immediately qualified to the point of making the simple fact meaningless. The West, in our opinion, does not need a new theory, *vis-à-vis* Africa; it has had all the theory it needs for two hundred years, and that theory is, indeed, the true genius of Western institutions.

Permit me to point to the recent decision of the United States Supreme Court, in the cases involving the segregation of children in schools by race, as a pure and very simple expression of what is here regarded as the very great and noble tradition of the Western world. One feels that the West would save itself a tremendous amount of misery regarding the future of Africa—and this means, in all truth, the future of the Western world—if we could but approach the problems that are in fact basic in as simple and direct a manner. That decision did not quibble or beg the question. Neither did the great and now fairly ancient political documents of the Western world; neither "Liberty, Equality, and Fraternity" nor "all men are created equal," are weasel words.

Our too human experience testifies how difficult it is to translate these fine phrases into reality. Now the Western world has the choice between translating its fine words into unequivocal practice or seeing newer words, not yet tarnished by deferred performance, captivate all of that other world—Africa as well as Asia—in which the simple people live.

One may agree heartily with Mr. Henry's opinion, that it is questionable to believe that political and economic problems are easier to solve in homogeneous than in plural societies. One may also be permitted to raise some timid questions of one's own.

Is it not easy to make too much of a difference between African and European mentalities on the basis of a presumed greater resistance to technology as a way of life? I have seen American farmers resist cattle-dipping far more violently than did Gold Coast farmers resist "cutting-out" of cocoa trees to eliminate swollen shoot. The resistance of the European peasant to change is proverbial. I think we can too easily make a case for a different psychology on the basis of experiences thought racially characteristic, experiences that are in fact the common experience of humanity everywhere.

I would link to this observation the need for noting that what may appear to be the "intractable problem"—the "challenge" the Western world has met in trying to export its technology and "scientific attitude of mind"—may in fact be a resistance to motives, attitudes, and presuppositions that accompany the exported technology, rather than resistance to the technology itself. I do not believe anyone has ever adequately explained why Japan so avidly and competently embraced Western technology during the same period when apparently the Chinese were resisting that technology. We have commonly heard it explained in terms of derogatory racialisms; the Japanese, says the man on the street, is an "imitator" —"just like a monkey." Indeed, precisely, the same explanation is likely to be given to those forms of ready adaptation characteristic of the African. We need, I think, to essay more fundamental analyses of the laws of cultural assimilation, the rates at which they proceed, and the principles governing differential selectivity of cultural aspects to be assimilated.

Nor would I agree with Furnivall, that ". . . economic development disintegrates and atomizes native society . . . in place of a whole people it creates a plural society devoid of any common social will." Certainly an obviously exploitative economic development will have such an effect; there is no basis for believing that an economic development based on the self-interest of the people involved need have such an effect. The testimony from countries where economic development has obviously been in the direct, nationalistic interest of the affected people—in old and tough cultures like Turkey and Japan, and now in Pakistan and Afghanistan, and in soft, underdeveloped cultures like the Gold Coast and Nigeria—refutes, I think absolutely, this theory. My own observations of the latter two countries suggest, indeed, how amazingly an economic and political development may both fuse a people and develop in a very short time an immense and accelerating common fund of social will. The difference between Africans in these new emerging states, as compared, say, to Africans in South Africa, is the psychological difference between the living and the dead; people with hope, and people without hope.

Africans, Mr. Henry reassures us, are people. For people in Africa, or Europe, or in Asia, I can think of no better specific to prescribe than that first formulated in the Western world two centuries ago, which set in motion a revolution that created my country and transformed his. Africans are people, they are natural men, they have natural rights, they are endowed by their Creator with certain inalienable rights. While this is neither the Fourth of July, nor Bastille Day, yet it is satisfying to recall the many African rebels who have come out of Lincoln University; which is to say, men who have struggled against Colonialism in the great tradition of Locke and Hume and Voltaire and Condorcet and Franklin and Jefferson.

If that be recidivism, I must prayerfully implore you to make the best of it.

the impact of Western education on the African's way of life

LORENZO D. TURNER

Roosevelt College

In this essay I have dealt specifically, first, with the content of the curricula provided in African schools and, secondly, have pointed out certain effects that the educational policies of the European powers concerned with African education have had upon three important aspects of the African's way of life: 1) his economic condition; 2) his religion; and 3) his language and literature. Since the curricula in African schools vary greatly in the different regions, each region will be treated separately.

I. *The curricula in African schools*

British territories

West Africa. The Africans are further advanced educationally and in most other respects in British West Africa than they are in other regions of Africa south of the Sahara. Brief reference to the educational situation in the Gold Coast and Nigeria, the largest and most progressive of the four British territories of West Africa, will be sufficient for the purpose of this paper. In these two regions self-government is in the offing. In fact, it has already been achieved in the Gold Coast, which expects to have dominion status in the British Commonwealth of Nations by 1956. In these two countries education is directed largely by the Africans themselves. The nationalist movement, which is far

147

advanced here, calls for the preservation of what its leaders consider the best in the traditional culture and the adoption of the best from Western culture. The number of Europeans is relatively small, but Western culture has been rapidly spreading for many years, and the relations between Europeans and Africans are good. Such racial clashes as have occurred during past months in Kenya would be unthinkable not only in the Gold Coast and Nigeria but anywhere else in British West Africa, because here the Africans are in possession of their land. Though at present literacy here is enjoyed by a relatively small portion of the total African population, development plans indicate that this situation will be greatly improved in the near future.

In the Gold Coast primary education in Ashanti and the colony will be free and universal by 1957, and places are to be provided for 405,000 children as against the enrolment for 1950 of 212,000. The number of primary school teachers is to be increased from 6,900 to 13,500. There will be considerable expansion of facilities also for middle schools, secondary schools, teacher training, and technical education. A longer period is indicated for the attainment of objectives in the northern territories. Higher education is provided at the University College of the Gold Coast, at Accra, where in 1952 there were 482 students and a full-time teaching staff of 95, not including the staff of the Extra-Mural Department.

In Nigeria there is a ten-year plan providing for the development of all forms of education, but universal primary education is not likely to be attained soon. Even for a four-year primary course to be available for all children in Nigeria the cost would be £5,900,000 each year as against the present budget of £2 million for all types of primary and post-primary education. In Nigeria as a whole only one child out of every four children is receiving any form of education; and in the northern provinces, where over half of the country's people are to be found, scarcely one child out of every twenty-seven is attending school. Higher education in Nigeria is provided at the University College at Ibadan, where in 1952 there were 368 students and a full-time teaching staff of 80, not including the staff of the Extra-Mural Department.

Unlike the Europeans in some other colonial governments, the British encourage the use of native languages and literatures in African schools. This will have important bearing on the process of acculturation. In most of the four-year primary courses in British West Africa the vernacular is used as the medium of instruction for the whole of the course with English being introduced as a subject of instruction toward the middle of the course and thereafter given increasing attention. To make this practice really effective, however, a great deal more vernacular literature will have to be made available than exists at present. In addition to the traditional school and college courses, considerable emphasis is being put on adult informal education throughout British West Africa.

East and Central Africa. In this area the Africans are less advanced educationally than in British West Africa. The principal territories are Nyasaland, Northern Rhodesia, Tanganyika, Uganda, and Kenya. The British government has been firmly established in this region for less than fifty years, and education organized and sponsored by the government is often only twenty-five years old and sometimes less. Life is predominantly rural. Since the European population here is larger in proportion to the total population than in British West Africa, the ultimate goal is complete self-government racially on a partnership basis.

The most thoroughgoing account of the present status of education in this region is to be found in the *Report of the East and Central Africa Study Group,* of which A. L. Binns was chairman. I shall give the gist of a few of the many significant recommendations made by the Group:

1. Since this region depends for its existence almost entirely on agriculture, and since agriculture is at present conducted for the most part by primitive and wasteful methods, the attack on agricultural ignorance should be made simultaneously by the schools and the agencies of adult education. In the middle school, agriculture should form the starting point of a group of studies in which practical and theoretical work is closely integrated, and in the secondary school the importance should be emphasized of the school farm and of a course in agriculture up to the School Certificate standard. The work of the Faculty of Agriculture at the University College of East Africa should be a great asset to the entire region.

2. The Group recommends eight years of education for all children of the region and a secondary education for 25 per cent

of the child population. This goal should be reached within the next twenty-five years. Not one of the territories visited had succeeded in getting as many as 50 per cent of its children through a four-year course.

3. Concerning the educational work of the missions and the churches, it is recommended that these should continue to be closely associated with the work and government of schools, but the professional supervision of all teaching except that of religious education should remain in the hands of qualified officers appointed and employed by the government; and that eventually all grant-aided schools should become at the same time state schools and religious schools, with governing bodies representative of the African local authorities and the African church or churches. It is felt that the period of pioneer work in education by the churches is over; that since they have played so small a part in adult education work, and since some of their work is educationally unsound—such as that in thousands of small scattered "bush" schools where "many facts are absorbed, but many minds are deformed in the process"— the churches might divert the money and energy so freed into channels of adult education, the rewards of which would be much richer and the life of the churches stronger.

4. Regarding the language problem in the schools of East and Central Africa, it is recommended that in the four years of the primary school the vernacular should be the medium of instruction throughout except to a limited degree in the final year. It should be continued in the middle school in a suitable group of subjects, while English should be used in others to an increasing degree. In the senior secondary schools English should be the language of instruction. Swahili should gradually be eliminated from all schools as a *lingua franca*, and there should be developed at the University College of East Africa a school of African languages.

5. There should be immediate expansion of library services, education for women and girls, and a technical education which should be based on eight years of general education and which should maintain the closest relations with industry.

6. Finally, it is suggested that the ideal school, if it were acceptable to parents, would be an interracial school; and it is felt that initiatives in this direction should receive moral and financial aid from the government.

Higher education in East Africa is provided at Makerere College (the University College of East Africa) at Kampala, Uganda. The college is open to students of all races, but at present there is only one European in attendance. In 1953 there were nearly 400 African men students and about 20 women. At present almost all of the academic staff are Europeans—there were 56 staff members in 1952 —but there will be an increasing number of African teachers as persons with suitable qualifications become available. For Central Africa a university college is scheduled to open in March, 1956, at Salisbury, Southern Rhodesia. It is to be interracial. Admission will be solely on the basis of educational attainments and character, but living accommodations and social functions will be separate for Europeans and Africans. The expected enrolment at the opening is 65 students (20 European men, 20 European women, and 25 Africans). A staff of 15 professors, a senior lecturer, and a librarian is planned. The site of the institution covers 450 acres. It appears that the college will be independent of the Southern Rhodesian government. The Colonial Development and Welfare Fund will advance $3,500,000, and the Central African government will probably provide funds for recurrent costs. The student body will be made up principally of students from Northern and Southern Rhodesia and Nyasaland, but some are expected from the three High Commission Territories of Bechuanaland, Swaziland, and Basutoland, and a few probably from the Belgian and Portuguese territories and possibly from the Union of South Africa.

Southern Rhodesia

As regards the quality of education for Africans in Southern Rhodesia, there is much to be desired. It has been estimated that there are about 340,000 African children of school age here and that between 50 and 65 per cent of these are in school. Ninety-eight per cent of all African pupils are taught in schools erected and maintained by missions with government aid. The government has recently, however, undertaken to build, equip, and manage its own schools. About 50 per cent of the children in school are in the lowest two of the eight classes, and in 1943 (latest available statistics) only 55 out of every one thousand reached Standard VI. In 1950, of the 5,939 African teachers employed in aided primary schools, 70.5 per cent were untrained; and of these, 1,300 had not passed beyond Standard V. In the *Report of the Native Education Inquiry Commission* (1951), of which Alexander Kerr was chairman, it is recommended that as the necessary accommodation is made available, a system of free and compulsory education be introduced in African townships, that the government should concentrate on the educational needs of Africans in towns, and mission societies on their needs in rural areas. Provision is made in the syllabuses for the study of the vernaculars. In the upper standards one and one-half hours a week are suggested. Some adult education is at present being given in sixty-seven community schools aided by the government and located mainly in rural areas. At the present time there is no provision for Africans in Southern Rhodesia to obtain instruction in commercial subjects, but the Commission recommends that certain courses in commerce be made available to Africans in government secondary schools. It is of the opinion, however, that since shorthand would be of little use to them, it should not be included in the list. Some attention is given to agriculture—three hours a week up to Standard III, and four hours a week from Standards IV to VI. There has been no higher education in Southern Rhodesia for Africans, but in 1951 there were twenty-four Africans attending universities in the Union of South Africa, principally at Fort Hare University College.

The Union of South Africa

In the Union of South Africa education for Europeans is financed to the extent of about 50 per cent by the Union government, the remaining expense being met by provincial taxes. With minor exceptions education is free and compulsory for all Europeans, their population being about 2,640,000. In the early days the idea of educating natives was strongly opposed. Money derived from European taxation, it was felt, should not be spent on educating the native. Gradually this view changed and small annual grants were made to mission societies for native schools; but the principle that Africans should pay for their own education prevailed and the native poll tax was used to finance African education. In 1945, or thereabouts, this principle was abandoned and the government accepted financial responsibility for aiding native education; it still has not accepted full responsibility, however, as it does for European education. There are about 8,500,000 natives in the Union and about 4,500 African schools with 15,000 teachers and 650,000 pupils. More than 50 per cent of the African children are in the sub-standards, as compared with 20 per cent of the European children; and only about 4 per cent receive post-primary education, as compared with 24 per cent of the European children. Education is not compulsory for Africans, and the large majority of those who go to school leave after Standard II. In theory, a Bantu language is the medium of instruction up to Standard IV, but in practice English is used as the medium much sooner. In both theory and practice the syllabus used in the African primary school is different from that in the European. In the secondary school, however, the syllabuses are the same because the Africans insist that they should be. The Africans are demanding the same kind of education that the Europeans receive. The Dutch Reformed Church missions and Afrikaner educationists, on the whole, favor a special "African" type of education for Africans. In keeping with the *apartheid* doctrine Nationalist theorists are stressing instruction in the vernacular and insisting that African education be based on tribal traditions.

In the *Report of the Commission on Native Education* (1951), it is recommended that the Union Department of Native Affairs control African education; that all African primary schools be placed under the control of the Bantu local authorities and all post-primary schools under that of the Bantu regional authorities; that greater use be made of Bantu languages; that an increasing share of the financial burden be borne by the Africans themselves; and that the churches be gradually eliminated from the direction of African education, but that religious instruction be made a compulsory subject in all African schools. One of the members of the Commission, A. H. Murray, submitted a minority report in which he says that with religious instruction in its present form in African schools, it would be better to remove the subject entirely from the curriculum. Leo Marquard, in *The Peoples and Policies of South Africa,*[1] says that the implementation of this Commission report "will be strenuously opposed by African teachers and by most of those Europeans who have devoted their lives to African education."

Some provision has been made in South Africa for Africans to receive higher education. There are nine residential universities and the University of South Africa. Non-Europeans attend four of these regularly and for the time being are admitted to graduate courses at a fifth (Rhodes University College) provided such courses are not offered at Fort Hare University College. The four universities regularly attended by Africans are Fort Hare, for non-Europeans only; Cape Town and Witwatersrand, for Europeans and non-Europeans in the same classes; and the University of Natal, for Europeans and non-Europeans in separate classes. At Cape Town and Witwatersrand non-Europeans attend lectures but do not live in the same hostels as the European students and are excluded by practice and tacit agreement from many student social activities. African students are also permitted to take correspondence courses in the Division of External Studies of the University of South Africa. Cabinet ministers in the Nationalist government have stated that the universities of Cape Town and Witwatersrand will be compelled to conform to the government's *apartheid* policy. Fort Hare, the South African native college in the Cape Province, was founded in 1916. It is supported partly by missionary and private aid and partly by government aid. Of the 324 students enrolled in 1946, 29 were Indian and 35 Negro. In 1949 there were 343 students, including 40 women. The range of studies is considerably restricted. The staff consists of the principal, 10 professors, 7 senior lecturers, and 9 lecturers.

French territories

In the French territories education is free and is controlled largely by the state. Pupils are boarded and clothed free of charge and in some instances are given spending change. The French language is the medium of instruction, though in French Togoland

[1] Oxford University Press, 1952, p. 191n.

and the French Cameroons (trust territories) teachers in mission schools may use the vernacular as a medium. Since instruction in the vernaculars is not allowed, except in such rare instances, very little vernacular literature has been produced. Native studies are conducted outside the normal educational system in museums and departments of research. Mission work is rather rigidly controlled and, on the whole, does not play a very important part in the general educational scheme. Education is interracial and aims to further the development of French civilization. There is a two-fold educational system: 1) the European, which is restricted to European children and African children coming from French-speaking homes; and 2) the native system. In the former there are infant schools, primary and secondary schools, and lycées. The secondary schools and lycées are equivalent in curricula and equipment to corresponding schools in France. Students can thus qualify in Africa for entrance into French universities. These Africans are essentially French in spirit and culture.

In the native system there are popular schools, complete in themselves, technical schools, and higher schools. The native system is designed to meet the needs of the masses who will be assimilated much more slowly than the elite. In these schools emphasis is put on vocational training. Students receiving technical education are fitted to meet the needs of village life and to work in industrialized areas, government departments, and factories. In Moslem areas there are schools for the sons of chiefs. These are under government supervision and give instruction in Koranic law and philosophy as well as general French education. The purpose is to draw the Moslems closer to France. There are also in the French territories teacher-training schools, craft schools, adult education courses, a veterinary school, many of whose graduates enter the government veterinary services of the different colonies, a school of midwifery, where government nurses are trained, a medical school, in which students are prepared to be medical assistants for the state service, and a marine engineering school, where Africans are trained for the French naval service. Military training is compulsory. Education in the French territories thus allows the African little freedom of choice as to his nationality. It is designed to make of him a good Frenchman.

The Belgian Congo

Missions, particularly Catholic, play a much more important role in African education in the Belgian Congo than in the French territories. There are "national" and "foreign" missions, the former receiving state aid. The few state schools are usually managed by religious bodies. There are three grades of schools: 1) lower primary, offering a two-year course under an African adviser who, in turn, is controlled by an inspector appointed by the appropriate mission; 2) higher primary or middle schools, headed by a European who is usually a Catholic missionary; and 3) secondary schools. There are also schools for medical assistants, schools for midwives, teacher-training schools, schools for training clerks, technical schools, and domestic-economy schools for girls. All education is free, and until recently it has not been interracial. Now secondary schools are open to all on an interracial basis. There are also schools maintained by various industrial concerns in which the instruction is given by Catholic missionaries. In some of the companies there are technical schools where Africans are trained as skilled laborers. In this respect the situation differs from that in the Union of South Africa. Native languages are used as the media of instruction in the African schools of the Congo. In the past higher education has been denied the Congolese. At present, however, a university related to Louvain University in Belgium is being established at government expense. It is to be called Louvain University of Leopoldville and will open in October, 1954.

Ruanda-Urundi. In general the educational situation in Ruanda-Urundi (trust territory) follows the pattern of that in the Belgian Congo. Plans are being made here also for a university which will be put into effect at some time in the near future.

Portuguese territories

In Mozambique, Portuguese East Africa, there are primary and technical schools for Africans, each extending over a period of three years. The course in the technical schools includes apprenticeship to a trade. There is a school of arts and crafts for Africans in each district. The Portuguese language is the medium of instruction, but the vernacular may be used in the primary schools for oral teaching. For children living within three kilometers of a school, education is free and compulsory between the ages of 7 and 12. There are state schools and mission schools. Since 1935 it has been illegal for non-Catholic missions to receive state aid. In 1938, or thereabouts, the Catholics took over the education of the Africans. The schools for Europeans, however, are still state property. Before 1938 a Protestant Swiss mission had about eighty schools; it now has only fifteen. There is one teacher-training school now under Catholic control. It is felt that the Protestant missions retard the spread of Portuguese culture. There are a few Africans who attend European high schools, but comparatively few complete their courses. In Angola and Cape Verde a few finish and go to Portugal for further study. There are at present between fifteen and twenty Africans from Angola studying in Portugal. There is one from Mozambique in the United States doing graduate work at Northwestern University. It appears that more emphasis is placed on agriculture for Africans in Angola than in Mozambique. The Portuguese policy resembles the French more than it does the Belgian policy in that it tends toward the Europeanization of the African; but in some ways it differs from the French, as, for example, in its giving greater authority to religious bodies.

II. *Some effects of Western education on the African*

There are many ways in which the African has been affected by the impact of Western education as described in the foregoing pages. I shall discuss briefly three aspects of his life that have been influenced vitally by the educational policies of European powers operating in Africa: his economic condition; his religion; and his language and literature.

His economic condition

One of the unhappy results of European contacts in Africa is that the African in abandoning many of his traditional means of earning a livelihood frequently cannot find adequate substitutes under the new system. One would suppose that the education which the Europeans have devised for the African would be adequate, in quality and amount, to equip him to make the necessary adjustments to the new way of life with a minimum of discomfort to himself. For the large majority of Africans, however, this is not the case. In such areas as the French and the Portuguese, where education is free, a limited number of Africans are assured of a modicum of training in elementary, secondary, and vocational subjects which fit them for jobs requiring limited skills. An even smaller number have educational and employment opportunities that appear not to be limited, but the price these few pay is that they lose their identity as Africans and become French or Portuguese citizens. Even though under present conditions they accept such terms, it is reasonable to suppose that as the nationalist movement continues to spread in British West Africa not only will the elite in contiguous non-British areas be affected by it but eventually the uneducated masses also. One wonders, therefore, how long the masses will remain content in their present condition and how long the elite will be able to withstand the impelling political pressure from British West Africa.

In many areas where education is neither free nor universal, such as in some of the British territories, few Africans can qualify for jobs requiring even limited skills. In Central Africa, technical training for Africans is scarcely higher than that of the trades school. In Northern Rhodesia, where racial discrimination prevails in all walks of life, the policies of European trade unions have made it virtually impossible for a class of skilled artisans to be developed. Since there are so few job opportunities, there is little incentive for the African to improve his educational status. Throughout Central Africa there is need for technically trained Africans in the government services, but there are not enough men available with adequate training. Last year the Commission on Higher Education for Africans in Central Africa reported that in Northern Rhodesia, with an African population of 1,930,000, there were only six fully qualified African teachers in secondary schools and teacher-training institutions for Africans. In Nyasaland, with a population of 2,540,000 Africans, the Commission was informed that the immediate needs in African education were for only six African teachers a year with diplomas and two a year with arts degrees. The members of the Commission also observed that the public libraries they visited were not accessible to Africans either because of the operation of the color-bar or because the subscription rates were higher than they could afford.

The employment situation for Africans in Southern Rhodesia is ironic, to say the least. The following quotation from the *Report of the Native Education Inquiry Commission* (1951), p. 9, is pertinent to this discussion:

> Section 60 of the Industrial Conciliation Act [1945] implies that Africans may be employed in any skilled industry, trade or occupation, provided their wages and conditions of service are not inferior to those of the European skilled employees; but we were told that employers would not apprentice Africans in any trade because if they were to do so the European journeymen and apprentices would stop work. . . . In short, the European legislates to compel his trade opponent to compete with him on level terms, while, at the same time, preventing him, by other means, from competing at all. The opponent can hardly be blamed for thinking that the more liberal and not unreasonable attitude expressed by the legislation is mere humbug. . . . A bar that is imposed in such circumstances therefore becomes a major obstacle to successful African education.

In the secondary schools of the Union of South Africa, the Europeans and Africans use the same syllabuses and supposedly receive comparable training that fits them for certain jobs. These jobs are open to Europeans but are not available to Africans. For the Europeans there are official vocational-guidance and employment services to link the European school system to the economic system; but for the Africans the educational system and the economic are not co-ordinated. Such a situation results not only in wastage and in unemployment for the African but in frustration, and it engenders bitterness on the part of the African toward the European. It is said that because of rising costs the mine-owners would like to abolish the color-bar and use Africans in skilled jobs, but the European miners' unions oppose this.[2] The same situation obtains in the building and other skilled industries. The skilled trade unions will not admit Africans to membership. There are African trade unions, but they have no legal status.

In West and parts of East Africa, however, educational and eco-

[2] Leo Marquard, *The Peoples and Policies of South Africa*, p. 132.

nomic systems are becoming better co-ordinated for Africans. In the Gold Coast and Nigeria there have been established colleges of arts, science, and technology, and in Nairobi, Kenya, the interterritorial, interracial Royal Technical College has been founded. These are postsecondary institutions. They will provide further general education and technical training, and many of their courses will provide instruction in co-operation with government departmental or industrial training schemes. Such institutions will no doubt play an important role in the future development of Africa. Another encouraging development, which was begun a few years ago in British West Africa and has since spread to East and Central Africa and the Belgian Congo, is the establishment of university colleges. These in the years to come will contribute enormously to the economic well-being of Africans. Africans are also availing themselves of the opportunity to obtain higher education in the universities of Europe, America, and elsewhere. In 1952 approximately 2,750 African students (many of them on government scholarships) were studying in universities and other institutions of higher training in the United Kingdom, and at present there are 900 African students in the United States, most of them from British West Africa and Liberia.

His religion

No one who visits Africa today can fail to observe the influence of the Christian religion in almost every phase of the African's life, the remoter regions not excepted. Christian missionaries have contributed importantly to this state of things. In most regions they were the first to carry Western education and the Western religion to the African, and to them the African probably owes more than to any other group representing Western civilization. Most of the African schools are still operated by the missions. They play a significant role in British, Portuguese, and Belgian territories and a much less important one in the French educational system. But, as I have already indicated, in several of the British areas there is a definite trend toward government supervision of all teaching in the African schools except that of religious education. In South Africa, the view seems to be that the churches should be gradually eliminated from the direction of African education but that religious instruction should be a compulsory subject in all native schools.

In spite of the enormous influence which Christian missions have exerted on the life of the African, it should not be assumed that where the missions have been at work for many years all traces of the native religion have been destroyed. Anthropological studies that have been and are being made reveal something of the great tenacity of traditional religious practices throughout Africa south of the Sahara in spite of the tremendous impact of Christianity and Mohammedanism. Many of the Africans who proclaim their allegiance to the Christian faith still operate, consciously or unconsciously, under the influence of their early native religious environment. The form of the service in many African churches, in even the more Europeanized areas, furnishes ample proof of this. A little more than two years ago in the Yoruba country of West Africa I recorded on wire the entire Sunday service of several African Christian churches, including the prayers, the sermon, and the musical numbers. All of the services were in the native language. Of the five musical numbers rendered by the choir and congregation in one of the churches, three were Christian songs and two were songs in praise of native Yoruba deities—Ogun, the god of war, and Ifa, the god of divination. These two native songs were much more enthusiastically rendered and got a greater audience response than the Christian ones. As the native songs were being sung the entire congregation of about 300 persons, young and old, arose and danced with all the grace and pleasing abandon of which the African is capable. In addition to the organ, which was played by an educated African, at least six native instruments were used by members of the choir—three drums, two rattles, and a gong called *agogo*. The minister's sermon was a curious mixture of native religious lore and the teachings of Jesus Christ.

In the Union of South Africa in 1949 there were 1,211 Bantu separatist churches listed by the Department of Native Affairs. The separatist movement there has two main branches—Ethiopianism and Zionism. The Zionist churches have the following characteristics:

a) They are based on a Bantu syncretism, a mixture of Bantu animism and Christian faith, a blend of old magic and new Christian ideas. The old tribal magician, the *Isangoma* of the Zulu, has today a rival in the Zionist prophet.

b) They are led by bishops or prophets many of whom claim supernatural powers.

c) Most of the churches are not interested in conducting schools but some are.

d) They do not insist on marriage by the church or according to civil laws but recognize Bantu customary unions.[3]

Among the reasons given for the founding of these separatist churches are the color-bar imposed by European missionaries, the desire for independence in church matters, the reaction of Bantu clergy to church discipline, and the desire to establish tribal schools and to own a church that will be in accord with tribal customs.

Most of the educated Africans whom I know readily accept the Christian theory and philosophy of life 'but feel that the practical application of this theory is not always made by the Europeans with whom they have to deal in Africa. They also feel that the missions do not have the proper respect for the African's indigenous culture. A prominent Gold Coast attorney, Ako Adjei, educated in England and America, says:

> The Christian church in Africa has never respected or tolerated the traditional institutions of African society. . . . It is difficult for Europeans and Americans to believe that there is something noble and sublime in African religion and in African moral ideas that is worthy of respect by the civilized world. . . . Belief in an Almighty God, love of one man for his fellow human beings or what we usually call the universal brotherhood of mankind, a belief in life after death and the existence of a spiritual world are fundamental in African religious ideas. . . . [These] and other fundamental Christian beliefs were common in African religious philosophy long before the first Christian missionaries set foot on the [African] continent. . . . It is the Christian church . . . that Africans have found to be destructive of the traditional and indigenous institutions of our society.[4]

Diedrich Westermann says that there are two schools of thought among missionaries. Followers of one school have a negative atti-

---

[3] *Report of the Commission on Native Education, 1949–1951*, p. 22.

[4] Ako Adjei, "Imperialism and Spiritual Freedom: An African View," *The American Journal of Sociology*, Vol. L, No. 3 (November, 1944), pp. 193, 194, 196.

tude toward African cultures. They have nothing to learn from the findings of anthropologists. To them the institutions and outlook of the West are the ideal, and to transplant this ideal is the aim of their work. Where native institutions are different from our own, they are unchristian. Representatives of the other school, he says, utilize the findings of the anthropologists. They believe that there is a variety of cultures, each with its own features and its own values. Their first task is to make themselves familiar with the civilization of the people among whom they are working. "Pagan religion for them is an object of deep interest, and worthy of that respect which a cultured man brings to every form of spiritual life." [5] Apparently the missionaries with whom Mr. Adjei had had dealings all belonged to Mr. Westermann's first group. Westermann says that the second attitude—the sympathetic one toward African life and institutions—is gaining ground in Africa.

One factor to be considered in a discussion of the effect of Western education on the religion of the African is the rapid spread of Mohammedanism in many parts of Africa. Many Africans find more in common between their native religion and Mohammedanism than between their native religion and Christianity. Apart from the fact that Mohammedanism permits of polygamy to the extent of four wives, many Africans find other attractions in this religion. The agents of Islam whom they meet are themselves Africans who can usually establish a more harmonious relation with another African than a European can. The Islamic costume and ritual and the readiness of Islam to preserve a large number of the native animist ceremonies also appeal to Africans. The Christian missions, on the other hand, are opposed to animist practices and polygamy. Fernando Rogado Quintino, in his discussion of religious institutions in Portuguese Guinea, points out that Islam embraces two-thirds of the area and nearly half the population of the colony and that the "few Christians are detribalized individuals who have been driven away from the agricultural activities which are the basis of the native economy." He thinks that Christian missionaries should show greater tolerance

[5] Diedrich Westermann, *The African Today and Tomorrow* (London: Oxford University Press, 1949) , pp. 104–105.

toward native practices.[6] At the Conference on African Education held at Cambridge, England, in September, 1952, attention was given to the subject of Moslem education in British tropical Africa, where there are many millions of Moslems, and one of the recommendations made was that in order "to bring about understanding and co-operation between Moslems and non-Moslems for the general good of their countries' progress, a Chair of Islamics should be established in each of the growing universities of Africa." [7]

His language and literature

The impact of Western education on Africa has brought about many changes in the status of African languages. Such activities as the following have been significant in this respect: the emphasis placed upon the teaching of the vernaculars in the schools, accompanied by the preparation of grammars and other textbooks and of dictionaries to facilitate classroom instruction; the making of translations of the Bible and of the lyrics of European and American hymns and the publication of other religious works; the editing of collections of African folklore in the vernacular, together with translation in the European language; the extensive research done by European and American scholars in African linguistics, anthropology, and sociology; the offering of courses in many African languages at universities in England, France, Germany, and other European countries—these and the many other activities that have accompanied European contacts generally in Africa have enhanced the prestige of several African languages and dialects and caused these to be known and used more extensively than others. Some have become languages of communication over wide areas. There have also emerged creolized languages, such as the Creole of Freetown, Sierra Leone, which is acquiring a literature of its own. Creole life in Sierra Leone, which started during the last decade of the eighteenth century when ex-slaves from the United States

[6] Fernando Rogado Quintino, "The Secret of Beliefs—Religious Institutions in Portuguese Guinea," *Boletim Cultural da Guiné Portuguesa* (Bissan), (July, 1949), pp. 419–88; (October, 1949), pp. 686–721.

[7] *African Education: A Study of Educational Policy and Practice in British Tropical Africa* (1953), p. 174.

and the British West Indies returned to make their home in Africa, furnishes an example of one of the earliest permanent contacts of Western civilization with West Africa. There have also arisen pidgin forms such as West African pidgin-English, which is spreading rapidly throughout British territories and is a source of great annoyance to teachers of English in African schools.

A considerable body of African literature in the vernaculars has been produced by the Africans themselves who are products of Western education. This includes plays, novels, short stories, poetry, essays, biographies, letters, diaries, historical and philosophical treatises, legal and theological works, and other varieties. The establishment by the International African Institute of an annual competition among Africans for manuscripts in the vernacular got a ready response from the Africans and has increased their interest in creative writing.

The extent to which native languages and literatures are used in African schools and colleges will have important bearing on the future civilization of Africa. The missionaries have consistently advocated the use of the vernacular, especially in the religious education of the African. In the British and Belgian territories and in South Africa considerable attention is given to the vernacular, particularly in the early stages of the African's education, and there is developing in these areas a native literature which should greatly facilitate the teaching of the languages. Under such circumstances those features of the indigenous culture which the Africans consider worthwhile have a much greater chance of survival in the modern world than they do in areas such as the French and Portuguese territories where a study of the vernaculars in the schools is prohibited. Africans generally, like other peoples, do not wish to relinquish their mother tongue. They know that without it their education would be incomplete, for only by means of a people's language can there be preserved the best that its culture has produced. In those regions where the Africans are acquiring self-government and are gaining control of their own education, ample provision will be made in the curricula of their schools and colleges for instruction not only in the native languages and literatures but also in African music, art, history, religion, philosophy, and other disciplines stemming from their indigenous culture whose enduring values they realize they cannot afford to ignore.

commentary

E. FRANKLIN FRAZIER

Howard University

Professor Turner has not only provided in his article a comprehensive view of the educational situation in Africa, but he has also indicated some of the results of the impact of Western education upon three aspects of African life. I shall not attempt to add to what he has said concerning the three aspects of African life with which he has dealt except a few remarks in regard to the use of the vernacular in instruction. My brief comments will be directed to some phases of the impact of Western education on African societies not included in his essay, namely: (1) its effects on family life; (2) some consequences of the technical education of the urban and rural masses; and (3) the problem of the education of the elite.

It is generally recognized that in discussing Western education in Africa one cannot ignore the traditional social organization and cultural background of the African peoples. But there seems to be less awareness of the fact that the education of the African today is tied up with the nature of new societies that are coming into existence as the result of the impact of European civilization. For example, the refusal of the French to utilize the African vernaculars was the logical result of their policy of developing an elite which would be French in culture and associate themselves with the latter in the administration of their African colonies. As a result of the two world wars which brought about an awakening of the African masses, French policy has been forced to plan for the use of the vernacular in elementary instruction at least as a part of a broader program of education. It should be pointed out, however, that the awakening of the African masses and the emergence of nationalistic movements have stimulated the demand for the use of the vernacular in education not only in French but in other colonies as well.

The problem of the use of the vernacular in instruction has not been solved either by the change of policy on the part of the French or by a wider use of the vernacular in those colonies where it was employed. Aside from the problem of creating a literature for instruction, there is the larger problem of giving instruction in a language which would provide a tool for communication and participation in the new African societies which are developing. These new societies or more inclusive social groups include people speaking many different languages. If one fails to take account of this important fact, it may appear that the use of the vernacular would provide the most natural means of developing literacy among Africans. Moreover, it would appear that the use of the vernacular would enable Africans to find stability and a sense of personal identification with their traditional culture. But as the result of the social and economic changes which are occurring in Africa, the use of the vernaculars in education may become the means of retarding their intellectual growth and social development. In South Africa, for example, where it is proposed to make widespread use of the native languages, African leaders see in this new appreciation of the African cultural heritage on the part of the whites an attempt to prevent Africans from acquiring European culture in order to keep them divided and in a subordinate status. As African societies are increasingly brought within the orbit of the Western economy and especially where they are becoming a part of so-called multiracial communities, one cannot deny that intellectual and social development depends upon acquiring a European language. In those parts of Africa where nationalistic movements have developed most and self-government has advanced most, the acquisition of a European language has been one of the means for overcoming tribal particularisms.

Having made these remarks on the vernacular, I shall turn now to the main part of my comments. It is hardly necessary to emphasize the fact that in considering social changes in Africa one must begin with the effect of these changes on the traditional family system. The polygynous joint family is the most important element in the traditional societies. Polygyny, as it has been pointed out, "is only one aspect of a system where cooperation in tilling the fields and herding cattle is provided by a group of people bound by the obligations of kinship and marriage . . . ." [1] One of the most important functions of the traditional family system was the education of the child, that is, education in the broad meaning of the term. It was in the family that the child acquired the values and learned the skills and techniques which were part of the African cultural heritage. Moreover, it was the family that played the primary role in the formal instruction given during rites that prepared the individual to assume the status and obligations of an adult member of society. Although industrialization and urbanization and new modes of agricultural production have been the most important factors responsible for the destruction of the traditional family system, the role of Western education cannot be overlooked, nor should it be underestimated.

As Western education has caused the African to break with his traditional culture, the family has lost to a considerable extent its function as an educational institution. This has had tremendous consequences for the socialization of the individual. Long ago Mary Kingsley made the observation that the native educated in the missionary school was unfit to live in European or native society. One of the results of Western education has been to create confusion and conflicts in family and marriage relationships. It has created conflicts between the generations and it has tended to erect cultural barriers between men and women. This latter result has been due to the fact that it has generally been the males who have received Western education, and they have found it difficult to form satisfactory marriages with women whose habits and mental outlook and values have been molded by the traditional culture. Of course, where an educated elite has been large enough to create a society of its own and Western education has become a part of its traditions, Western education has ceased to be a disintegrating force. Nevertheless, it is necessary not only to point out but to emphasize the disintegrating effect of Western education on African family life because so many people in Western society, especially in the United States, have unqualified faith in the beneficient and magical power of formal education.

As the traditional family system, which was based upon co-opera-

[1] Arthur Phillips (ed.) , *Survey of African Marriage and Family Life* (London: Oxford University Press, 1953) , p. 1.

tion, is undermined by changes in the modes of production and pecuniary rewards for labor on an individual basis, the African is developing a type of individualism that is alien to his traditional culture. This individualism is being encouraged by Western education with its emphasis upon individual competition and other values of a competitive society. There is implicit in these values a certain rationalistic and materialistic attitude toward people and nature which is transforming the intellectual and emotional life of the African.

Here some comments are in order concerning the impact of Western education on urban and rural masses in Africa. I am referring to education in its broadest meaning as including technical education and the application of scientific methods of agriculture. Professor Turner has indicated the limitations and restrictions placed upon the African's acquiring technical training where such training would make him a competitor of white workers. This tends to emphasize the fact that education must be considered in relation to the type of new societies that are evolving in Africa. In South Africa the attempt to create a community based upon racial caste in which the African is restricted to unskilled labor is being undermined as much by the economic forces within the community as by the political struggle which is developing. On the other hand, in those areas of Africa where the problem of the competition of white and African workers is not present, the technical education of the urban and rural masses is accepted as necessary for the economic and social development of the areas.

But here I would like to point out another aspect of the influence of Western education on the African. The technical education of the urbanized native and the application of scientific methods in agriculture are tending to transform the mental outlook and personality of the African. Labor is losing its social character and is ceasing to be a co-operative endeavor in which religious and magical practices and ritual are involved. The earth which the African regarded as his mother from which he drew sustenance is losing its sacred character. Of course, this process of secularization is not proceeding at the same rate in all areas. Moreover, as the African acquires education and nationalistic movements develop, his leaders are beginning to question the desirability of abandoning the traditional African values in regard to labor and the relations of men to each other in society. This brings us to the problem of the education of the elite.

That the emergence of the elites is often called the "problem of the elites" suggests its importance in the evolution of new societies in Africa. The so-called "problem of the elites" really resolves itself into the question of the type of advanced education which should be provided African leaders. It has been argued that a purely European education tends to create a class which has little sympathy with the masses and practically no understanding of their problems. They become *déracinés*, and because of their lack of roots in the traditional African community, they are preoccupied with political and personal ends. This is undoubtedly a question that deserves considerable study and it is to be noted that UNESCO and the International Sociological Association have plans for studying this phase of African development. However, in commenting on Western education in relation to the creation of elites, I would like to indicate what I regard as the two important aspects of the problem which require study.

The first aspect concerns the role of the elites in the structure of the new societies that are developing in Africa. From this standpoint, one may say that there is more need for engineers and other highly trained technicians and social scientists and social workers who can deal with problems of social organization than there is a need for lawyers. However, when statements like this are made, some people object on the ground that such education would restrict the intellectual development and mental horizon of the Africans to practical problems. But nothing of the kind is implied in such a statement. For if the leaders in the new African societies are going to make a real contribution to the development of these societies, they must master modern science and technology and acquire whatever valid knowledge the social sciences have to offer. The other phase of the study of the elites concerns the study of the personality of the leaders. This aspect of the study is related, of course, to the role of the elites in the new societies that are developing. It involves more especially the question of identification with the masses and the traditional culture and the character of the nationalistic movements of which they are leaders. Here it seems that the social sciences would have an important place in the education of the elite.

The necessity for providing education in the social sciences for the African elite is inextricably bound up with the social and cultural transformation which is occurring in Africa. The world outlook and traditional values of the African peoples are being undermined and swept away by new techniques of production and administration. The result has been social chaos and personal disorganization. In some of the nationalistic movements which are stirring the illiterate and semi-illiterate masses, there are evidences of a return to forms of thinking and social practices which have no place in the modern world. While this is understandable, it tends to emphasize the important role of the educated elite. The significant question is then: Can the elite be educated in a manner so as not to lose their identification as Africans and build a new society in which traditional values can be utilized? Since the answer to this question often involves, as I have said, the personalities of the elites themselves, the education of the African elite acquires primary importance in the new societies that are developing in Africa.

three   **ELEMENTS OF**
POLITICAL AND SOCIAL UPHEAVAL

geography of
sub-Saharan race relations

EDWIN S. MUNGER

American Universities Field Staff, Inc.

We are approaching mid-point in the decade of decision for racial philosophies and practices in Africa. In four years we have seen the rise of African nationalism to new power and strength and its spread to all parts of the subcontinent. The Gold Coast now has a fully African legislature. We have seen the birth of a great new state in Central Africa, at present dominated by Europeans. We have seen the increasing polarization of racial forces in the Union of South Africa.

This essay is concerned with the political, economic, and social relationships of the European, Asian, and African communities. It would be impossible within the compass of this essay to discuss even in the most cursory manner all of these relationships for all the racial groups in all of sub-Saharan Africa. After having spent four years in all parts of the sub-Sahara for the purpose of observing these relationships, I am humbly conscious of my own limitations in view of the complexity of the problems encountered in the field.

We will consider, therefore, some aspects of sub-Saharan Africa as a whole—a whole nearly three times the size of the United States—and select significant racial relationships for the final five years of this decade of decision.

Racial demography

Race relations are like arguments: it takes two parties to make them. In Map 1 we have an index of the degree of multiraciality

175

in sub-Saharan Africa. This area is broken down into individual countries, the separate colonies of French West and Equatorial Africa, the provinces of the Belgian Congo, territories of the Federation of Rhodesia and Nyasaland, and the provinces of the Union of South Africa.

The political and economic influence of the minority of non-Africans is at present all out of proportion to their numbers. This is not surprising. The influence of Africans who have been educated outside of the continent, and therefore may also possess technical knowledge and a facility in the languages of commerce, is even more disproportionate to their numbers.

Despite the small numbers of non-Africans in the total population, we can make a major division into those areas of sub-Saharan Africa where over 99 per cent of the population is African and those where the percentage is less. The opposing cores of these thus defined "uniracial" and "multiracial" areas are clearly shown to be in West Africa and the Union of South Africa, respectively.

Many factors, for which space to discuss in detail is lacking, help to explain this distribution of the non-African population. Perhaps as important a reason as any was best expressed some years ago by Nnamdi Azikiwi when he remarked, "The greatest friend of the Nigerian people has been the mosquito."

Certainly world political developments, climate, and disease have played their part in forestalling the establishment of a large European population in West Africa. All of these factors may change completely with new political alignments, modern technology, and public health developments. Nonetheless, African nationalism on the west coast has, at least in what we may soon be calling the former British colonies, ended the probability of large-scale European settlement.

Conversely, whatever predictions may be made by Professor Toynbee or African nationalists about Europeans leaving major portions of Africa, we cannot anticipate the bulk of the European population in the South leaving unless cataclysmic changes occur, probably involving the very lives of those Europeans.

We will therefore have for many years beyond the present decade of decision both uniracial and multiracial parts of Africa. This is important to remember because it seriously limits the degree to which many kinds of problems worked out and lessons learned in

FIGURE 1

FIGURE 2

FIGURE 3

FIGURE 4

uniracial Africa can be applied to multiracial Africa and vice-versa. Although, like most boundaries, the line between the two areas is a blurred one in many places (and there are minor exceptions on both sides of it), it does essentially divide two different kinds of Africa which have different kinds of racial problems. Under what constitution and with what success the Gold Coasters will govern themselves is far removed from how Tanganyika may strive to represent fairly three economically and ethnically different groups in its legislature. In the Gold Coast, lines of cleavage are primarily regional; in Tanganyika they are racial. Even the tripartite character of Nigeria, which reflects cultural differences, is not as politically schismatic as the racial groups of South Africa.

Intra-national racial characteristics

Racial distributions within countries are as important as between countries. Let us first consider urbanization; secondly, the location of racial conflicts; and thirdly, the degree of concentration of the European population.

Increasing urbanization south of the Sahara exerts a powerful influence upon race relations through the Westernization of the African population. It is in the cities that the racial groups, as groups, come into contact and sometimes into conflict.

Nearly 40 per cent of the total population of the Union of South Africa is urbanized. The drift to the towns began with the Africans, closely followed by the Indians in Natal. In 1891 only 35 per cent of the Europeans in the Union lived in towns and cities, whereas today the figure is over 75 per cent. In part this reflects an immigrant preference for towns. However, there has been a distinct movement in recent years of Afrikaans-speaking people from the platteland and the small dorp to the large cities. This movement underlay the great political success of the Nationalist party in the last general election in capturing seats in the industrial triangle of the Rand and Pretoria.

The city has been the geographic point of collision between European and African ways of living, between those Africans who desire a Westernized existence and the Europeans who they sometimes feel deny it to them. The "mass uprootedness" of Africans, which Professor Frankel calls the most baffling disease of Africa, is endemic in all the large cities. The resulting frustration and confusion, coupled with the advantages for organization which cities give, have contributed to physical protest at many points.

That cities are the foci of sub-Saharan race relations is clear from an examination of riots and rebellions of recent years. African-European disturbances involving the loss of lives have occurred in Abidjan, Accra, Enugu, and Sao Tome in West Africa, and there were wartime mob scenes in the Belgian Congo at Matadi and Luluabourg, and immediately postwar in Kampala.

The greatest rebellion in Africa in the twentieth century, in which probably 40,000 Malgache died, had its start in Tananarive. Its failure can be attributed in part to the indecision of the urban Hovas, who instigated the rebellion, to support the Sakalavs and other rural tribes when the hostilities began.

In South Africa the Passive Defiance Campaign was almost entirely confined to urban areas. The greatest physical violence there has been in the large cities such as Durban, Kimberley, East London, and Port Elizabeth.

Mau Mau could be cited as an exception in that the grievance over rural lands has been put foremost in the listing of its causes, and because of the gangs' retreat to the forested slopes of the Aberdares. However, the urban African population has been intimately involved in the struggle, as illustrated by Operation Anvil in May, 1954, when out of 30,000 Africans gathered up in Nairobi, the authorities felt they had to hold 19,000 for detailed screening.

Now we turn to a different concept. If urban areas are the sites of racial conflict, what is the effect throughout the sub-Sahara of varying degrees of concentration of Europeans within a single urban area?

As a rough index of this, Map 2 shows the percentage of Europeans living in the largest European town or city out of the total European population of each area. The same territorial and provincial breakdowns used in Map 1 are used in Map 2. The map measures not urban-versus-rural distribution but the relative pre-eminence of a primary city over secondary and tertiary cities and the countryside.

The highest concentration of Europeans lies in uniracial Africa,

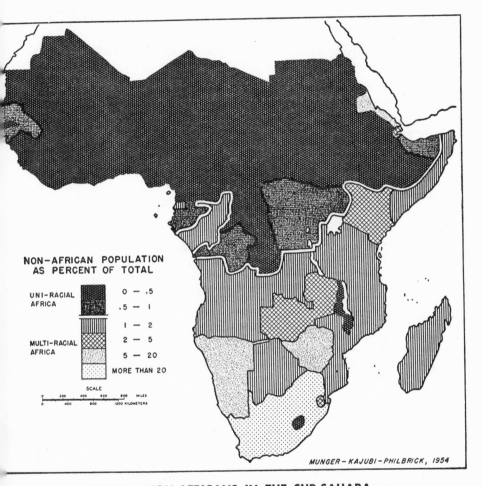

NON-AFRICAN POPULATION
AS PERCENT OF TOTAL

UNI-RACIAL
AFRICA

MULTI-RACIAL
AFRICA

	0 — .5
	.5 — 1
	1 — 2
	2 — 5
	5 — 20
	MORE THAN 20

SCALE

MUNGER-KAJUBI-PHILBRICK, 1954

MAP 1. NON-AFRICANS IN THE SUB-SAHARA

reaching 75 per cent in arid Senegal, Mauretania, and French
Somaliland. As would be expected, the pre-eminence of any one
city is much less in the Union of South Africa, even after provincial
breakdowns, because of the rural population and proliferation of
small towns in the Union. This degree of moderate concentration
does not apply to all of multiracial Africa. Between the cores of

uniracial and multiracial Africa we have a broad area where less than 25 per cent of Europeans are concentrated in a single city.

The degree of European concentration appears to have little or no correlation with where racial conflict bursts forth, except to suggest that where the concentration is very low and the percentage of non-Africans to Africans is also low (Map 1), there has been a minimum of physical conflict. This area of low concentration also corresponds in part with an area of political indecision we will discuss later.

Middle economic group

In most parts of sub-Saharan Africa there is an important minority of the population which is non-African and also different from the controlling European group in nationality or culture. These Asians or Europeans acquire their significance because they are largely engaged in trade. Their commercial activities lie above the petty trading of most African women on street corners or in the rural market place and below the large corporate operations of most European trading companies, and in all cases of such elephantine firms as Unilever. This middle economic group of non-African political or ethnic aliens is often the target of racial antipathy on the part of both Africans and Europeans of the colonial power. It is both a buffer group and at the same time a complicating factor in African-colonial European relationships.

First let us identify this middle group, which is functionally similar everywhere but varies regionally by race and nationality. In West Africa it is made up mostly of Syrians and Lebanese; in East Africa and Central Africa of Pakistanis and Indians, who also fill that niche in Natal, but less so in other parts of South Africa because of provincial immigration barriers. In the Belgian Congo it is cosmopolitan. The middle group is mostly Portuguese in the West and up the Congo River; Indian and Pakistani in the East; Greek in the center and East. In checking the register of the hotel in Kongolo patronized by traveling merchants, we found that out of the last two hundred entries fourteen men had written down Rhodes and seven Cyprus as their European home.

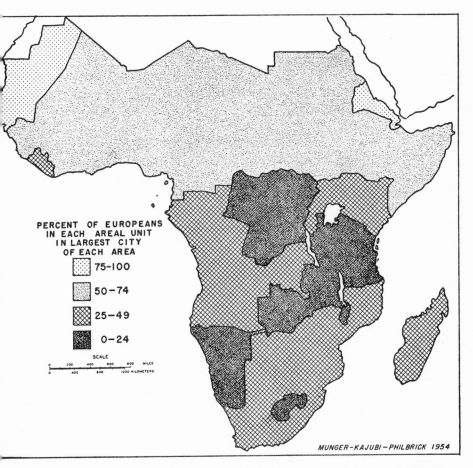

PERCENT OF EUROPEANS
IN EACH AREAL UNIT
IN LARGEST CITY
OF EACH AREA

75-100

50-74

25-49

0-24

SCALE

MUNGER-KAJUBI-PHILBRICK 1954

MAP 2. CONCENTRATION OF EUROPEANS IN LARGEST CITIES, BY COUNTRY

Dislike of the middle group is expressed by many kinds of criticism. The charge is often leveled that they are poor colonizers, that legally or illegally they send their accumulated wealth out of the country in which it was earned and where it is needed for future development. They are condemned for their lack of civic virtue and participation in sports, charities and community projects.

The middle group is accused of being a barrier to African advancement because it monopolizes trade and its individuals perform some jobs Africans aspire to fill. A Kikuyu high-school boy voiced his dislike of Indians: "I don't know enough to be the general manager of the railroad and take the European's place, but I could (pointing to the station) learn the job of that Indian clerk selling tickets."

The Zulu-Indian riot in Durban in 1949, with its terrible toll of pillage, arson, rape, and murder, showed how deep the antipathy lay between the storekeeping group and the consumers, between the bus owners and drivers and the passengers. European merchants also protest against sharp practices and the diligence with which Indians pursue trade and their willingness to live in the back of their shops and pare their overhead to the bone. The commonest cliché heard at least once daily in every town from Kampala to Cape Town is that "Indians can live on the smell of an oily rag."

Whether this human adaptation to the gasoline age is true, or whether the allegations are fair or slanderous, they are common beliefs which affect racial attitudes. Can we discover what factors, real or imagined, are most important in creating this widespread attitude? Fortunately, in the Portuguese province of Mozambique we have almost a laboratory in which to observe two groups similar in origin which act differently toward, or at least are reacted to differently by, the Europeans and Africans. I refer to the "Portuguese Indians" (largely from Goa with a few from Diu) and those formerly called "British Indians" (from the rest of the Indo-Pakistan subcontinent).

British Indians are strongly discouraged from coming to Mozambique; practically speaking they are discriminated against in the granting of trading licenses. In fact, their numbers declined by about 20 per cent in the decade ending in 1950, whereas they increased everywhere else in Africa.

On the other hand, Mozambique has not discriminated against Portuguese Indians, whose numbers have shown a slow but steady increase over the same period. These Goans are numerically prominent in the government and participate widely in cultural affairs. The difference in treatment, with its demographic consequences, has arisen because the Portuguese believe that the Goans make good citizens and that by and large the British Indians do not. Why this difference?

First of all, a few people attribute it to the amount of Portuguese "blood" in the Goan community. Actually this is probably quite low, but the belief does influence some Portuguese and a few Goans.

Secondly, there is a religious factor. The Catholicism of the Goans (99 per cent), even when nominal, goes a long way toward their acceptance by their Portuguese coreligionists, whereas the various Indian beliefs are a barrier to mutual confidence.

The third point, of greatest weight to the African population, is occupational distribution. It is estimated that over 90 per cent of the Hindus and non-African Moslems in Mozambique are directly engaged in trade, usually at the retail level, but that over 80 per cent of the Goans are in administrative posts, as clerical employees of the government or of business firms. The petty, imagined, or sometimes real grievances and antagonisms which build up between a racial minority group selling to a consuming and poorer majority is not a new story.

Fourth and probably the most potent force is nationality. The barriers between Portuguese nationals—whether born in Lisbon, Novagoa, Loanda, or elsewhere on Portuguese soil—is melting away, but the barriers between Portuguese nationals and aliens in the overseas provinces is stiffening. When making a house-to-house survey in the larger towns of Goa, this writer found that every fifth family had ties with another province of Portugal. This force of nationality, implying a people subscribing to a common goal as a community, contributes importantly to the felicitious relationship between white and brown Portuguese.

One additional factor that Europeans or Africans in Mozambique do not mention in assessing their attitudes is numbers. Elsewhere on the east coast some Europeans view every Indian as standing for a hundred more people back in India who would like to migrate to Africa. This feeling does not arise with the Goans. The result of all these factors, and perhaps others, is a markedly different attitude toward two sets of immigrants from the same part of the world.

The middle group in Africa not only has relationships with colonials and Africans, it is often a relay point in ideas about one group in the minds of the other. The picture which builds up concerning the British people in the minds of Acholis in northern Uganda is filtered in part through the ideas and expressions of the Indians who run the local *dukas*.

Similarly, attitudes toward the middle group on the part of the Africans are often conditioned by the dominant European nationality. There is evidence that the groundwork for the Durban riot was laid over a long period of time by European comments to Africans regarding Indians. Some of the uneducated Zulus were dumbfounded when European police finally intervened to protect Indian families from slaughter, when those Zulus thought they were carrying out European wishes.

Racial philosophy and practice

We have considered some demographic and economic aspects of race relations south of the Sahara. These have only limited correspondence with the boundaries delimiting control by one European country or another. Within each territory, however, there is substantial agreement among the European population in their attitude toward Africans. The Europeans in Kenya have a group attitude, as do those in Northern Rhodesia, in Madagascar, and in the Sudan. Despite the political difference between the United party and the Nationalist party in South Africa, they and the great bulk of the European population are in substantial agreement on what the broad policy of the government should be toward non-Europeans.

The dependent territories are governed under British, French, Belgian, Portuguese, and Spanish colonial policies, which represent five dramatically different solutions to similar problems. The differences between those nations which have incorporated or expect to incorporate parts of Africa as integral parts of the mother country, on the one hand, and those nations which look for eventual independence of the African territories, on the other, is not a difference that carried over into distinctly different racial policies. French and British racial policy toward Africans in West Africa has much in common despite the contrast in ultimate political goals. Each of the colonial nations is reasonably consistent on racial matters throughout its own territories, although British policy in uniracial and multiracial territories requires copious draughts of traditional British flexibility.

Keeping in mind that we are discussing racial philosophy and practice, taking the sub-Sahara by political units, two cores stand

out clearly: one where the spirit can be summed up as "integrationist," and another subscribing to the opposing spirit, which is
"segregationist." The cores of these beliefs lie in uniracial and in
the most multiracial parts of Africa, respectively. These integrationist and segregationist areas are delimited on Map 3.

Between the two contrasting philosophies are various shades of
racial theory and practice. These territories stand at the crossroads

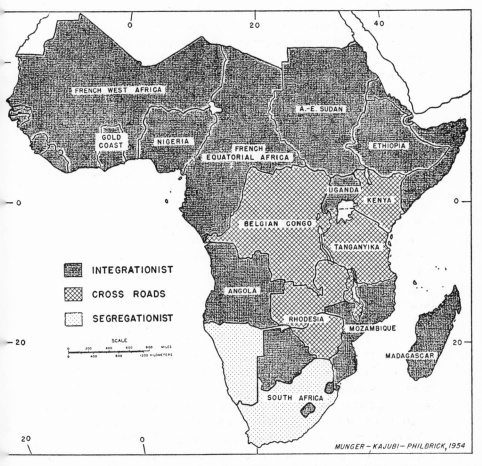

MAP 3. SUB-SAHARAN RACIAL PHILOSOPHY AND PRACTICE

of racial ideas south of the Sahara. The division of sub-Sahara Africa into these three groupings is arbitrary, although based upon published records and my own personal field observations. In delimiting the crossroads, attention has been given to both theory and practice in racial affairs. The two are not always consistent in Africa. In some cases sufficient time has not elapsed to indicate definitely whether or not practice will conform to theory. The crossroads include both uniracial and multiracial territory interlaced. They coincide in part with the area of least European single-city concentration.

It is far from inevitable that the choice at the crossroads has to be complete integration or complete segregation; but just as two streams can be near each other at a continental divide yet flow into different oceans, so there are two broad philosophies into which racial ideas in Africa are flowing. In time the opposing streams of thought may erode headward, working back until they meet and become one and the same stream, but when and where this divide will come is open to speculation.

We must note anomalies in the two broad groupings on either direction of the crossroads. West Africa is relatively homogenous in adhering to the integrationist philosophy, but there are pockets of inconsistency. In the French cities with the largest number of Europeans (and the most European women) there is an operational segregation in many social aspects, along with a political differentiation. Legal discrimination exists in the Republic of Liberia, where an African coming to settle from another part of the continent enjoys a favored position vis-à-vis a migrant from Europe. The spirit of integration has less than full application to all the African residents of Spanish and Portuguese territories.

At the south end of the continent, the segregationist policy of the Union has been more clearly defined in recent years. Politically and socially, policy is much more rigid now than before World War II. There has been a stiffening of the social barriers in universities, in housing, and in transportation facilities. Simultaneously, the segregationist approach has been under increasing economic pressure—to the point where South Africa now employs more Africans than before in semiskilled and even skilled operations, sometimes by means of the device of defining skilled jobs as semiskilled to allow Africans to fill them. Even intermingling on the job of European and non-European employees occurs. Changes in the employment pattern are most noticeable in the garment industry of Johannesburg, less so in general manufacturing, and scarcely at all in government and mining.

The colored [1] community is finding its traditional adherence to European culture in conflict with a growing political identification with non-Europeans. The resulting dichotomy is evident in the rival Cape Town newspapers (*The Sun* and *Torch*), rival teachers organizations (TEPA and TLSA), and competing political parties (NEUM and CPNU).

Another inconsistency characterizing much of multiracial Africa is the difference in racial philosophy held by European settlers in each territory compared with the ideas of their kin "at home" in Europe. The differences of view between the Kenyans and the Churchill government, while less extreme than when a Labor government was in power, are still strong enough to make the post of governor of Kenya one conducive to schizoid tendencies.

The attitude of settlers from Flanders in the Kivu region of the Belgian Congo diverges markedly from that of high administrative officers in Leopoldville, who come from a different social level, sympathize with a different political party, and come originally in many cases from a different economic stratum in Belgium herself.

Exceptions aside, the integrationist viewpoint appears to be expanding its influence from its West African core throughout most of sub-Sahara. The expression "Gold Coastism" has come into common use in Northern Rhodesia in the past two years, and South Africa's newspaper *Die Transvaler* was led to remark that whenever Dr. Malan speaks there is a good chance he will mention the Gold Coast.

The segregationist spirit of the Union is also expanding throughout the crossroads. Afrikaans-speaking settlers at Thompsons Falls in Kenya have asked for religious and educational support from the Union government, and a remark frequently heard in Nairobi is that South African troops should be brought in to clean up Mau Mau because some of the United Kingdom troops do not have the right attitude toward Africans. Former Premier Paul Reynaud

[1] Persons of mixed blood.

has been looked upon as a man to link the ambitions of settlers in French Africa with the segregationist ideas of the Union.

These opposing philosophies are now like gusts of wind swirling over the crossroads, but like a cold front, they may herald a coming storm. It is to the crossroads we must look for clues to the storm's path.

The crossroads

On Map 3 the crossroads of current sub-Saharan race relations are delimited as lying between the area where the racial spirit is essentially integrationist and where the spirit is segregationist. The area consists of three political units: the Belgian Congo and Ruanda-Urundi, controlled by a highly centralized administration; the Federation of Rhodesia and Nyasaland; and Kenya-Tanganyika, which are loosely tied through the East African High Commission.

The two East African countries are dissimilar in many aspects of race relations, not the least of which is the influence of the United Nations upon Tanganyika. They are similar, however, in their major racial grouping of Africans, Asians, and Europeans and in that the racial path they will follow in the future is by no means irrevocably set. Racial policies in Kenya strongly affect Tanganyika, and conversely to a lesser degree.

The third mainland country under the East African High Commission, Uganda, continues to travel the integrationist road. Proposals to federate East Africa, which were seriously discussed long before federation was an important topic in the Rhodesias, have so far foundered upon the fears of the people and leaders of Uganda that their country would be in time drawn into a larger segregationist state. Indeed, the exiling of the Kabaka of Buganda was directly related, according to Mutesa's own statements, to fears of closer union with Kenya and Tanganyika.

The Federation of Rhodesia and Nyasaland is the key to the racial future of the crossroads. Its racial policies and practices stand out as the crucial ones. Whereas the militant and potentially expansionist center of integrationist philosophy lies in the Gold Coast and Nigeria, which are physically far removed from the cross-roads, the Union of South Africa borders on the Federation and is in a better position to influence developments within the Federation. If the segregationist policy is to prevail throughout the crossroads, the first indication will, in all probability, be the encroachment on Rhodesia-Nyasaland of its racial ideas.

The Rhodesian federation is the key to the crossroads despite the fact that the Belgian Congo is larger, much richer, and militarily more powerful. The Federation does have more than three times as many Europeans, but cultural and political factors are even more important. Rhodesia and Nyasaland will have much more influence upon Kenya and Tanganyika because of their common national heritage, the linguistic ties of most of the European population, and common political allegiance. It has been seriously proposed by legislators in the Federation and in Kenya and Tanganyika that they should all become one political unit.

If there emerges on the eastern shore of Africa a bloc consisting of the two Rhodesias, Nyasaland, Kenya, and Tanganyika (and possibly Uganda), then this new political entity would dominate the racial philosophy of the entire crossroads including the Congo. Therefore, the first step in that direction, the Federation of Rhodesia and Nyasaland, makes the Federation the key unit in shaping the future racial orientation of crossroads Africa.

Federation of Rhodesia and Nyasaland

The Federation will be dominated for many years at least by Southern Rhodesia, or, more accurately, by Southern Rhodesians, who have provided the bulk of the leadership in government, business, and society. Northern Rhodesia and Nyasaland together have a majority in the federal legislature, but this is the high point of their influence. The legislature meets in Salisbury; the new university is being built there; even the head offices of the great copper companies of Northern Rhodesia are moving there. Southern Rhodesia contains 75 per cent of the Europeans in the Federation, and in the realm of race relations it will—and so the Africans of the North have feared—set the racial pattern.

One man towers over this dynamic scene. To be brief and dogmatic, federation was achieved in a few scant years of serious effort because Prime Minister Sir Godfrey Huggins wanted it. This astute, if often testy, politician has been in politics so long and has made so many speeches to so many groups that it is possible by selective quotation to picture him as the most bigoted, anti-African, hypocritical European in Africa. By other quotations he can be characterized as the greatest friend of the African people since David Livingstone. These sharply contrasting pictures of Huggins as a simon pure saint or a simon pure Legree have their counterparts in the present status of race relations in Southern Rhodesia.

On the one hand, no person has been killed in Southern Rhodesia over racial friction in this century—since the end of the Mashona and Matabele fighting. Relationships in the rural areas are essentially paternalistic, borrowing many of the good qualities in such relationships from the rural Europeans of the Union.

The police force of Southern Rhodesia is composed of an outstanding body of men, mostly recruited in Great Britain, with a fine *esprit de corps*. The police are senior to the army in status. Relationships between the European officers and troopers and the African sergeants and constables with whom they work closely, on the one hand, and the general African population, on the other, are excellent. One does not sense the immediate antipathy in an African throng to the presence of a European policeman which is common some places.

Urbanization in Southern Rhodesia has been relatively recent and rapid, and there have not yet grown up African gangs or the bitterest kinds of slum conditions in which they often arise. There is less feeling of community against community than there is to the south and, so far, less African nationalism in Southern Rhodesia than in any other British territory in Africa.

At the same time, however, laws and conventions affecting Africans as distinct from Europeans more closely resemble those of South Africa (which country, before federation, included Southern Rhodesia within its appellate system) than any other part of Africa. These embrace the carrying of passes, a practical economic color bar, division of the country into European and African lands, and almost total social discrimination with respect to theaters, restaurants, schools, and residential housing.

Historically and legally, race relations in Southern Rhodesia are clearly segregationist. Indeed, Southern Rhodesia, with fewer problems (or at least newer ones) than the Union can be pointed to as a country where the maximum benefits can be achieved from a paternalistic, segregationist racial philosophy with a minimum of the undesirable aspects.

Despite past tranquility and the smoothness of present-day relationships, the prevalent feeling among leaders in postwar Southern Rhodesia was that the country was too small to long continue its own racial philosophy. South Africa was gradually incorporating Southern Rhodesia in every way but politically as a sixth province of the Union. A few people saw this as a large scale plot organized by the Broederbond although that idea had little support in influential circles. Attention was given to immigration from South Africa. The Prime Minister's Secretary maintained a large chart showing sources of European immigrants to Southern Rhodesia; and steps were taken without fanfare to limit the flow of Afrikaans-speaking people into Southern Rhodesia.

Pragmatically, the Prime Minister decided (according to private statements) that the form of segregationist belief in South Africa was not going to succeed, or would not succeed over the long run in Southern Rhodesia. Not from motives of idealism, but from what he and prominent leaders considered realism, the decision was made against consciously casting their lot with South Africa or allowing the same result through the impact of economic and social forces and direct immigration.

To the north the integrationist philosophy of West Africa was in postwar days being extended more and more rapidly under the aegis of the Colonial Office to British-held territories, including Northern Rhodesia. The Southern Rhodesian fear of a policy they considered wrong was ameliorated when the Labor party lost power in Britain, but the possibility of the much berated socialists regaining control remained.

This political background is essential to an understanding of why the Southern Rhodesians have now embarked upon what seems to the writer to be a major change in their racial philosophy and practice. To reduce the ties to the South, to cast their weight northward, and hence to counteract the policy of total integration, a number of compromises had to be made to persuade the House of Commons to create the Federation.

The major political distinction with respect to racial policy between South Africa and Southern Rhodesia has been the common voters roll, that is, a common roll for Europeans and non-Europeans. It never existed in the Boer Republics, and the roll long ago excluded Africans in the Cape. Strong efforts are now being made to exclude the colored in the Cape. In Southern Rhodesia the common roll has so far meant virtually nothing in practical politics —only two thousand Africans are eligible and only one quarter of them normally vote—but with the growing prosperity of Africans, which will qualify them to vote, it is a means whereby African participation can be expanded without parliamentary action.

The election to office of two Africans in Southern Rhodesia, with the support of a European party, made possible under the constitutional provision for six African members in the federal parliament, marks a tremendous jump in African political participation from insignificant advisory bodies in rural areas to the highest legislative body.

A marked change is underway in the spirit of race relations in Southern Rhodesia. Perhaps this was best summed up for this writer by an African newspaper editor in Bulawayo. Hove explained it this way: "In 1936 when a European came toward me on the sidewalk, I would step into the street to let him by. Now I get out of his way but stay on the sidewalk." That was in 1952. Today the editor is an African Member of Parliament whom some Europeans are pleased to shake hands with on the street.

The change in the past two years has been greatest at the upper levels of society. The Governor-General took the step of inviting selected Africans to tea *inside* Government House instead of on the lawn as in the past. This distinction often strikes Americans as humorous but marks a real change in Rhodesian mores. The Prime Minister laid down personal orders to the railroad that an African newspaperman must have equal treatment on the Royal Train during the Queen Mother's visit. Equal academic opportunities have been agreed upon for the new university in Salisbury. Change is evident in the business community, where a group of young businessmen are raising $140,000 to endow a chair of race relations at the university. European voters in a high-income suburb of Salisbury elected to the territorial legislature a war hero who had taken the lead in organizing interracial gatherings.

Southern Rhodesia's referendum on federation, the elections for the first Parliament, and the recent territorial elections were fought primarily on racial issues. Huggins' side in these scraps favored a kind of partnership with Africans, while the opposition (which eventually named itself the Confederate party) was greatly alarmed by the prospect of African advances within the European sphere. The Confederates used the "Do you want your daughter to . . . ?" arguments. The approval of the Federation by 63 per cent of the voters, the landslide for Huggins in the federal elections, and the obliteration of Huggins' opposition (including sitting M.P.'s) in the territorial election have all been construed by some observers as pro-African. This seems to be an unwarranted assumption, although the trend is correct. The European voters of Southern Rhodesia have three times resoundingly shown they do not wish to be anti-African; and while not pro-African, they are not unduly alarmed over prospects of a somewhat more integrated society. Individual voters had many reservations concerning the new status of Africans, and the mind of the mythical average voter was not made up to a shift away from segregation, but it was flexible enough so that the prestige of Sir Godfrey Huggins and his party's organizational strength more than tipped the scale.

It is of great significance for the future of Southern Rhodesia that Mr. Public does have a fairly open mind. I administered an adapted form of the Thematic Apperception Test to 2,000 Africans, Europeans, Asians, and colored, both adults and adolescents, in the urban centers of Southern Rhodesia. These were designed not to bring out the personality structure of any individual, rather to distill out a group attitude or attitudes on racial matters.

Only the briefest account can be given here. The kinds of situations on which reactions were sought are suggested in the four pictures. There was a general lack of stereotyped response by any one group. There were group differences but also a wide range of attitude within each group. The dress and manner of the figure in picture 1 and what many described as a startled reaction on the part of the central figure led a minority of both Africans and Europeans to suggest impending violence on the initiative of the figure identified as African.

In picture 2 violence was also suggested by a minority and a right and wrong side indicated. Just over 60 per cent of the Europeans suggested the figure on the right was a European and was in the right, the figure on the left an African and in the wrong.

Just under 60 per cent of the Africans, nearly all of whom made the same racial identifications, indicated the European was at fault; and just over 40 per cent of those indicating a right side put the European on it.

Similarly in picture 4, there was a cleavage along racial lines, but over one-third of those tested assessed blame to their own race. Some Africans made derogatory remarks about *tsotis* (criminals), and some Europeans suggested the European's reaction to the well-dressed African was unfairly hostile. All this gives a distinct impression, although I can give you only a small part of the evidence, that there is a large area in which racial attitudes are not petrified—that there is a fairly large reserve of sympathetic understanding between the two major racial groups.

A second notable characteristic was a difference in racial identification on the part of European adults as against adolescents. In picture 1 a large minority of European high-school girls (22 per cent) considered the figure on the left to be a European in a shadow. A much smaller number of European boys also thought this. Interestingly, the only adult group which was not almost unanimous in identification of the individual as an African was a large class of young African police recruits who had just arrived in the city from the rural areas. Here clothing apparently led to identification as a European.

In picture 3 the character sitting down facing you was drawn to suggest definitely but not absolutely a colored man. He was so identified by 87 per cent of the colored people taking the test and by 82 per cent of the Asians. In contrast, both African adults and adolescents identified him almost equally one-third as European, one-third as colored, and one-third as African. The Europeans split evenly between European and colored. All of this may reflect the small number of colored people in Southern Rhodesia. The group has not stabilized to the extent of the Cape community. Their European ancestry in most cases is only one or two generations back, not five or six, which is more common in South Africa. The correlation between colored and Asian identification is probably explained by the smallness of the communities, which are much closer together than in the Union. The colored and Asian schools are on the same grounds in Salisbury and there is an interchange of colored and Asian teachers.

The final point for the purposes of this paper is that in picture 4, where Americans frequently see a sex conflict, this did not arise in any group result. Some European women spoke of low-type European women who did not wear slips, but only a few cases showed any confusion over the girl with one dark and one light arm; only three people referred to the girl as colored and these three all gave the locale as Cape Town.

In very few cases were extremely hostile views expressed. The language varied, which may suggest different conventions or attitudes. In this context an upper-middle-class group of Jewish professional women all used the term "African." A girl's softball team of lower-middle-class and lower-class Europeans used "native," "Kaffir," or "munt," the latter being commonly used as a derogatory term for Africans in Southern Rhodesia. But hostility toward another race was mild on the whole when expressed. Europeans spoke of poor bicycling habits of Africans and so did some Africans; while some in both groups thought the European in picture 2 might be losing his temper unreasonably.

There are relatively few colored people, as we have said, or Asians in Southern Rhodesia; proportionately far fewer than in South Africa, Mozambique, Nyasaland, or the three East African territories. This is probably a great advantage for Southern Rhodesia in meeting its racial problems. Third and fourth groups not only complicate relationships but, as we have seen with the middle economic group, may serve to exacerbate European and African relationships.

One reason Southern Rhodesia has few flare-ups between its different races may lie in the makeup of its European population. The country lacks the aristocratic layer of British society which has long been evident in Kenya; it also lacks the large numbers of poor whites present in South Africa, who have needed in the past and do need today special legislation to protect them from economic competition with Africans. Southern Rhodesia is the most egalitarian English-speaking society in Africa.

Conclusions

The climate of Southern Rhodesia is amenable to change from what is now basically a segregationalist policy toward a modified form of integration. The trend in this direction is more in spirit than in law, and the trend is one that could reverse itself within Southern Rhodesia, although this prospect is not likely.

Southern Rhodesia will in large measure determine the racial philosophy which animates the Federation, of which it is a member. The success of the Federation depends largely upon what this racial philosophy becomes. Nyasaland, much like Uganda in East Africa, is unhappy at the prospect of permanently belonging to a political bloc in which the racial spirit is segregationist. Sir Godfrey Huggins was reluctant to include Nyasaland within the Federation, but the Colonial Office was adamant, and the Prime Minister now expresses a feeling of responsibility for the previously economically undeveloped country.

With its influence on the British-settled crossroads countries, the Federation of Rhodesia and Nyasaland is the key which will unlock the door for either an integrationist or segregationist spirit to dominate that great part of Central and East Africa which now stands at the crossroads.

Sub-Saharan Africa with its two major regions, one uniracial and one multiracial, is midway in the decade of decision for racial philosophies. No one can predict its course with certainty. Anthony Trollope, visiting the Union of South Africa in 1877, remarked that it "is a country of black men—and not of white men. It has been so; and it will be so."

Lord Bryce, writing in 1899, or fifty-five years ago, observed that "anxieties must press upon the mind of anyone who in South Africa looks sixty or eighty years forward. . . . Whatever those difficulties may be, they will be less formidable if the whites realize, before the colored [Negro] people have begun to feel aggrieved, that they have got to live with the natives, and that the true interests of both races are in the long run the same."

How interested both Trollope and Bryce would be to look at Africa today, and with us look into tomorrow. We can expect to see by the end of the last five years of this decade of decision the crossroads of racial philosophy well on the way to fitting the integrationist or segregationist pattern. The evidence today from the Rhodesias is for a swing toward integration, but only time can write the final judgment on this and on its importance to the world.

commentary

WILLIAM O. BROWN

*Director, African Research and Studies Program,
Boston University*

Dr. Munger has delineated in broad outline the varying forms of
race contact in Africa south of the Sahara, indicated some of the
major factors of race conflict, reviewed trends in race relations, and
high-lighted the philosophies and ideologies associated with race
in this region. He devotes special attention to practices, philosophies,
and trends in the Federation of the Rhodesias and Nyasaland, suggesting that developments and decisions here may well influence
fundamentally developments in race relations elsewhere, particularly
in British East Africa.

My assignment is not, however, to summarize Dr. Munger's able
presentation or to review his conclusions. The essay speaks for
itself. Mine is the more difficult task of evaluating and supplementing the analysis given. With this aim in mind, I shall raise
certain points for clarification (some of these queries suggesting
minor dissent from Dr. Munger's analysis) and outline a few tentative generalizations on the sources and character of race conflict
in the region under review.

Points for clarification

As I read Dr. Munger's article I am somewhat troubled by (a) his
failure to define more specifically the concepts of race and race
relations; (b) the meaning and relevance of the terms integrationist
and segregationist practices and policies as they relate to racial
situations reviewed; (c) the idea that the content and form of race
relations in Africa, particularly in British Central Africa will be

partially determined, at least in broad outline, within the next five years; and (d) the assumption that developments in this region of the Federation will be crucial for British East Africa and the Belgian Congo. Each of these points will be considered briefly.

a. *Race and race relations.* Dr. Munger does not explicitly define the concepts of race and race relations. He refers to Europeans, Asians, coloreds, and Africans as racial groups and discusses various aspects of the relations between these groups. As he recognizes, these varied and seldom homogeneous aggregations are not merely distinguished by physical characteristics, but more important, they tend to diverge in historic traditions, cultures, and ways of life, as well as in their relative economic, social, and political roles. Physical characteristics make for easy and quick identification of groupings which are essentially historical in origin and cultural in character. These physical characteristics play little role in race relations until they are defined as socially significant and become operative factors in social action.

In the analysis of race relations in Africa, therefore, it is essential that we identify the way in which "race" becomes an active force in economic, social, and political relations. Generally speaking, race relations in Africa, or elsewhere, are only incidentally related to biology; essentially these relationships are social in content and form. Even in South Africa, where great importance is attached to race *per se,* the significant factors in race relations are not the physical differences, existing or imputed, but the basic divergencies in history and culture as between the various so-called racial components in the South African complex. The emphasis on race as a physical reality conceals the Europeans' fears that Africans, Asians, and coloreds as social groupings may share with them a common society and compete for place and status in a common world.

b. *The meaning and relevance of the integrationist and segregationist concepts.* As analyzed by Dr. Munger, the integrationist approach seems to apply to situations in which ideas associated with race interpose no significant barrier to the economic, social, political, or status aspirations of the African, although in practice there may be some restrictions. Under the segregationist régime, on the other hand, race does limit (as is evident in the attempt to separate the races spatially and to restrict them to separate spheres) economically, socially, and politically. In its extreme form, as manifested in South Africa, for example, the ideal is reciprocal isolation of the races to the obvious disadvantage of the non-Europeans, though economic forces, as Dr. Munger suggests, compel a measure of integration in practice. The purer form of integration Dr. Munger finds in British West Africa, with the ideal sanctioned in French and Portuguese territories. What he terms the "crossroads" areas of British Central and East Africa and the Belgian Congo reflect a more fluid situation and are placed between the extremes of the South African segregationist and the West African integrationist positions.

If I interpret the meaning of these terms correctly, I doubt if they are entirely applicable to the divergent situations they are meant to encompass and identify. I would assume, for example, that integration means little when applied to uniracial situations such as exist in British West Africa. Actually, the ideal in British West Africa is not integrationist but rather economic, social, and political control by Africans. The European will remain (if he does remain) not on his own terms but presumably on terms drawn by Africans. The problem of the European, therefore, is not to "integrate" the Africans but to find a niche which suits both his interests and those of the Africans who move constantly toward total assumption of political power. This is not the situation in French or Portuguese territories; here the Africans lack the power to impose adaptations on the relatively small European settler elements. In theory, at least, racial ideology in these latter territories fixes no barrier to a shared world for Africans and non-Africans. In these territories it is doubtful whether the European settler elements will in fact support or practice the model of integration described as existing in British West Africa, although actually no serious race problem exists as yet in these French and Portuguese regions.

If this analysis is correct, the concept of racial integration is not significantly relevant when applied to West Africa since race is only a minor factor, divisive or otherwise, in this region. There is of course a serious problem of integration if we consider the numerous, diverse, and complex tribal and cultural groupings which are divided socially, although they may share a common habitat, participate in a more or less common economy, and are subject to a common territorial or external political authority. This problem, however, is outside the scope of Dr. Munger's essay, though the situation indicated does have a significant bearing upon the future of these territories.

The racial situations of South and East Africa diverge so basically from those of West Africa and represent such a completely different cluster of realities that they are not actually comparable. In these regions a critical race problem exists, particularly in the Union of South Africa. Realistically considered, integration on the West African model is not susceptible to export to these areas. Fundamentally, developments in West Africa will probably have little real effect on racial situations in South Africa or on what Dr. Munger refers to as the "crossroads" areas of British East and Central Africa; nor can we expect influences from the South and East to diffuse or appreciably alter the West African pattern. Essentially, these situations are at such variance as to make comparisons more or less meaningless and the assumption of significant reciprocal influences dubious.

c. *The period of decision in the Federation.* I am unsure about Dr. Munger's emphasis upon the "decade of decision," or the idea that developments in race relations in the Rhodesias and Nyasaland will provide within the present decade, particularly during the next five years, the clue to the future character and content of race relations in this region. Such may conceivably be the case; certainly we can expect basic changes. The nature of these changes, however, and their impact on race relations cannot be assessed with any measure of certainty. It is doubtful if anything approaching definitiveness in the content, trends, and form of race relations will be clearly observable by 1960. The situation is much too fluid, the variables involved far too complex and trends too uncertain to justify anything more than the broadest type of prediction.

d. *The impact of developments in the Federation in the crossroads areas.* I am in partial disagreement with what appears to be Dr. Munger's assumption that present developments in race relations in the Federation of the Rhodesias and Nyasaland will profoundly influence interracial situations in Kenya, Tanganyika, or the Belgian Congo. My own guess is that developments in these areas are more likely to be basically determined by the complex interplay of forces indigenous to each of these territories than by an external model established in the Federation territories. Even assuming the unlikely prospect of a common political system for British East and Central

Africa, the racial realities in Kenya or Tanganyika will still diverge sharply from those of Southern or Northern Rhodesia. These realities, while they will be affected by outside influences, are more apt to be the crucial factors in the content, form, and ideology of future race relations in British East Africa or the Belgian Congo.

Generalizations on
nature and sources of race conflict in Africa

Dr. Munger's essay devotes some attention to the nature and sources of race conflict in Africa south of the Sahara. The following generalizations are designed to reinforce the ideas suggested in his discussion of this problem.

a. Problems of race and race conflict are primarily limited to the areas of European and alien settlement, that is, to areas in which non-Africans are either dominant or play a major role in the economy, social system, or internal political and power arrangements as *permanent* settlers. The areas of potential or actual conflict, therefore, are largely restricted to the Union of South Africa, British Central and East Africa—I would not exclude Uganda, given its large population of Asians—and to the northeastern Congo. As permanent European dwellers increase in urban areas of French West and Equatorial Africa and in the rural and urban areas of Portuguese Africa, the probability of race conflicts will be enhanced, even conceding the wide tolerance of the French and Portuguese in matters of race contact.

b. Broadly stated, the sources of race conflict in these varied areas of Africa are to be found in the complex of interrelated changes generally described as economic, social, and political. Under a régime of change, Europeans, Asians, Africans, or other racially or culturally distinguishable groupings become involved in a common economy, are drawn into a more or less common society, and are subject to the laws and authority of the only political system that counts. Within this context racial contacts multiply, interests collide, competition for place and status increases, race consciousness grows, people once relatively isolated discover their "race," and defensive racial doctrines emerge. As Dr. Munger correctly observes, this conflict is most evident in urban and industrialized areas, since it is in such areas that the impact of change is most deeply felt. Under such conditions, Africans tend to lose their traditional identifications and rootage and are compelled by force of circumstance to participate in a new and complex world, dominated by men of alien ways and systems. It should be stressed, however, that potential and actual race conflicts are not limited to the urban and industrialized areas of Africa, as is clearly shown by developments in the rural regions of non-African settlement. While race conflict may be more latent than overt in such areas, it nevertheless exists and may be expected to increase.

c. If the approach suggested in the above paragraphs is valid, we may expect an intensification of race and other forms of social conflict in Africa during the years that lie immediately ahead. As the situation and trends referred to extend and deepen, the struggle for bread, status, and power will sharpen, shaping up along lines of basic cleavage such as tribe, ethnic group, race, or even class. This will be the case particularly in the dynamic areas of European and alien settlement, where race may well become a potent and divisive symbol. Perhaps the most favorable reading of the future permissible is that adaptations can be worked out and adjustments made which will minimize violence and maximize tolerance and orderly development. Actually, however, there is no known preventive or guarantee against conflict, violent or otherwise, given a dynamic situation in which peoples of divergent backgrounds and cultures meet and interact and are compelled by need and circumstance to share resources and operate within a more or less common economic, social, and political framework.

fears and pressures
in the Union of South Africa

CORNELIS W. DE KIEWIET

President, University of Rochester

Bernard Shaw once insisted that no man should address an audience on a serious subject without first disclosing his qualifications. I have been absent too long from the Union to have the intimate command of detail of an expert. This essay is rather an effort to express a few of the thoughts about South Africa which my involvement in American life has stimulated.

In this country our interest in South Africa is still greater than our knowledge. There are few editorials and fewer reviews that reveal any real understanding of South African life. The official policy of *apartheid* in South Africa has become a very convenient device for a display of highmindedness. Because *apartheid* is not a very pleasant phenomenon it simplifies the task of critic and reviewer. Words of regret and indignation make good copy for readers whose reaction to colonial problems has been deeply and adversely influenced by the traditional anticolonialism of American history. This adverse feeling is today much strengthened by the recognition that old empires are dissolving and that uprising and emancipation are in the air of Asia and Africa.

Since it is natural that we should use the experiences of our own history as tools for comprehending the experiences of others, let us begin by using the most fundamental of all American historical experiences as a means of entering more understandingly into the complex life of South Africa. The American Revolution can in one sense be compared with the Boer War of 1899–1902. The Boer War

203

is the basic crisis of modern white South Africa. It ended the separatism of colonies and republics and led directly to their union in one state. There is, however, a profound difference. The American Revolution ended the separatism of the colonies and established the nation. After the Revolution, American society no longer contained two contestant groups who continued their quarrels and differences over the issues of the Revolution. The Boer War, on the other hand, left two groups within the new society who differed in their interpretation of their country's basic crisis. Although the similarity and compatibility of Afrikaner and English were always greater than their differences, the differences were great enough to impose upon the postwar generation the effort to make the adjustments, concessions, and compromises without which a harmonious white population would be impossible. The first generation after the Boer War had the historic assignment of trying to purge itself of the past in order to meet the requirements of the present, of determining whether similarity and compatibility could be cultivated and differences subordinated. Only by agreeing to treat the Boer War as a rupture with the past could South Africa come to grips with the problems of the new age.

It is important to be clear about this historic assignment because it was in large measure responsible for the postponement of the major assignment of South African history, which is the native problem. The characteristic affliction of South African life for over a hundred years has been this lag of a generation behind the rest of the world. South Africa is a land in which history is incomplete. Trekking, quarreling, and war caused it to miss the settling and appeasing touch of the liberal Victorian generation. A new world has appeared and South Africa is not ready to meet its demands. This is why reflective observers have a sense of anachronism in studying South African problems. At the end of the nineteenth century South Africa was fighting the battle of separatism when Australia, New Zealand, and Canada had won the battle for consolidation. In the middle of the twentieth century, South Africa is struggling to maintain a colonial policy of racial ascendancy for the whites and economic and political subordination for the natives, when world opinion in general has consented to the abandonment of this type of relationship in Indonesia, Burma, India, and elsewhere.

It is difficult to decide whether the experiment of creating a homogeneous white community is still continuing or has already failed. Why success is far from complete has many explanations. *Iliacos intra muros peccatur et extra.* English speaking leadership, to give one illustration, committed the blunder of building up the new universities at Cape Town and Johannesburg without giving a full and satisfying place to the use of the Dutch language. The consequence was the erection of separate Afrikaans-speaking universities which aggressively cultivated a sense of racial and cultural difference and weakened the influence of the universities. A principal function of universities is to draw men's attention to alternative forms of explanation and conduct, to carry on the never ending task of burying the past so that the present may live, and above all to insist on the human compassion which is the hallmark of the liberal mind. Of all forms of liberalism, that expressed by young Afrikaner intellectuals is the most precious to South Africa. South African intellectual life is becoming dangerously depopulated of men in a position to challenge the loose slogans, the false economics, and the reaction of *apartheid*. It has become more difficult for liberal or dissenting minds to survive in the leading Afrikaans universities. The result is a lack of challenge and contest. Though academic freedom is honored in all the universities of the Union, the atmosphere of the Afrikaans universities does not sufficiently discourage the growth of racial and cultural authoritarianism in South Africa.

At a moment when the great Western powers, like America itself, are in need of all the humility and all the openmindedness they can muster in order to achieve a new vision of their place among the people of the earth, South Africa is engaged in an effort to twist itself into a shape which history has vetoed in other and greater societies. The Boer War left a large section of the Afrikaner population with the sting of defeat and a painful memory of past grievance. They could not turn their faces from the past, with the result that their minds were dominated by the desire to be purged of their defeat and to recapture what had been violently taken from them. Thought and emotion flowed obstinately back to the past. Yet what in the nineteenth century a sympathetic world was inclined to regard as an understandable rebellion against the power of the British Empire has increasingly come to be regarded as willful reaction.

There is cause for gloom. It is very difficult to avoid the use of words of intellectual dissent and moral disapproval. Yet it is good advice for us to avoid the smug and doctrinaire assumption so widely held in this country that South Africa has entered upon a fatal course that can only lead to tragedy and disaster. I shall therefore not follow the predictions of those who announce that in fifty years there will be no whites left in South Africa or that the generation of those under twenty-one is doomed to bloody catastrophe. To be sure, the policies of *apartheid* will each year increase the sum of frustration and suffering, each year make more likely the chances of social and economic turmoil. Yet to conclude that the course of events is set for disaster is still unwarranted.

｜It is not a foregone conclusion that liberal thought is dead. Nor are the exponents of *apartheid* men without conscience or compassion. It is not in a keen sense of freedom and justice that they are deficient. In the management of democratic institutions their record is excellent. South Africa is not a remote rural economy in which discrimination and helotry can persist simply because a ruling class wills it. There are still spokesmen for policies that are wise and practical. South Africa is a modern industrial state. In the modern world, industry and economics lean strongly toward enlightened practice.｜There is hope in gold and uranium, in the industrial centers like Johannesburg and Durban, in the flow of progressive economic thought from Great Britain and America, in the compulsion of any modern government to seek prosperity for the people and solvency for the state.

An assessment of the reasons for fear and hope is called for. There seems very little prospect that in this century the different racial groups in the Union will open their veins to one another sufficiently to lay the basis of a society more marbled and grizzled by a blurring of the hard lines of separation between African, European, and Indian. It is even possible that the aggressive distinctions now drawn between English and Afrikaans language and culture have severely checked the intermingling of Dutch and English that was going on. Even less attainable seems the growth of a cosmopolitan white community which some farsighted people see as the escape from the rivalry between Afrikaner and English.

The attitude of the Union to the colored people, the fruit of earlier miscegenation, calls for very special attention. I have sometimes recommended that South African scholarship pay special attention to those periods in history or those parts of the earth where different racial stocks have become fused or amalgamated societies. A study of Brazil should cast important light on the racial problems of the Union. In South America the Spaniards and Portuguese did not impose an impassable barrier of political and economic segregation against the *mestizo* and the *mulatto*. In spite of social distinctions these gradually improved their place in Latin American society. In the old Cape the groundwork was laid for a growing community of interest between the whites and their half-caste offspring. The effort today to thrust the Cape colored folk outside that community repudiates an invaluable alliance. The effort to drive the colored folk off the common roll is far more a measure of racial intolerance and political unwisdom than the restraints upon the native population. The ability of the European population to maintain itself as a privileged group could only be enhanced by a shrewdly calculated and sympathetic alliance of interest with the colored population. To this population one is tempted to add also the Indian population. The arbitrary exclusion of about a million people in these two special groups from the major privileges of modern society increases the numerical preponderance against the white population, provokes additional domestic and international bitterness. The modern independence and prestige of India have very demonstrably strengthened the Indian population of the entire east coast of Africa. They have acquired a greater self-consciousness than they formerly possessed. That increased ambition and urgency for an improvement in their position will flow into their midst from India seems inevitable.

The rise of India to eminence in the modern world is very likely to affect South Africa in another way. The withdrawal of Great Britain from India has created a power vacuum in the Indian Ocean and the Middle East. The weakening of the British position in the Suez Canal and the slow rotting of French prestige in North Africa will probably enlarge this area. South Africa exists on the very edge of a great power vacuum. Potentially India is an obvious candidate for influence and prestige in the Indian Ocean. At the moment three distinct forces are struggling for expression in Indian diplomacy and foreign policy. The first is the quite inevitable anticolonialism or anti-imperialism which has resulted from the generations of British rule. From forces deep within her religious culture, India derives a pacifism or rather neutralism that leads India to stand aside from the confrontation of the massive power of Communism and the West or from negotiating a reconciliation between them. More obscure, yet both logical and discernible, is the prospect of a positive entry of India into the affairs of the Indian Ocean. Popular and official sympathy has been aroused by the struggle of Indians in Kenya, Tanganyika, and South Africa to improve their political status. The concept of a more active relationship with India is very appealing to a small but energetic group of Indians in Africa who see India as the proper heir to the opportunities which may be opening up in this area. India's role on the African shore of the Indian Ocean is potentially very great. At least it can be assumed that India will lose no opportunity of using its prestige and influence in behalf of the Indian population in South Africa. The submergence of Indians under the discriminatory laws of *apartheid* has therefore some very special hazards for the Union.

In the decision to impose severe measures of segregation upon natives, colored folk, and Indians alike there is one quality which arrests attention. It is more than consistency. It is a quality almost of integrity, of total belief in the right of white civilization to maintain itself, of complete faith that *apartheid* is a goal to be courageously sought whatever the danger and sacrifice. It has the power of moral compulsion over the minds of its followers, bred of racial pride, national zeal, religious fervor, and historic anger. *Apartheid* may commit South Africa to great international embarrassment, frustration, even disaster, yet its zealots are refreshingly and naively un-Machiavellian.

It was Machiavelli who declared that for those who entered a province it was important to win the favor of its inhabitants. The day will come when historians under greatly changed circumstances will raise again the question why a European minority that had decided to maintain its ascendancy over the native majority could so undiscerningly and unwisely alienate two other minority groups who in most things stood so much closer to the white than to the native population. *Apartheid* in its extreme form is in clear danger of forcing the entire non-European population into a bitter and intractable league against the whites. The establishment of several frontiers to safeguard the privileged economic, political, and social interests of the European population creates the necessity of arming these frontiers with the legal and physical power needed to maintain them. These frontiers are a dividing line between the rule of law and the exercise of restraint, between the exaction of obedience and the daily freedom of the democratic Western world, between an open future for the few and a closed future for the many. Their artificial and arbitrary character, the fact that they are at variance with the powerful forces of economic life, make it necessary to examine the difference between *apartheid* on paper and *apartheid* in practice.

The persuasion of a few academic idealists that *apartheid* is attainable by giving up native labor and accepting the drastic economic consequences is the fantasy of a dream world. No process, abrupt or gradual, could possibly divorce white from black in this generation. Town and country are alike in their hunger for more native labor. Some of the legislation of *apartheid* is actually a device to pump labor from the towns to the politically powerful farms. The indispensable gold mines live precariously in the narrow margin between costs and the inflexible world price of gold. Labor for the mines must either be very cheap or very efficient. Thus far the economics of mining has amounted to an ingenious manipulation of cheap labor and great technological efficiency. In the Rhodesian copper belt the lesson is already being slowly learned that the proper alternative to low cost, inefficient, sulky, and unreliable native labor is efficient, willing, and dependable native labor at better rates of pay; in other words, with a higher standard of living. A growing labor shortage has within it a compulsion that the laws of *apartheid* are already finding it difficult to resist. There is hardly a form of European enterprise that is not vitally dependent upon native labor. One of the greatest forces working to the advantage of the native is the need of the European for his services. From north of the equator all the way down to the Union of South Africa there is a serious and growing labor shortage. The mining companies developing the new Orange Free State gold fields are desperately in need of a greater labor force. Every European immigrant, every new appropriation for a railroad, every dollar invested in a new mining venture make the shortage more critical. In spite of artificial and arbitrary barriers the pressure is mounting against low wages and the color bar. The need for their labor places important weapons in the hands of the native population.

Physical or geographical *apartheid* is also a practical impossibility. There are more millions living outside the native reserves than inside them. Geographic *apartheid* might be more feasible if, taken together, the reserves could maintain the native population. This they are notoriously unable to do. Apart from some wool in Basutoland, the native population has benefited little from the rise of world prices for staples like the coffee and cotton which have brought prosperity to parts of Tanganyika and Uganda. In the Union the specialized export crops are almost entirely monopolized by European agriculture. If possible, the native population is even more dependent upon the industrial activities of the great towns than the whites themselves.

The Union cannot remain unaffected by the changes and events in the rest of Africa. The physical weakness of the metropolitan powers and the important change in world sentiment toward the colonial relationship have redressed the balance of power within most African territories. This is true in both French and British areas, in North Africa and Africa south of the Sahara. Throughout Africa the position of the natives relative to local European communities and to colonial administrations has become stronger. This is clearly shown in the widespread unrest which seemed inconceivable even fifteen years ago.

African unrest is still more local than general in character. The reciprocal flow of influence across African frontiers is still very difficult to discern or prove. Even though a few West African university students talk romantically and vaguely of armies marching upon the Union or of Nigerian planes flying over its cities, anything like a Pan African movement seems too remote to be considered. Yet if we place side by side the political changes in the Gold Coast and Nigeria, the new level of urgency to which the Mau Mau rebellion has raised native problems in the East African territories, the formal acceptance in the Central African Federation of an experiment in multiracial co-operation, then the conclusion seems sound that the trend of events in great areas of Africa is toward an adjustment of relations between the native populations and their European rulers. That the political leaders of the Nationalist party recognize this fact is shown by their many hostile pronouncements upon events in West Africa, Kenya, and the new Federation to their immediate north.

A far deeper meaning must be given to the slow rise, especially in the Union, of a positive anger against the white man, of a refusal any longer to accept the Fabian idea of co-operation and compromise. In the minds of a significant few, the frontier of *apartheid* is being redefined as a frontier of repudiation and conflict. For over a hundred years it has been an axiom of British colonial policy that through the generations the natives of Africa would slowly rise in the scale of civilization to share in its benefits. It was assumed that the European liberal would strike an alliance with the emergent African and that together they could utimately establish conditions favorable to a generous and dignified co-operation within a single society. Today liberalism is becoming discredited in the eyes of the emergent African who feels that its promises have been endlessly deferred and its assurances betrayed by discrimination and a white monopoly of Africa's favors.

There is ample evidence that this feeling of differences which cannot be reconciled has seeped down into the awareness of even lowly folk. In Alan Paton's book *Cry, The Beloved Country*, the central incident in the story is the symbolic murder of the liberal. The victim, Arthur Trevelyan Jarvis, spent his days in the service of the depressed and demoralized natives of Johannesburg. The murderer, Absalom Kumalo, was a partly detribalized and partly urbanized native. Jarvis, the liberal, had his hand outstretched to help him in his passage into the difficult and dangerous world of the white man. Between the two men, though they had never met, was an implicit alliance, for the life-work of Arthur Trevelyan Jarvis was to build the means of co-operation between his race and the black man. His brutal and pointless death is the figurative repudiation of the liberal spirit, the symbolic rupture of the alliance between the conscience of the white man and the emergent modern spirit of the black man.

In actual fact and in real life, the breakdown of an earlier sense of community between educated native leaders and liberal white leaders is very plain to see in the Union of South Africa today. Many native leaders openly express their loss of faith in the patient process of education, negotiation, and compromise. In its stead have come a hard racial animosity and a belief that the white man will only yield when compelled by force. Moderate native leaders complain that they risk losing their own native following by consorting too closely with even the friendliest whites. It would be a gross exaggeration to say that the divorcement between white and black is complete or even very far advanced. Yet it is true to say that in more than one of the territories inhabited by Europeans the natives are recognizing and learning to use the power they possess. In the copper belt there already exist native trade-unions that have conducted successful strikes. In areas as far apart as Johannesburg and Nairobi there are indications that native leaders are beginning to see that they can wage a damaging cold war against European economic life through boycotts, surreptitious sabotage, and short, jabbing wildcat strikes. There was a spectacular and successful boycott in Johannesburg in 1947 against buses because the company had raised the fares. In 1953 there was a sudden boycott of buses in Nairobi, of Asian restaurants, and of cigarette purchases. Against political subordination, discriminatory civil and penal laws, restriction of movement, denial of the right of free association, and social ostracism, native sentiment and a shrewd leadership seem to be steadily rising. Strikes, boycotts, and passive resistance have disclosed an ability to plan and engage in coherent action, which until recently was supposed to be lacking in native life. There are signs that native leaders are beginning to recognize that civil disobedience is far more powerful than riots. It hits harder, is more difficult to control, and can hold its following better.

There is some evidence that the régime of crime and violence amongst the native urban population has an implicit component of protest against the prevailing order. It takes no exceptional knowledge and discernment to see that the coming of the white man set in motion forces which thrust the natives out of the orderliness of the tribe into the alien environment of the white man's economy. There they collided with a legal system which they could not understand. They saw the white man's goods, yet could not readily buy them. Taxes, bus fares, fines, high cash prices for food, clothing, and rent were a whip that lashed them into efforts, legal and illegal, to lay their hands on money. The collapse of their own order produced a violent crisis of transition marked by crime and corruption which persuades many people that race relations are best conducted by the police. The coexistence of crime and political discontent is a grim augury for the future.

One of the major misconceptions of *apartheid* is that native and European are totally separated from each other by irreconcilable differences of culture. True, the differences which exist are great and obtrusive. Yet they cannot blind any attentive observer to the important degree to which large elements of the native population have been deeply drawn within the framework of white society. The assumption that there is a distinct place for the native naturally circumscribed by language, tribal affiliation, economic needs, and inveterate social habit is nonsense. In an increasing degree the native population is being detribalized and Westernized, urbanized and industrialized, inextricably intertwined with the white community. His dependence upon cash is as Western as are most of his crimes. Even his ulcers are the result of the strain and anxiety caused by existence within white society. It is too simple to say that African natives are restless merely because they are oppressed. Africa has been going to school with the West, with its industrialism and its political thought. There is a story of a young Nigerian who enrolled at the famous London School of Economics in the days when Harold Laski and others of his persuasion were assailing the capitalist system and all of its works. After a term or two an acquaintance asked him how he was getting on. "Oh, famously," he replied, "I have learned what my grievances are!" There is restlessness because there is enlightenment. Men see opportunities to which they were blind in their primitive state, and they reach after them because of the discernment the West has taught them. The French Revolution took place not because life at the end of the eighteenth century became intolerable but because men became impatient to seize the legacy which the Enlightenment and the Industrial Revolution were making available. The urge to independence, the ambition to learn, the passion for human dignity are the gifts of civilization. That they are acquired and expressed in pain and suffering is a familiar phenomenon in history.

The noise of speeches on *apartheid* leads to the impression that the relations between the races can only be described in the language of breakdown and conflict. But these are manifestations of a deeper process of adjustment and assimilation. His dirty shack in the slums of Johannesburg, his pyorrhea instead of the fine teeth of tribal days, his acquisition of the goods of white society by work or theft, his religious cults, the invasion of his language by new and strange expressions—all these and much more are the signs that the native has moved in large numbers well within the frontiers beyond which the laws of *apartheid* now wish to thrust him. That it is easy to demonstrate the powerful hold that the old beliefs and habits of the tribe still have upon him cannot disprove that he is a member of the total South African community, unripe as yet for its highest privileges and opportunities, weighed down by his illiteracy, a clumsy fit, demoralized and often frightened yet irreversibly a part of the total life of South Africa. The true problem of South Africa is to what degree and by what means the process of adjustment and integration is to be continued. It would be easier to drive the white man out of South Africa than the black man out of the society the white man has created.

Even as it is necessary to recognize the deeper process of adjustment and integration beneath the unpleasant surface of tribal collapse and urban degradation, so is it necessary to recognize that no statute book of segregation laws can confine all initiative and power in the hands of the white minority. The native's position within white society and the dependence of the total economy upon his services yield to him a power and initiative of which neither police nor prison can deprive him. His power is disorganized. His initiative is implicit, the consequence of the multiple acts of his daily existence. The mass of natives is only dimly aware of the fact that the flow of their lives and destiny is not inflexibly in the direction set by Parliament and the courts.

A turning point in South African life will come when what is still implicit becomes explicitly recognized. The study of this process is vitally important. A growing number of native leaders is already entirely capable of applying the analytical and descriptive concepts of modern economics and sociology to South African life. Their minds are receptive vessels for the vocabulary of criticism and censure that no bans on books can prevent from seeping in from those quarters where South African problems are discussed, whether in Western Europe, America, or behind the Iron Curtain. If it is wise at all to talk of crisis, then crisis in South African affairs will arrive when what is recognized by a few becomes the conscious public opinion of the many. Such a growth in self-awareness will redraw the picture of the white man in their minds and transform the entire world of native thought, feeling, and action. The meaning of bus strikes, boycotts, and passive resistance is not entirely in their degree of success or failure. They are outward signs of the transfer of new thought and comprehension into the minds of the bulk of the native population. They are steps toward the enhancement of power and initiative. This is not a prophecy. There is perhaps a sort of race between the forces that tend to violence and those that may open a new and constructive chapter in human relations. The time has come to speak of these.

The apostles of full *apartheid* are visibly losing ground. Wide rifts have opened up between word and deed, between legislation and practice. Very impressive is the great variety of expedients suggested in articles and speeches to carry out the principles of *apartheid*. The writers and speakers are so baffled that they have fallen into haphazard and random efforts to fit the hard facts of economic life into a contradictory ideological mold. It is an effort to make the right picture out of the wrong jigsaw pieces. Yet this random groping of confused men for working arrangements seems also to be a preparation for compromise and concession. A number of forces may lead to a shifting of ground. The first depends upon the compulsion upon any modern government to protect the prosperity of the people and the solvency of the state. The practical application of total *apartheid* would mean economic suicide for South Africa. Since Mr. Malan claims that the abandonment of *apartheid* would mean race suicide, the cynic might claim that South Africa has to choose between economic or racial suicide. This extreme and even inaccurate statement of alternatives nevertheless suggests the direction in which coming administrations in South Africa may be compelled to move.

The new gold fields in the Orange Free State, the techniques of uranium extraction, and other favorable economic developments have helped the present government to produce a surplus and to reduce taxes. Having gained power on the racial issue, it is altogether possible that the Nationalist party, possibly after the death or retirement of Malan, will move toward adopting a platform based on maintaining its fiscal and economic achievements. As soon as this happens a new meeting ground and area of compromise will become available.

Beneath the racial tensions of *apartheid* there is a further struggle which would be too simply put if it were called a struggle between town and country. In the legislation of *apartheid* there is clearly expressed the suspicion of the rural areas toward the new industrial areas. The suspicion is reinforced by the divergence between the anachronistic thought of the Nationalist party doctrinaires and the needs of modern industry. The effort to inhibit the settlement of natives in urban areas is more than an attack on the movement of natives into urban areas, more than an effort to control the squalor and criminality of city slums, more than an effort to direct native labor to the farms. It is an attack on the assimilative and integrating character of modern industrial communities. The flow of natives into the towns is a migration into the white man's world.

The urban centers of South Africa are overwhelmingly the principal supports upon which the prosperity of the country rests. Without these supports all talk about the purity of white civilization tends to become meaningless. The greater industrial areas are in fact engaged in an active process of economic integration between the races. This process is dictated by the inescapable needs of industry for a constant supply of labor. It is becoming yearly more imperative that such labor be more dependable, more experienced, more adjusted to the habits of a modern industrial society. In consequence there is a fundamental quarrel between the natural integration of urban life and the unhistorical effort to impose "disintegration" upon the vital centers of South African economic prosperity. It is an extremely serious issue whether the opponents of *apartheid* can maintain a stable lodgement in the major cities and whether business leaders, industrial leaders, together with their engineers and economic advisers, can compel political leadership to recognize that the real problem of South Africa is how to make the most effective use of its total manpower, and that prosperity and solvency can in the long run be maintained only in an atmosphere of racial co-operation.

The struggle will be hard, and the road to wisdom may pass through tragedy. The new native-resettlement bill of the Nationalist government provides for a native resettlement board which would compel and override city councils which refuse or fail to carry out the provisions of resettlement legislation. What is termed industrial reconciliation legislation seeks to impose a greater degree of separatism upon the not altogether reluctant trade-unions. Such legislation would even more strictly separate the areas and levels of economic activity open to the different races, forbid the creation of mixed trade-unions, and force separate branches upon those that are already mixed. South African trade-unions are not unselfish bodies, and municipal councils are not always heroic. The political influence of Nationalist party sympathizers in the municipalities and trade-unions is a powerful fifth column. Yet there are signs that a new United party may be arising out of the ashes of the old. There is a tendency for the United party to become more frankly an urban party, more closely identified with the interests of the industrial centers. This involves a willingness to admit that the economic integration of the races cannot be reversed. The growth of a political party committed to economic integration as the only foundation for prosperity would force a reappraisal in all political life. It would force the apostles of *apartheid* into a more obdurate position but, in the long run, would be likely to dissolve out of the Nationalist party those elements who talk *apartheid* but condone and practice integration. The extent to which the present controversy shifts onto economic grounds is of vital importance and merits the closest scrutiny.

I am not afraid of being caught in error by stating that the economic and industrial needs of South Africa are at variance with the racial policies of the present government. The error would be in not sufficiently recognizing the opposing forces that arise in the intellect and the spirit. The schooled mind that has read the past and can calmly survey the present knows that a revolution has begun in the modern world, a revolution that hangs like an overtowering wave over the heads of all those who try to maintain special privileges of race and authority over others whom they term natives, subject races, or colonial peoples. The effort to establish a provincial and aristocratic civilization with power and wealth in the hands of a privileged minority stands in contradiction to the revolt against the ascendancy of the West in the rest of the world, conducted by more millions than South Africa has thousands. The independence of India, Burma, and Indonesia; the self-government of the Gold Coast and the ill temper of Egypt and the Arab world; the Supreme Court decision against segregation in the United States; the insurgence of Viet Minh and the belligerence of China—these are all manifestations in different ways of the same phenomenon: the death of the nineteenth century. That is why the unhistorical and anachronistic temper of Malan's South Africa is of such intense interest. This is possibly why so many people within South Africa write novels about their country and why so many people outside South Africa read them.

There was a time when I was disposed to blame the South African universities for doing too little to develop the intellectual and spiritual resources that would be adequate to the immense difficulty of the country's problems. In explanation I would have made the following points. The first has already been made. The total impact of the universities was reduced by their separation into English- and Dutch-speaking institutions. Following the habit of universities in pioneering societies, they spent more money and effort on medicine, engineering, and the sciences than on the humanities, which were incalculably the country's greatest need; and unfortunately the sciences have not thus far rewarded their support by their brilliance or productiveness. The humanities were stodgy and uncreative. Today I am held back from an easy and maybe unfair indictment by my knowledge of the great difficulty which our older and more experienced American universities have in combatting forces that offend the intellect and outrage the spirit. But above all am I held back entirely by the knowledge that there is coming from the universities a dignified and courageous spokesmanship. This spokesmanship has come from the universities of Natal, the Witwatersrand, and Cape Town. The two latter institutions in particular have spoken and acted in support of opening their doors to gifted students of all races. In a memorandum from the University of Cape Town to the government commission to inquire into "The Practicability and Financial Implications of Providing Separate Training Facilities for Non-Europeans at Universities," the Senate of the University reported the following resolution adopted at its meeting on April 20, 1954:

> 1. The Senate of the University of Cape Town notes the appointment of a Commission to "investigate and report on the practicability and financial implications of providing separate training facilities for non-Europeans at Universities." In authorizing its delegates to give evidence before this Commission, the Senate:

(a) Wishes to make it known that it is opposed in principle to academic segregation on racial grounds;

(b) Believes that separate academic facilities for Europeans and non-Europeans cannot be equal to those provided in an open University;

(c) Reaffirms its conviction that the policy of academic non-segregation, which as far as possible this University has always followed, accords with the highest ideals of the Western democracies and has contributed to inter-racial understanding and harmony in South Africa;

(d) Desires that the University be permitted and enabled to carry on its functions under the same conditions as hitherto, and that nothing be done to impede the University's policy of academic non-segregation.

2. The Senate authorizes its delegates, acting in the spirit of these resolutions, to give such evidence as may seem to them to be relevant.

The future is not easy to read. The dangers are very great. But there is also promise. There is the danger of the growth of resentments that finally can no longer be appeased. Leaders of the non-European population cannot accept the basic assumptions of *apartheid*. Behind them are growing numbers increasingly able to recognize the discrimination of the segregation laws and to resent the humiliation and harassment of their daily application. Here is a road that could lead to disaster and cause much blood to soak into the land. Yet against South Africa's policies of segregation and discrimination are ranged powerful forces. Briefly, they are world opinion, the realities of South African economics, the requirements of industrial efficiency, and the hardening temper of the natives themselves. There is no need to be equivocal or hesitant about making such a statement. Even those who speak most loudly of a violent showdown with the natives look apprehensively over their shoulders at world opinion. It is still entirely possible to speak of another road of intelligent discernment, economic self-interest, and humane wisdom which may yet join the main highways of today's world.

Finally, if we bespeak compassion for the non-European we must bespeak it also for the European. If the present régime is doctrinaire and unhistorical, its critics must avoid the same faults. Even as there is no legislation that can bring about absolute segregation, so also is there no law or pronouncement that could swiftly reconcile the differences and frictions of history, of uneven levels of culture and ingrained belief. Those who seek assuagement and relief must seek it, and seek it patiently, for all who inhabit this troubled land.

commentary

ARTHUR KEPPEL-JONES

University of Natal

One reason why South Africans find it difficult to solve the problems of the present day is that they persist in fighting the battles of fifty or a hundred years ago. Dr. de Kiewiet drew attention to this. What he did not say is that he is our greatest authority on what was happening in South Africa a century ago, and therefore especially qualified to speak about people who act as though they were still living in the pages of his books.

He modestly disclaimed any special knowledge of the present South African situation, on the ground that he has been too long out of the country. The disclaimer is belied by his expert analysis. There is perhaps just one way in which his long absence may have misled him, though we must hope that even in this his judgment has been correct. I refer to his belief in the capacity of South Africans to think and act rationally.

The central theme in Dr. de Kiewiet's essay is that the policy of *apartheid* is incompatible with the broad facts of economics in an industrialized and developing country. He implies that when *apartheid* and its advocates are wrecked on this rock, liberal policies will be accepted as the necessary alternative; that white South Africa will choose what it calls racial suicide rather than economic suicide. Will this happen? That is the main question to be asked and answered in any appraisal of South Africa.

Apartheid was originally supposed to mean a policy of separating the white and the black races into two different countries, each racially homogeneous. But it must never be forgotten—and Dr.

de Kiewiet has underlined this too—that this is not an actual policy. The government which is supposedly devoted to this ideal was returned to power on this slogan, is now in its seventh year of office, and has not taken one single step in the direction of territorial separation. This is the best proof that total *apartheid* would mean economic catastrophe and that even a few steps toward it might cost the government its life.

So an utterly different policy is followed, but for the sake of political consistency it is called by the same name. This is a policy merely of white racial supremacy and privilege in a mixed society. Now the question must be put, will this be wrecked on the economic rocks as pure *apartheid* would have been, so leaving liberalism or racial integration as the only remaining possibility?

The word *economic* must be stressed. A policy that obviously impoverished white men might be abandoned because white voters turned against it. Whether they would turn against it for other reasons is quite another question.

It is true that the present policy obstructs the economic development of South Africa. It makes labor immobile and prevents industry from making the best use of the business resources it could profitably use. So the industrial color bar has been difficult to enforce. Africans are increasingly employed in semiskilled and even in skilled work.

But at this moment the government has a bill on its program which will enable it to close these loopholes. Industrial growth will then be retarded, but it will not be catastrophically reversed. The objections to the policy of race privilege, from the European point of view, will be slight and not widely perceived. And on other grounds it might be heartily supported, since it accords with the old and familiar social pattern and is fortified by deep racial prejudices.

If the actual policy of the South African government is not to be abandoned for economic reasons, the tensions and stresses that Dr. de Kiewiet described can only increase. The question that then arises is whether the white electorate will reverse the policy in order to escape from these. Such a reversal could come in either of two ways: by a change in the policy of the present government; or by the removal of that government from power.

Both these possibilities are conditioned by the fact which distinguishes the South African problem from those of other societies where the European and the African races are intermixed. This is the deep historical division within the white group, to which Dr. de Kiewiet referred at the very beginning of his essay.

The Nationalists regard themselves as the political embodiment of a nation, rather than as a party in the usual sense. The long struggle of that nation against a hostile environment culminated in the political victory of 1948. For reasons which to them seem well-founded, the Nationalists believe that the very survival of their nation depends on the continuance of their party in power.

Yet its tenure of office is really very precarious. It has not yet won the support of a majority of the white electorate. Only through certain lucky accidents in the electoral system has it been able to gain and retain power. The need to increase its majority in Parliament was one reason for the attack on the colored vote, and an important reason for giving Southwest Africa overrepresentation in the Union Parliament. The fear of losing this grip led to a discouragement of white immigration, however obvious it might seem that this alone could give the white population any hope of a long tenure of power.

The cause of the racial problem is the demand of the Africans for a share of political power. But clearly even a small concession in this direction would tilt the electoral balance against the Nationalists. Their hostility to such a concession is therefore based on national and political as well as racial considerations. Moreover, racial prejudice and fear lie so near the surface of the European consciousness that an appeal to these is the obvious if not the only way to win the floating votes that might otherwise go to the United party. Thus the National party is committed by the logic of its position to a philosophy of racialism. This might conceivably be modified if the United party were to collapse as an effective opposition, but the prospect of this is much more remote than it was a year ago.

For the same reasons a split in the National party is unlikely. No one will take the responsibility of causing a split which Afrikaners have come to equate with national suicide.

The hope to which Dr. de Kiewiet pointed therefore depends on a swing of the electorate to the United party and also on a quick movement of that party in a liberal direction. This is to suppose that large numbers of voters now dominated by fear and color-consciousness will sublimate these emotions and radically change their opinions. Dr. de Kiewiet pointed to two forces which might cause these things to happen.

The first is the pressure of world opinion. Unfortunately, the people who keep the present government in office are, as a rule, the very people who are most insensitive to this pressure. Their sense of grievance and of persecution and of being misunderstood inhibits a positive response to the pressure of outside opinion. Here the chief hope lies in their discovering, in some practical way, how world opinion affects their security and their prosperity.

The second force is the growing resistance of the non-Europeans within South Africa. As things now appear, this factor is more discouraging than any of the others. One would hope that South Africa might react to this as Britain did to the resistance of Ireland and of India. But, as South Africans like to point out, the Irish and the Indians were not living in England. For a hundred years the white and the black South Africans knew one another as enemies at the other end of a musket or a spear. The memory of those days is too easy to revive on both sides. A threat of effective resistance by the non-Europeans is less likely to wring concessions from the whites than to unite them in a sense of common danger and a refusal of all concessions.

There have been enough signs of this tendency to make the Africans suspicious of all white men, including the liberals. Their refusal to co-operate with white liberals weakens the liberal case in the eyes of the Europeans. Thus we are in a vicious circle, with resistance on either side serving to consolidate the other in stronger resistance and antagonism.

In this picture of doom there are two rays of light which could, if they shone for long enough, change its design. One is Christianity. The African Christians are a minority and have not been very vocal as a group. But they have bonds with the white Christians which could become the strongest of all the links between the races. Among white Christians, and notably in the Dutch Reformed Church, there is some heart-searching and hard thinking going on about the relations between racial discrimination and the Gospel. The Gospel has not so lost its hold that it can be easily defeated in this argument. In many unexpected places one sees Christian doctrine asserting itself in opposition to the social doctrines traditional in South Africa.

The other ray of light comes from the rest of the Western tradition, of which Christianity is the core. Constitutional democracy, science and other aspects of Western thought and practice are a part of the very heritage which white supremacy is supposed to be a means of defending. One by one the inconsistencies between South African practice and the Western moral, intellectual, and political tradition are being brought to view.

In each case—on censorship and the freedom of the press, the rule of law, scientific integrity, the competitive economic system, the punishment of crime, free intercourse with the outside world—South Africans have to make their choice between two systems, each of which has for them the compelling force of old tradition. The question is whether they will knowingly abandon to the black man the guardianship of those values which have been the only valid justification for the supremacy of the white.

The choice—between racial supremacy on the one hand and Christianity and the whole Western tradition on the other—is not an easy one for most white South Africans to make. The conflict in their minds over this is probably more responsible for their emotional tension than the conflict between races. If they could easily choose white supremacy at this spiritual cost, they would be handling the present situation more calmly and with more assurance and humor than they are.

These are some of the factors that lie behind Dr. de Kiewiet's theme. One can only hope and pray that time will justify his guarded optimism.

the emergence
of African political parties

JAMES S. COLEMAN

University of California at Los Angeles

Introduction

Political parties are regarded as institutions characteristic of modern democracy; they are also considered to be indispensable for its success and survival. On the one hand a democratic order is necessary in order to provide and guarantee those freedoms necessary for political parties to emerge and to function. On the other hand, political parties are necessary for popular government in the modern state in that they serve as instruments to integrate interests, to provide leadership, and to facilitate a periodic choice of alternatives by the common man. In short, political parties and democratic government presuppose and require each other.[1]

The concept "political party" has tended to be used very loosely to refer to any group within a given society which strives to control or to exercise political power, irrespective of its ends, means, or the character of its organization. In a broad sense, therefore, any ad hoc or continuing organization ranging from the Roundheads of the Long Parliament to the Communist party of the Soviet Union would be considered a party. In turning to the politics of emergent Africa it is tempting to use this broader concept of a party, not only

[1] In the words of the Donoughmore Commission: "The Parliamentary system of government is essentially dependent for its success . . . on the existence of parties. . . ." *Ceylon. Report of the Special Commission on the Constitution,* 1928, Cmd. 3131, p. 41.

because we are confronted with a wide range of political movements pursuing power for different ends, and by a variety of means, but also because of the varying degree to which freedom of association exists and the assumptions of democracy and party government prevail. To do so, however, would be to perpetuate a form of uncritical classification of socio-political movements characteristic of journalistic descriptions of non-European political systems and situations. On the other hand, in seeking greater precision there is the danger of becoming bogged down with a confusing jargon and an elaborate conceptual apparatus. It is believed both of these extremes can be avoided by distinguishing certain broad categories of organized activity.

For the purpose of this survey, a distinction will be drawn between the following types of political movements:

1. *Pressure Group:* An organization which endeavors among other things to *influence*, but not to control, government on behalf of the special interests of its members. The early proto-nationalist organizations of educated African elites on the west coast and of European residents in Dakar, Nairobi, Leopoldville, or Lusaka would fall squarely in this category. Today economic-interest groups are most typical and include Chambers of Commerce, employers' associations, settler unions, co-operative and provident societies, farmers', traders', and marketwomens' associations, communal and kinship unions, and so forth. The pressure group presses for favors, or for the redress of grievances, within a status quo which it does not challenge; and its instruments include the petition and *voeux*.

2. *Nationalist Movement:* An organization formed to achieve self-government (e.g., the CPP in the Gold Coast in 1950); or to secure absolute political equality within a broader Euro-African grouping (e.g., the RDA in French tropical Africa in 1948), or within a plural society (e.g., the proscribed Kenya African Union). In a colonial context such a movement normally suggests final *African* self-determination and, consequently, the extinction of the European presence; but in the light of the racial composition of many of Africa's emergent political units, the alternative goal of equality is included here. A national movement has as its *raison d'être* the final realization of a purely political objective—independence or equality, depending upon the context—which involves *control* over government; and therefore it represents a fundamental challenge to

the status quo. It has many weapons—constitutional or extra-legal—such as press invective, mass meetings, general strikes, boycotts, as well as agitation within councils and assemblies.

3. *Political Party:* An organization which competes with other similar organizations in periodical elections in order to participate in formal institutions and thereby influence and control the personnel and policy of government.[2] It accepts the constitutional status quo, at least for the time being. The *Bloc Démocratique Sénégalais* in Senegal or the Ghana Congress Party in the Gold Coast are political parties in this sense. The weapons of the party include the usual campaign pyrotechnics and propaganda, and in some instances intimidation or bribery.

The dividing line between these various categories is not sharp; indeed, depending upon circumstances and the stage of development, some organizations could quite properly fall in any one or all of them. There seems to be, however, a fairly typical pattern of historical development. In the first generation after the European intrusion, African political movements were proto-nationalist pressure groups petitioning for tax relief or very limited representation. As a result of the great social changes and ferment created by the Western impact, new second and third generation elites emerged and formed nationalist movements that categorically demanded change. Insofar as they won constitutional reforms these nationalist organizations tended to take on by equal measure the functions of a political party.

The extent to which pressure groups become primarily nationalist organizations, and the latter in turn become primarily political parties, has varied among the several territories. In British West Africa and French tropical Africa the transition has been fairly smooth; in British East and Central Africa, African movements continue to take the form either of pressure groups begging for favors, of nationalist movements agitating for constitutional reform, or of conspiratorial and terroristic movements dedicated to violence; and in Belgian and Portuguese Africa, organized activity has not moved beyond the pressure group stage.

[2] It is the narrower concept of the "legal" party described by Max Weber that is used here. See his *The Theory of Social and Economic Organization* (London, 1947), pp. 373–78.

In the light of these different patterns of development it is necessary at the outset not only to state rather arbitrarily what is meant by the concept of "political party" in its African setting but also to clarify the concept of tropical Africa as an area. The great diversity which characterizes the land, peoples, and governments of this area has tended to be obscured by the common colonial status as well as the persistence of the popular conception of the "Dark Continent." This has resulted in inaccurate generalizations not only about Africa's physical and cultural realities, but also about the nature of polical problems and the direction of political developments. The many sharp contrasts that characterize the political situations of this area have only recently become manifest.

Two major factors help to account for these sharply divergent patterns of political evolution. The first relates to the colonial policy of the imperial powers. Insofar as the emergence and development of African political parties is concerned, there are three respects in which colonial policy has been significant. One has been the degree of freedom allowed Africans to organize political associations and carry on political activity. Another element has been the institutional framework established by the colonial power, especially constitutional provisions for popular participation in government via the electoral process. A final feature has been the declared political objective of the colonial relationship—territorial self-government (British Africa), Euro-African assimilation (French and Portuguese Africa), or protracted European tutelage (Belgian Africa). The second major factor concerns the resident non-Africans —the "settlers." Important considerations here are the number involved; whether or not such aliens are politically conscious and claimant; whether they are settled farmers, as in the Kenya highlands, urban technicians, as in the Belgian Congo, or merchants, such as the Levantines in West Africa or Indians in East Africa; and whether they are members of the same race and nationality as the imperial power. Each of these several variables, individually and in combination, has been of crucial significance in the emergence of African political parties.

In applying these selected criteria to the broad area of tropical Africa, it is believed that most territories fall into one of four categories, each of which is characterized by a distinctive set of political relationships and pattern of development.

Group I: *Emergent African States* (Gold Coast, Nigeria, Sierra Leone, Uganda, and Togoland and Cameroons under United Kingdom Trusteeship), the distinguishing feature of which is the assumption of ultimate African self-government in an African state; and, as a consequence, the predominance of African political parties.

Group II: *Territories Belonging to Euro-African Unions* (territories of French tropical Africa), the unique features of which are the absence of an assumption of territorial autonomy and common participation by resident Europeans and indigenous Africans in political institutions and processes in both the metropole and Africa, and, consequently, the important role of metropolitan as well as African political parties.

Group III: *Emergent Multiracial States* (the territories of the Central African Federation, Tanganyika under United Kingdom Trusteeship, and Kenya), the distinguishing features of which are the coexistence within each territory of two or more unassimilated ethnic groups, the absence of an assumption of ultimate African self-government, the partial or total devolution of imperial power into the hands of politically conscious and claimant non-African groups, and, hence, the predominance of non-African—mainly European—political parties.

Group IV: *Territories Without Political Parties* (Belgian, Portuguese, and Spanish territories), the key characteristic of which is the present nonexistence of those preconditions necessary for the emergence of political parties (European or African).

The foregoing classification of African territories is based upon political realities rather than constitutional theory. According to the latter, Portuguese and Spanish territories should belong to Group III, as they are in each case politically assimilated to the metropolitan country. In consideration of the authoritarian character of the one-party political systems of Portugal and Spain, however, they must be placed in Group IV. Again, because of the reluctance of the Belgian government to declare rigid and absolute political goals or to provide the procedures or institutions for popular participation—African or resident European—in the government of the Congo, it is too early to forecast which pattern of party development will characterize the Congo of the future. There are signs pointing in all three directions—an African state, a plural society, and a *Congo-Belge* union. Pending the devolution of additional power from Brussels and the democratization of the central government of the Congo (as distinguished from native councils), however, political parties for all practical purposes do not and cannot exist.

As this study is concerned with the emergence of African political parties, attention will be focused primarily upon party development in the territories falling in the first two categories; namely, emergent African states and Euro-African unions. It is only in these areas that one finds an electoral system and an institutional framework that either assumes or provides for African political parties. Insofar as the emergent multiracial states are concerned, the special obstacles and problems connected with the development of African parties will be briefly examined. As thus limited, emphasis will be placed upon selected factors which have contributed to or conditioned the origin and evolution of African parties. European and other non-African parties will be treated only insofar as they have affected that development.

Political parties in emergent African states

Selected factors in the origin of parties

There are certain special features regarding British West Africa which help to explain the unique pattern of party development in the emergent African states of the Gold Coast, Nigeria, and Sierra Leone. One is the earlier and more intensive intrusion of Western influences and forces of modernity. These have brought into being in far greater numbers than elsewhere those individuals and groups—intellectuals, professional men, and a nascent middle class—which are predisposed toward Western-style political activity. Another factor is the absence in this area, for special historical and climatic reasons, of a politically conscious and claimant alien group, or groups, which could arrogate to itself, or induce the imperial power to devolve upon it, full control over the personnel and policy of government as well as the destiny of the emergent states. This has meant that the new African elites have been comparatively unfettered in their pursuit of self-government, not only because they have not had to face obstacles erected by fearful settlers but also because they have enjoyed a self-assurance and a confident expectancy that their vision of the new society in which they would be masters was in fact a realizable ideal.[3]

A third factor has been prevalence of certain democratic assumptions and institutions to a greater and more meaningful degree than elsewhere on the African continent. Like the new Asian states, the West African territories have been the unplanned beneficiaries of the indiscriminate application of the Durham formula to all British colonies. The institution of the Legislative Council was established in the west coast colonies in the mid-nineteenth century when different imperial assumptions prevailed. It has always carried with it the strong implicit assumption of a progressive climb up the constitutional ladder to the finite goal of responsible self-government. Moreover, this has been buttressed by official declarations to the effect that self-government is the final goal of the policy, although until the nineteen-forties British officialdom, when thinking of Africa, had in mind what Baron van Asbeck has called *native* autonomy as distinguished from *Western* autonomy.[4] Nevertheless, the Legislative Council and the finite goal of self-government, when coupled with the prevalence of certain limited freedoms (association, speech, press, and movement), have provided British west coast nationalists with a forum, mantle of legitimacy, and an area of freedom in which they have been able to drive inexorably toward the full realization of responsible African self-government.

The foregoing situational factors—the early emergence of an uprooted and claimant minority, the absence of a dominant alien community, and the prevalence of certain limited freedoms and

[3] The psychological stimulus to political consciousness and the drive for change and power which is derived from an awareness of opportunities is vividly described in the writings of Eric Hoffer, especially his *The True Believer* (New York, 1951), p. 48.

[4] For Baron van Azbeck's distinction between the two types of self-government see A. F. G. Marzorati, "The Belgian Congo," *African Affairs*, Vol. 53 (April, 1954), pp. 104–112. For British West African territories this distinction was most emphatically drawn by Sir Hugh Clifford of Nigeria, in 1920, when he scoffed at demands by educated African nationalists for self-government and stated flatly that "real national self-government" could be realized only through the "local tribal institutions and the indigenous forms of government." See Joan Wheare, *The Nigerian Legislative Council* (London, 1950), pp. 31–32.

adaptable political institutions—helped to provide a setting conducive to or permissive of the emergence of organized nationalist movements. The latter, through constitutional reform, have developed into political parties. But other forces and influences have been operative. One of these has been the strong attraction of the emergent African elites to parliamentary democracy, a system that both assumes and requires political parties. In part, this attraction is the result of certain strong conditioning factors operative in a British colonial territory, such as the fact that most political institutions and developments—whether at the center or in native administration—are defined and rationalized in terms of Western democracy, or the fact that these elites are largely the product of Christian missions and Anglo-American institutions of higher learning. These influences have encouraged or stimulated emulation of Western political patterns or stressed the supremacy of certain values realizable only through democratic institutions.

In another sense, this attraction to parliamentary democracy has been and is opportunistic. As Western institutions, in response to nationalist pressure, progressively took on more form and substance, it became increasingly evident to nationalists that it was not only possible but also easier and quicker to gain their ends—freedom for their people, welfare, personal aggrandizement, or whatever the case—if they worked within the evolving political structure sanctioned by the British colonial governments. In that way they encountered less imperial resistance; in short, constitutionalism paid bigger dividends. To the extent that opportunism has been a factor, this channeling of nationalist energy into constitutional political parties demonstrates in striking fashion the powerful influence of colonial institutions upon the political patterns of the emergent African states.

African nationalists have had their energies directed into constitutional political parties not only because of the influence of the institutional framework but also because of the character of colonial nationalism. Modern nationalism wherever it appears carries with it certain strong democratic implications because of its reference to the people. In a colonial milieu it tends to be ultra-democratic. For one reason, Western colonial powers are most vulnerable when confronted with the contradiction between democratic pretensions and the inescapably paternal character of a colonial system. Another reason is that in most colonies the impact of modernity and the operation of the colonial system have brought about a reversal in status of leadership groups—the older traditional elites have been eclipsed by the new Westernized elites. Like most leaders in a post-democratic world, the latter are obliged to assert and justify their claim to power by an appeal to the people through the use of democratic symbols. Thus, the new elites are the leaders and the prisoners of both nationalism and democracy. Political parties are not only useful instruments for acquiring power; they are also the only legitimate and respectable vehicles for pursuing power in a democratic order.[5]

Another factor facilitating the emergence of parties was the very considerable organizational development that occurred prior to and during the Second World War. Very early in the colonial period Christianized Africans either founded or were given control over independent African churches. Beginning in the early nineteen-thirties there commenced to spring up in most of the urban centers an increasing number of kinship associations, youth clubs, literary societies, farmers' co-operatives, community leagues, and tribal unions; and in the early nineteen-forties the British government gave strong official support to the organization of trade-unions.[6] During and immediately following the war, the overwhelming majority of the educated elements in Africa and students in England and the United States were engaged in one way or another in organized nationalist activity. This backlog of organizational experience was very important in the development of a political party system. The earlier associations provided the framework for the assertion and maturation of leadership as well as a training ground in the techniques of organizational management, and in stratagems for manipulating a mass following. Moreover, in many instances, cultural organizations or nationalist movements simply

[5] See Daryll Forde, "The Conditions of Social Development in West Africa," *Civilisations,* Vol. III (1953), p. 581; Cf. Rupert Emerson, "Paradoxes of Asian Nationalism," *The Far Eastern Quarterly,* Vol. XIII (February, 1954), pp. 140–41.

[6] For this early organizational development see Thomas Hodgkin, "Towards Self-Government in British West Africa" in Basil Davidson and Adenekan Ademola (eds.), *The New West Africa* (London, 1953), pp. 65–70.

assumed the character of a political party, in which cases there was continuity both in personnel and organizational structure.[7]

Most nationalist movements and political parties were formally brought into existence as the result of the initiative, dynamism, and enthusiasm of a new leadership. In analyzing the character of this leadership one is struck by the decisive importance of the unusual leader. Certain individuals, driven by insatiable ambition or high idealism, have appeared upon the stage at the critical moment to crystallize energies and articulate aspirations. They have emerged as leaders possessing a charisma and a religious symbolism that seems to defy opposition or resistance. The origin, unity and strength of such parties as the CPP of the Gold Coast and the NCNC of Nigeria cannot be explained or understood without an appreciation of such "men of destiny" as Prime Ministers Kwame Nkrumah and Nnamdi Azikiwe. In other instances, however, one finds the appearance of strong, well-organized political parties which are not solely dependent upon the personality of one man. The unity, strength, and success of the NPC of northern Nigeria, the Action Group of western Nigeria, and the SLPP of Sierra Leone can be explained partly in terms of such strong and able—but uncharismatic—leaders as the Sardauna of Sokoto, Prime Minister Obafemi Awolowo, and Dr. Milton Margai. Yet in each instance, either because of the personality of these leaders or because of the nature of the interests they represent, there has evolved what approximates a collegiate form of party leadership.

The really decisive factor—the precipitant—in the formation of political parties has been constitutional reform providing for (1) the devolution by the imperial government of a sufficiently *meaningful* and *attractive* measure of power to induce or to provoke nationalist leaders to convert their movements into political parties

[7] On the Ivory Coast M. Felix Houphouet's *Syndicat Agricole Africain* provided the organizational base for his *Parti Démocratique de la Côte d'Ivoire*. See F. J. Amon D'Aby, *La Côte d'Ivoire dans La Cité Africaine* (Paris, 1951), pp. 48–61. In western Nigeria the Action Group capitalized upon the organizational structure and leadership groups of the Yoruba cultural organization *Egbe Omo Oduduwa;* and, in northern Nigeria, the Northern People's Congress was first formed as a cultural organization which declared itself a party during the 1951 elections. The NCNC in Nigeria and the CPP in the Gold Coast were both nationalist movements converted to parties for electoral purposes.

and (2) the introduction or refinement of institutions and procedures, such as an electoral system, which would make it technically possible for parties to seek power constitutionally. The several sociological factors and historical developments previously discussed have provided the social groups and an institutional setting indispensable for and predisposed toward the emergence of parties. But the latter did not formally come into being until the introduction of very substantial constitutional reforms in these territories during the period 1950–53.

Special factors affecting party development

In the development of political parties during this formative period, one fact commands attention: as of January, 1955, none of these territories had achieved full self-government in the sense that the British "presence" had been terminated. Whether the British departure would have led to one-party dictatorships of the left or right, chaotic internecine strife between warring tribes or factions, or democratic party systems the equal of many of those in the West, it is impossible to state; there have been and are signs pointing in all three directions. In any event, the "presence" has been a factor that has influenced party development in two crucial respects. By providing visible evidence of "Western imperialism," it has tended to perpetuate nationalism and the "struggle for self-government" as a major factor affecting most aspects of the political life of these territories. The political process is dominated by interparty struggles to capture and monopolize nationalist symbols.[8]

A second consequence of the persistence of the "presence," in the qualified form it has taken, is that it has enabled nationalism to become institutionalized without losing its *élan*. Broadly based nationalist movements have become political parties commanding

8 This has been the case particularly in the struggle between the CPP and the Ghana Congress Party in the Gold Coast and between the Action Group and the NCNC in western Nigeria. It has also been an operative factor in the struggle between the BDS and SFIO in Senegal and the RDA and its opposition in the Ivory Coast. Cf. M. N. Roy, "Asian Nationalism," *The Yale Review*, Vol. XLII (Autumn, 1952), pp. 100–101, and Robert A. Scalapino, "Neutralism in Asia," *The American Political Science Review*, Vol. XLVIII (March, 1954), p. 52.

large parliamentary majorities, thereby attaining the ideal of a parliamentary system—a government of the day supported by a safe majority whose members are united by a common interest (in this case, the cement and enthusiasm of nationalism). At the same time, because of the continued "presence"—which has been adaptable, indulgent, and astute—the majority party has been able to retain its leadership over the nationalist movement (and therefore a safe majority in Parliament) by continued agitation for full self-government and by blaming "imperialism" for shortcomings or failures in government policy.[9]

Considering the cultural heterogeneity of most colonial territories, it was to be expected that tribal, regional, and sectional differences would be uncovered and sharpened with the approach of self-government. While standing upon the threshold of independence, the leaders of the various groups have been able for the first time to perceive the emerging power clusters and to calculate their role in the new order. For some, it raises hopes and ambitions and is a provocation to fresh activity and renewed pressure. In others it creates doubts and awakens or stimulates an awareness of belonging to a distinct cultural group, whether that be defined in terms of kinship, religion, level of material development, or a "community of fate" whose members simply share a common fear of being dominated by another group. Apart from the northern territories, these inter-group tensions are largely absent in the Gold Coast not only because of its greater cultural homogeneity and economic development, but also because of the powerful leadership of Prime Minister Nkrumah and the integrative influence of the Convention Peoples' Party.[10]

Elsewhere, however, this subterritorial group-sentiment or consciousness, referred to as tribalism or regional separatism, has been one of the decisive factors in determining party alignments. Thus,

[9] See David Apter, "Political Democracy in the Gold Coast," in *Africa in the Modern World*, Proceedings of the Twenty-Ninth Institute of the Norman Wait Harris Memorial Foundation (Chicago, in press).

[10] In emergent Africa, as in Southern Asia, there tends to be a fairly common developmental pattern in which broad and loosely knit nationalist coalitions, united in the early stages for the purpose of achieving independence, tend to disintegrate into religious, tribal, or socio-economic parties as they approach the goal of independence. Cf. Sydney D. Bailey, *Parliamentary Government in*

in the case of the Sierra Leone Peoples' party, the bond of unity has been a mixture of apprehension, shared by leaders in the protectorate, regarding the historically dominant position of the Creoles of Freetown; a common awareness of being far more under-developed, and therefore weaker, than the colony; and a tacit agree-ment to use their unity plus their numerical superiority to achieve and hold power in the emergent state of Sierra Leone. In the case of the Action Group of the Western Region of Nigeria, one finds a medley of Yoruba cultural nationalism, a common opposition to what has been made to appear as the threat of Ibo domination, and a consciousness of a higher per capita income in the Western Region which does not invite dilution. In the case of the National Council of Nigeria and the Cameroons of the Eastern Region of Nigeria one finds an Ibo self-consciousness rallied around the per-sonality of Prime Minister Nnamdi Azikiwe, who has acquired and retained effective monopoly over both Ibo tribal and, in some respects, Nigerian national symbols. Finally, in turning to the Northern Peoples' Congress of northern Nigeria we discover a common bond in the Moslem religion and Islamic Hausa culture and a common apprehension regarding the more advanced peoples of the southern regions.

In each of the above instances, it is clear that the principal explanation for the emergence of strong majority parties is that such parties are the carriers and symbols of an overriding group consciousness, referred to loosely as tribalism, regionalism, and, in certain contexts, communalism. This conclusion is further strengthened by analysis of the character of the opposition parties. In Sierra Leone, the National Council has been exclusively a Creole affair; in western Nigeria the NCNC has tended to draw its main strength from the non-Yoruba elements of the Western Region; in eastern Nigeria opposition tends to be crystallizing around non-

Southern Asia (New York, 1952) , pp. 15–17. In both the Gold Coast and Nigeria the process of disintegration and fragmentation continues as a consequence of the progressive awakening of ethnic or religious minority groups. Thus one finds the recent emergence of the Northern Peoples' Party in the northern territories, and the National Liberation Movement in the Ashanti region of the Gold Coast. Similarly, in Nigeria the Coastal Peoples' Party amongst the non-Ibos of the Eastern Region, the Middle Belt Peoples' Party amongst the non-Moslem groups of the Northern Region, and other new parties have recently appeared.

Ibo groups; and in northern Nigeria the Northern Elements Progressive Union has derived much of its strength from the non-Hausa groups of the middle belt. In most instances, therefore, opposition leadership has discovered that support is most easily aroused by appealing to the group consciousness of minority groups in the territory concerned. Yet, once these general tendencies are noted, it should be emphasized that many African party leaders have been strongly impressed with the need for transcending tribalism or regionalism. The leadership of the SLPP has included prominent Creoles, and party programs have appealed to the unity of Sierra Leone. Similarly, the leadership of the Action Group in western Nigeria includes prominent non-Yorubas; and, ever since 1938, Prime Minister Nnamdi Azikiwe has publicly eschewed tribalism. Even in northern Nigeria the Fulani-Hausa leadership of the NPC is addressing increased attention to leaders of the middle-belt groups.

Another factor conditioning the development of parties has been the influence of the institutional framework within which they were born and have been obliged to function. In some respects, the institutions established by the new constitutions were conducive to the development of a "political party system"; in others they clearly were not. On the positive side one can list the fact that it has been the British system of parliamentary government—at the central level, at least—that has provided the model for African leaders and the standard according to which their expectations have been calculated. A distinctive feature of this system is the assumption that full and absolute "executive" power within a society is legitimately exercisable by the leadership of the majority party, including power over local government. The visions of boundless opportunity, of playing a decisively important role, and of having control over events and destinies which such a system engenders are powerful stimuli for self-sacrifice, discipline, and united action on the part of aspiring party leaders and followers. Moreover, the image of the consequences of not belonging to the majority party is sufficiently unattractive to provoke a "band-wagon" or "wave-of-the-future" psychology on the part of nonparty electors, including chiefs. It could be argued that both factors have been operative in the politics of the west coast and are in part the inevitable result of the perceived implications of the establishment of the British majoritarian system of government.[11]

When transplanted, and thus shorn of historical restraints derived from habit and convention, that system carries with it the potentialities—indeed, for some the enticements—of a "cabinet dictatorship," which is the same thing as saying a dictatorship by a tiny coterie of party leaders. Moreover, as most African politicians are modernists, they desire to supersede chiefs and the older elites ensconced in the traditional structure; therefore the attractions of a *unitarian* as well as a majoritarian political system are very strong.

In preparing the new constitutions, very little consideration seems to have been given to the institutional requirements for an effective party system. In some instances, such as the awkward system of representation in the Nigerian House of Representatives—which effectively prevented party government at the center—the neglect of these requirements was due in part at least to the overwhelming need to achieve compromises between differing African viewpoints. Apart from such instances, however, there appears to have been a common feeling in officialdom that a party system was either premature or undesirable. One current of thought was the fear that the fragile structure being constructed might be wrecked in its early stages if there was a "rush of party politics to the head." Another line of argument was that constitution-making in Africa was and should be an experimental and pragmatic process in which adaptation and synthesis of Western and African institutions was preferred over blind emulation and wholesale transplantation. Finally, at the time the constitutions were drawn up, as the Secretary of State for the Colonies publicly stated, an "established and well-tried party system" did not in fact exist; moreover, the assumption was that as elsewhere it would take some time to develop.

Beyond these attitudinal explanations there was the fact that the British faced a major dilemma that created serious institutional complications. Ever since Lord Lugard had popularized—and the Colonial Office had adopted—the policy of indirect rule for British

11 This has meant that as election trends are perceived the emergent majority parties have acquired sudden landslide accessions of strength as a result of "independents" or *attentistes* declaring their membership in the victorious party. This was a phenomenon characteristic of early party development in modern Europe.

African territories, officials had been preoccupied with the task of finding, creating, modernizing, and democratizing "native administrations." During the late nineteen-thirties, when the Westernized elite became increasingly claimant, a drive was launched by officialdom to integrate these "educated elements" into the "N-A" system. In the meantime, the Second World War intruded and not only arrested this development before it could get under way but also stimulated a new ferment and unleashed new forces which at the end of the war burst forth as militant nationalist movements. The nationalists were first and foremost modernists and centralists. They therefore found the N-A's dull and unsatisfying as arenas for the display of their talents and the realization of their aspirations. They also suspected, with no little justification, that the British authorities were endeavoring to seduce them into a preoccupation with "local government" in order that they would be less attracted to the central apparatus—the British "scaffolding."

The institutions established by the postwar constitutions of British West Africa were strongly influenced, therefore, by a British effort to reconcile the two tendencies. Their solution was to fuse the partially democratized N-A system with an Africanized "scaffolding." The instrument for achieving this integration of traditional and secular institutions was the electoral system. Except for municipalities such as Freetown, Accra, Kumasi, Secondi-Takoradi, Lagos, Port Harcourt, and Calabar, which elected a few representatives directly, entry into the central political structure was via indirect election, which in most instances meant through the N-A system. This channeling of legitimate political activity through the traditional structure had several interesting and important consequences. In the first place, it forced modernists—the party politicians of the urban centers—to carry their appeal to the N-A councils of the most remote bush villages. Elections were not the esoteric pastime of the barristers, clerks, and marketwomen of the main centers— a rally of the faithful, as nationalist leaders desiring direct elections would have preferred; rather they involved campaigning throughout the countryside, with the courting or intimidation of the traditionalists. The result was an unprecedented political awakening, a mobilization of groups previously untouched and inert.

In addition to this wide-scale political mobilization, there have been other more specific consequences of the forced use of the indirect electoral system in the early stages of the development of new parties. One of these concerns party strategy and campaign technique. The party struggle has in many instances been dominated by the drive to capture and control N-A councils. National parties have sought to outmaneuver each other in order to get on the popular side of local issues, which might thereby give them a majority in the N-A council-cum-electoral college. Thus, local issues —chieftaincy and boundary disputes, education rates, or the allocation of market stalls—have in some instances become crucial party issues. Again, with the progressive democratization of local councils, local political parties that have emerged have been courted by national or regional parties seeking alliances in order to establish a firm organizational base in the local communities. Finally, in many instances, certain forms of bribery became an accepted technique for party success, mainly because the indirect system of election—now replaced by systems of direct election—made bribery both technically feasible and financially possible.

Once in power, majority parties have endeavored to bring about radical changes in both local government and the electoral system. In part this has been due to their desire to render local government more democratic and efficient, in which respects it has merely meant accelerating or consummating developments already instituted by the British. In part it is a reflection of their resolve to reduce or extinguish the power of traditionalists and chiefs who have tended to be obstructionists or who are tainted by alleged collaboration with the colonial authorities. It has also been the result of the desire of party leaders to establish a secure local base amongst the masses in anticipation of future elections. Thus, during the past two years in both the Gold Coast and Nigeria, leaders of national political parties have had as one of their major preoccupations the drive to fill democratized local councils with safe majorities; a pattern of activity known to Latin Americanists as *continuismo*.

This initial quest for country-wide support forced upon party leadership by the indirect electoral system may, in the long run, prove to have been an important contribution to democratic government in at least two respects. First, the channeling of the corrosive dynamism of the modernists through the traditional structure, coupled with their use of central power after victory to hasten the democratization of that structure, has tended to undermine or reduce what remained of the power of the traditionalists. This accelerated disintegration of the old order has been a sociological development indispensable for the development of a modern party system. Another factor is that fairly wide-scale popular participation has been enforced by the structure of the political process during the formative stages of these emergent states. This may have established not only a pattern of political expectations on the part of the general populace, but also a set of predispositions among party leaders to feel the continued need for broad popular support in the exercise of their power, even after the "presence" is withdrawn.[12]

Another fact which suggests that a regular party system was not contemplated by the new constitutions was the absence of any provision for majority party leadership to become the "government of the day." Despite this, however, in each territory (each region in the case of Nigeria) the elections produced strong majority parties with a leadership that not only could be clearly identified, but also one that demanded the full rights and privileges normally accorded the leadership of a majority party in a parliamentary system. After initial hesitation, British officialdom accommodated itself to this unplanned development and conceded the demands of party leaders within constitutional limits. The reason for the concession is perfectly straightforward—they were confronted with majority political parties under leaders who represented the only organized power of consequence in the territories and without whose co-operation they could not govern. In short, party government has been established despite early official discouragement and institutional obstacles.

The special case of Uganda

In turning to Uganda, the only other emergent African state clearly identifiable, we confront a historical, cultural, and political situation which in certain respects is not unlike that found on the British west coast. It is, of course, a British territory. There has been a similar policy regarding the non-alienation of land.

[12] The influence of cumulative political experience in the use of democratic institutions acquired during the transition to self-government may be the decisive factor in the future political orientation of the emergent African states.

There are relatively few European settlers and many signs of a growing African middle class, yet there have been and are decisive differences that have prevented or discouraged the development of modern political parties.

One major difference is the existence of a highly developed and comparatively well-integrated African state—the Kingdom of Buganda. Pursuant to the Agreement of 1900 between the British and the Kabaka, as well as the general British African policy of using established forms wherever possible, the archaic state structure of the Kingdom was retained at the time the Protectorate was established and has been slowly adapted to modern conditions and requirements. As it has evolved, the Kingdom has tended to absorb the energies and attract the loyalties and sentiments of the new elites that have emerged from the Western impact. As a consequence there has been very little pressure, from educated Baganda at least, for pan-Uganda political development along Western lines. Indeed, one of the major wellsprings of nationalism in Buganda is opposition of many Baganda—both modernists and traditionalists—to the current British effort to integrate the remodeled archaic state of Buganda into the emergent modern state of Uganda.[13]

This absence of nationalist pressure for participation in the central institutions of Uganda has very decidedly delayed their development. Moreover, despite the recent reforms in the Uganda Legislative Council, the Governor in his recent address before that body indicated that for the immediate future at least no provision exists for party government.[14] However, as all African members in the new Legislative Council are indirectly elected through district councils, there is not even a technical need for political parties. Uganda missed the powerful opening wedge of at least a few directly elected representatives who could become, as on the west

[13] See cable from Uganda National Congress to Secretary of State for the Colonies: "The campaign by British officials preaching a unitary State is designed to perpetuate the unpopular, outmoded Legislative Council, retarding political progress towards self-government." *East Africa and Rhodesia* (February 25, 1954), p. 803.

[14] ". . . the relations between the Government and Representative sides of this council are not the relations of a Government and Opposition. . . . I look to the whole of the council as a united team to promote the well-being of the country." *East Africa and Rhodesia* (February 11, 1954), pp. 725–26.

coast, a core group for the expansion of the role of Legislative Council.

Until 1945 the political structure of the Kingdom of Buganda was representative mainly of the Mengo ruling classes—an aristocratic landowning group. Primarily in response to the ever-growing demands from educated elements and the new social groups created by Westernism, a limited measure of popular representation, via an indirect electoral system, was instituted in that year for the Great Lukiko (the Buganda National Parliament). The agitation for political reform came primarily from organized pressure groups such as the Uganda Welfare Association, trade-unions, traders' associations, and in 1949 by the more militant and suspect Bataka Movement. There are several actual or potential sets of opposed interests within Buganda society which could become the basis for party formation at such time as the electoral system, the method of election to and composition of the Great Lukiko, and the Kabaka's cabinet are reformed so as to provide the institutional setting for a party system. At the moment, the principal line of cleavage is between the Mengo ruling classes and the newer popularly elected elements; but as yet these two groups have not crystallized into parties. It is possible that the recent increase in the elected element in the Lukiko will accelerate an orthodox party development. In the meantime, the crisis surrounding the Kabaka's deposition tends to obscure the situation.

Political parties in French tropical Africa

The pattern of party development in French tropical Africa presents several interesting contrasts to that characteristic of the emergent states of British West Africa.[15] One reason for this difference is that until 1945 French colonial institutions and French policy regarding the freedom of association, speech, and press did not

15 See Thomas Hodgkin, "Political Parties in French West Africa," *West Africa* (February 20, 1954), pp. 157–58; and his "Political Parties in British and French West Africa," *Information Digest* (The Africa Bureau), No. 10 (August, 1953), p. 15. Also Kenneth Robinson, "Political Development in French West Africa," in *Africa in the Modern World*, Proceedings of the Twenty-Ninth Institute of the Norman Wait Harris Memorial Foundation (Chicago, in press).

allow for African political activity outside of Senegal. Another is that in the postwar period Europeans have moved into tropical Africa in ever-increasing numbers, and in such territories as Senegal, Sudan, Ivory Coast, Guinea, Cameroons, and Chad, they are an actual or potential factor of importance in the developing political situation. A third fact, stemming from the assimilationist philosophy underlying the French Union, is the absence of an assumption of ultimate territorial self-government. In short, the social and institutional setting which the new French African elites have confronted has been markedly different from that of their British counterparts.

Apart from these more general elements in the situation, there are two special features of the institutions of postwar French Africa and the French Union that have had important implications for party development. The first is what Thomas Hodgkin has referred to as the "metropolitan axis" of political reference. The French Constitution of 1946 not only makes representation in the National Assembly the most meaningful political right possessed by Africans but it also perpetuates the strong centralist and unitarian character of the French administrative and political system, in which all power and decision effectively remain in Paris. This has resulted in the development of close-working relationships between African and metropolitan leaders and parties from which mutual benefits are derived.

African *députés* have been fully alive to their "pressure-group" status and the power they possess in the floating vote—a power that has been decisive on several occasions in the National Assembly. In order to exert influence over policy they have developed a variety of devices, of which two should be noted. In some cases they have become *apparentés,* individually or as an African party, to one of the metropolitan parties (e.g., the alliance of the RDA first to the Communist party and later to the UDSR). In other cases, African *députés* have formally joined metropolitan parties and have become prominent in the leadership hierarchy. On their side, metropolitan party leaders have sought to secure added parliamentary strength not only by courting African *députés* but also by organizing party branches in Africa and by running party candidates in African territorial elections. For example, as early as 1928 the SFIO established a section in Senegal in order to capture the seat of its *député.* These interactions and relationships between Africa and the metropole have been a powerful stimulus not only in the political awakening of the African, but also in the actual formation of parties.

A second institutional factor of special significance relates to the role of the territorial assemblies. Territorial parties first sprang into existence as vehicles for the election of representatives to the Constituent Assemblies in Paris in 1945–46 and subsequently for the election of *députés* to the National Assembly. Since the constitutional reforms broadening the functions of the territorial assemblies and establishing an electoral system, however, these territorial parties have acquired greater importance and meaning as instruments for the election of representatives to the territorial assemblies. These assemblies, like the *Grands Conseils* at the federation level, are patterned after the *conseil général* of the departments of metropolitan France and are therefore neither legislative nor parliamentary bodies. Although they have been given rather wide powers over financial and budgetary matters at the territorial level, and even exert considerable indirect influence upon policy questions reserved for the metropole, they nevertheless are founded upon assumptions quite different from those of the legislative councils of British Africa.

The French concept and practice of parliamentary government, coupled with the unitarian character of the French political system, tend to assign a rather negative pressure-group role to political parties. It is in the French tradition, more because of sociological and historical reasons than institutional factors, to regard the political party as a vehicle for representing interests rather than, as in the British tradition, a positive instrument for the integration of diverse interests, the formulation of public policy, and the provision of leadership that ultimately becomes the government of the day. The crucial difference, in sum, is that leaders of French African political parties neither pursue nor anticipate receiving what is normally conceived as the *raison d'être* of political parties—the *meaningful* exercise of executive power.

Within these limits, what approximates a party system has developed in several of the territories. Thus, for example, in Senegal the *Bloc Démocratique Sénégalais* (BDS) commands an overwhelming majority in the *Assemblée Territoriale* and is therefore in a position to manage the affairs of the Assembly by its control of the chairmen of the committees, and particularly the *Commission Per-*

manente. The same holds true in the case of the RDA in the Ivory Coast, the *Union Voltaique* in Haute Volta, and the *Mouvement d'Evolution Sociale en Afrique Noire* (MESAN) in Oubangui-Chari. In some cases there have been electoral alliances, such as between the *Parti togolais du Progrès* and the *Union des Chefs et des Populations du Nord Togo* in Togoland. In other cases there have been Euro-African coalitions formed in the territorial assembly, such as the one between the all-European *Rassemblement du Peuple Français* (RPF) and the all-African *Union Soudanaise* against a second all-African party, the *Parti Progressiste Soudanais* (PPS) in the Sudan. This latter example points up the unique and potentially powerful role that European *colons* and their parties can play in territorial politics by exploiting their floating vote.[16]

These three selected factors—the metropolitan axis, the limitations of the territorial assemblies, and the interpenetration of French and African political parties in the politics of the metropole and Africa—have very decisively conditioned party development in French Africa. In addition to these factors, there are two other respects in which party development has been different from British areas. The first concerns the role of civil servants in party politics. In French areas, African *fonctionnaires* are permitted to seek election to and become members of the territorial assemblies. In British territories, African civil servants are forbidden from engaging in political activity pursuant to the long-established British tradition regarding the political neutrality of the Civil Service. This difference has been explained in terms of the political nature of the Legislative Council as opposed to the technical character of the territorial assembly. The importance of the difference can hardly be exaggerated. In any event, these different policies have had and will continue to have serious implications regarding the composition of leadership groups, including especially political parties. Apart from those who have joined private firms, become traders, or pursued professional careers, the best educated and the most talented elements in the new elites have tended to join the Civil Service.

16 In the recent municipal elections in the Ivory Coast the African leaders of the RDA and the European representatives of the Chamber of Commerce formed a common list on which Africans were in the proportion of two to one under the rubric *Union pour la Défense des Intérêts d'Abidjan.* This Euro-African electoral coalition won over 90 per cent of the votes. *Le Monde* (June 4, 1954), p. 4.

As a consequence of the drive for rapid development in all fields, as well as the nationalist slogan to hasten the departure of European expatriates, there is every likelihood the Civil Service will continue to absorb a disproportionate share of upcoming talent.

Another significant difference between the two systems relates to the role of traditionalists in elections and in political parties. The effect of the indirect electoral system and the N-A's upon British African parties has been examined. In some instances, such as the Protectorate of Sierra Leone, the northern territories of the Gold Coast, and western and northern Nigeria, party leaders were obliged to court, intimidate, or follow the chiefs. In French tropical Africa the situation has been quite different not only because of the direct electoral system but also because of the radically different policy of the French regarding local government and the functions of traditionalists. Once this basic difference is noted, there is considerable evidence to suggest that in certain French areas the traditionalists play an important role in parties and elections, particularly in the northern areas of French Togoland and the Cameroons. In balance, however, that role is markedly less significant than has been the case in British areas.

Despite these several differences, there have been certain similarities in the development of parties in the two areas. In both, the party leader has played a crucial role as a unifying symbol or by giving a sense of direction and purpose. Moreover, it has been a leadership that, despite its Westernization and modernism in outlook and behavior, has desired or felt obliged to link itself in varying degrees with African culture. One of the most highly sophisticated and cosmopolitan African leaders, Leopold Senghor, has reflected this "back to Africa" theme.[17] Also, with few exceptions, most party leaders are "of the people" in the sense that they have achieved their positions through dint of personal talent rather than birth or privilege. The chief difference in the new leadership groups of the two areas concerns the issue of racial or color consciousness. In British areas it tends to be sharper and perhaps more bitter. In part this is but a reflection of the two contrasting policies of identity (French) and differentiation (British).

[17] This same tendency is revealed in the recent dual appointment received by Mr. Obafemi Awolowo, namely, the Prime Ministership of the Western Region of Nigeria and a Yoruba chieftaincy.

A second common feature has been the decisive importance of constitutional reforms in precipitating wide-scale party activity. The broadening of representation and the extension of the suffrage, as part of the dramatic reforms of 1946, served as an open invitation to party formation.

Another similarity has been the overriding importance of cultural differences in determining party alignments. In some cases, such as MESAN in Oubangui-Chari, or the BDS in Senegal, the party has sought with considerable success to integrate diverse groups and interests. In most cases, however, sectional, regional, or tribal sentiment and interests have been the principal bases for party unity, thereby reflecting the weakness or nonexistence of territorial or national sentiment. Thus, in Haute Volta, the *Union Voltaique* represents principally the interests of the Mossi peoples of the eastern part of Haute Volta. In the Sudan the PPS is not only the party of Fily Dabo Sissoko but it also represents the Malinké peoples of the Sudan. In Dahomey the parties are divided on regional lines, the PRD *(Parti Républicain Dahoméen)* in the South, and the GEN *(Groupement Ethnique du Nord)* in the North. A similar party sectionalism follows the lines of a basic north-south division in French Togoland, French Cameroons, Chad, and the Moyen-Congo. With the exception of the latter, the basis for the split is the same as in Nigeria and the British Cameroons: namely, the sharp cultural cleavage between the more conservative Moslem peoples of the North and the more adaptable and modernist southerners. The intrusion of the cultural factor is perhaps most dramatically illustrated, however, in the complex party alignments that have developed in the two Togolands. A case study of this small area would provide many fascinating insights.

There are other bases for party alignments which have not been unimportant. One has been the issue of nationalist militancy, with particular reference to positions taken on various questions relating to the European connection. Another issue concerns the difference between groups regarding political party strategy (i.e., programmatic versus tactical appeals to the electorate). A final cause of party alignments has been the personality factor. Competition, jealousies, and animosities within the ranks of the new party elites all too frequently have been the source of party splits and party differences.

All of these phenomena, of course, have been characteristic of early party developments elsewhere and need only be noted here.[18]

African political parties in plural societies

In turning to the plural societies of British East and Central Africa, one enters a new world in which the concept of an African political party seems out of place. In fact there are no African parties—at least as the concept has been used here. It is proposed, therefore, to examine briefly a few of the factors connected with the failure of conventional African parties to emerge, as well as the possibilities regarding their future development.

The analysis of other African areas suggests that certain special developments or situations are required for, or are conducive to, the birth of parties. Specific factors have been the rise of new social groups that are increasingly discontented and assertive: the emergence of a dedicated and inspired leadership; the development of nationalist movements with an integrating and purposive ideology; the freedom to organize and pressure for reform; and an institutional framework and political climate in which parties are both legitimate and able to play a meaningful function. On each of these counts, whether as a result of special historical circumstances or because of the very nature of a plural society, the emergent states of British East and Central Africa fall short. The new social groups of these areas are considerably less developed than those on the west coast, particularly in terms of a middle class and a sizable group of intellectuals and professional persons.[19] Powerful leaders have emerged, including such inscrutable figures as Jomo Kenyatta,

[18] The issue of nationalist militancy has been in part the basis for differences between the CPP and the Ghana Congress Party in the elections in the Gold Coast, between the RDA and its opposition parties in Senegal, Ivory Coast, and the Cameroons; and it has been one of the main issues separating the NPC and NEPU in northern Nigeria. Since 1951, however, there has been a progressive move in many areas to a more central party position and greater moderation. See Robinson and Hodgkin, n. 15, *supra.*

[19] In view of the fact that African leadership has tended to come from those groups educated abroad, the difference in the number of African students pursuing higher education in the United Kingdom in 1952–53 is quite revealing: East and Central Africa, 751; West Africa, 2,548.

as well as more responsible personalities such as Eliud Mathu, J. Z. Savanhu, and Godwin Lewanika. But, this leadership has been confronted with a social situation that has been either unready or unexploitable.

Nationalist movements not unlike those on the west coast have appeared, but the political environment has been unfavorable to their maturation. By definition, a plural society deprives a nationalist movement of its finite goal. In such a society nationalism is unable to generate that *élan*, dynamism, and purposive energy that comes from the hopeful anticipation of a total realization of the nationalist dream: namely, *African* self-government. Moreover, within these plural societies there has been considerably less freedom for nationalist activity. Under such thwarting and limiting circumstances, emergent African leadership has tended to be wasted in messianic and puritanical religious movements, or it has been attracted to terrorism as a violent means of breaking the bonds of the plural society, or it has reconciled itself to accommodation and conformity to the dominant elements in that society. In any event, it has been impossible to repeat the west-coast pattern whereby broadly based nationalist movements have been peacefully converted into majority political parties in emergent parliamentary systems.

The principal barrier to the emergence of African parties is not the mere existence of a plural society. French Senegal is a plural society with a European population equal to that of Kenya, but it also has one of the most highly developed African party systems on the continent. The obstacle is clearly most pronounced in a British colony and stems from a combination of three factors: the existence of a plural society; the indiscriminate application of the Durham Formula to that society; and the uncritical adoption of the British majoritarian system of concentrated parliamentary sovereignty. Within the political climate and institutional framework that develop from these factors, there exists little scope or purpose for African parties.

There are several important respects in which the plural societies of this area differ. Southern Rhodesia and Northern Rhodesia clearly belong in one category in which the full implications of the foregoing factors are increasingly being realized. Kenya's development along similar lines may have been arrested by the Mau Mau experience, the small size of the European community, the existence of a large Asian community, and the fact that a sobered imperial government intruded to impose its will. Nyasaland has acquired the character and disabilities of a plural society only to the extent that it forms a part of the new Federation, a fact which helps to explain the power generated by the Nyasaland National Congress in its opposition to the new scheme. Of all these societies, however, Tanganyika has not only enjoyed better race relations in the past but also her different racial groups are commencing the climb up the constitutional ladder with the basic assumption of racial parity. Clearly the future development of African political parties in each of these areas will take a markedly different course.[20]

With the foregoing limitations and qualifications in mind, what are some of the principal factors that will condition or affect the growth of African political parties in these plural societies? It is suggested that a clue may be found in the vague concept of "partnership," which is at the center of the political theory upon which the new states are based. Implicit in this concept is the assumption that Africans will *not* exercise central executive power, at least for the foreseeable future. This in turn means that African parties will be obliged to take on the character of an institutionalized pressure group. They will exercise influence only to the extent that they exploit the power of the floating vote. There is the possibility, therefore, that they will be able to play a role not unlike that of African *députés* in the French National Assembly. Indeed, there are probably many stratagems the new African MLC's could learn from African *parlementaires*. Although the six elected African members of the Legislative Assembly of the new Federation of Rhodesia and Nyasaland have publicly denied their intention of forming an "African bloc," it is not impossible that the potentialities of such an arrangement will lead to the organization of something approaching a political party.[21]

---

[20] For the socio-economic bases of possible party alignments in Kenya see M. Parker, "Social and Political Development in Kenya Urban Society," *Problèmes d'Afrique Centrale*, No. 15 (1st Quarter, 1952), pp. 12–19. See also W. J. M. Mackenzie, "Representation in Plural Societies," *Political Studies*, Vol. II (February 1954), pp. 54–69.

[21] In view of the fact that the two African MLC's from Southern Rhodesia are elected directly on a common roll, by European as well as "civilized" African electors, whereas the MLC's from Nyasaland and Northern Rhodesia are elected

A second element in the theory of partnership is that the great mass of Africans will continue to "develop along traditional lines." The perpetuation of the native authority system as well as the device of indirect election will be positive deterrents to the growth of mass parties. On the other hand, of the four indirectly-elected Africans in the Legislative Assembly of the new Federation, the two from Nyasaland were members of the Nyasaland National Congress, and the two from Northern Rhodesia have been prominent leaders of the Northern Rhodesia National Congress. To the extent that these two nationalist organizations have been the instruments for deciding the election of these four candidates, one might argue that they have already taken on the quality of political parties. It might be recalled that political parties first came into being in the territories of French tropical Africa for the purpose of electing one or more *députés* to the National Assembly. Is it not similarly possible that parties of a limited character may develop within the Nyasaland Protectorate Council, in Zomba, and the African Representative Council, in Lusaka, for the purpose of electing their four representatives to the Federal Assembly? Indirect election through a remodeled traditional system may be a damper upon party development but not necessarily a positive barrier.

Finally, the concept of partnership—as interpreted by its enthusiasts—includes the ideal of "equal rights for all civilized men." This suggests the possible development of not only a common electoral roll but Euro-African political parties as well. The development of Euro-African organization and leadership in the case of the Socialist Party of France (SFIO) provides an interesting precedent. The SFIO, of course, took the initiative. Thus far there appears to have been no trend in this direction—certainly not from the dominant European parties of those plural societies where direct elections are held. Moreover, only a small number of Africans in

indirectly by all-African electoral colleges, it is improbable that such an African bloc will emerge, at least for the next five years. Because of the overwhelming majority held by the all-European Federal party, there would be very little opportunity in any event for such a bloc to exploit its floating vote. Dauti Yambi, in speaking for the MLC's said recently they "would not just be an African opposition, but an opposition consisting of all those who want to further the cause of the African people." *Information Digest,* No. 14 (February–March, 1954), p. 14.

the Rhodesias have acquired the means or demonstrated the desire to become registered voters on a common roll.[22]

The foregoing observations cover but a few of the many complex factors involved in the development of African parties in the plural societies of British East and Central Africa. One cannot escape the conclusion that the social and institutional setting allows very little scope for the emergence of parties. There seems little prospect for them to be able to transcend the status of a pressure group or a mere vehicle of opinion.

Conclusions

It has been stated that political parties and modern democracy require each other. It is not simply the existence of parties that is important; rather, it is the existence of a structured party-system functioning in what has been called a "climate of political party government." The key to this system in its ideal form is the presence of a free, responsible, and reasonably united opposition, prepared to become the government of the day. As there has not been a transfer of executive power to African parties in French tropical Africa, the development of an opposition in its idealized version is not possible.[23] The role of African parties in this area, for the foreseeable future at least, would seem to be that of an ever-present opposition "checking" the government in the tradition of Alain's *le controleur*. If and when African parties develop in the very different setting of the plural societies of East and Central Africa, it is likely that they will be limited to a similar role.

Only in the emergent states of British West Africa has there been a transfer of executive power to African party governments against which an organized African opposition could be called into being. But even here the only area where a strong and united opposition

22 By November, 1951, there were 453 Africans on the common roll in Southern Rhodesia and only four in Northern Rhodesia.

23 The question of the devolution of greater executive power to the territorial assemblies was the subject of a very broad debate in the French National Assembly in which M. Jacquinot, Minister for Overseas France, and M. Senghor (Senegal) and Dr. Aujoulat (Cameroons), leaders of the IOM, were the principal participants. See *Journal Official de l'Assemblée Nationale* (April 9, 1954), pp. 1908–38.

exists is in the Western Region of Nigeria. The reason in this instance is the prevalence of a remarkably unique set of circumstances which, suffice it to say, do not reflect a government-opposition difference on ideological grounds. In short, an opposition and a party system in its idealized sense have not yet emerged. One of the main reasons has been the absence of an ideal institutional framework within which such a development could occur.

It is unrealistic, if not captious, to evaluate African political realities at this stage in terms of an idealized system approximated in only a few countries of the world, and there only because of certain unique historical circumstances. The role of African political parties in the politics of emergent Africa should be appraised in terms of their usefulness as instruments for achieving desirable ends within the extremely narrow limits that they have been allowed to function. By this standard the performance rating of African parties has been quite high. There have been oppositions that have endeavored with some success to educate public opinion where it exists. The parties have been the vehicles for the emergence of a new leadership that is "of the people," and in an over-all evaluation this new group contains many remarkable and outstanding men. Moreover, the parties have been the medium for expressing, frequently in almost catalog fashion, the aspirations and objectives of thoughtful Africans. In this sense they have participated in the formulation of public policy. Their most important and indispensable contribution, however, has been their powerful role in the difficult task of socio-political integration. While the "cultural factor" has been divisive and frequently overriding, the parties in many instances have been incomparable instruments for building a broader unity. It is in this sense that parties such as the BDS in Senegal, the MESAN in Oubangi-Chari, the CPP in the Gold Coast, and the three major parties in Nigeria should be appraised.

A final observation that emerges from the present analysis relates to the transcendent importance of the institutional framework in shaping and conditioning political patterns during the transition period from colonialism to self-government or new forms of African participation in the political process. In a somewhat different context, this same fact has been observed by Carl J. Friedrich: "Party development appears . . . greatly affected by the policy of government in the period of the beginnings of parliamentary, representative government." [24] In the fashioning of new political institutions during this crucial gestation period, when behavior patterns and group relationships are still somewhat malleable, it is vitally important that constitution-makers realize the creative nature of the task upon which they are engaged.

commentary

NORMAN STEVEN-HUBBARD

*Former Area Specialist, United Nations Secretariat,
and Former Director of Technical Training,
East Africa High Commission*

Dr. Coleman's categorizing of political activity, on a broad distinguishing basis, of the various types and kinds of such activity as found in Africa, and in fact everywhere where there exist greater or lesser elements of free political association, would appear to achieve a good workable balance between imprecise and amorphous concepts of socio-political movements, on the one hand, and the fractionating requirements of pedantic definition, on the other.

While it is correct to assume in general (and the developments in West Africa provide very tidy evidence for this) that there would seem to be a natural pattern of development from pressure groups, through a nationalist movement to a full-fledged political party, this evolutionary pattern can be either inhibited or modified by many factors inherent in the African scene. It could also be mentioned that political associations, more especially perhaps of numerically minor groups in positions of privilege of one kind or another, can have confusing characteristics of more than one category. It would be correct perhaps to say that the white community of East Africa is politically organized within a context of aims and objectives that have characteristics of the pressure group, a sort of

---

[24] *Constitutional Government and Democracy* (Rev. Ed., New York, 1950), p. 414.

localized nationalism, and a political party. Although sub-units of this kind of Africa's total population are peripheral to the main thesis of Dr. Coleman's essay, the behavior patterns—political behavior included—are significant in those areas of the continent where there is, without doubt, the greatest likelihood of serious future disaffection and dysfunction. It could also be said that, in some real respects, the political aggregations among the Baganda have here at least a superficial similarity, and their activities in the political field have multiple motivations that do not fit too snugly into a tight scheme. This observer, having lived for several years among the peoples of Uganda, has on several occasions come across non-Kiganda opinions which, with a change of substantive content, bear some resemblance to African criticism of the dominant minority in Kenya.

Dr. Coleman has concisely analyzed the special Uganda situation, which is generally one where there has been, up to very recently, a record of quiet and stable and relatively successful development. Within the economic and political realities of today, the broad basis for a good deal of this success, namely the separately negotiated agreements between the four kingdoms and the United Kingdom government which were arranged in the early years of the century, seems now to be a potent factor militating against further smooth development. It is hard to see around what foci emergent political parties will form until provincial passion is channeled into a more definite political ideology.

It could also be brought out that the political affairs of territories contiguous to the Protectorate, in particular Kenya, have exercised a profound influence over African political thought; and it is likely that fears of a spreading "settler" philosophy have tended to make the Baganda more insistent upon the protections written into the early agreement. This raises the larger question of the influential factors at work in one territory consequent upon developments in not only contiguous territories but in those areas that may be physically far away. These effects may be very significant indeed, and although difficult to weigh and evaluate, one cannot but be aware of their importance to the thinking of most Africans who read newspapers and listen to the radio. The extremes of policy, namely the Gold Coast situation and the Union of South Africa situation, are inflammatory material for African's thoughts and make for a psychological climate that will have its effect on the eventual colorations of political activity at all stages. No doubt Dr. Coleman is well aware of this interplay, which is likely to become more significant as communications improve throughout the continent, but it is believed that the interpenetrations of various political developments of a contemporary nature could, with merit and value, be made a subject of further and more detailed study.

Dr. Coleman has succinctly brought out the special—one could almost say unique—features operating in British West Africa, which have been of paramount importance to the development and maturation of political parties now existing there. It is of particular significance when he states that "they [the Africans] have enjoyed a self-assurance and a confident expectancy that their vision . . . was in fact a realizable ideal." The psychological and ideological power inherent in this situation has tremendous virtue and has been the greatest single factor in the success of the modern parliamentary machinery now being established in the area. This factor is in effect a summation of the other factors enumerated in the essay. Alfred North Whitehead once stated that "moral education is impossible without the habitual vision of greatness"—this could be paraphrased in this context as "political maturity is not possible without the habitual vision of greatness." One cannot but be impressed with the confidence and vision of many West Africans.

Looking ahead somewhat, the next stage in the maturation process, more especially in the Gold Coast, is one of exceptional interest for Africa as a whole; that is, what kind of opposition party or parties are likely to arise when the alien "yoke" is finally lifted? The aims of the CPP have been largely identified with the "divinely inspired" objectives of Kwame Nkrumah, the cornerstone of which has been freedom from metropolitan control. Now that the scapegoat is on its way out, now to all intents and purposes "off stage," the integrative forces will necessarily have to undergo a shift from the emotionally centered charismatic focus to much more realistic forces involved in the hard economic and political facts of life. This will obviously lead to an increasing growth and prominence of opposition parties, which are at present of very limited function and almost impotent. The springs of this opposition would seem to be those areas where traditional authority systems still struggle and the small reservoir of independent intellectuals, some of whom see Kwame Nkrumah and the powers of the CPP as a potential danger to democratic principles and practices. Should the masses of the CPP become disenchanted, now that Nkrumah has undertaken almost complete responsibility so that the hard facts of life will have to be reconciled with past and present promises, the charisma will begin to fade, and thus party opposition will become more meaningful and real, and the real party struggle will be on. It would seem that not only local economic considerations will play a large part in this future struggle but, as the Gold Coast national economy can hardly be called safely diversified, the state of world markets will play a profound part in future parliamentary politics.

Dr. Coleman tends to shrug off a little hastily the possibilities of African political aspirations in the so-called plural societies. It is readily admitted that the application of the criteria he lists so clearly to explain the emergence of meaningful political activity in the developed party format would seem to present an unpromising picture as far as East and Central Africa are concerned. The special factors he lists are impressive and no doubt determinative to a very large extent, but it is sure that the one listed first, namely the rise of new social groups that are increasingly discontented and assertive, is by no means lacking in the plural societies; and there are elements, still in great measure unformed and plastic, of most of the other factors enumerated.

To one who has lived and worked in these areas, it is hard to find much realism in the concept of a partnership in a plural society. This concept is sophisticated and Western-centered and has little real meaning for any of the groups involved. The racial in-group feelings are altogether too powerful and dominate strongly so many conceptions, political, cultural, and economic, that partnership raises no enthusiasm from anybody, least of all from Africans. One gets the impression, whatever the rationalizations formulated, that the ideology of partnership within a plural society is a somewhat desperate line of defense against the dangers perceived as a consequence of nationalism. It is a nationalism still embryonic, ill-formed, and ill-organized, but none the less psychologically generative of vast power in the developments of the future. Taking into account the excitement and stimulus generated by West African developments, on the one hand, and the deep fears engendered by policies being followed in South Africa, on the other, the chances of quiet and stable development in Eastern and Central Africa are limited. If this is correct, nationalism is more than ever likely to become meaningful and dynamic and thus lead to the growth of political action groups that would approximate to the forms and functions of parties. It is hardly conceivable that leadership will not arise. With the current fluidity of social, economic, and political climate in both East and Central Africa, generated by slowly rising standards of living, greater exposure to Western cultural patterns, the influence of democratic world opinion on the motivations of territorial and metropolitan governments, and the sheer need for patterns of adaptation and modification that is being realized as vital for the workable continuance of these areas of Africa as a functional part of the Western democratic scene—with these factors present it is likely that there will arise a social and political climate where more mature political action is not siphoned off into messianic and violent movements that have characterized near-past history.

The probabilities of Euro-African or Euro-Asian-African political action of a meaningful nature seem remote and unreal. The eventual political role of the Asian communities is obscure. If these communities were less divided among themselves and suffered less from divided loyalties, they would be, and might still become, a much more decisive factor in the political future of the plural societies. The unreality of cross-cultural political activity will remain until such time as unity of political thought grows out of a real and equitable economic and social base, that is, until a climate arises where members of each racial group have at least a minimal identity of aim and object. As this would seem to be a remote possibility at present, these areas must be looked at from a viewpoint that is more realistic than a loosely conceived partnership.

African self-government, despite policies and rationalizations to the contrary, is very much in the forefront of African thinking. The main hope of politically conscious Africans in these areas rests finally upon numerical superiority; and if the democratic principles of the West are to survive, this in the final analysis would seem to have some justification.

With this in view, Dr. Coleman's "precipitant factor," constitutional reform for meaningful devolution of imperial power and the refinement of political institutions, is of high significance. That there is an increasing demand from Africans for such constitutional reform is evident; and that power is being slowly devolved (not yet in meaningful quantity it is true) and that institutions are undergoing refinement processes is evidenced by a good deal of new legislative proposals and counter proposals, constitutional study groups, commissions of inquiry, and other similar activities, the results of which may lead to real changes in the social and institutional climate. The recent and continuing disturbance to the status quo in Kenya could very well precipitate the kind of social, economic, and institutional reform that would seem so very necessary for there to appear new and sanctioned political activity of a much more progressive nature. It is believed that the impact of such terrorist activity and the fears of its recurrence and spread to other areas is not a little significant. Insipient terrorism can become a powerful lever in future institutional and constitutional reform.

The Central African Federation seems so delicately balanced, subject to so many internal passions, and close enough to South Africa for there to be a good chance of a rising African nationalism, probably centered around the elected Legislative Council members from Northern Rhodesia and Nyasaland. The speed of social and institutional reform in Central Africa may be slower due to a strong complex of white vested interests, but in time, and not so very far ahead at that, as other areas of Africa take on a more democratic coloration, the rise of political activity of a party nature is probable. It is quite possible that the role of Tanganyika will play an important part in developments both to the north and to the south of this trust territory. The acceptance of racial parity there as a legislative base is already having a powerful effect, and as a precedent of a high order will make the goal for African thinking take on more confident expectancy—likely to help in creating a psychological climate that in turn could lead to some kind of party politics —even if such parties have almost no chance of undertaking full executive power for a long time.

Dr. Coleman's conclusion concerning the vital importance of the shaping of the institutional framework when new constitutions are being formulated, and when social deployment is still fluid, could not be more significant at this time of crisis in the history of Africa; it is to be hoped that those responsible for this tremendously delicate task will be conscious of their creative function and will be able to see beyond the clamor of expediency.

the Communist threat in Africa

MAX YERGAN

Specialist on African Affairs

The Communist threat in Africa is not just a possibility; it is an actuality. Indeed, the use of the word *threat* may be misleading. Africa is not only threatened by Communist activity in the sense of what may happen in the future. Communist intrigue in that continent is already a force to be reckoned with. There should be no surprise that the threat exists. The important need is that we should know more about it. What, for instance, does it seek to accomplish; how does it operate; how is its strength to be estimated so that we may not be misled by it; and, finally, how do we fight it, head it off, and defeat it?

The danger of the Communist threat in Africa should not be judged by the numerical strength of the Communist movement. For Communist strategists, numbers are at times unnecessary and frequently expendable. The Korean and Indochinese wars, where manpower losses have been colossal, are proof of this fact.

Communist parties usually, of course, try to swell their numbers. In France and Italy, they have succeeded in creating large political organizations, but where the party is small, illegal, or underground, its strategy tends to concentrate on the conspiratorial or the activity of a dedicated hard core in front organizations.

The Communist party, first of all, tries to give the illusion that it is concerned about the conditions of labor and living standards, colonial peoples, minorities, and national aspirations. This, as will be shown below, is often pure deception. Propaganda of this type is primarily a means toward achieving the political and military objectives of the center and dynamic of the Communist movement, namely, Soviet Russia.

The aims and methods of the Communist movement vary according to the particular needs of the Soviet Union—the Communist party within the Soviet Union, i.e. the Kremlin. Immediately following World War II, the feverish aim of the Soviet Union was to develop the atom and hydrogen bombs. Communist agents stopped at nothing as they sought throughout the world to aid this end. Their crowning accomplishment in England, Canada, and the United States, where, by the way, only small parties exist, was to produce a following of devoted traitors.

When, therefore, we speak of the Communist threat in Africa, let us be clear as to what we are discussing. We are talking about an international organization, a hard-core apparatus of dedicated, often efficient, unscrupulous men and women who may be surrounded by followers often unaware of the real nature of their leadership. We are talking about a new phenomenon in international relations.

The primary target of this apparatus, even in Africa, is to undermine the Western and free peoples. To strike at the West through Africa, Communists must try to weaken European and American economic interests; sabotage industrial and military installations; increase bitterness rather than encourage good will between white and nonwhite peoples; and channel the growing nationalism into violent interracial conflict by taking advantage of the real grievances of the Africans and the administrative problems of government. International Communism has another function, and that is to sabotage orderly political development among Africans, as in the Gold Coast.

It would be a mistake to assume that because the Communist movement is relatively small in Africa it does not have at its disposal the means, direction, and information with which to operate. In the winter of 1936, while living in South Africa, I visited the Soviet Union as a tourist. In a conversation with a Russian official, Mr. Lozovsky, I was naïvely amazed at his detailed grasp of facts about social and educational conditions in Rhodesia and the Union of South Africa. Although he had probably never visited these countries, he talked about persons in Africa, both European and African, as though he had conversed with them the day before. He really interested me when he described vividly and accurately the condition of the road between Thabanchu, in the Orange Free State, and Maseru, capital of Basutoland. His command of details was astounding.

A second illustration is even more to the point. Shortly after the close of World War II, there came into my hands a bulky document. When I examined it sometime later, I found it to be a rather full outline of a "History of Tropical Africa" (south of the Sahara) and a thesis entitled "The Approach to African History." This material was thoroughly Marxist in style and ideology and Communist in propaganda, obviously intended as instruction and source material for Communist officials. It was also clearly the basis for the instruction of Africans studying in the Soviet Union or in Communist schools elsewhere. It was something of a handbook of the Communist plan for Africa south of the Sahara. I made these documents available to the proper United States officials. They have also been useful to others who have some responsibility for helping to check Communist aggression in Africa.

The Communist threat in Africa has a solid basis in a resolution, adopted at the Sixth World Congress of the Communist International at Moscow in 1928, entitled "The Revolutionary Movement in the Colonies and Semi-Colonies." This resolution states in part:

> The revolutionary struggle in the colonies, semi-colonies and dependent areas constitutes from the standpoint of the world-wide struggle of the Proletariat, one of the most important tasks of the Communist International.

After describing some colonial difficulties to be expected, it went on to say:

> An especially great responsibility in this connection lies with the Communist Parties of the imperialist countries. This demands not only assistance in the matter of working out the correct political line, accurate analysis of experience in the sphere of organization and agitation, but also systematic education of the Party ranks, the creation of a certain minimum of Marxist-Leninist literature and its translation into the languages of the different colonial countries, most active assistance in the matter of study and Marxist analysis of the economic and social problems of the colonies and semi-colonies and the creation of a Party Press, etc.
>
> The native workers and the workers that have come from the metropolis must unite together in one and the same Party organ-

ization. The experience of the older parties in the matter of a correct combination of legal and illegal work must be utilized in accordance with the situation in the different countries.

The immediate task of the Communist Parties of the Imperialist countries on the colonial question bear a threefold character. In the first place, the establishment of regular connection between the Communist Parties and the revolutionary trade union organizations of the Imperialist countries, on the one hand, and the corresponding revolutionary organizations of the colonies, on the other hand.

The second series of tasks consists of genuine support of the struggle of the colonial peoples against imperialism through the organization of mass demonstrations and other effective activities of the Proletariat.

The Communists must mobilize the wide masses of workers and peasants in the capitalist countries on the basis of the demand for granting, unconditionally and without reservation, complete State Independence and sovereignty of the colonial peoples.

On March 2, 1951, twenty-three years after the Sixth World Congress, the powerful French Communist party through its daily publication, *L'Humanité,* declared:

At the present time French communists support all movements, all parties, all persons in the Overseas Territories who are effectively contributing to the weakening of the imperialist camp.

Six years earlier, in 1945, at the organizing conference of the United Nations in San Francisco, Mr. Molotov attracted worldwide attention and considerable support by proclaiming his country, meaning thereby the Communist party, as the only advocate of the freedom of the colonial peoples of the world. At the Geneva Conference of 1954, conveniently forgetting that Russia is the only expanding imperialist country of today, the same Mr. Molotov, with the same cynicism, again posed as the great defender of colonial peoples.

During the intervening quarter-century since 1928, a fateful war and the powerful course of events have translated much of what was a resolution on paper into actual fact. These changes never could have taken place without men to carry them through; without poverty and frustrations to exploit; and without blind and stupid policies and mistakes in some of the countries which Communists have overrun.

Many of the leaders who today head the Communist régime in

China were present at the Moscow Conference of 1928, as well as representatives from Indochina, Indonesia, India, and Africa. It must be recognized that the results they have achieved have been vast. Communist control, though often weak and unpopular, has been imposed upon one fourth of the human race, the Chinese people. Most of Southeast Asia is at this moment threatened by the same iron hand. A few questions are unavoidable.

Who is able to say that there cannot be widespread Communist gains in Africa? Over the years, we have been told the Communist plan, but we still wait for the fire to break out. Even where there are smoldering flames and a haze of smoke, our eyes detect too little and our minds and imaginations fail to display the bold discernment that the march of time demands.

The Communists enjoy an easy and unearned advantage because of our ineptitude. And even more serious is the fact that the free world is frequently missing the opportunity to show what democracy can do in Africa. Consider the easy though unearned and deceptive advantage which Communists enjoy in one aspect of cold-war propaganda. We permit them to choose and force some of the issues which we debate with them and around which powerful propaganda is made. These issues are fateful. One such issue is imperialism and colonialism. On no issue have the Communists been more effective than on this. Yet, on no issue are they more cynical and hypocritical.

There is in the world today but one expanding empire, but one dynamic colonizing force. That is the Soviet Union, now aided by a similar régime in China. According to a report of the United States Senate Subcommittee on Security Affairs, quoted by *United States News and World Report,* November 13, 1953, "Communist régimes dominate eleven countries populated by 800,000,000 people, occupying one quarter of the world's territory."

These Communist régimes are still expanding, still threatening, and still claiming that they are being threatened. They promise to end poverty and meet the food needs of the millions whom they control. Yet, in the past year, they have had to admit that they had not been able to increase their own production of grain and cattle since 1917. The empires of the Western powers, on the other hand, have become much smaller during the past ten years. And their colonial policies tend generally toward more self-government and improved living standards, even though progress is not always easy. Yet, with brazen cynicism and unbridled effrontery, Communist spokesmen pose as the liberators of colonial peoples and the champions of human freedom!

These Communist claims are widely known and attract a following in Africa. Two years ago, on a long tour in that continent, I had occasion to address several gatherings on the character of democracy. In a meeting at Lagos, Nigeria, I spoke as one who had at first hand seen Communist deception on racial problems. I spoke also as a Negro, one of many millions in the Western Hemisphere for whom the democratic idea and practice had meant a new life. The next day, I was attacked in a Lagos newspaper, *The African Pilot*. In an accompanying cartoon, a Nigerian, of all people in Africa, was shown with a rope around his leg described as "Colonialism" and saying that he could not make a choice among capitalism, socialism, and communism, until freed of colonialism. In a subsequent conversation with an editor of that paper, he made it clear to me that he was constantly hammering that view home and that it had "plenty of followers." This young man himself told me of his "political education" while a student abroad during World War II, and boasted of his regular contact with Communists overseas.

At Dakar, in June, 1952, I talked with an official of the *Force Ouvrière*. His comment was that he had "plenty of trouble with Communist activity in and around this city." Also, in Dakar, an article in the weekly paper *Afrique Noire*, June 19, 1952, argued that "French Imperialism is the most serious of all menaces to Black Africa. The promises of communism should be examined. This way of life should not be rejected without giving consideration to it; it may be the salvation of Black Africa." While in Dakar, I happened to talk with a Senegalese clerk employed in a shipping firm near the Hotel Croix du Sud. He talked freely about his "powerful Communist group" in that city, "to which I give my fullest support because it will liberate us."

It was in Leopoldville, Belgian Congo, on this same tour, that I met two young Africans who were hoping to go to a Communist training school in Prague, presumably Charles University, "to be further trained for work among our people here in the fight for freedom."

One of them said to me, "The Belgians and the Portuguese, whom I know well, are mistaken if they think we Communists will not one day be rid of them." Across the Congo River at Brazzaville, the African waiter in a small restaurant told me, with great show, of the "meetings which Communists of this place attend at these very tables." To my surprise, he pointed out a post-office worker who, he said, "is one of them." "These men," he said, "will bring us liberty."

It would not be correct to say that the appeal of the Communist movement in Africa is due altogether to our ineptness. Communist zeal has something to do with their achievement. On issues such as imperialism and colonialism, however, Communist propaganda is even helped by anti-Communist writers and publications of the West.

For instance, *Time Magazine* of May 17, 1954, carried a lengthy and graphically illustrated article on imperialism. The waning empires of Britain, France, and other European countries were described. Even the United States was included among the "colonial powers." But no mention whatsoever was made of the Communist empire which began business only thirty-seven years ago and today is the dominant imperialist power of the world.

This is not generally recognized because of the smoke-screen of Communist propaganda against colonialism. Even though many of the peoples whom they dominate are of the same color and culture and live on the same continent, the essentials of imperialism are there. That is, the economy and political life of the "liberated" country are rigidly controlled by Moscow and now Peiping in their own interest.

The issue of colonialism is at present most loudly raised by Communists. It is sufficiently echoed, both wittingly and unwittingly, by people in non-Communist Asia and Africa and in the West to do serious harm to the Western cause.

Communist anticolonial propaganda deals largely with an out of date picture of imperialism. Large areas have been turned by Britain, the United States, and Holland into independent and self-governing states. Other areas have been set well on the road toward that goal by France and Britain. Relationships are changing, even though sometimes painfully and unevenly.

Again, some of the critics of Africa help Communist propaganda by the character of their purely adverse and condemnatory criticism of policy and administration in Africa. A glib, superficial approach to the difficult and complex aspects of race relations is a dangerous approach. The facts and effects of history, however undesirable, cannot be laughed off or easily solved. Nor can standardized and conventional solutions be insisted upon for the unique type of race relations such as exist, for instance, in Central and Southern Africa. As Dr. Rita Hinden points out in an article in the *Manchester Guardian*, December 9, 1953, the aim in Africa must be "democratic self-government." She adds to this the clarifying statement that "democracy is not just a matter of forms and institutions—it is a set of values, and institutions are only a means for safeguarding them."

No contribution is made to the solution of Africa's problems by those who, in writing about them, try to set one section of the white race against another or to make one section appear worse than another. Such distinctions have no warrant in the facts of European habitation of Southern Africa. A neat sensational phrase about "settlers and savages" or the mere castigation of Dr. Malan accomplishes nothing save to provide more grist for the Communist mill. Many individuals and organizations that express themselves on Africa fall into this error. Africa deserves better of those of the West who would write about her. A constructive approach is the urgent need.

Even if Africa had no special problems, and if the West showed greater strength and wisdom, Communist strategists would still find "causes." Without doubt, however, the Communist appeal to Africa owes much to unsound, outmoded, and indefensible policies within Africa. It is in this respect that there exists a serious and potentially fatal weakness in the free world's approach to its own interests and to its responsibility and opportunity in Africa.

The most serious problem-area in the continent is South Africa. A large European population of 2.5 million, domiciled for three centuries in that temperate climate, alongside of 10 million Africans, Asians, and colored people, are factors that make the problem serious. Great economic assets in land and minerals and the consequent need for a large supply of labor add to the complex character of the problem.

The rock on which South Africa's future is sure to founder is the desire of most of its now dominant white population to have their cake and eat it. The heart of their problem is this: Can two races culturally different and numerically very unequal, as are Africans and Europeans in that country, live together with dignity, justice, and self-realization for all? If they can, then there is no alternative to a solution of problems based on the concept of ultimate equality. No race on earth would ever willingly accept anything less.

If there is strong evidence and feeling that the two races cannot live together, under the conditions mentioned above, then a serious though not unprecedented alternative remains: that is, to live in separate areas. But that is a most hard solution. It means, first of all, that equity and justice must characterize the separation if future conflict is to be avoided. It means, secondly, that industry and agriculture will lose much of their present African labor which will be occupied in their own territory.

A mutually acceptable beginning toward the solution of the racial problem in Southern Africa will surely speed solutions in other parts. The new state of Rhodesia, for instance, has some problems close to those of South Africa, but it has committed itself to the principle of economic and political citizenship for Africans. That principle has yet to be tested and realized under the existing conditions. There are evidences that it will make substantial progress. It can even be a success. But there are difficult problems ahead.

The quickening pace of world events has made the Communist task in Africa easier. African nationalism, though less advanced than its Asian counterpart, has made tremendous strides in the last ten years. To the extent that nationalism becomes anti-white or is made a channel for anti-Western activity, Communists will encourage and exploit it. Where nationalism seeks to build democratic institutions, in co-operation with the West, Communism will try to wreck it.

The deepening racial crisis in South Africa and the consequences of the Mau Mau uprising, tragic for both European and African, must be scored as losses for the free world and therefore as Communist gains. These troubled areas, as well as territories like the Gold Coast and Nigeria, are equal targets for the wrecking tactics of those who direct Communist strategy. Let us now look at some evidence of Communists at work in Africa.

On February 25, 1954, the Prime Minister of the Gold Coast, Dr. Nkrumah, made an important statement in his Legislative Assembly. He said:

Experience in this country and elsewhere has shown that membership and other forms of continuing association with the Communist Party may involve acceptance by individuals of a loyalty which, in certain circumstances, can be inimical to the State.

After pointing out how Communist infiltration interferes with the ordinary development of a young and rising state like the Gold Coast, and after making it clear that Communists will not be employed in the administration of his country, in the departments of Education, Labor, Information Services, Police, Army, and overseas representatives of the Gold Coast government, Dr. Nkrumah went on to make the following statement:

I would also like to add that in recent months foreign organizations have been taking an increasing interest in our affairs as we approach the goal of self-government. Large quantities of pamphlets and magazines are being sent to this country from abroad. All of it is tendentious and some of it is designed to stir up trouble which may obstruct or destroy our movement in this country for self-government. Again, certain persons in this country are being given free air passages to attend conferences behind what is generally known as the Iron Curtain, with all expenses paid; and scholarships are being offered Gold Coast students to attend conferences and seminars organized by communistic organizations. The government is taking measures to deal with this aspect of the matter.

In the light of the above, it is clear that the Communist threat in Africa is directed as much against democratic development and progress among Africans themselves as it is against those European powers and peoples who are related to Africa. This form of Communist activity operates both within the continent as well as from without. Communist fronts in New York, as well as in Paris, London, and Bombay, are responsible for correspondence and literature of a subversive character which are mailed to all parts of the African continent.

The Liberian Review, Vol. 3, No. 1 (1st quarter 1954), carried an article called the "Red Menace" written by its publisher, Henry B. Cole, who says:

I make bold this statement after interviewing independent observers who have the facts at their command. The job of these people, both Africans and Europeans, has been to keep track of what is going on. The communist pattern they have unearthed makes alarming reading.

Quoting from *Intelligence Digest*, described as a monthly publication in London and privately circulated, Mr. Cole says:

> The latest article has stated that since 1933 there has not been a class at Lenin University, Moscow, without at least one representative from Liberia and one from Ethiopia.[1]

He says further:

> That Russia has a plan for West Africa as a whole, including Liberia, has been repeatedly exposed by a section of the West African Press. The *Daily Echo* of Accra recently went so far as to name the Russian officials in Moscow charged with the responsibility of carrying out the plan. In October last, the *Sunday Times* of Lagos in a front-page headline "The Red Menace" in Nigeria, particularly and West Africa generally, exposed a communist plan of training West African agents and went so far as to publish a photostat document to support its case.
>
> Intelligence records show that every year, through communist free trips to London or France about 100 West Africans reach Iron Curtain countries and receive communist indoctrination and training. These Africans are recruited from trade unions, from sailors, stranded students, and unemployed, or through other agents.

Mr. Cole concludes:

> These Africans are trained quietly and return to their stations in as unobstrusive a manner as possible to indoctrinate and train more men. If the Liberian Government does not know about this until now, it is not alone. Other governments were in the same position until recently.

The trade-union movement is another channel which the Communists seek to use for their purposes. As is well known, the trade-unions throughout the democratic and free world have had to exercise constant vigilance to prevent Communists from infiltrating and controlling their organizations. The powerful trade-unions of

---

[1] The Liberian government, through its Embassy in Washington, presented at the conference, in which Max Yergan's article was delivered, an official denial that any Liberian "has within recent years applied for or has been issued travelling documents to visit Russia or any other country dominated by the Soviet Union, either for the purpose of education or on any other business." The official statement of the Liberian Embassy added that "the records of the Department of State of Liberia show that only one Liberian went to Moscow over two decades ago for the purpose of education. This particular student returned to Liberia some years ago." *(Ed.)*

North America and Europe, and in some other countries outside of the Iron Curtain areas, have succeeded, on the whole, in this necessary task. They have exposed and expelled the completely Communist-dominated World Federation of Trade Unions.

In several African countries, particularly in West Africa, including both French and British areas, the Kremlin's organization, the WFTU is active. It is known that the statement made by the Gold Coast's prime minister quoted above had particular reference to the Communist WFTU. According to Mr. Isau, of the Nigerian Teacher's Union, Lagos, Nigerian Communists are active and are in contact with British, French, and American Communists through the WFTU.

Southern Rhodesia is the scene of more recent Communist activity in Africa. According to *Rhodesia Herald* of June 7, 1954, the Prime Minister of Southern Rhodesia, Garfield Todd, issued on June 6, at Umtali, a warning on Communism in that territory:

> I challenge you as I would challenge all our citizens, to fight the foe within our borders. . . . Make no mistake about it, the foe is here, and because he is slimy and underhanded and as hard to grip as quicksilver he is all the more dangerous and real.
> This is the year when his master has called for bigger and better strikes, and I would not have believed that in this country we would so soon have seen the familiar pattern.
> We may not have many members of Communist organizations among us, but we have some of these people.

In a different way, Africans living in French possessions are the victims of Communism in France. All European powers holding colonies in Africa have made progress in their administration during the past ten years. The boldest and most forthright advance has been made by the British Colonial Office. The granting of constitutions and large measures of self-government to the Gold Coast and Nigeria are evidences.

In contrast, France's effort to achieve real colonial reform has been only partially successful. The existence of the powerful French Communist party is even more responsible for this than the French die-hards. The French Communist party is the principal vehicle for the execution of Soviet policy in West and Central Africa, and its influence extends beyond French colonial frontiers into British, Belgian, and Portuguese territory.

I had no great difficulty in ascertaining and checking this information on a tour through Africa in 1952. Through its main instruments of action, the RDA *(Rassemblement Démocratique Africain)* and the CGT *(Confédération Générale du Travail),* the French Communist-dominated labor movement, French Communists are able to do the Kremlin's job of sabotaging progress in Africa. Their activities achieved results in Toga, Dahomey, and the Ivory Coast territories of French West Africa, and in the island of Madagascar, off the coast of Southeast Africa.

In 1948, Communists succeeded in provoking a violent uprising in Madagascar, which was put down by French military force with considerable ferocity. This was a great success for the French Communist party which for several years continued to exploit sympathy for the victims in France and in Africa.

In the British colonies, Communists are active though they do not enjoy the powerful support from the British Communist party that the French Communist party provides in French Africa. Nevertheless, there is evidence that Communists were active in the riots which caused twenty deaths in Nigeria in 1949.

The main task of furthering Soviet policy in East Africa has fallen to the Indian Communist party in co-operation with the party in Britain. The large Indian communities in British East Africa and in South Africa have provided Indian Communists with a good base for operation. This is not to suggest that the Indian communities in Africa are Communist dominated. The contrary is true. But a small disciplined Communist minority is all that is required to execute directives from the Cominform.

Nowhere is the Communist influence more dangerous than among African students abroad. There are over ten thousand African students in France, Great Britain, and in the United States and Canada, and perhaps fifty in India. C. L. Sulzberger of the *New York Times* reported in that paper on January 18, 1953, that there were "forty Africans studying at Charles University in Communist Prague, and an unknown number in the Soviet Union." He stated further: "Several left-wing leaders now study in Indian universities and are being encouraged to come by a New Delhi government keenly aware of the effects of racial discrimination."

For the most part, African students abroad represent the highest levels of African culture and achievement. The Communist parties of France and Britain as well as of America, but particularly France, engage in most intensive political and propaganda activities among these African students. They are the future African leaders, and their visits to Europe and America should provide them with the groundwork on which they can build the future partnership of their countries in the West.

But their experience abroad too frequently has the opposite effect. In Paris, the pseudo-intellectual circles of the left bank, the jazz clubs, the student hostels, are often centers of the most intensive anticolonial, anti-American and anti-Western propaganda. It is here that African intellectuals foregather, because they find a minimum of racial discrimination. It is here that the Communists make the greatest show of interracial social contact. It is of the highest importance that we do not lose these students by default.

South Africa is a most fertile area in the African continent for Communist activities. This is due to several factors. South Africa has the largest white population in Africa, and among these Europeans there is Communist strength. There is also marked conflict between the government and the nonwhite population of nearly ten million, which includes nearly one million people of mixed blood and nearly a quarter-million Indians. There are Communists in the leadership of the organizations belonging to all parts of the nonwhite population. Writing again from Johannesburg, C. L. Sulzberger, in the *New York Times* of January 21, 1953, said:

> The reason diplomats expect trouble sooner rather than later is not simply because of conditions in South Africa but because an organization has been formed to combat them. At the head of this is the "Franchise Action Committee" made up of Negroes, Indians and colored, plus a few whites. It is openly dominated by the African National Congress and the South African Indian National Congress, and there is no doubt also that extreme leftists and communist elements are edging into controlling positions.

A dispatch from Cape Town, by the correspondent of the *New York Times,* carried in the *Times,* March 28, 1954, describes a meeting held at Durban on March 21, attended by representatives of three Communist-dominated organizations named by the correspondent as "The Indian National Congress," the South African colored peoples' organization, and one for whites called "The Congress of Democrats." The *Times* article states:

The communist organ, *Advance,* says the meeting was an important step toward the convening of a "Congress" of the people.

The article continues:

> Walter Sisulu, General Secretary of the African National Congress, has been addressing groups here on his trip to Soviet Union, Communist China and the Eastern Europe Soviet satellite states late last year. . . . The communists are launching bitter attacks on the new liberal party, whose president is the brilliant member of Parliament, Margaret Ballinger.
>
> Mrs. Ballinger and her friends fought for the communists' right to sit in Parliament when two were expelled. The reward of the liberals is the bitter animosity of the communists.

The influential South African Indian National Congress was, until last year, led by Dr. Dadoo, known to be a Communist. Other Indians, including Mr. Naidoo and Mr. Singh, are also prominent Communists within the Indian Congress. Communists exercise a powerful influence in the African National Congress. Among the known Communist leaders within it are: John Marks, of Cape Town; David Bopape, of Johannesburg; and Moses Kotane, also of Johannesburg. Kotane was trained in the Soviet Union; all three have had contact with Communists in Europe.

Speaking before the South African Parliament in June, 1950, during the debate on Communism in South Africa, D. L. Smit, Secretary of Native Affairs, under General Smuts, and now a member of the opposition in the South African Parliament, said:

> The fact is, the communists are well organized in all the big towns, and with the skillful propaganda they are sowing among the people, their influence is gaining ground steadily, particularly in the urban and industrial centers. There they find a fertile field in the grievances and resentment of the non-Europeans, and they exploit to the full extent, matters such as bad housing, bad social conditions, the pass laws, police raids, and the poverty of the people. The natives are being told that the Communist Party is the only party that will stand up and fight for their rights. And it is apparent to anyone who is in touch with these developments that communist agents have been active in fomenting many of the disturbances that have occurred in recent times. . . . Only last Sunday, the General Secretary of the Communist Party, a native named Moses Kotane, addressed a meeting of natives in the East Bank location in my own constituency, with all the paraphernalia of his party. . . . In Johannesburg, there are no less than 18 communists on the native advisory boards and town-

ships' committees, and nobody should underrate the gathering strength of the Communist Movement.

With cynical cunning, Communists stress the slogan, "Africa for the Africans," by which, of course, they mean Africa for the Communists. This yields the same return as their slogan "Asia for the Asians." It can only be counteracted by genuinely cultivated friendship between Africans and the people of the West, upon a realistic application of the principle of partnership in administering and developing Africa and upon the common recognition, by Europeans and Africans, that Communism is to both races a deadly foe which can only be dealt with effectively by the combined forces of free Africans and Europeans.

There arises here the important question of that African leadership which is moderate and reasonable on the main issues. It is this leadership which is also overwhelmingly pro-Western and anti-Communist. There can be no doubt of its existence. Dr. Nkrumah symbolizes it on the West Coast, Mr. Mathu represents it in East Africa, and Dr. Xuma reflects it in South Africa.

The existence of this leadership imposes a definite moral as well as political responsibility upon white Africa and the related West. This African leadership always has the double responsibility of facing the normal problems of black-white relationships and of resisting Communist attacks and infiltration upon itself. It should be accorded the greatest sympathy, understanding, and co-operation. This leadership cannot, at its own level, avoid contemplating the tragedy of the anti-Communists of Indochina, who are the victims of their loyalty to authority as well as to their principles.

Closely related to this is the question of Communist infiltration and seizure of hitherto non-Communist organizations—a well-known and universally followed Communist tactic. It has happened, for example, to the African National Congress of South Africa. The pattern is familiar. A few experienced Communists can turn the trick by making demands and setting a program which the more reasonable leaders will not follow. A demogogic exploitation of the real grievances of the people follows, and the action is generally complete; Communists have the reins.

There is a lesson from this pattern which African leaders and government officials have every reason to apply. For the African leadership, the lesson is to shun Communists as they would poison. Communists must be kept out of all organizations. At the same time as effective action is carried out on crucial problems, vigilance must be exercised to detect Communists or their spokesmen. There can be no compromise on this issue, for, to organizations in every country in the world, Communist participation has been the kiss of death. Experience makes possible the universal affirmation: "You cannot do business with Communists."

Upon government in Africa there rests the inescapable responsibility of avoiding action which handicaps and isolates the moderate though nationalistic African leadership. To avoid such action, there should at all times and places be an effective relationship between such leadership and government. Under the circumstances, government can well afford to take the initiative in establishing such relations. The Communist foe of both African people and government makes a main point of seeking to cultivate African leaders; in too many instances he meets with success. The anti-Communist forces on both sides of the racial line must, in this respect, be ahead of their common enemy.

If Communists at the moment had no contact whatsoever with Africa and no influence upon events in that continent, the objective facts of African life would themselves be a most compelling invitation to Communists to "come in and fish." But there is nothing hypothetical or academic about the situation. Communists, white, African, and Asian, are active in South Africa as well as in other parts.

Africa's present racial divisions make her an easy victim all the more vulnerable to the Communist threat, Cominform-directed. The forces, both within and without, that divide the people of Africa serve the purpose of softening up the continent and of making it easier for the Communist enemy to take over. Let us consider briefly this fact. It goes to the heart of the strategic and political aspect of African problems.

In the military sense, no part of Africa is strong enough to defend itself alone. The continent is relatively safe militarily, mainly because the free world of the West will defend it. But the successful defense of Africa is more diffcult because of its internal divisions and weaknesses. These divisions along lines of race and color, exploited as they already are by Communist propaganda and agents on the spot, could possibly nullify and would certainly weaken the strongest military defense.

Since it is easily possible for Communist strategy to take advantage of racial conflict in Africa to the disadvantage of Africans and Europeans, and to the disadvantage of the free world, one fact stands out: A compelling conclusion confronts the people of Africa, white and black, to begin searching for ways and means of placing much more emphasis upon unity, co-operation, and partnership than upon the advantages which may appear to result from division.

Admittedly, this is a difficult task, but its difficulties do not begin to compare with those which will flow from the increased conflict which Communists are out to inspire. One advantage in acting *before* the crisis is deeper and more widespread is that steps may still be taken with discipline and order.

It is necessary to realize that the entire world is a divided one, that the division is along ideological lines, and the loyalty of Africa, definitely and effectively on the free-world side, requires urgency and wisdom.

To achieve what is in mind, the first act for all concerned in Africa is the hardest: It is the act of genuine friendship. It is only upon the reality of interracial friendship that confidence can be created. Seldom have men been confronted with such a task as now faces Europeans and Africans in those parts of the continent which are most explosive and, consequently, in the greatest need.

It is necessary to entertain actively a vision of the coming together of Africans and Europeans at all responsible levels on a friendly basis. The vision should be speedily implemented. In the light of the nature and imminence of the Communist threat in Africa, no pride or ambition should stand in the way of what is needed to avert the threat. The only force that can avert it is effective understanding, unity, co-operation, and partnership among the various racial groups in the explosive parts of the continent.

The gulf between the European and African races in many parts of the continent is so deep and wide that a most serious and high-level approach is required to bridge it. Something along the lines of a department of interracial education, co-operation, and friendship ought to be seriously considered for most parts of Africa south of the equator. This approach would be but part of the present movement toward interracial conciliation, but it could be a large and most effective part if there is the will and imagination on the part of white and black to go forward to a new level of relations.

In making the above proposals, I tread humbly and cautiously. No one could be more sensitive than I to the feelings, the points of view, the pride, fears, and hopes of the people in the troubled parts of Africa. I do not deny that I think long and hard and with deep sympathy about the Boer population, in particular, and the white minority in Africa in general. As a Negro myself, I do not know how to describe adequately the depth of the feeling I have for the complete welfare of what I think of as my people—the black population of Africa.

To mention all of these various peoples and to think of the generations behind them out of which stem their present problems is to become aware of what may appear to be insoluble differences. But the nature and the imminence of the Communist threat in Africa compels us to see all of Africa's problems in a new light and from a new point of view. To see them in this manner is to have an added sense of the need and will to solve them.

It seems to me that it is altogether unrealistic to regard the main issues in Africa today only in terms of conflict between white and black. In the final analysis, there is but one issue confronting the entire world today: That is between the pro-democratic forces of the free world and the masters of the Iron Curtained Communist world. Africa will stand or fall on the outcome of that issue.

The reality of the Communist threat imposes an inescapable responsibility upon white and black in Africa, and upon the free world in its relation to Africa. That responsibility is to find speedily the basis for vastly increased mutual confidence, co-operation, and partnership between African and white man. There should be open-mindedness in seeking for new methods of solution of problems along equitable and just lines. A dramatic display of the will to understand and co-operate is needed. Symbolic of this would be the coming together, say, of Dr. Malan and Dr. Nkrumah, or individuals at a comparable level.

To the above, the Communists offer an alternative: More racial conflict throughout Africa, the spread of the Mau Mau pattern, and the destructive weapon of widespread sabotage in industry. I think the evidence shows that the situation in Africa is as simple as that.

Why cannot the sense of realism and the capacity of Europeans and Africans for friendship avert this tragedy and help save Africa and the free world?

commentary

ROBERT D. BAUM

*Chief, African Branch, Division of Research for
Near East, South Asia, and Africa,
Department of State*

Dr. Yergan's discussion of the Communist threat in Africa raises many thought-provoking problems. However, I shall confine myself to further analysis of one of the most important channels of Communist infiltration mentioned by Dr. Yergan, the African trade-union. I intend to focus on certain characteristics of the African labor movement which affect Communist efforts to gain or maintain control.

Trade-unionism among Africans is relatively new except for the northern and southern extremities of Africa, hence the recency in tropical Africa of Communist efforts to organize the workers. Progress in organizing labor has been impeded by a number of factors. The low level of industrialization and the high proportion of migratory or unstabilized labor has left many territories with only a relatively small permanent labor cadre working in industry, mines, or on plantations. Relatively few educated Africans in colonial territories have shown themselves capable of or interested in becoming trade-union leaders, partly because they, as well as the rank and file, feel that political advancement for Africans is the real key to improvement of economic status. The independent territories have lacked the inspiration or guidance of a metropolitan labor organization. Moreover, some governments have shown themselves averse to a strong, independent labor movement which might have political overtones.

The adaptation to African conditions of a Western institution formed in a quite different context is difficult enough. Like most other newly developed African leader-follower relationships, trade-unionism is complicated by factionalism, not only personal and regional but also cultural and, particularly, tribal. As a result, stable trade-union organizations on a territory-wide basis are rather rare. African labor leaders, relatively little experienced in union activities, tend often to see the trade-union more as a vehicle for personal and political advancement than as a tool for furthering the economic and social welfare of the worker. Consequently, there are Africans who welcome approaches from agents of the Communist-front World Federation of Trade Unions, not because of any love for Communism but because the WFTU appeals to their anti-imperialist sentiments. Association with this international organization may enhance their local prestige, especially if a by-product should be funds or paid trips abroad to Communist-inspired international conferences. Even the Communists are becoming aware, after certain unrewarding experiences, that the interest of some of these African travelers in Communism is largely nominal.

Organizational discipline of African labor unions varies widely in its effectiveness. Its imposition tends to be sporadic and to lead to fragmentation. Rank and file adherence is often spotty and nominal with little long-term interest in the obligation of dues. Because of insufficient member-interest in attending meetings or elections, key positions in certain unions are sometimes captured by small but well organized Communist groups which often include Africans who become oriented to Communism while students in the metropole. In other unions individual Communists, little concerned over the adequacy of dues, may even seek to lower payments to the level of Communist-controlled and externally aided unions on the plea of "competition."

The social, political, and economic environment within any African territory significantly conditions, as we all know, the prospects of African trade-unionism and Communist penetration. Having considered thus far some of the characteristics of the African labor movement in general, let us illustrate by reference to specific territories some of the effects of these conditioning factors.

The areas where African resentment and sense of frustration are most virulent—the Union of South Africa, French North Africa, and Kenya—offer fertile fields for Communist efforts. Yet, regardless of their potential for the future, the Communists have not had any substantial success in their efforts up till now, although they have had limited success in the Union of South Africa. One of the many possible explanations of this fact in South and North Africa lies in the difficulty confronting Communism in overcoming African racial suspicion in territories where it also seeks the support of the European worker. Communism could probably approach the African worker more easily if in such areas it could confront him in the guise of an essentially African movement, but this it can do only at the expense of antagonizing possible European converts.

In South Africa it was the anti-white suspicion of Africans which first led to the ouster of European Communists from the loosely organized but once powerful Industrial and Commercial Workers' Union prior to its collapse in 1929, and anti-white suspicion is an important element in forestalling Communist control today of the most important native unions. While it is indeed probable that the repressive nature of recent legislation, designed, according to the Minister of Labor, to kill native unions, will drive native labor unions underground and closer to the Communists, Communism has not yet found a bridge between the European and African worker in order to achieve its main purpose.

In French North Africa also, where the wedge of nationalism impedes French efforts to find an acceptable formula for welding Moslem and European aspirations, Communism, already in control of the dominant European labor federation (the CGT), finds itself suspect among many Moslems. This suspicion derives not only from Communism's European ties but also from its foreign ideology and the subservience it implies to another external authority. Nevertheless, those Algerian and Moroccan workers who are actively interested in trade-unionism, being able to exercise their choice only among three European-controlled federations, apparently prefer membership in the Communist-dominated CGT. This may be partly because of religious scruples against joining the Christian CFTC and because neither it nor the non-Communist CGT-FO has especially encouraged Moslem workers or shown that it would particularly serve their purpose. In Tunisia, on the other hand, where Moslems have long had their own labor organizations, the largest labor federation, the all-Moslem UGTT, is not only strongly nationalist but also anti-Communist. The nationalist parties in all three North African territories largely resist Communist blandishment, but sheer desperation could conceivably eventually drive them in that direction.

In Kenya, the other African territory where a form of nationalist tension runs high, African trade-unionism is largely undeveloped despite earlier efforts of an Indian Communist (who was exiled in 1950 to the Northern Frontier Province) to organize and gain control of the labor movement. Here African resentment has taken the form of Mau Mau, apparently without leadership or direct inspiration by Communists.

African territories on the threshold of independence, like the Sudan and the Gold Coast, with burgeoning trade-union movements, must cope with Communist efforts to gain control. Faced with a multitude of problems, their young and relatively inexperienced governments are going through difficult transitional periods. They must contend not only with economic problems which vitally affect the stability of their fragile and predominantly one-crop economies but also with competing political and social forces which are opposed to the existing government. Amid such unsettled conditions, labor factionalism provides an opening for Communist efforts to undermine stability.

The Sudan faces future difficulties in the postwar rise of the powerful Communist-dominated Sudan Workers Trade Union Federation, one of the largest in the Arab world and covering hotel employees as well as rail and river transport workers. It owes its strength partly to the freedom of trade-union organization allowed by British authorities and to the skill of anti-British organizers educated in Egypt, but primarily to the fact that it alone of the existing politico-economic groups has a relatively comprehensive social and economic program for the worker. Here as in no other place in Africa, the Communists, at least for the moment, have made a successful move along lines familiar elsewhere to unite workers and peasants. The Peasants Federation, established by Communist-oriented organizers, includes in its membership a large number of workers in the recently nationalized Gezira cotton project. Last December the Peasants Federation led a demonstration of 15,000 Gezira peasants in favor of a greater share in the control of this scheme.

In the Gold Coast, as Dr. Yergan has noted, Communist efforts to infiltrate the labor movement and the government have provoked warnings and corrective action by Prime Minister Nkrumah. Although the efforts of WFTU to capture control of the Gold Coast TUC have been thwarted, some of the individual Gold Coast unions, as well as some in Nigeria, still contain Communist-oriented leaders who will continue to bide their time while taking advantage of future opportunities to follow the Moscow line.

Government policy toward African labor organizations can help or hamper the growth of free trade-unionism. Thus in South Africa, where African organizers have found lack of government support or encouragement, they have turned to left-wingers and sometimes Communists as the only available source of guidance. Where, on the other hand, government actively encourages and recognizes the bona fide African labor union, as in Northern Rhodesia, the unions have an opportunity to develop with an appreciation of their role and responsibilities and to conduct their negotiations, in the words of Rhodesian officials, "with restraint and ability."

To be sure, freedom of labor organization may, as in the Sudan, facilitate Communist tactics, but this is the risk which democratic policy must always assume and guard against by proper counter-measures. It is for such purpose that the anti-Communist International Confederation of Free Trade Unions has a regional office in Accra and a representative in Nairobi and that it offers Africans training courses in trade-unionism and the advice of experience.

French policy toward African trade-unionism appears to approve the organization of local trade-unions as integral parts of those in the metropole and the guidance of local Africans by the more experienced European members. In French West Africa the affiliation of the strongest labor group, the CGT (except for the branches in Upper Volta), with the Communist-dominated CGT in France has given the Communists leverage even though they apparently have not been able consistently to manipulate it. While in the immediate postwar period relationships with the metropolitan CGT were relatively close, the ejection of the Communists from the French government in 1947 and the repudiation of Communist support by the African political party RDA, in 1950, have been reflected in the tendency of the West African CGT affiliates toward greater independence of direction.

During the past year the local units of CGT, joined by other unions in French West Africa, have participated in intermittent strikes and, along with moderate African political leaders, in the controversy over implementation of the new labor code. While this activity gives the appearance of bona fide trade-unionism, it also follows the present WFTU tactical line of "unity of action" with non-Communists as a means of further consolidation of power.

The focus of my discussion has been the African labor movement because it is precisely through the workers—and through the returning overseas students—that the Communists have concentrated their greatest efforts thus far in Africa. Their success in the labor field has been quite limited; but with increased economic and social development the number of wage earners is bound to increase, and, with this growth, the opportunities for Communist exploitation of the labor movement will increase. At the same time the free trade-unions of the West will also have greater challenge and opportunity to render active assistance and encouragement to the native trade-union movement in Africa.

four   **RECENT DEVELOPMENTS
IN THE AFRICAN DEPENDENCIES**

the Gold Coast and Nigeria on the road to self-government

KOFI A. BUSIA

University College of the Gold Coast

In the Gold Coast today, the government is in the hands of an all-African cabinet consisting of eleven ministers, including the Prime Minister. There is a legislative assembly of 104 members, all Africans, elected by universal suffrage. Men and women have the vote on equal terms, and there is one woman member of the Legislative Assembly. The colony is at the final stage of becoming self-governing. When the Governor's reserved powers and the over-riding legislative powers of the British Parliament are removed, it will become fully self-governing.

In Nigeria, each of its three regions, North, East, and West has its own regional assembly and its regional ministers, in addition to a Central Council of Ministers drawn from the Central Legislative Council. The Central Council consists of the Governor, six official ministers, and twelve African ministers. There are further changes on the way to give Nigerians more responsibility in a federal government. Self-government is not far away, and some Nigerian politicians have set 1956 as the deadline.

Both in Nigeria and the Gold Coast, political parties have already emerged. At the recent elections in the Gold Coast (June 15, 1954), the following parties put up candidates: The Convention People's Party, The Ghana Congress Party, the Moslem Association Party, the Northern People's Party, the Ghana Action Party, the Anlo Youth Association. In spite of this multiplicity of parties, there is the danger of a one-party rule in the Gold Coast, for the Conven-

289

tion People's Party won 70 of the 104 seats. As 14 independent candidates were returned, and the rest divided among four parties, it can be seen that the opposition is not likely to be very effective.

Nigeria has three main political parties. The National Council of Nigeria and the Cameroons is the oldest and the only really nation-wide party, though its main support comes from the Ibo province of the Eastern Region. The Action Group derives its support from the Yorubas of the Western Region, and the Northern People's Party from the Hausas and other Moslem communities of northern Nigeria.

The legislatures of the Gold Coast and Nigeria are unmistakable copies of the British House of Commons. The procedures and ritual of Westminster have been transported wholesale and have been successfully mastered. It seems to have been an unquestioned assumption that both territories should adopt the parliamentary institutions and constitutional procedure of Britain, and African legislators of the Gold Coast and Nigeria have proved themselves capable of mastering this aspect of British culture.

Only a decade or so ago, West African leaders visualized self-government mainly as a constitutional and legal issue. Their goal was to obtain constitutions which would give full powers of legislation to the colonies, so that they could be masters in their own house.

In the last few years, "self-government," as used and understood by West African nationalists, has had a much wider connotation. It embraces not only legislative powers but economic and social development as well. Its meaning includes the attainment of full sovereign nationhood as well as freedom from economic exploitation, ignorance, disease, and want; it is also the assertion of racial equality and of confidence in the ability of the African to build modern nations out of the colonies now under foreign rule.

This new conception of self-government is the outcome of a long historical process, and the problems of the Gold Coast and Nigeria as they advance toward self-government must be appraised against that historical background.

Both countries have had long contacts with Europe, and particularly with Britain. Phoenician ships are believed to have sailed along the Guinea coast. It is not conjecture but a historical fact that Portuguese navigators sailed along the Guinea coast during the fifteenth century. A Portuguese navigator, Fernando Po, discovered the island that bears his name, and by 1520, Fernando Po was already a famous Portuguese settlement noted for its sugar and other tropical crops. It was from Fernando Po that a Gold Coast farmer took cocoa pods home to the Gold Coast to begin an industry to which the country owes its present economic prosperity.

Nigeria and the Gold Coast were drawn closely into the orbit of European history by the slave-trade. West Africa was the reservoir of labor for plantations in America and the West Indies. Portuguese, Dutch, Danes, English, Swedes, and Brandenburghers sent ships there for slaves. It has been estimated that during the second half of the eighteenth century 100,000 slaves were annually exported from the west coast to America and the West Indies. The castles and forts which the European states built along the African coast to facilitate their trade stand as memorials of the period. More important than this, many observers of the West African political scene who bemoan what they consider to be too rapid an advance often forget that along the West African coast there are families who have been in contact with Europe for many generations. Some of them have European blood in their veins. Of course, in addition to this historical fact, the real answer to such critics is that their time scale is irrelevant within the context of cultural borrowing and assimilation.

The abolition of the slave-trade in the nineteenth century was succeeded by expeditions of discovery. Mongo Park explored the Niger, and subsequently Oudney, Clapperton, and Denham moving southwards from Lake Chad reached Kano and Sokoto, and Lander, another British explorer, reached Lagos and the river Benue. Trade followed in the wake of these discoveries. There was a period during the middle of the century when the British were uncertain whether to withdraw from the Gold Coast and Nigeria or to take over the administration of these colonies from merchant companies. But the scramble by European powers for possessions in Africa after the Congress of Berlin, in 1885, induced the British to abandon their vacillating policy and to assume responsibility for the two colonies. British influence in the Gold Coast and Nigeria has been exercised over several centuries through trade and commerce, in administration, education, and the spread of Christianity. The cumulative effect of the impact has revolutionized society in both countries.

In the economic sphere, through trade, mining, agriculture, and industry, the self-sufficient economies of isolated villages and tribes have been displaced. Expanding trade and commerce with Europe have led to the opening up of Nigeria and the Gold Coast. Forests have been cleared to grow cash crops for European markets. A network of road and rail and of telegraph and telephone services provides communications within each colony and between the two colonies. The improved means of communications developed to meet the needs of trade and industry have led also to the growth of towns, and to increased mobility.

New employment opportunities were offered. In agriculture, money could be earned from growing cash crops: cocoa, coconut, peanuts, or palm kernels. The Civil Service and trading firms offered employment of all types—unskilled, semiskilled, and skilled; technical, clerical, and professional. Those who went to school and could fill these posts acquired a new social status in their communities.

A large number of men and women took to earning their living by trading and distributing the products of industrial countries. All this has led to increasing specialization and differentiation of economic activities, as a result of which a new class structure has emerged.

Particularly noteworthy is the emergence of a new class of wage-earners, for this has come to have political significance. In the Gold Coast, the Convention People's Party derives its strength from the support of the wage-earning class, particularly in the towns. Traditional skills and functions have become obsolete, especially in the towns, and those who have mastered the new skills have achieved new statuses which challenge traditional ones.

The European administration also imposed European methods of education through schools and colleges where European skills and values were propagated. Literacy opened the door to social advancement and provided yet another source of change in the social structure. The introduction of European education is of sociological—as well as political—significance. It is the educated minorities of Nigeria and the Gold Coast that have pressed for political and constitutional changes and demanded self-government for their respective countries. It is from among them that political leaders have arisen to fill the new roles that each constitutional advance places in the hands of Africans.

The colonial policy of Great Britain, as repeated by successive British governments, has been to train the colonies for self-government. In the Gold Coast and Nigeria this was to be achieved through indirect rule, as expounded by Lord Lugard and his successors. The British government had a dual mandate in the colonies. This was the advancement and welfare of the colonial peoples themselves and the development of their resources for the benefit of mankind generally. The advancement and welfare of the colonial peoples could best be secured if the British administration discovered and used native institutions and authorities as instruments of government. In this way, the best of tribal values and traditions would be preserved, and the transition and adaptation to meet modern needs would be achieved with the least dislocation.

In practice, this admirable policy made traditional councils and chiefs junior partners or agents of the alien ruler. In the Gold Coast, the support which the chiefs enjoyed from the British government tended to free them from traditional constitutional checks. They were often able to flout the will of the people or to stifle its expression. They tended to become more autocratic than they otherwise could have been. This is why the new nationalists in the Gold Coast denounced the chiefs as "reactionary imperialist stooges." The evolution of local government under the policy of indirect rule was too slow and not sufficiently sensitive to changes in the social structure resulting from trade and commerce and education. Thus, the Gold Coast, and to a lesser degree Nigeria, has reached the threshold of self-government without a firm foundation of local government.

The Second World War accelerated the pace of change. Both those who served in the armed forces and those who remained at home were affected by it. Those who enlisted learned new skills. Their horizons were widened, and their expectations for higher standards of living on their return to civilian life were raised.

Civilians enjoyed higher incomes from war work, from commodities specially needed for the war, or from remittances from relatives in the armed forces, which put more money into circulation; but there were fewer consumer goods available, and inflation and profiteering assumed proportions never known before. There was general discontent with the rising cost of living.

After the cessation of hostilities, the methods of the colonial governments in Nigeria and the Gold Coast, as well as the methods of the Imperial government in Britain, seemed slow and ineffective in dealing with the problems of resettling ex-servicemen, of lowering the cost of living, and of making more consumer goods available; and the general discontent found expression in the demand for freedom from "imperialism." There is, thus, a very close connection between the recent constitutional changes that have taken place in British West Africa and the economic conditions that prevailed at the close of the Second World War.

In the Gold Coast, the popularity of the slogan "self-government now" was due to the fact that it was represented as the seizure of power as well as the lowering of the prices of all consumer goods, increases in wages, reduction in taxation, the expansion of health and social services, free education, and the immediate implementation of vast schemes of development. Self-government would bring immediate material benefits to all.

This throws light on the major problems facing Gold Coast and Nigerian political leaders. What they aim at and what their countrymen expect of them is that they should establish simultaneously a parliamentary democracy and the welfare state. It is the prospect for the achievement of this double task that we must consider and appraise.

In both Nigeria and the Gold Coast British rule provided a framework for the administration of each colony as a unit; but the units were artificial creations imposed from above, rather than a growing integration from below. The tribes along the Coast had longer contacts with the British, and both in Nigeria and the Gold Coast this historical accident led to wide differences in the development of the different regions of each colony. Neither the Gold Coast nor Nigeria was a nation. In the Gold Coast, the concept of nationhood is gaining popular acceptance. *Ghana* stands for the concept of a united Gold Coast. But the sense of nationhood is still incipient. The formation of regional parties such as the Northern People's Party and the Togoland Congress attests to the strength of tribal sentiment; nevertheless in the Gold Coast there are no deep dividing issues, and it should not be long before a sentiment of nationhood gathers around *Ghana*.

The size of Nigeria and the accidents of history have made it more difficult for a sense of nationhood to develop there. The northern and southern parts of the colony have differences of tribe, culture, and religion. The North has for centuries been influenced by Moslem culture and religion and considers that it possesses a culture superior to that of the South. The South, on the other hand, gave less resistance to European civilization, and consequently clerical and administrative posts in the North are held by Southerners who are therefore often in positions of authority vis-à-vis the Northerners.

The administrative framework provided by the British did not bridge the gulf of cultural and religious differences within the regions. As late as 1946, The Richards Constitution recognized the strength of regional and tribal differences, which had existed throughout the period of British rule and provided for three regional legislatures loosely linked at the central legislature.

The cumbersome nature of the 1946 Constitution was apparent, and it was not welcomed by Nigerian nationalists. It had hardly been tried when a committee was set up in 1948 to consider "how far there can be devolution from the center into the regions, and whether it is possible to conceive of a kind of Federation in Nigeria in the place of a highly centralized parliament of the kind which has probably been visualized by some of the agitators in Nigeria in days gone by."

To ascertain the views of the public, provincial and regional conferences were held, and finally a central conference consisting of regional representatives was held in Lagos. The Committee submitted its report in 1949, and early in 1950 a new constitution was worked out.

This Constitution which came into force in 1951 established a central legislature for all Nigeria and three regional legislatures, one each for the northern, eastern, and western regions. It has been criticized as being too complex in form, as perpetuating regional differences, as being cumbersome in electoral procedure, and finally as dooming Nigeria perpetually to having coalition governments.

Accordingly, changes have been worked out in a conference which was held in London (July–August, 1953) and Lagos (January, 1954) under the chairmanship of Mr. Oliver Lyttleton, then Her Majesty's Secretary of State for the Colonies.

A federal form of government on the basis of semi-autonomous regional legislatures has been proposed, and the necessary changes will be incorporated in an order-in-council.

The system of election will be simplified, and there will be separate elections to regional and central legislatures. Each regional legislature will have a general power to make laws for the region, and there will be a federal legislative list restricting the subjects on which the central government can make laws. This is why Nigerian leaders are studying the constitutions of Australia and the United States.

It can thus be stated in respect both to the Gold Coast and Nigeria that one of the problems of self-government is the awakening and fostering of loyalties wide and strong enough to maintain unity and the responsibilities of nationhood. The prospects for the Gold Coast are better because it is smaller in size, and because the regional differences are due mainly to differences in economic and educational development rather than to deep-seated cultural or religious differences.

A legacy from the policy of indirect rule remains, in that a suitable system of local government has to be devised which is capable of performing the functions that must now devolve on local councils. The struggle for power between traditional rulers and the new class of popularly elected representatives in local councils and regional and national legislatures appears less acrimonious in Nigeria than in the Gold Coast, but it is an important issue in both. The philosophy of indirect rule does not appear to have considered the role of the chiefs when Britain finally relinquished power, after the transplantation of British parliamentary institutions. Under the new conception of democracy, the ordinary citizen demands a more active participation in administration and government, and elected ministers exercising wider powers strive for their authority over the chiefs to be recognized. It is a struggle which should be seen in terms of competition for prestige and status within the community, as well as the desire for efficient democratic administration. On the other hand, chieftaincy is deeply rooted in the traditions and prejudices of West African peoples. In many of the tribes, the chief is not merely an administrative head; he also fills a sacral role; he symbolizes the unity of the tribe and its culture and provides it with a sense of continuity in time and space. So, for both countries the choice lies between the adaptation of an old institution that enshrines much of the peoples' cultural achievements to a new situation, or the radical elimination of chietaincy as an outmoded institution. Neither operation will prove easy; and the issue divides political parties and is a source of internal dissensions.

Togoland, in the Gold Coast, and the Cameroons, in Nigeria, present their own peculiar problems. Both regions were former German colonies which were divided and placed under French and British trusteeship. There are political leaders in the Gold Coast who wish to see a unification of the two tribes in both the British and French territories of southern Togoland into a separate self-governing state with the right to choose which territory it wishes to join, and the form of such alliance or federation. With the possibility of the Gold Coast becoming self-governing within the next two or three years, the future of the trust territory of Togoland has become a burning issue. The British government has already announced that it will not be prepared to administer Togoland as a separate trust territory after the Gold Coast has attained independence, and is advocating the integration of that part of Togoland under British trusteeship with a self-governing Gold Coast. Nationalists in southern Togoland do not accept this, and if the results of the recent elections in the Gold Coast be taken as a guide, those advocating unification have strong support. In Nigeria, there is a similar demand for the Cameroons to be administered separately, and already this has received recognition; but the final position of the Cameroons has still to be decided. These are matters which bring the Gold Coast and Nigeria into international politics; the question of the date for the granting of self-government for the Gold Coast is related to the future of Togoland, for the area and boundaries of a self-governing Gold Coast have to be determined, and that involves the question of Togoland under British trusteeship. As Nigeria approaches the goal, a similar question will arise with regard to the Cameroons.

Parliamentary democracy has been represented as a way of life; a way of life the success of which depends on the discipline, understanding, and degree of responsibility that the individual citizen can shoulder. Constitutional advances both in the Gold Coast and

Nigeria have been won through the activities of the educated people who form a minority. In neither country is the literate section put above 15 per cent. No attempt to estimate the prospects of parliamentary democracy in the Gold Coast and Nigeria can be realistic without a consideration of this fact and of the new political parties which have been formed. These are revolutionary times in West Africa, and the political parties, especially the Convention People's Party in the Gold Coast, bear unmistakable marks of revolutionary movements elsewhere: the charismatic leader; fanatic devotion; intolerance of opposition; mass support; party slogans and rallies; and efficient organization. This situation imposes severe tests of morality and discipline which cannot be ignored. This makes the need for strong and effective opposition parties pertinent and urgent.

European observers of the West African scene often ask for the differences between the existing political parties of Nigeria or the Gold Coast, and they expect answers which will enable them to place these parties in categories with which they are familiar in their own political history: conservative, socialist, liberal, communist, left-wing, right-wing. These labels are often inappropriate in the context of the Gold Coast or Nigeria. The parties are agreed on self-rule; and the differences are mainly in internal policies, such as the approach to the reorganization of local government, the position of chiefs, the rate of development of a particular region, behavior and interpersonal relations, or the details and the manner of implementation of plans of development. It is possible that in due course the familiar European labels may become applicable, but at present they befog rather than clarify our knowledge of the aims and characters of the parties of Nigeria or the Gold Coast. The issues and the historical and social situations are different and still in a state of flux.

The creation of a welfare state demands technical knowledge, efficient personnel, adequate resources of capital, manpower, and natural resources. Both the Gold Coast and Nigeria suffer from the lack of trained personnel, adequate capital, and technical knowledge. The lack of personnel and technical knowledge is in part a legacy of the lack of a clearly defined policy of education under the British administration. As a result of this, the educational system was not sufficiently geared to the social needs and goals of the people.

While political leaders are aware of the need for outside help, nationalism and the fear of economic exploitation dictate caution. There is a serious dilemma. The countries must be developed, and for this they must have foreign aid; but they must beware lest they win political freedom and yet submit to economic serfdom; and they must also see to it that they do not purchase economic and technical aid at the expense of political freedom. The problem is one of establishing the right kind of relationships with Britain and other countries and corporations that have the personnel, capital, and technical knowledge, and one of arriving at arrangements which will provide adequate security and profits for foreign investments as well as sufficient protection for the peoples of the Gold Coast and Nigeria.

But both countries have set their feet firmly on the road to self-government and are within a few yards of the goal. There is an awakening sense of nationhood; remarkable successes have been achieved in trade and commerce; there are bold schemes to exploit the natural resources of power, timber, mineral, and agricultural wealth; determined efforts are being made to overcome the disabilities of illiteracy, disease, and poverty. Above all, both countries have faith in the democratic way of life, born of their own political experience and nurtured by British ideals and institutions which they have accepted. There are indeed difficulties and shortcomings; but they are recognized to be so because the leaders and the best informed citizens of both countries measure themselves by the best examples of contemporary democracies. Their goal is to be admitted as self-governing dominions within the British Commonwealth of Nations. Whether that club will be prepared and ready to admit them is a challenge which the present members of the club have to face.

What both Nigerian and Gold Coast citizens and leaders need to consider most at the present time is the warning given by John Stuart Mill:

> If we ask ourselves on what causes and conditions good government in all its senses, from the humblest to the most exalted, depends, we find that the principal of them, the one which transcends all others, is the qualities of the human beings composing the society over which government is exercised.

The close relationship that Mill sees between politics and character is as relevant to the Gold Coast and Nigeria as anywhere else. The creation of the welfare state means the assumption of wider activities and powers by those who govern. The opportunities for public dishonesty correspondingly increase. The democratic society cannot be built unless dishonesty and corruption are overcome or at least effectively curbed. The test for the Gold Coast and Nigeria in this sphere will prove more severe than learning to work the constitutional machinery and acquire the technological competence necessary for building a democratic welfare state. Our hope is that we will pass the test and be able to take our places as respected members of the community of nations and make our contribution toward the peace of the world and the enrichment of human life.

There has been much implied criticism of British colonial policy in the above presentation. This is because I have attempted to throw light on the problems that still remain to be solved, on the assumption that in a publication of this kind it would be more profitable to examine problems that lie ahead. It is inevitable that a statement of what remains to be done should uncover what was done badly in the past or was left undone altogether.

There is no lack of appreciation of the difficulties or the achievements of the British government. The fact that both Nigeria and the Gold Coast have made such rapid strides in the last few years that they are within reach of self-rule is itself a testimony to the achievements of the British administration, as well as of the colonial peoples themselves. Ten years or so ago, even the most sympathetic and best-informed British experts on colonial affairs estimated that it would take at least a hundred years for the Gold Coast or Nigeria to become self-governing. They have had to revise the time span of their prognostications.

In the sphere of education, for example—although the criticism has been offered that no clearly defined policy was followed by the British and that the education provided did not take sufficient account of the social needs and goals of the colonial peoples—it nevertheless produced enough educated people not only to demand self-government but also to be able to shoulder the responsibilities involved.

There are colonial powers that have had clearly defined policies of education in their dependent territories. The education provided has been designed to serve political ends. They have made sure that the type of education given has been such as to discourage their colonial peoples from political activities and only fit them for certain specific occupations.

Whatever faults there were in the educational system of British West Africa—and it is submitted that there were serious ones—it should nevertheless be recognized that it made constitutional advances possible and produced Africans capable of taking political responsibility.

Similarly, an answer could be made at least to mitigate the force of the criticisms leveled against local government. The philosophy underlying indirect rule was in its day an enlightened one; but fidelity to the doctrine seems to have blinded its devotees to the realities of social change. It could be pointed out, however, that both in Nigeria and the Gold Coast the need for reforming the local authorities has been recognized for some time, and efforts have been made to improve them. In Nigeria, for example, a committee of the Eastern Regional House of Assembly was set up in 1948 to review the then existing system of local government in the eastern provinces and to make recommendations for their improvement. Similar committees were set up in the Gold Coast, and in 1951 the Legislative Assembly passed ordinances to establish new local councils. But in both countries more suitable systems have still to be devised.

Attention has also been drawn to the need to develop a sense of nationhood, and the peculiar difficulties of Nigeria in this regard have been indicated. The progress of scientific invention and technological change perpetually face mankind with the problem of combining smaller political units into larger ones and of enlarging man's sense of civic obligation to embrace wider communities. It is not a problem peculiar to the Gold Coast or Nigeria. In this context also, the part that the British administration has played in developing the conception of nationhood and in providing both a foundation and a scaffolding for administration on a national scale should be duly recognized.

There are no criteria for determining when a colony is "ripe" for self-government, and hence the period when a colony feels itself able to take over responsibility is one when relations with the imperial power are liable to become strained. There is usually a

difference of opinion between guardian and ward as to whether the
ward has come of age or not. In the Gold Coast it took a nation-
wide boycott, an ex-servicemen's protest, the bloodshed of ex-servicemen and civilians, and a period of tragic disorder before the British
government woke up to the need for making constitutional changes.
Nigeria had a similar period of agitation, riots, and labor strikes.
In such an atmosphere, much ill-feeling is engendered, and it is to
the credit of British administrators as well as the nationals of
Nigeria and the Gold Coast that the present constitutional experiments have had so smooth a running.

The British government itself has to face moral tests no less
severe than colonial nationalists. As the colonies approach the
time of their independence, the logical implications of British policy
become real. British officers in the Colonial Civil Service are faced
with the possibility of their careers being cut short because they are
no longer needed. They have to seek employment elsewhere and
sometimes face keen competition. They naturally feel anxious and
insecure and expect guarantees of security or adequate compensation.

Further, in both Nigeria and the Gold Coast, much British capital
has been invested in mining, industry, trade, and development; and
investors wish to be assured not only that their capital will not be
expropriated but that they will continue to procure adequate
returns.

A question in which some nationals of Nigeria and the Gold Coast
are interested at the moment is where Britain's interest will mainly
lie at this final stage. Will it lie in taking responsibility to ensure
that, when it finally hands over full powers of self-rule to the
Gold Coast and Nigeria, the highest standards of probity and
efficiency will be maintained, or will Britain's prime concern now
be to secure adequate gratuities and compensation for British
personnel and the protection of British financial interests? These
are not mutually exclusive alternatives, but the way in which Britain
interprets its duty and directs the conduct and actions of its representatives in the two colonies will be different according as one or
the other is given priority. On the other side, there have been
scandals of corruption both in the Gold Coast and Nigeria. It would
be sheer complacency to ignore these red lights warning of danger.
They do indicate that the British government and Parliament, if
they are to accomplish the task of tutelage successfully, should not

regard the achievement and maintenance of high standards of efficiency and probity in administration as matters for which they are no longer responsible in Nigeria and the Gold Coast.

With regard to British personnel and capital, Nigerian and Gold Coast political leaders have not only recognized and acknowledged their need for foreign personnel and capital, at this stage of their development, but have also promised to provide adequate safeguards for both. Assurances to this effect have been given in the legislative assemblies of both territories.

Since these assurances were given, the Secretary of State for the Colonies has announced that the Colonial Service will, as from October 1, 1954, become the Overseas Civil Service and that when a colony becomes self-governing the British government will enter into an agreement with the government of the former colony guaranteeing that colonial officers who remain after the transfer of power will not suffer any change in conditions, and that there will be adequate compensation in the event of premature retirement following constitutional change. Such officers will remain members of the Overseas Service and be available for transfer.

"Universal education," wrote John Stuart Mill, "should precede universal enfranchisement," and it is generally agreed that democracy is the form of government which makes the biggest demands on the intelligence and watchfulness of its citizens. Some critics have therefore considered it hazardous that self-government should be granted to the Gold Coast and Nigeria when they have such a high degree of illiteracy. If assurances beyond what has already been achieved and demonstrated by both countries are still needed, they can be found in the emphasis that has been placed on community development in both countries. The aim is not only to combat illiteracy but to harness the energy of every citizen for self-help and social betterment. It is the awakened alertness, the widespread efforts for individual as well as community improvement, the construction and works of development in progress on all sides that give an index of the social revolution going on in Nigeria and the Gold Coast today.

The problems which I have attempted to spread before you give evidence of the growth of the two colonies toward maturity and independence. The political situation in the Gold Coast and Nigeria today presents both a challenge and an opportunity: a challenge to race prejudices and myths; and an opportunity for the kind of interracial co-operation which spells hope for our complex and divided world.

commentary

HAROLD COOPER

*Former Public Relations Officer
of the Nigerian Government*

Dr. Busia has, to borrow a metaphor from Philip Guedalla, walked with a remarkably sure step over the still-hot lava of recent West African politics. I commend his daring and congratulate him on the safe completion of his journey.

I shall follow him only on to those patches of lava which have shown some signs of cooling. This will involve hopping from one patch to another, a performance which I hope I can execute with reasonable grace.

Dr. Busia has charted for us not only past mistakes but future dangers. Many of the latter are likely to arise from overconfidence. The people of the Gold Coast appear to expect, for instance, that with the dawn of complete self-government the welfare state will spring fully financed from the head of Prime Minister Kwame Nkrumah. This optimism is scarcely surprising. The notion that imperialism is the root of all evil finds its natural complement in the belief that independence will be the fount of all good. I have always felt that the worst crime the British have committed in the colonies has been unintentional. They have provided a continuous and costly distraction, like a stranger who is walking to and fro in a room where someone else is trying to work. In the end the work is forgotten in the heat of argument with the intruder. "It will all come right when we get rid of the British" is a healthy slogan insofar as it gives priority to the task of attaining freedom. It is unhealthy if it also results in a neglect of problems which, under an ideal arrangement, would be resolved in advance of independence instead of being left to bedevil the efforts of founding fathers of the new state. Much has been written about tribal disunity in Nigeria. It is fashionable to seek an explanation for it in the alleged devotion of the British to the policy of "divide and rule." But to detect the cause of an ailment is not enough. There should also be an attempt to cure it. The achievement of national unity in Nigeria should be an essential part of the campaign for freedom, not a separate salvage operation hastily undertaken in the wake of that campaign.

Dr. Busia has mentioned that British officials in the Gold Coast (and I was once among them) were slow to realize that the period needed to achieve self-government could be calculated in years instead of centuries. He is right in supposing that we thought it wise and proper to make haste slowly. That was partly because it is a tradition of British workmanship to do things thoroughly. We found it hard to adjust ourselves to the idea of turning out dominions on a mass-production basis. Or, to put it differently, we looked on the Gold Coast as a ward to whom it was our duty to give the best possible schooling before he went forth to make his own way in the world. It was easy enough for us to take this attitude, of course, because the ward was paying the tuition fees. If we could have had our way, he would have stayed on and worked for his Ph.D. and perhaps done a few years of research after that; and we were grieved when instead he insisted on taking his A.B. examinations at the end of his freshman year and leaving college as soon as he passed them.

There is another factor which helps to explain why we have constantly been overtaken by events and never seem to hear the winged chariot at our back until we are almost crushed beneath its wheels. The clamor for self-government in the Gold Coast and Nigeria has come, Dr. Busia tells us, from the "educated minorities" in the two countries. The absence, outside the big towns, of popular, articulate support for these "agitators"—has led to the drawing of facile assumptions about the loyalty of the masses. If anything can be said of the masses in most colonial territories, it is that they are inert, uninformed, unawakened. To construe this inertia as a positive manifestation of satisfaction with existing conditions and of dislike for any change that might be suggested is the same as contending that any voter who stays away from the poll in the next American elections must be an ardent Republican. What should arrest attention in any situation of this kind is not the quiescence of the illiterate ten thousand, but the malaise of the educated half-dozen.

What political forces, it should be asked, are strengthened by the steady spread of enlightenment? In the Gold Coast and Nigeria the answer to that question has never been in real doubt. The primary and secondary schools have for years been the breeding grounds of nationalism. That, as Dr. Busia has hinted, is a singular tribute to the type of education which the British have imported from their own land. Lord Mansfield said, in a famous judgment of 1772, which helped to sound the death knell of the slave-trade, that "whoever breathes the air of England must be free." It is equally true that whoever goes to school and is immersed in English literature and English history and English philosophy must feel the exhilerating attraction of freedom and must, if he has applied himself intelligently to his lessons, become at any rate a nationalist and perhaps an agitator. After all, most of us are prone to agitate about the things in which we believe.

Dr. Busia warns us that events in West Africa are testing the strength of the system of indirect rule. I am glad he has recognized the honesty of the motives which inspired the adoption of this system. It is altogether humble and prudent to give colonial peoples an opportunity to adjust their own political institutions to the needs of the modern world, rather than to require a baffled conformity with practices which, however admirable, may be alien to their tradition. But the secret of sound political health is constant growth —the sort of decorous mutability that enabled England to start with a conquering Norman duke and eventually produce a Ramsay MacDonald, to live comfortably enough at one stage under the theory of the divine right of kings and then move on, with only one serious convulsion, to the strict but splendid limitations of constitutional monarchy. In West Africa, this capacity for growth has been stunted, although precisely the opposite effect was intended. The chiefs, who were to be groomed for the responsibilities of enlightened and progressive leadership, have instead come to be chided and even vilified as reactionary "stooges"—like Dr. Busia, I cannot escape the horrid word—of the European interloper. In part, the chiefs themselves are to blame for this because so many of them chose to assess their new position in terms of personal or dynastic safety and to welcome the British rajas as a convenient air-raid shelter in which they could retreat whenever the bomb splinters of public indignation began to fly. But the British are far from blameless in the matter, although the idea that they consciously used the chiefs as puppet rulers of a myriad satellite régimes is an exaggeration. The original mistake lay in treating the chiefs not as intermediaries, through whom to negotiate, but as subordinates, through whom to transmit orders. The British genuinely felt that they deserved the loyalty of the chiefs. The chiefs took note that this loyalty was earnestly craved, and as a matter of simple gratitude they provided it. Thus grew up the comfortable legend that the way things were being done must be all right because the chiefs approved of it, even if some of their less perceptive subjects did not. There was a grave temptation to measure a chief's usefulness by his devotion to British rule and his belief in British infallibility. The true yardstick—his willingness to speak out frankly in the interests of his people, even if this meant opposing official policy—tended to get lost in an eager exchange of courtesies.

In recent years in Nigeria there has been a vigorous attempt to "democratize" the native administrations, which is the same as saying to reduce the power of the chiefs. The object is to repeat on the lower levels of government the reforms which have come with such a rush at the top—or to dismantle the lesser imperialisms simultaneously with the dismantling of the central imperialism from which they draw their authority and to which they look for protection. It is doubtful if this effort is being made in time. At least some of the chiefs, unprepared for the changed conditions which will follow the transfer of power, seem likely to share the fate of the Indian princes.

Perhaps the most doom-laden sentence in Dr. Busia's essay was that in which he referred to the international status of the Gold Coast and Nigeria once they have achieved independence. "Their goal," he said, "is to be admitted as self-governing dominions within the British Commonwealth. Whether that club will be prepared and ready to admit them is a challenge which the present members of the club have to face." Much, in terms of human destiny, may hang upon the response to that challenge. It may determine whether racial antagonisms in Africa are to be resolved by giving substance to the hazy dream of partnership or whether the continent is to be split irrevocably into two embattled and embittered camps. For it is a delusion to suppose that the Gold Coast and Nigeria, having won freedom for themselves, will silently acquiesce in its being withheld indefinitely from their neighbors. Despite the reassurance offered by some of the writers in this book, it seems to me that the gulf between the two Africas—between black Africa and settler Africa, or integrated and segregated Africa, or uniracial and multi-racial Africa, call them what you will—is opening at a frightening rate. The opportunity for friendly high-level contact afforded by the Commonwealth association may be the last chance to bridge it.

French Africa and the French Union

KENNETH ROBINSON

Nuffield College, Oxford University

It has become a commonplace that the major problems of contemporary Africa center on the resolution of the strains and tensions resulting from the impact of the West on African society. To an ever-increasing and rapidly accelerating extent, demands for the more or less radical transformation of Africa into a part of the modern world are being voiced by many of those Africans whose lives have been affected by these processes. And although such Africans are still a minority, often a small minority, such demands elicit sufficient response from other, less vocal, elements in the population to ensure them a substantial and increasing measure of general support. But, just as the initiation of this process of social change was the outcome of demands made on Africa by the rest of the world—demands for supplies of raw materials, for the provision of land for European settlement, and for the acceptance of Christianity—so it continues to be fed by such external demands, especially in respect of the provision of raw materials. These inevitably extend the area subject to such induced social change and also increase its intensity or depth. Moreover, one of the older external demands has taken on a new form; an important original cause of colonialism is to be sought in the inability, as well as, on occasions, the unwillingness, of precolonial societies to provide those minimal assurances of law and order without which the individual agents of these various external demands could not operate. Today, this external demand for guarantees of political stability has assumed a new guise, that of anxiety that the political structures which

311

replace the colonial system will be able to contain and channel the pressures resulting from rapid and uneven social change sufficiently to ensure a reasonable degree of political stability in Africa. There is, of course, sufficient justification for this preoccupation in the actual needs of the territories and the welfare of their peoples. But it has recently been reinforced by the struggle between East and West and the anxiety that arises from their fear that the passion for the modernization of their countries (a passion which consumes so many of the Western educated African elite) should result in their acceptance of the Communist formula, presenting as it does precisely the attractive possibility of very rapid modernization to be brought about by the dictatorship of an educated and dedicated elite.

Neither African demands for modernization nor Western pre-occupations with political stability carry with them any necessary implication that the political structure which is to replace the colonial system must be that of the Western national state, still less that it must entail a Western democratic form of government or, in any real (as opposed to a merely formal) sense, a sovereign, independent state. But one of the fundamental underlying drives which finds expression in this demand for modernization seems to be a deep-seated urge to secure acceptance, both of Africans as individuals and of their countries, as equal in status with the people and countries of the rest of the world. Since this is at least formally organized on the basis of sovereign, independent states, it is natural that the model of an independent state should seem to provide the essential basis for a successful emergence into the modern world as members of a community equal in status with others elsewhere. Although natural, this is not inevitable, at any rate not logically inevitable, for it is possible that both the demand for modernization and the passion for equality might be satisfied completely within some larger political unit. If by nationalism is meant the demand for modernization and the passion for equality of status, rather than the attempt to secure the realization of these aspirations by the creation of a separate national state, nationalism is indeed, as has been said recently, "the inevitable end-product of the impact of Western imperialism and modernity upon African societies; it is also the inevitable assertion by the Africans of their desire to shape their own destinies." [1] The central political problem in Africa today derives from the emergence of African nationalism in this wider sense. This does not, of course, mean that organized, self-conscious, nationalist movements exist in every territory, but the eventual appearance of movements rejecting European domination and the demand, in one form or another, for modernization and equality for Africans must be regarded not only as inevitable but as a natural phenomenon, one of the necessary consequences of the changes made and the forces released in the African environment by Western contact. The object of this essay is to consider the extent to which the over-all organization and structures of the French Union appear, as we near the end of the first decade of its existence, to offer the possibility of accommodating political pressures of this kind which have made, or are making, their appearance in various parts of French Africa.

The French territories in Africa, which together cover about one-third of the area of the continent and include about a quarter of its 200 million inhabitants, fall into three major areas, apart from French Somaliland which will not be especially considered here: French North Africa; French tropical Africa; and Madagascar. There are of course great differences not only between any one of these areas and another but also within each area and indeed within the individual territories themselves, diversities so great that it might well be contended that it was impossible usefully to consider the various parts of French Africa in any sense together. For many purposes, there is unquestionably great force in this view. But there are two features which all these areas of French Africa exhibit: first, some of the political and psychological consequences of that social change induced by Western contact which have just been discussed; and second, that they are all under French rule. This latter characteristic is particularly important because of some of the fundamental habits of thinking of most French politicians, administrators, and businessmen. The tendency to think of metropolitan France and the overseas areas as constituting in some sense one unit, a *bloc français,* or as evolving toward the more complete

---

[1] J. S. Coleman, "Nationalism in Tropical Africa," *American Political Science Review* (June, 1954), p. 426; cf. also the remark of Dr. Aujoulat, Deputy for the Cameroons, "La réclamation essentielle des Africains tient en un mot: Egalité," *Marchés Coloniaux du Monde* (July 14, 1951), p. 1863.

realization of that unity in a French Union is a habit of thinking deeply rooted in French history and experience. As contrasted with the habits of political thinking characteristic of the British, which typically considers each territory as an essentially separate entity, this French approach means that what happens in respect of any one French territory is more likely to be considered as having some relevance to other French territories. Moreover, this tendency is reinforced, in the kind of political structures which have been developed to give expression to this habit of thinking, by institutional mechanisms which are in fact likely to mean that pressures felt in any one territory will be translated into more general pressures affecting the structure as a whole. There is thus an important practical sense in which it is more meaningful to think of these very diverse parts of Africa which are under French rule as being interrelated in a French Africa than it would be in respect of British Africa; though, as we shall see, it is possible to exaggerate this point and to overlook some important contrary tendencies which operate to differentiate North Africa in particular from the other overseas areas under French rule.

The French Constitution of 1946 may be thought of as having recognized the possibility of two alternative destinations for French dependent territories: on the one hand, the traditional objective of assimilation or political integration with metropolitan France; and on the other, a new possibility of association with the French Republic in a French union in which a common policy in external affairs and a pooling of resources for defense would be reconciled with the grant of self-government or autonomy in internal affairs. But these two possibilities did not, in fact, stand on the same footing. Assimilation, as an overseas department of France, represented the logical carrying through of a French policy and practice of very long standing. It was not particularly difficult to convert the four colonies of Martinique, Guadeloupe, Réunion, and Guiana into departments identical, at least in all constitutional and juridical respects, with those of metropolitan France: even before the war they had already advanced very far along this road; and a model was, in any case, at hand in the metropolitan departments themselves. Moreover, each of these territories was, both demographically and economically, very small in comparison with metropolitan

France.[2] From the political point of view, not only was their incorporation as overseas departments a more realistic method of meeting the demand for equality of status than any attempt to establish them as separate self-governing units could have been, but it raised no serious problems as regards their "weight" in relation to metropolitan France. They could, for example, be assigned representation in the various metropolitan assemblies on the same basis as metropolitan departments, without any danger to metropolitan predominance. Moreover, all their inhabitants had for many decades enjoyed equal status as French citizens; difficulties about the representation of the very small minority of French settlers had long since been overcome or at least overridden.

Very different was the situation in regard to the other formula of the new Constitution, that of the associated state. This was not a model for which French experience provided any precedent. There was no political structure within the French system which could be pointed to as showing what the meaning of such internal self-government really would be in practice, nor was there any experience of the working of the kind of political relationship between such a self-governing territory and the French Republic which the new Constitution had implied in the word "Associated," but which it had defined only in the most general terms. Moreover, this new model was intended to be applied to areas of quite exceptional difficulty, namely Indochina and the two North African protectorates. In the former, the outcome of World War II had been the formation of a combined nationalist front, which was actually in control of substantial parts of the country, had been recognized as constituting a government, and was under a degree of Communist leadership. In North Africa, the fundamental political problems had only an indirect connection with the particular issues with which the notion of an associated state was intended to deal, that is to say, the relationship between France and an autonomous state associated with France in matters of common concern, especially defense and foreign policy. The real issue, both in Tunisia and Morocco was, on the contrary, that of the terms on which

2 K. E. Robinson, "The End of Empire: Another View," *International Affairs* (April, 1954), gives some account of departmentalization in the French West Indies.

Frenchmen settled in these countries were to participate in any future autonomous Tunisian or Moroccan government. The notion of an associated state, for it can hardly be described as anything as precise as a model, offered no guidance on this point.

Although the Constitution of 1946 had thus set up these two alternative possibilities, it assumed that in fact most French dependencies would not for some time yet achieve either the status of an overseas department or that of an associated state, and it seemed to contemplate that those that did not might ultimately evolve either in one direction or the other. Meanwhile they would be assigned a kind of transitional status to which the label of "overseas territory" was applied. This new régime, which was that established in French tropical Africa and Madagascar, involved some very considerable changes as compared with the old colonial system: the extension of citizenship to all the inhabitants and the abolition of the special legal code previously applied to all noncitizens; the extension of the franchise to many, though by no means all, of the new citizens; the representation of all these territories in the French Parliament, as well as in the new consultative Assembly of the French Union; and the creation of wholly elected territorial assemblies with some important powers in connection with the budget and finance.[3] These changes involved some genuine shifts in the locus of political power, but it should be noticed that they were all changes in the direction suggested by the assimilationist model of the department rather than that which might have been suggested by the notion of an associated state.

Algeria did not fit very readily into any of these categories, and its position was separately defined in the Organic Law of 1947. It represented a combination of a somewhat modified version of the departmental model with many features, peculiar to Algeria, for which parallels were to be found among the overseas territories, rather than in either of the other categories. Only on certain subjects were metropolitan laws to apply to Algeria automatically, though others could only be regulated by such laws. On all other subjects a special body, the Algerian Assembly, might decide to

[3] For the constitutional changes in 1946, see K. E. Robinson, "The Public Law of Overseas France Since the War" (Oxford, Institute of Colonial Studies, 2nd Edition, 1954) and, for their impact in West Africa, K. E. Robinson, "French West Africa," *The Fortnightly* (September, 1950).

apply metropolitan legislation, with or without modifications, or make regulations peculiar to Algeria. All such decisions required the approval of the metropolitan government; but if this was not given, the metropolitan government was required to notify the French Parliament as well as the Algerian Assembly. The three Algerian departments of Oran, Constantine, and Algiers remained departments but, unlike either metropolitan or overseas departments, the main public services were organized on an Algerian basis, under the Governor-General, who was also, as previously, responsible for the administration of the southern territories, which were to be "considered as departments." Algeria continued to have its own budget, distinct from that of metropolitan France or those of the three Algerian departments, and this was voted by the Algerian Assembly. For the election of Algerian representatives in the French Parliament, as well as for those to the Algerian Assembly and to the general councils of the three Algerian departments, the great majority of the recently enfranchised Moslem Algerians had been placed on one electoral roll, while Europeans and a relatively small number of Moslem Algerians had been placed on another. Each of these electorates was represented by the same number of members in each of these bodies, although, of course, the latter electorate was considerably the smaller. A similar system of two separate electorates had been established in most of the overseas territories; but any such differentiation between citizens was, of course, unknown in any metropolitan department or in the new overseas departments. This electoral differentiation between citizens, the limited extent to which French legislation automatically applied to Algeria, the special administrative régime existing outside the three Algerian departments, and the recognition of Algeria as a separate entity expressed in the institution of an Algerian Assembly, with quasi-legislative powers, and an Algerian budget, are all features which are difficult to reconcile with any contention that Algeria has been fully incorporated in metropolitan France on a basis of political and juridical equality in the same way as the new overseas departments.

What general comments does experience since 1946 suggest on the present and future viability of these different political structures set up in the French postwar settlement? The actual carrying through of assimilation, in the sense of complete political incorporation, in the new overseas departments as well as the considerably increased representation of the overseas territories in the French Parliament has resulted in an increasing appreciation that, if in fact departmentalization were ever to be completely realized in all the overseas territories, there would be almost as many members of the French Parliament representing overseas France as there would be French metropolitan deputies. There is also an increasing appreciation, at least on the part of politicians and officials, that in the twentieth century the political incorporation of overseas territories will be considered by the people of these territories to imply the extension to them of all metropolitan social-welfare legislation and the provision of social services on the same basis as in the metropolitan country. Indeed it would not be too much to say that, from the point of view of the new overseas departments, this has come to provide the most important motive in their support of assimilation. Since, however, social and economic conditions are vastly different, such developments have involved and are likely to continue to involve large metropolitan subsidies to the new overseas departments, as well as the application to them of social-welfare legislation which may be quite inappropriate to their actual social conditions. These practical disadvantages of "departmentalization" would, of course, be very much more pronounced if an attempt were made to apply this formula to the tropical African territories and Madagascar. The traditional objective of complete incorporation with France as an overseas department thus tends to appear to Frenchmen a less satisfactory solution to the problems of colonial policy than it once did, nor is it any longer claimed by the political leaders of the people in French dependent areas.

On the other hand, the attempt to define the character of the French Union and to fill out in detail the nature of the relationship with France implied in the status of an associated state appears, to a foreign observer, to have been much more seriously discouraging. In view of the strong centralizing tendencies characteristic of French political thinking, this would have been a difficult task in any event, but it was undertaken in circumstances which were bound to help confuse many of the issues: many controls, which in a desperately fought and bloody war the French could with some justice insist on retaining in practice, could with conviction be represented by ardent nationalists as proof that the "independence within the

French Union" accorded to an associated state meant no more than
the maintenance of French rule. What conclusions Frenchmen or
the inhabitants of other French dependent territories will draw
from this experience cannot yet be clear. Will they, like François
Mitterand,[4] conclude that the notion of an associated state is merely
the dangerously thin edge of a wedge which must inevitably lead
to total independence? Or will they come to distrust the legalism
which sought to define every aspect of the association (in particular
French juridical, economic, social, and financial rights) with meticu-
lous precision and which also resulted, to quote a member of the
Assembly of the French Union, in "a régime which, whether you
like it or not, recalls that of capitulations."[5] The final version of
the expression of this relationship of association—in which the
unconditional independence of the associated state was first proclaimed, and then an agreement, affirming their desire to associate
freely within the French Union as sovereign states equal in rights
and duties, concluded between the new associated state and France
—may, if other precedents are any guide, come to be considered,
at least by nationalists in other areas under French rule, as their
starting point in negotiations.

In these circumstances, it is not surprising that neither of the
two possible objectives for colonial policy which the Constitution
of 1946 set up should today seem wholly satisfactory models for
the future of the overseas territories or those in North Africa.
Although it continues to be asserted that Algeria is a part of France,
it hardly seems plausible that complete incorporation and organization on the departmental model will satisfactorily provide for
Algeria's future political status. As for Morocco and Tunisia, for
which it was certainly hoped that the status of associated states
would provide, their titular rulers have consistently refused to
accept this position; and, as it has now developed under the impulse
of events in Indochina, many Frenchmen may not be anxious to
see it applied to these two protectorates, in which France's direct
and indirect interests, strategic, economic, and human, are so much
greater and more widely felt than in Indochina. On the other hand,

[4] F. Mitterand, *Aux Frontières de l'Union Française* (Paris, 1953).

[5] A. Salvary, *Journal Officiel, Débats de l'Assemblée de l'Union Française* (February 13, 1950), pp. 55–56.

if the relationship of an associated state, as most recently defined, should be successfully developed in respect of Laos and Cambodia, it would no doubt come to provide a working model to which French opinion might be more inclined to turn.

As has already been remarked, the most intractable political issue in French North Africa is not the association of the protectorates with France in matters of foreign policy and defense or even the maintenance of their existing close economic ties. French claims to a special position in these matters have been frequently, if somewhat vaguely, admitted by many, though not all, nationalists. The basic problem is the future position of the substantial numbers of Europeans who have, since the annexation of Algeria more than a century ago, been encouraged to make their homes there: almost a million of them in Algeria, more than a quarter of a million in Tunisia, and some four hundred thousand in Morocco. Only in the Union of South Africa does European settlement on this scale exist elsewhere in Africa, and, in any consideration of French policy in this area, this significant comparison should never be forgotten.

Besides the pressures for modernization and equality which have been pinpointed as the central feature of nationalism, in the sense in which it is being used in this essay, nationalist activities in all three of the French North African territories have included other elements, and all these various strands have been of differing degrees of importance from territory to territory and from time to time. The extent to which they have resulted in separate nationalist movements or groups or been uneasily combined in one group has also varied. But in all three territories, there are backward-looking elements, deriving their inspiration from the rejection of Westernization, emphasis on past glories, and reliance on popular and traditional elements in Islam. There are also groups inspired more specifically by modernist reforming movements in Islam and emphasizing religious doctrines. There are Westernizing nationalists, such as Ferhat Abbas in Algeria and Bourguiba in Tunisia, whose original aims were directed to the achievement of some token of equality with or acceptance by the French and whose demands have become more uncompromisingly nationalist as the years have passed. There is a certain ambivalence about the pronouncements of these groups, due in part to their change of outlook through time, but also due to pressures from the other nationalist groups and the tergiversations of French policy especially since the war. Finally, there are groups more consciously aimed at mass discontents, such as the Movement for the Triumph of Democratic Liberties in Algeria, led by Messali Hadj, and some Communist-directed organizations.

The present situation in Algeria differs from that in the two protectorates in a number of respects. Some Algerian nationalists have been imprisoned or banished, and their poor showing both at the elections for the Algerian Assembly, in 1947, and in the parliamentary elections, in 1951, has been claimed to be the outcome, at any rate in part, of administrative interference during the elections; [6] but the relative quiet which has characterized Algeria in recent years can hardly be wholly accounted for by such factors and appears to indicate, to some extent at least, a greater degree of acquiesence in the present régime than is to be found in the two protectorates. Moreover, it is not possible in Algeria, as it is in Tunisia and Morocco, to appeal to the formal recognition of its continuous existence as a national state, which is implied in the protectorate treaties and the maintenance of their respective rulers and separate governmental machinery. It is more difficult to evaluate another factor in the relationship between France and North Africa which predominantly concerns Algeria. For several decades now, large numbers of Algerians and other North Africans have found work in France. Although this migrant labor, largely concentrated in a few major industrial areas, formed the basis of Messali Hadj's original movement, the *North African Star,* and has recently been the source of much Communist activity, it can hardly be doubted that it increases the ties of many Algerians with France, as well as perhaps causing some politicians to consider the possible consequences were this outlet for surplus Algerian labor to be closed. The position of North African Europeans is also stronger in Algeria than in either of the two protectorates. Their absolute number as well as their relative proportion is greater; their present position is reinforced by their strong representation (fifteen members) in the French Parliament, by the overriding control of Algerian affairs which, inasmuch as Algeria is not a protectorate, there is greater expectation the French government will retain, and

6 Ch-A. Julien, *L'Afrique du Nord en Marche* (Paris, 1952), pp. 331 ff.

finally by the electoral arrangements which in effect ensure them equal representation with Moslem Algerians in all the representative bodies. Although these latter are rejected by the extreme nationalists, they have, nevertheless, been operated since 1947.

In Tunisia, successive attempts by the French government to give effect to its declared policy of the grant of internal autonomy by stages have run into difficulties on both sides. The French residents have seen in each of them a policy likely to result in the liquidation of their position and continue to maintain that any real transfer of power is premature. On the other hand, the Tunisians have become more and more suspicious of what they consider to be an unwillingness of the French to make any real change. They have seen in French attempts to ensure that the French residents in Tunisia should have a voice in the new institutions—which in practice has meant an attempt to ensure parity of representation of Frenchmen and Tunisians in municipal and government bodies—a fundamental limitation on Tunisian sovereignty, a perpetuation of the notion of "co-sovereignty," which they regard as a French usurpation. They have accordingly come to emphasize more and more insistently the need both for an over-all scheme of political development in which each stage would be precisely defined, as opposed to a mere reform, and the unequivocal recognition of Tunisian sovereignty in the establishment of all-Tunisian, as opposed to Franco-Tunisian, bodies. The reforms announced by the French in March, 1954, went some way toward meeting this latter point inasmuch as an all-Tunisian advisory assembly was established and the Tunisian cabinet included eight Tunisians and only four Frenchmen.[7] But on the vital question of the voting of the budget (the only real power the Assembly possessed) the members of an all-French representative body which was to advise the French Resident General were added to the Assembly, together with certain other members representing economic interests, in such numbers that, in this enlarged body, parity of representation of French and Tunisians was secured, while it was provided that the government might insist on a two-thirds majority for the rejection of its proposals. Although a leading moderate nationalist, M. Mzali, who had been a member of the

[7] Textes relatifs aux réformes promulguées en Tunisie, *Notes et Etudes Documentaires* No. 1855.

most nationalist cabinet since World War II (that of M. Chenik, 1950–52), was ready to form a government on the basis of these reforms, they were not acceptable to many of the nationalists, and terrorist outrages continued.

In Morocco, the position is more complicated and more difficult, though the basic issue is the same. In the first place, nationalist aspirations have been less widely diffused and essentially concentrated in the towns, and on two occasions in the last few years it has proved possible to rally the tribesmen of the hills to bring pressure to bear on the Sultan and indeed to bring about his deposition. Secondly, although Morocco is undoubtedly less developed, less Westernized than Tunisia, nationalist demands have been more violent and have consistently insisted on independence as compared with the internal autonomy which has mostly been the demand of Tunisians. Thirdly, while European residents are now said to number some four-hundred thousand, they are, in comparison with about 8 million Moroccans, a relatively smaller proportion of the population than elsewhere in French North Africa. Although Morocco is, of course, still less important economically than Algeria, its relative importance has been increasing rapidly, while its strategic importance has been signalled by the establishment of United States air bases. These various factors would in any case make it more difficult to arrive at a solution of the basic problem in Morocco than in Tunisia, but the situation has been exacerbated, some think irremediably, by the deposition of the Sultan in 1953 and the events leading up to it. But the demand for total independence, maintained by the Istiglal and apparently espoused by the former sultan is unrealistic in the sense that it could only be accepted by a French government after a major military defeat. The reforms,[8] to which effect was given by the new Sultan, once again sought to ensure French participation in the political institutions of the country in local government bodies and established the principle of parity of French and Moroccan representation in the major governmental bodies, the Council of Vizirs and the Council of Government.

In French North Africa, while there is an underlying problem of the over-all terms on which Franco-Tunisian and Franco-Moroccan,

[8] Documents relatifs aux réformes du Maroc, *Notes et Etudes Documentaires* No. 1827.

perhaps even in the long run Franco-Algerian, association will be expressed; and this is particularly likely to give rise to difficulties in Morocco. The immediate problems are thus the negotiation of a program for the transfer of real powers in internal affairs to a Tunisian or a Moroccan government, and the terms on which it will be possible to safeguard the interests of the French resident population. It must be recognized that the principle of equal representation proposed by the French, while unacceptable to most nationalists, nevertheless compares more than favorably with what has been done elsewhere in Africa in the face of similar problems of multiracial societies. On the other hand, it is clearly not possible to secure a sufficient degree of support or acquiesence from nationalists for such an arrangement, within the framework of the rest of the political structure, for it to afford a basis for future development. Neither the departmental model nor the notion of the associated state in themselves offer any solution of this problem. Unless, however, it is tackled immediately, the prospects of any long-term solution are certain to decline. To an outside observer, it would seem that in Tunisia, at least, there is still a prospect of arriving at a solution, since the need for co-operation with France in foreign affairs and defense is generally admitted. It might be possible to arrive at some solution of the problem of French participation in Tunisian institutions on the basis of a system of reciprocal citizenship if this formed part of an over-all scheme which would be capable of satisfying a sufficient number of Tunisians that real self-government, within a framework of continued association with France, was going to be brought about. Although the successful development of a form of Franco-Tunisian co-operation might no doubt have some repercussions in Morocco, the position there is basically more difficult. Mendès-France in his investiture speech [9] indicated his intention of resuming discussions in North Africa. Whether any French government will be strong enough to persist in any policy on the lines which seem essential, against the certain opposition of the French residents in North Africa and their lobby in Paris, or whether any way can be found of reconciling the legitimate need of the French residents to feel that their position is

[9] *Journal Officiel, Débats Parlementaires, Assemblée Nationale.* Seventeenth Session (June, 1954).

adequately protected with the determination of nationalists to establish the "sovereignty" of their countries—these must both be considered very open questions. It is not inconceivable, but time is running out.

In French tropical Africa, much of the period since 1946 has been taken up with digesting the changes made by the new constitution and the other measures taken just after World War II. These were considered by many of the African political leaders to have involved too many concessions to colonialism and too little real acceptance of Africans as fellow citizens, and much political activity has centered around attempts to secure further advances in this direction. In particular, in the first few years, attention was concentrated on the limited franchise established for Africans, the system of the two electoral rolls—one, in effect, for Frenchmen and one for Africans— and the question of equal pay in the public service. Substantial advances have been registered; the franchise was very considerably extended in 1951 [10] when the changes made by the new electoral law increased the number of African citizens entitled to vote in tropical Africa and Madagascar from some $1\frac{1}{4}$ million, in 1946, to some 5 millions, in 1951. The attack on the system of dual electorates has not so far been generally successful, but the extension in 1952 of the common roll from Senegal, where it was maintained in 1946, to Togoland will make further changes of this sort inevitable sooner or later. In the meantime the number of members of territorial assemblies elected by the African electorate (who were in every case already a majority as compared with those elected by the other, essentially French, electorate) was everywhere increased in 1952.[11] The Lamine Gueye Law of 1950, which sought to secure the application of equal pay to African and French civil servants, may not have been wholly effective in preventing the payment of special allowances to the latter, who are, after all, serving away from home; but it has considerably increased the African wage bill of the administration.

Political parties and their leaders have shown a marked trend toward a more moderate position, reflecting the rightward shift in French metropolitan politics since 1947. Apart from those parties

[10] Law of May 23, 1951.
[11] Law of February 6, 1952.

in the two trust territories that are preoccupied with the issue of the eventual reuniting of the British and French portions of Togoland and the Cameroons, it can be said that there are no nationalist parties, in the sense of parties openly campaigning for separatism or independence. On the other hand, there are many indications of the widespread preoccupation with the modernization of their countries and the demand for equality which characterize nationalist psychology. Indeed, the move from the more doctrinaire and more violent manifestations of this outlook was expressed most notably in the African democratic rally *(Rassemblement Démocratique Africain)* between 1946 and 1950. The moderate approach and greater willingness to collaborate with the administration is expressed in that party today or in Senghor's Democratic Senegalese Front *(Bloc Démocratique Sénégalais)*, which has also been characterized by an increasing emphasis on African interests and issues and, more recently, a greater preoccupation with the need for a larger measure of real power locally.[12]

Apart from the fact that the powers of the territorial assemblies are very limited even in financial and budgetary matters, where legislative powers are most real, in French West Africa and French Equatorial Africa the division of powers and functions between the component territories and the group as a whole has the effect of still further limiting not only the powers of the territorial bodies but also their revenues. The demand for greater real powers for the assemblies, and for a greater measure of association between them and the administration, in the person of the Governor or Governor-General, is still voiced in very moderate terms; but it has been made clear by Senghor and the deputies from other parts of Africa who are associated with him in the parliamentary group called the Overseas Independents (IOM) that they look to the development of a real measure of local autonomy within a genuine federation of metropolitan France and the overseas territories as the objective. They have declared opposition both to departmentalization and to the associated-state conception, and they

12 K. E. Robinson, "Political Development in French West Africa," *Africa in the Modern World,* in press. L. S. Senghor, "La Méthode et la Doctrine du Bloc Démocratique Sénégalais," *Marchés Coloniaux du Monde* (March 27, 1954), pp. 813–15.

express their aim in the phrase "an autonomous state within the French Republic."

The position of Madagascar is a most difficult one to assess. On the one hand, it is only sixty years ago since the last queen of what had been treated by both British and French as an independent state was finally sent into exile by the French, who had annexed the island. That this kingdom was essentially the organization of the people of the high plateau who had succeeded in imposing their rule to a varying extent on different parts of the island and that it had often degenerated into a cruel and bloody tyranny does not necessarily deprive it of the glamor required to provide a basis for backward looking nationalism. Moreover, even if it is true that there are numerous groups in the island whose material culture and economic organization vary considerably, it is nevertheless the case that they all speak one language and have many beliefs and customs which are closely related if not identical. Among the *merina* people of the central plateau, the most advanced and Westernized group, the recollection of their independence has never died; and there have been some nationalistic groups, both of a cultural and a more directly political kind. The First World War saw an alleged plot to kill the French organized by a group of this kind, and its leaders, pardoned in 1922, were among those who, toward the end of the Second World War, began to organize a new nationalist party, which was in fact formally organized in Paris in 1945. The candidates of this party, the Malgache Democratic Renovation Movement (MDRM), were elected to the French Parliament by overwhelming majorities in 1946. Their program was not very precise, but they spoke of Madagascar either as an "associated state" or a "free state within the French Union." A rebellion broke out in March, 1947, which, after the first few days, was concentrated in one area along the southeast coast and among people who were not of the *merina* group. The responsibility for this tragic disaster, in which French official figures put the total deaths at eighty thousand, remains obscure. Although the leaders of the MDRM confessed to having organized the initial outbreak, they later withdrew these admissions on the ground that they had been extorted under pressure. Whatever the precise degree of their complicity— and it seems probable they were responsible at least indirectly—there are two conclusions that it is necessary to draw. First, there are in Madagascar some of the elements from which a nationalist party can most easily derive inspiration: the consciousness of a historic past; linguistic unity; and a substantial measure of common beliefs. Secondly, although the memory of this disastrous rebellion may be likely to discourage any further attempts of this kind for some time, and the leadership of the party has been largely disrupted, the rebellion was extremely localized, and little actually occurred in the part of the plateau where the *imerina* live, or in most other parts of the island. Therefore, it would be unwise to assume that no such nationalist movement will ever rise again, although since 1948 overt political activities in Madagascar have been of a very moderate kind, largely preoccupied with social and economic problems. An announcement made in 1953 by the Catholic hierarchy suggests, moreover, that it would be a mistake to conclude that nationalism has disappeared. "Always wanting to give an answer to the real preoccupations of Christians and aware that there are many who ask themselves about the legitimacy of their desire for the independence of their country," the Madagascan bishops stated that "the church, like the natural law, recognizes the freedom of peoples to govern themselves"; and, later in the same statement, they declared: "we recognize the legitimacy of the aspiration to independence and also of every constructive effort to achieve it." [13] Nevertheless, it would be going beyond the evidence to conclude that it would be impossible to secure substantial support in Madagascar for a development on the lines of much fuller local autonomy within a federal relationship with France, provided such a development is not too long delayed.

What are the prospects of such changes in the political structures of the overseas territories being made? At the end of a lengthy debate on policy on the overseas departments and the overseas territories, the Minister of Overseas France made a statement on April 9, 1954,[14] in which he asserted that "it was without uneasiness that the Government could contemplate increasing powers for the local assemblies, in order to associate them more intimately with the management of the affairs of the territories." He pointed out that a bill was already before the Assembly to increase the powers

13 *Le Monde* (January 26, 1954).

14 *Journal Officiel, Débats Parlementaires, Assemblée Nationale* (April 9, 1954).

of the Territorial Assembly in Togoland, empowering it to make regulations for the application of laws and decrees when those laws and decrees included provision for such application, and to establish a "council of government," a body which would provide a liaison between the Assembly and the head of the administration which would be given some powers of decision. Similar arrangements were contemplated in the Cameroons and in West and Equatorial Africa. Arrangements were also in contemplation for the establishment of local councils in each of the administrative units, rural as well as urban, in each territory, which might have their own budgets, and would be similar to those already established in Togoland and the Cameroons. He also advanced his own suggestions for the main lines of future development. Parliament should reserve to itself the major issues involving the French Republic as a whole; the present purely advisory powers of the Assembly of the French Union should be extended to include legislative powers in certain matters specifically delegated to it, subject to the right of Parliament to review any such decisions; the territorial assemblies should be more closely associated with local regulations and should be able to reach decisions on any subject not reserved to Parliament or the Assembly of the French Union, though these would be subject to executive approval, as they would be effective only when issued as a decree; finally, councils of government should be established as intermediaries between the territorial assembly and the head of the territory. Although these proposals appear timid in some respects, particularly in regard to the financial powers of the assemblies, they are certainly in the right direction. If developments of this kind can be brought about without undue delay and if a larger autonomy within a genuinely federal division of powers could be recognized as the objective, it is not impossible that the desire for equality could be accommodated. It must, however, be recognized that the ideas put forward by Jacquinot are only a beginning, and it is essential that such an increase in local autonomy should be effected very soon if it is not to be overtaken by the development of more pressure of this kind.

One of the great difficulties which beset the French in dealing with these manifestations of nationalism, in the wide sense given to that word in this essay, is precisely that there are no models to which they can point to show what the ultimate objective is. However reasonable their attempt to build a larger multiracial unit, instead of adding to the numbers of small and doubtfully stable political units in the world, they are attempting this in a world in which new states are constantly emerging. They are thus subject to a sort of political "demonstration effect" in which, for example, the grant of independence to Libya and self-government to the Gold Coast increases the likelihood that more specifically nationalist pressures will develop in French Africa. A recent paper by a French West African student entitled, significantly, "The Only Issue—Total Independence," contrasts some of the relevant facts for Senegal and Libya, and concludes, not unnaturally, that Senegal is more ready for independence than Libya.[15] There is evidence that nationalist views of a most extreme kind are developing among students from French tropical Africa: it is always difficult to assess the significance to be attached to student attitudes; but we have too much evidence of the importance of returning students in nationalist movements in Africa, as in Asia, to neglect the marked impression that specifically separatist, African nationalism is marked in their attitude today, as opposed to the more assimilationist forms of the demand for equality which have up to now been current in French tropical Africa.

In North Africa, in tropical Africa, and in Madagascar, the conception of the French Union is faced with major challenges. Much of what was written into the Constitution of 1946 was inevitably transitional, particularly in relation to the overseas territories; important changes have already taken place. So far as tropical Africa is concerned, there do not seem to be major obstacles to a development of the kind necessary to contain and channel the emerging nationalist pressures such as would be provided by large-scale European settlement or by the basis for the development of separatist national feeling afforded by such factors as linguistic unity and the awareness of a historically distinct existence as these exist in Madagascar. But the beginnings of a more separatist kind of nationalism can already be detected; and, if sufficient satisfaction is to be given to the demand for equality within the French system

15 Les Etudiants Noirs Parlent. *Présence Africaine*, No. 14, pp. 144–84.

to channel this nationalist pressure into acquiesence in a multi-national French Republic, there will have to be some real changes in the distribution of power between France and the overseas territories to provide a real measure of local autonomy.

The North African problems are by far the most dangerous which confront the French Union, and in fact none of the conceptions included in the French Union structure deal with the basic issue of the terms on which a large and economically vital French resident community is to participate in political life in Tunisia or Morocco. The same problem exists in Algeria, and the existing dual electorate arrangements cannot be expected to survive indefinitely, particularly if other arrangements are made in Tunisia. This problem, which has not so far been solved in other similar countries, is rendered exceptionally difficult in North Africa by the protectorate status of Morocco and Tunisia, the importance of French interests in North Africa (not only economic but strategic), and the means by which direct political influence can be brought to bear on French governments by the Algerian members representing the French residents, not only in Algerian matters but in any relating to North Africa. Nevertheless, here too, time is running out, and if there is to be any hope of a long-term solution it will have to be agreed upon soon. As General Catroux has said, these problems "can be dealt with if France, for its part, grasps the importance of the political and psychological evolution of Tunisia and Morocco and satisfies their desire to manage their own domestic affairs, and if the protectorates for their part relinquish their attempts to deprive France of the right . . . to remain on their territory." [16]

[16] G. Catroux, "The French Union," *International Conciliation* (November, 1953), p. 236.

commentary

RAYFORD W. LOGAN

Howard University

Since I find myself in almost complete agreement with Dr. Robinson, I will indicate a point of difference, make what is perhaps an important addition, and devote the rest of the comments to French tropical Africa. I visited this area last summer, and Dr. Robinson states his most definite conclusion about it.

Dr. Robinson appears to have made the reverse of the medal more important than the obverse when he states that "the real issue, both in Tunisia and Morocco, was . . . that of the terms on which Frenchmen settled in those countries were to participate in any future autonomous government." Perhaps a more accurate statement would be that the problems of these associated states were rendered more difficult by reason of the presence of a large number of French settlers.

While the potential influence of Communism on African nationalism was mentioned, the influence of Islam in tropical Africa was overlooked. Alphonse Gouilly gave the following percentages of Moslems in the total population as of January 1, 1946: Mauritania, 95 per cent; Nigeria, 90 per cent; Senegal, 85 per cent; Guinea, 80 per cent; Sudan (which at that time included Upper Volta), 60 per cent; Ivory Coast, Dahomey, and Togoland, 10 per cent.[1] Another writer estimated that, in 1950, 77 per cent of the inhabitants of Chad Territory were Moslems.[2] The percentages have probably not decreased in recent years. The French government

[1] Alphonse Gouilly, *L'Islam dans l'Afrique Occidentale Française* (Paris, 1952), p. 291.

[2] Albert N'Goma, "L'Islam noir," *Présence Africaine,* Special Number 8–9 (March, 1950), p. 338.

has, in fact, been accused of favoring Mohammedanism at the expense of Christianity.[3] Christians in West Africa last summer condemned the French government for facilitating the pilgrimage by sea and by air to Mecca. They asserted that the returning pilgrim, exploiting his title of El Hadj, became both a cultural and a political agent for the Crescent. Al Azhar University, in Egypt, is generally believed to be the principal center for sending Middle Eastern Arabs to tropical Africa and for training Africans to join them in propaganda and agitation. A considerable number of Syrian and Lebanese merchants and money-lenders use their daily contacts with Africans to propagate Moslem ideas of brotherhood and equality.

The importance of Islam in Africa is twofold. On the one hand, the dynamic influence of Arab nationalist movements in French North Africa, the granting of independence to Libya, and the emerging self-government in the former Anglo-Egyptian Sudan can hardly fail to send a tremor through Moslem tropical Africa. Perhaps proposals to create a new French state of Sahara [4] stem in part from the desire to establish a buffer between North and tropical Africa. Second, as a French official in West Africa suggested last summer, a real danger to continued French control lies in a possible uniting of Communism and Islam.

The danger must not be exaggerated. It is a commonplace that the African Moslems are not true converts, that they wear their new religion only as an outer garment. But Gouilly makes the same comment with respect to Africans converted to Christianity.[5] In any event, the political influence of Islam is weakened by other factors. Many Syrian and Lebanese merchants and money-lenders are accused of overcharging Africans. Many "white" Moors consider themselves superior to Africans whose forefathers they once held in slavery. Nomadic Tuaregs, for example, have refused to accept African teachers for their children. Some African pilgrims to the Moslem Holy Lands have experienced discrimination, which they attribute to racial prejudice. Whatever the final assessment

3 Gouilly, *op. cit.*, pp. 247–66.

4 *Le Monde* (February 24–25, 1952), pp. 1, 3; *Climats* (July 16–22, 1953).

5 Gouilly, *op. cit.*, p. 274.

of the influence of Islam in tropical Africa, it requires careful and continuing study.

Dr. Robinson's uncertainty as to future developments in Tunisia and Morocco has been justified by recent events. But he is convinced that "there will have to be some changes in the distribution of power between France and the overseas territories so as to provide a real measure of local autonomy." I am in complete agreement with him that in this way, rather than in political integration in the French National Assembly, lies the future of French tropical Africa and perhaps of Madagascar.

The number of deputies from these territories, 39 out of 627, is too small to exercise a decisive voice in legislation. Some of them are Frenchmen and some are Africans. These overseas deputies vote with their respective parties from the extreme left to the extreme right. More important than the absence of a sizable overseas bloc is the fact that metropolitan France simply is not going to permit African and other non-metropolitan deputies to determine French policy on EDC, the Schuman Plan, the Saar, North Africa, and a host of domestic questions.

Many French Africans, including students in Paris, recognize this fact. But by the same token an increasing number is demanding the right for the territorial assemblies to settle problems that have little or no direct bearing on French foreign or domestic policies. It was the French National Assembly which decided that only Togoland, like Senegal, should have a single electoral roll for the election of members of the territorial assemblies. The National Assembly fixed the ratio between Africans and Frenchmen in these assemblies. The National Assembly postponed definition in 1951–52 of the powers of these assemblies and voted the new labor code for them. The National Assembly will determine which and how many of the municipalities in tropical Africa will be fully elected or partly elected and will be permitted a mayor with administrative powers. The recent proposal to grant to the Assembly of the French Union legislative powers is not satisfactory even though it has proportionately a larger number of overseas deputies than has the National Assembly.

Spokesmen for tropical Africa are increasingly demanding not only more control by the territorial assemblies over budgetary, financial, and regulatory matters but also final authority on such political, economic, and social matters as those enumerated above. These larger questions are becoming more urgent as a result of the increase in the number of French settlers, especially in the Ivory Coast. Almost every plane and boat bring "petits Français" who compete with Africans for jobs. Some Africans received 6,000 West African francs, about $35 a month, for doing the same work for which Frenchmen received almost four times as much. Sometimes Africans were discharged after training Frenchmen for a job. In the large department store, Pariscoa, in Abidjan, all the salespeople were French girls. Spokesmen for African workers demanded the complete and immediate application of the new labor code, especially the forty-hour week. Spokesmen for the Chambers of Commerce in Dakar and Abidjan, on the other hand, vehemently berated the "stupid" members of the National Assembly for trying to introduce a labor code that would, they asserted, surely lead to bankruptcy.

African trade-union leaders are therefore beginning to join African political leaders and *évolués* in demanding the single electoral roll in all the overseas territories and final authority on political, economic, and social matters for the territorial assemblies. Some of these trade-unionists are also beginning to seek the election of members of the territorial assemblies who will be their representatives. Since the CGT in tropical Africa is perhaps directly affiliated with the Communist-controlled CGT in France, Communists may find an opportunity to regain the ground they lost when the *Rassemblement Démocratique Africain* publicly renounced its affiliation. And in French tropical Africa the last letter in CFTC, the *Confédération Française des Travailleurs Chrétiens,* is *croyants,* or believers, so as to include Moslems as well as Christians.

What, now, is the outlook for the constitutional relations between French tropical Africa and the French Union? African spokesmen oppose "departmentalization" since it would not sufficiently increase their representation in the National Assembly, give the territorial assemblies the desired final authority, or assure the appointment of Africans to higher administrative posts. It matters little whether they achieve their aims through association or federation. Léopold Senghor, one of the most influential of the African overseas deputies, told me in 1952 that he envisioned the evolution of the overseas territories to associated states. In a speech at Dakar,

July, 1953, he urged a "France, not 'one and indivisible,' but one and divisible." [6] Self-government is the goal. Nationalism as defined by Dr. Robinson is beginning to find expression even in terminology. Old African *évolués* do not object to *indigènes;* the next generation prefers *autochtones;* the most advanced insist upon *Africains.* But neither terminology nor constitutional change leads at the present time to a desire for a complete break with the French Union or with France.

Finally, self-government for French tropical Africa would certainly sharpen the conflict between "Gold Coastism" and "Malanism." A solid belt of self-governing territories from Senegal to Jibuti would make it difficult for Belgium to maintain her policy of "enlightened paternalism"; Portugal her minimal representation of her overseas provinces in the Portuguese National Assembly; the Union of South Africa its policy of *apartheid;* Kenya, the Central African Federation; and Tanganyika their tortoise-like procession toward participation by the African majorities in their own government. There is already talk of a "Mason-Dixon line south of the Sahara." [7] The future of French tropical Africa therefore poses questions that are important not only for the French Union but also for the peace of the world.

[6] As reported by observers of the *Pères Blancs.*

[7] Eugene P. Dvorin, *Racial Separation in South Africa* (Chicago, 1952) , p. 183.

recent developments
in Belgian Africa

GUY MALENGREAU

Professor, University of Louvain

During its first thirty years as a colonial power, from 1908 to the eve of the Second World War, Belgium was able to pursue freely, continuously, and unhampered, a considered and prudent colonial policy marked by that patient empiricism so much in keeping with the Belgian temperament.

Since it was unnecessary to be preoccupied unduly with international public opinion, which was generally indifferent, or with the demands of native public opinion, which was as yet unformed, Belgium was able to devote its principal efforts to developing the economy of the Congo. There was great need of this, for despite its copper, uranium, and diamonds, the Congo with its calcinous soil and its five inhabitants per square kilometer, is a poor country whose national income after the war did not exceed 15 billion Belgian francs and whose ordinary state budget still hovers around $160 million per year.

The primary need was a transportation system. In order to assemble the capital necessary for this, great sacrifices, such as extensive land concessions, had to be made in the early years and human potential had to be put to work even though this involved taxing the natives, authorizing the recruitment of labor, and instituting compulsory cultivation.

Since Belgium was principally concerned with assuring a certain degree of economic prosperity for the Congo without which progress of any sort was impossible, it expected to postpone until later the

337

elaboration of new political and social forms. Native policy was aimed at maintaining the traditional structures, at least to the degree permitted by the inevitable weakening of native institutions under the stress of European occupation with its modern techniques.

The Congo during these thirty years might therefore have remained primarily a vast field of economic activity, despite the political and social preoccupations of the territory's administration, had it not been for the activities of the missionaries, whose influence was the greater since they comprised so large a percentage (20 per cent as late as 1948) of the non-native active population.

While certain schools patiently labored to train the qualified personnel necessary for the state and for business, the missions pursued their work of evangelization and mass education, achieving the extraordinary result of converting 40 per cent of the population to Christianity in two generations and of attracting to their schools about 50 per cent of the children of school age and more than 70 per cent of the boys. And this was done without seeking spectacular results or forcing the growth of some exceptional individuals, as would have been the case with a prematurely established higher education system.

Need I recall here that in educational matters Belgium has always considered that it is necessary to develop a broad and sound base of elementary instruction before passing on to secondary or higher education.

This example is characteristic of Belgian colonial methods. Uninfluenced by extremist theories or by preconceived ideas, unwilling to take any action precipitately, Belgium has always preferred a slow but sure evolution to brusque and rapid changes which weaken the whole structure.

The error of the colony's government was, no doubt, to rely almost exclusively on European mining or agricultural enterprises for the economic vitalization of the country, for these were more concerned with making their investments profitable than with assuring the stability of the Congo's economy.

By exporting its riches, was not Belgium running the risk of someday leaving behind a Congo that had been bled white, a Congo which in the long run would be poorer than it had been before?

King Leopold III, then heir to the throne, revealed his anxiety in this regard in 1933, when he reproached some of his compatriots for believing that the future of the Congo rested solely on the prosperity of private businesses and for not attaching sufficient importance to the development of native agriculture, "to the establishment of a peasantry in the most integral form possible, allowing the native to acquire private property and to enjoy the economic freedom guaranteed him by our colonial charter."

The world depression, by revealing the extreme fragility of the Congo economy, had been a serious warning. But it was difficult to escape from administrative routine and the pressure of private interests. The inertia of the natives themselves presented an equally formidable obstacle. While the *Union Minière du Haut Katanga* continued to export copper, the *Forminière* to export diamonds, the *Géomines* to export tin; and while oil drums and cotton bales were piling up at the port of Matadi, the colonial government quietly pursued the paternalistic role which has been, to the present time, one of the essential characteristics of Belgium's colonial methods.

World War II was to transform the situation completely in a few years. Although the Congolese contributed heavily to the war effort, we must remember that the hostilities brought substantial profits to the Congo and speeded up an evolution which till then had maintained the slow and sure rhythm favored by prudent and wise administrators.

The intense economic activity of the war years; the efforts demanded of the population, particularly in harvesting rubber and producing strategic minerals; the stationing of a native expeditionary corps in Egypt, the Middle East, and Burma; the spectacle of dissensions among the colonizing powers; the withdrawal from the tasks of native policy by the officials of the territorial service called on to dedicate all their efforts to the war; the complete breakdown of communications with metropolitan Belgium—all these factors in a few years transformed the Congo. Those who, like myself, had known the Congo on the eve of the war and saw it again six years later had difficulty recognizing it. The prodigious development of industrial and urban centers had been accompanied by a profound change in native mentality.

The anxiety and insecurity into which the disintegration of his traditional social patterns had plunged the native was compensated for to a great extent by the constant solicitude of a paternalistic administration. The latter had succeeded without difficulty in winning the unquestioning confidence of the natives, always in quest of a father or mother on whom to rely; and their filial attitude accorded full well with a state of total dependence that eliminated the need to exercise initiative or to concern themselves about the future.

War had assuredly not raised the prestige of Europeans. And in addition to this loss of prestige, a certain disaffection had grown up between colonials and natives. Brought by force of circumstances to increase the production of raw materials requested by the Allies, exhausted by a prolonged stay in the tropics, kept at home in the evening by wife and children (a different situation from that of the bachelors of previous years), the majority of the Europeans had let their man-to-man contacts with the peoples of the interior slip and had relaxed their solicitude toward the natives. The bitterness on the part of the natives at this was the sharper since, being no great individualists, they had difficulty accepting solitude and abandonment. "The Whites don't like us any more," they were saying after the war; and the administration, knowing how easily hatred can spring from confidence betrayed, looked uneasily on the strangely unsmiling faces of the Negroes.

On the other hand, the effort required of the peoples of the interior had emphasized the dislocation of the traditional social forms. Enforced statutory labor had weighed on the mass of peasants more than ever before, and their exodus to the cities was taking on disquieting proportions. In 1939 Leopoldville had a population of 40,000. In 1945 the number was approaching 100,000, and today it is near 300,000. This exodus to the town, the growing number of natives employed in white-collar jobs, and the progress of education which some people consider to be too bookish, suddenly brought to the fore the problem of the évolué and his growing discontent. These évolués are individuals who, having lost confidence in what we might call the Bantu order of things, are seeking to regain their internal equilibrium through the assimilation of our Western culture. This cannot be done overnight; hence their bitterness and sense of deception, which are more deeply felt because their progress has provoked manifestations of the "color bar." This latter development seemed to be supported by previously enacted discriminatory legislation. Such discrimination, which was justified at first by the widely differing levels of culture, was becoming intolerable for those Africans who had attained a high degree of civilization and whose mores, habits, manner of living, and even ways of thinking were daily approaching those of the Europeans.

Another sequel of the war was the somewhat artificial development of a native trade-union movement, which the government, however, succeeded to a large degree in channeling. European employees, whom isolation from the mother country protected against forced repatriation, had taken advantage of their situation to unionize and at the same time to foster the organization of native unions capable eventually of giving weight to the European workers' demands. The measures taken by the government to prevent the native unions from becoming subversive in character and the natives' ignorance of the aims and methods of unions went a long way toward discouraging most of these initatives. But the movement did exist and the paternalistic attitude toward labor relations was growing obsolete.

Lastly, we must indicate the growing agitation undertaken by a minority of settlers supported by nearly all of the Congo press. This minority has not only made continual appeals for government aid to save their marginal undertakings from disaster but has also begun to agitate for greater Congolese autonomy and for participation by themselves in the councils of the government which they accused of showing too great a partiality in favor of the natives.

Such was the situation in the immediate postwar period. The Belgian colonial authorities had difficult problems to face; and it is the solution of these problems which preoccupy them today.

Their first concern was to try to remedy the extreme vulnerability of the Congo's economy which is a result of the insufficient internal market and of the economic hemorrhage resulting from the volume of exports. When we recall that the duties and taxes imposed on the *Union Minière du Haut Katanga,* whose production is almost exclusively for export, made up a third of the 1952 Congo budget, we can realize to what extent this budget, on which all the public services of the colony depend, is at the mercy of export factors.

Even before the war the legislature had decided to free from taxation those profits of colonial companies which were to be reinvested internally. But occasional steps likely to favor the industrialization of the country indirectly were not enough. Efforts on a vast scale were needed. Thus the ten-year plan, worked out in 1949 and begun in 1950, came into being. The plan provided for new investments amounting to approximately 50 billion Belgian francs, half of which was to come from public sources and half from private. Since then, public participation has reached more than 40 billion francs. The public investments provided for in the ten-year plan were destined for the amelioration of transportation facilities (12,712 million francs of the original amount), for the construction of electric power stations (1,909 million francs), for scientific equipment and public services (1,865 million francs), for water facilities (1,052 million francs), for the development of native agriculture (1,388 million francs), for education (1,338 million francs), for hygiene (1,978 million francs), and for the extension of tenant-farming (586 million francs). The execution of the plan is proceeding normally and its provisions have already been largely surpassed. By December 31, 1953, more than 15 billion francs had already been earmarked, of which more than 11 billion francs had been invested. The repercussions of the plan on the economic and social expansion of the Congo are not doubtful. The industrialization of the Congo is proceeding rapidly; it has doubled in the course of the last five years and is six times the prewar figures.

Moreover, the government of the Congo has engaged resolutely in a program of increased wages for the natives. This project has been opposed by some employers who plead the low production of native labor and wish to subordinate an increase in wages to an increase in the productivity of the worker. The government has not allowed itself to be turned away by these objections, since it is convinced that an increase in productivity can proceed from the higher wages and that these raises are the only means of bringing enterprises to economize on labor and to make a serious effort toward the rationalization and mechanization of their operations. Thus the average wage of the native worker, with adjustments for monetary differences, is almost five times that of 1939. This increase has taken place especially since 1948.

One index of the growing importance of the internal market can be found in the fact that the economic development of the colony has been proceeding gradually during the last few years, while since 1951 world markets have manifested evident signs of weakness. The collapse of the prices of oil-producing crops, whose importance in the prewar Congolese economy is well known, was barely felt by the economy as a whole. If it had occurred in the inter-war period, it would have had an immediate and catastrophic repercussion on the economy of the Congo.

Another indication of the importance of the internal market is the success of the 2 billion franc loan launched in January, 1954, in the Congo and immediately subscribed. From the 15 billion francs it attained in the immediate postwar period, the national income of the Congo reached approximately 40 billion francs in 1952.

It seems at present that the Congo is going to be able to escape the normal fluctuations imposed on it by its position as a raw-material exporter. This is a remarkable result obtained in a few years, and it deserves to be noted.

I noted previously that one of the consequences of the war was an increasing movement of the rural population away from the traditional areas. While in 1938 the native population residing outside the traditional areas amounted to 851,578, or 8.33 per cent of the population as a whole, in 1946 the number had reached 1,589,195, or 14.9 per cent, and in 1954, 2,586,919, or 21.51 per cent of the total population. This last figure represents 32 per cent of the taxpayers, i.e. of the adult and healthy males. These percentages would be even higher if calculated only on the basis of the men between the ages of 20 and 35.

This migration threatened to create a dangerous disequilibrium between the industrial centers and the countryside, and ultimately to deprive the former of their source of food. At the same time the proletarianization of the natives, of which the Duke of Brabant had warned the colonial government as early as 1933, was increasing.

A reaction was needed. In order to awaken interest in country life, it was necessary first to reduce the obligatory labors in the public interest which weighed heavily on the people of the interior and which the war effort had increased, particularly with regard to the upkeep of the road system. Very strict directives were issued for the utilization of machinery and for the execution of these works by paid labor as much as possible.

It was especially necessary to assure the peasants a sufficient income by increasing their productivity without seeming to constrain them. At the same time, exhaustion of the soil, the danger of which was being felt in some regions, would have to be avoided.

Thanks to the efforts of the INEAC, whose important role in agronomic research need not be restated here, and thanks to the initiative of certain colonial business firms like the *Compagnie Cotonnière Congolaise,* a *paysannat indigène* (or settlement system for African agricultural communities) was instituted in many sections of the colony. This system is a plan of native colonization directed and sustained under government auspices.

The system, inspired largely by the traditional methods of native cultivators, consists simply in delimiting a certain area of sufficiently fertile land, in grouping therein the fields of the native cultivators along a rectilinear base, and in making them carry out a given program following agricultural methods capable of safeguarding the fertility of the soil and even of increasing its productivity. This formula was put into execution on a vast scale. There were about 140,000 divided plots at the end of 1953. The colonial government foresees the extension of this *paysannat* system to about 400,000 native families.

It is too early perhaps to say whether this system is capable of assuring real prosperity for the native peasantry, but it has generally been welcomed by the interested parties and at present is substantially increasing their incomes. Just a few years ago the value of these incomes was a few hundred francs, while today they attain 8,000 to 9,000 francs.

But this formula by itself would certainly be insufficient if it were not coupled with production and consumption co-operatives permitting the native to sell his crop at a good price and to acquire his necessary tools at the best terms. This was the origin of the decree on native co-operatives of August 16, 1949. At the end of 1952 there were forty-eight such co-operatives comprising approximately 75,000 members. These co-operatives have not yet produced all the results we could have expected, and the revision of the 1949 decree is under way at present.

Among the efforts to ameliorate the situation of the rural population, we must emphasize the activities of the *Fonds du Bien-être Indigène* (The Fund for Native Welfare). The Fund was established after the war to compensate the population of the interior for the exceptional effort which had been asked of it during the war years. The Fund possesses a capital of a little more than 2 billion francs contributed by Belgium and the full profit of the colonial lottery, which permits it to spend each year about 300 million francs. In the six years since it began functioning, the Fund has undertaken expenditures totalling 1,696,146,375 francs. This amount is divided as follows, after deductions for administrative and investment realization costs: 775 million francs for medico-social activity; 308 million francs for equipping native rural collectives, of which 219 million francs went for their water supply; 313 million francs for teaching and for educational and cultural activity; 145 million francs for the rural economy. The Fund carefully concentrated its efforts in areas where they would be particularly efficacious. The equipping of native collectives comprises ordinarily the creation of social centers, the providing of a water supply, anti-insect campaigns, the seeding of ponds and streams, the development of livestock breeding, the improvement of means of communication, etc.

Though these many interventions designed to better the lot of the rural population might limit the migration to urban centers, it was still necessary to prevent the education received by an important percentage of the youth of school age from turning them away from agricultural occupations, as it was frequently accused of doing before the war. The reform of 1948 made a distinction between the education of the mass, in which an attempt is made to inculcate a taste for agricultural or artisan pursuits, and that of students selected on the basis of a higher mental endowment and expected eventually to continue to secondary or higher education. This reform, though excellent in principle, has not produced all the results expected, since the selection is made at the end of the first primary grade, at an age when the capacities and deep aspirations of the young student cannot be definitely ascertained.

Finally, we must note one more factor which is capable of stabilizing the Congolese economy. This is the creation of a savings bank by a decree of June 10, 1950. The success of this bank among the natives has exceeded expectation. At the end of 1954, two years after it had begun operations, the bank had opened 170,000 accounts for natives alone, containing more than 150 million francs. Total deposits were in excess of 1.5 billion francs. Needless to say, a bank disposing such a large capital fund can play a considerable role in the financing of socially useful enterprises.

All these measures tend to limit the overpopulation of the towns and to preserve the rural *milieu,* but they do not solve the labor-shortage problem which is still hampering many Congolese enterprises. In practice the government has given up the recruitment percentages authorized in 1925. High wages and all the attractions which the towns assume in the eyes of the natives are enough to bring the available labor to the industrial centers. There are few bush natives not tempted by the material advantages of the wage workers. Still it is not easy to satisfy the demand. The government has created in Brussels a special labor commission whose task is to outline the general framework for a labor policy. So far the work of the commission has not resulted in practical conclusions.

Meanwhile, certain businesses have made serious efforts to stabilize their labor force and the *Union Minière du Haut Katanga* has obtained surprising results in this regard. In 1950 only 24 per cent of the workers had less than three years of seniority, while 46 per cent had been employed by the *Union Minière* for more than ten years. The remaining 30 per cent had three to ten years of service.

In brief, the Congo is being progressively oriented toward a saner economy implying the existence of an internal market sufficient to lessen the effects of a sudden fluctuation in external demand. There is still a long way to go and many obstacles to overcome, but the business sense characteristic of the Belgian people will be of considerable advantage to the colony.

Such are the principal postwar innovations on the economic level and particularly with regard to the native economy. The colonial government has had to face other problems whose solution appears infinitely delicate. These are less susceptible to direct action because of their social character and because they have roots deep in the human soul which, in sub-Saharan Africa, has been so little explored.

Let us give some thought here to what we have called the problem of the *évolués.* Those who took the trouble after the war to seek out the basic reasons for the anxiety felt by the natives who had been at least superficially influenced by Western civilization came to the conclusion that this anxiety was the manifestation of a certain hopelessness. The legislative discrimination between natives and non-natives, the social barrier separating the two races, the actual exclusion of natives from supervisory positions, the caution with which natives were admitted to higher education—all this gave the educated native the belief that the colonist was deliberately preventing him from achieving civilization in the Western sense. Most of the educated natives aspire with all their being after a Western way of living, for although they may not always appreciate its true values, they consider it an assurance of success, and even more a source of privileges. In order to hasten their social rise, they are ready to repudiate those very values that they carry with them from their heritage and which constitute their true *génie*. To disappoint their hope would be to remove the joy of life from them.

Yet discriminatory legislation, caution in granting the natives higher education, and paternalism itself have never implied any wish on the part of the Belgian colonist to maintain the African indefinitely in a state of subordination. But even so, the educated native felt his confidence shaken and, blinded by his impatience as well as by certain foreign influences, he saw the star of his hopes fade. The government felt it to be its duty to restore the brightness of that star. I will not say that it has succeeded. Too much caution turns sometimes into cowardice. But on the other hand I cannot say that the government has not tried or that its efforts have been entirely repaid by failure.

The first measure taken to lessen the discontent of the *évolués* was the creation of a card of civic merit by an ordinance of July 12, 1948. Most of the educated were perfectly aware that their degree of culture did not permit their complete assimilation with the Europeans. But they did desire that the degree of achievement of the best of them be officially recognized and that their efforts be rewarded by a special status. They considered their position, juridically indistinguishable from that of the primitive peoples of the interior, intolerable. The Governor General therefore decided to recognize the existence of a special category of natives, leaving to the legislature the task of determining their juridical status. To these natives an official document would be given, i.e., the card of civic merit.

To receive this, a man must not be polygamous, nor have incurred certain penal sanctions specified in the ordinance. He must be 21 years of age—under certain circumstances, 16. He must be able to read, write, and do calculations, although exceptions are made for native notables, qualified artisans, and certain old workers. Finally, says the ordinance, a man must give evidence of good conduct and habits as a proof of his sincere desire to attain a more advanced degree of civilization.

Those who carried the card soon obtained the right to be judged, as they requested, by tribunals presided over by Europeans, and it was further decided that they could not be subjected to the penalty of flogging, which native tribunals at that time could still inflict in some cases. At the end of 1952, 485 natives had obtained the "card of civic merit," and the number is growing by 125 to 150 every year.

In 1947 the Minister of Colonies instituted in Brussels a special commission charged with studying the juridical status to be given to the civilized native population. The opinion of this commission was that the natives had to be convinced that the government had no intention of formalizing or institutionalizing discrimination founded on mere prejudice. Consequently, it was proper to look forward to a total assimilation with the European element of those natives whose complete Europeanization was attested by a tribunal.

The government felt that this was proceeding too rapidly. The government hesitated in beginning so radical an assimilation policy, mainly because it was not convinced that the status of the European population would necessarily be suitable for the native population, even if it were completely civilized. With its customary caution, the government decided on a gradual policy and took a series of legislative or regulatory measures eliminating from the laws all discrimination between native and non-native where such discrimination had lost its justification, particularly in the case of holders of the card of civic merit and of the *immatriculés*. The latter are natives to whom the provisions of the civil code apply because they have shown by their character and way of life a degree of civilization which implies an aptitude to enjoy the rights and fulfill the duties required by these written laws.

Since 1952 the *immatriculés*, like the holders of the civic merit card, and in contrast to their fellow natives, can benefit from certain forms of judicial procedure previously reserved to Europeans alone. On the other hand, they lose the benefit of other purely protective provisions, e.g., the *prononcé d'office* by the tribunal of restitutions and damages due to natives. They also have the right to enjoy all property rights contained in legislation without the safeguards established for the other natives whose inexperience might put them at a disadvantage. Other provisions were enacted in matters of transportation, access to public places reserved in principle to Europeans only, etc.

This is obviously only a beginning, and at the moment the colonial legislature is thinking of redrafting all previous legislation to make provision for the holder of the civic merit card and especially for the *immatriculés*. This would apply particularly in matters of penal law and judicial organization, in the matter of work contracts, etc.

Though there is no juridical color bar in the Belgian Congo—the discrimination still in force being justified on the cultural level —no one can deny that there does exist a racial barrier in social and personal relations. It was the government's task to do the utmost to prevent a separation of this sort from compromising the harmonious collaboration of all ethnic groups in the Congolese community of the future. In 1952 the government decided to admit native children with certain prerequisites of education and good character to schools reserved for Europeans, and to compel transportation companies to admit to first-class accommodations those natives willing to pay the price.

While the government was thus attempting to broaden horizons for the educated native with the aim of abating the disquiet which had arisen after the war, another problem demanded urgent solution. Any delay threatened to transform the great new settlements of natives into sources of disorder and immorality. The massive influx of population brought with it more and more critical housing shortages. The new city-dwellers were forced to crowd into lodgings never intended to house such numbers, where neither hygiene nor morality could easily survive.

On June 7, 1949, a decree established the *Conseil des Cités Indigènes et des Centres Extra-Coutumiers,* which was to create various bureaus primarily to construct housing units in the great native groupings. On March 30, 1952, this council was transformed into the *Office des Cités Africaines.* After prolonged hesitation, it set to work on a vast program of housing, with plans for tens of thousands of units, principally located in Leopoldville, where the shortage is more severe than elsewhere. It is at present building at the rate of thirty houses a day in Leopoldville. Thanks to a loan plan managed by the Treasury of the colony, it is possible to construct or to finance the construction of housing through the initiative of the natives themselves. More than 450 million francs of working capital is currently involved in this operation.

A slightly different procedure was attempted simultaneously at Elizabethville, where the native was invited to build his house himself with materials furnished on the best possible credit terms. This system has permitted the construction of thousands of dwellings and has temporarily solved the housing problem in this great city of Katanga.

This vast program of construction could not be conceived without a policy of urban planning. Thus the decree of February 21, 1949, was issued, giving local authorities more ample powers in this domain.

The number of social centers has been increased in these new population centers; there are more than 35 at present. One or two certified women social workers work in each of them, assisted by a graduate nurse. More than 55,000 native women visited the centers in 1952.

In line with these same social endeavors, we should note the effort made by missionaries, the government, and private organizations to occupy the native's leisure time with wholesome diversions. Many stadiums, some of which could rival the best in Europe, have been built in recent years. The number of auditoriums has been increased, and programs adapted to the native audience have been introduced on radio. In addition to the 115 stationary film projection apparatuses, 111 mobile units are in the service of the colony and are provided with some 900 films for the government's information service.

I mentioned that the war had brought about the development of a trade-union movement among the Europeans which was soon followed by a native union movement. One thing is certain (and all observers are in agreement on the matter) : the native workers understand only with difficulty what repercussions union action can have on the progress of the working class. Their filialism complements white paternalism, and this is one of the reasons why the natives show no inclination to join in a protective organization. Nevertheless, the formation of native unions was attempted after the war, and the government itself took the lead in regulating, through the ordinance of March 17, 1946, the creation and functioning of native professional associations. From another ordinance of May 10, 1946, native unions were born. The territorial administrator can sit in on all the meetings of the committee of the unions or the general congress, and he must be notified of the latter in advance. From this same ordinance arose the regional Commissions of Labor and Social Progress, which are tripartite groups comprising employers, workers, and representatives of the administration. Their job is to assure the protection and progress of the working class and to avoid management-labor conflicts. Local committees of native workers were also organized by the ordinance of March 17, and these are charged with enlightening the administration on problems touching the interests of workers of a particular region. Finally, native councils for each business have been set up which are to meet three times a year for the purpose of establishing and maintaining contact between individual employers and their native workers. These councils have had better results than the other organizations in the political and social education of the native workers.

This brings us to a final question, namely the political education of the natives and the preparation of the political forms of the future.

One thing is certain; the war has speeded up the disintegration of traditional political arrangements. As one proof of this I would take the increase in the number of "sectors." As opposed to chieftainships which were the traditional native divisions, sectors are administrative units more or less artificially created to replace the chieftainships when these became too ineffective a base for the administration of native interests. There were 1,212 chieftainships and 340 sectors in the Congo in 1938. At present there are 445 chieftainships and 509 sectors. Also, the number of organized urban groupings has grown from 28 to 45.

The inability of the traditional chiefs to insure the execution of administrative and governmental tasks is flagrant, as the official reports on the government and administration of the Belgian Congo for the last twenty years testify. This incapacity, due no doubt to a growing complexity of administrative problems and to the abnormal conditions in which the traditional authorities were called upon to exercise their functions, has led to increased intervention on the part of colonial authorities. The social and economic situation of the natives has not suffered thereby. But administrative paternalism has also resulted in discouraging the initiative and aggravating the inertia of the traditional authorities.

At any rate, new political structures were apparently necessary. It was at least the hope of the legislature, that the first experiments might be carried out in the new urban groupings. But the decree of 1931 had somewhat disillusioning results. Thus by 1945 most of these groupings, to which the 1931 decree had not been applied because they did not fulfill the desired conditions (particularly that of insufficient population), had to be organized along other lines. This amounted to maintaining them definitively under the direct administration of European administrators.

The government is perfectly aware that one learns by practice and that the political education of the natives is impossible unless they are given certain responsibilities and accorded an active share in the administration of their own interests. Unfortunately the native masses have difficulty in adapting politically; this makes the job of elaborating new political structures on the chieftain or village level particularly delicate. In every way it seems to be a long-term project.

Conversely, as certain concessions designed to lessen the discontent of the educated groups could not safely be put off indefinitely, the government of the colony took the decision to give certain members of the native elite a share in the exercise of colonial public authority. Since 1951 eight natives have sat on the Government Council; others are members of provincial councils, of the Commission for Native Protection, of regional commissions of the *Fonds du Bien-Être Indigène,* of consultative committees of the savings bank, not to mention the participation of natives in professional organizations, to which I have already alluded.

Though defensible for psychological reasons and from considerations of general policy, this measure was really a mistake on the political structure level. It amounted to beginning from the top what should have been begun at the bottom. What good is there in thrusting some individuals into positions of command without a corresponding promotion of the whole mass? What type of progress would there be if our colonial system were to disappear tomorrow to be replaced by the neo-colonialism of a native oligarchy? The Belgian colonial government is fully aware of this problem as is proved by the important speech delivered by the Governor General of the Congo at the opening session of the Government Council in 1952.

A reform of the fundamental document for native administrative organization (the decree of December 5, 1933) is at present being studied with a view to setting up councils on the local level in which the natives, the traditional chiefs as well as the new elite, may discuss their interests. It would be premature to discuss this here. At present in most of the territories there are consultative councils of natives functioning officially, whose task is to assist the territorial administrator in the exercise of his duties.

In Ruanda-Urundi the situation was different. Thanks to the prestige of the dominant class and to the client system by which the aristocracy held power, the traditional political forms had been maintained. The support which the Batutsi chiefs received from the government reinforced their authority though it could no longer be turned into despotism as was possible before. A policy of indirect administration would have been popular. To counteract the tendency towards despotism, Belgium has tried to democratize the existing institutions and to bring the native elite without the aristocratic Batutsi lineage to share in the exercise of power. This is the reason behind the important decree of July 14, 1952. While preserving the authority of the *bami* as this proceeds from custom and even extending their jurisdiction to areas previously reserved to the European authorities, the decree was careful to attach to each native authoritative office a council of notables. This council may, and in some cases must, be consulted by the authority in the exercise of its powers. This reform, the effects of which are already being felt, is a first step toward self-government in areas of Ruanda-Urundi and toward the democratization of the political regime in this region.

In judging that the moment had come to increase native participation in the administration of the Congo and Ruanda-Urundi, Belgium, while still faithful to its policy of keeping the elite in contact with the mass, also considered that it was time to create in

Africa an educational institution on the university level, open to native and non-native alike, to develop an intellectual and governing class that would eventually be capable of assuming the heaviest responsibilities of state.

The initiative was taken by the University of Louvain with the support of the government, and next October *L'Université Lovanium de Léopoldville* will open various departments and endow Belgian Africa with an important center of intellectual influence. Rather than adopt the easy solution of sending the Congolese to do their university studies in the mother-country, Belgium has preferred to avoid Africa's becoming a satellite of Europe in this domain. It has judged that in order to spread the influence of the culture it fosters, the university has to be located in the Congo itself, that the university has to be planted and grow in the soil which it is intended to enrich, in the way of the medieval universities of Western Europe.

When we examine the evolution of the Belgian Congo and Ruanda-Urundi in recent years, we find it difficult to discover spectacular reforms marking a radical turn from prewar policies. Belgians are a people of common sense, a profoundly realistic nation, whose constant guide is a cautious empiricism. If their colonial policy does not display evidences of boundless imagination or excessive boldness, its results do show stable and constant progress. Belgians have no colonial doctrine as such, for their faithful attachment to reality rules out preconceived notion. Neither the war nor the largely unjust criticisms of some international organizations has persuaded the Belgians to throw over their policy of common sense and prudence in favor of rash and apparently generous reforms from which the natives ultimately will be the first to suffer.

Let us admit that, so far, Belgium has not had to regret its attitude, although its tasks are far from easy, and in the relatively near future the evolution of the Congo will bring it face to face with extraordinarily complex problems. Not the least of these will be the political, juridical, and social organization of a pluralist society. For the number of European settlers has not stopped growing in the last few years and many now consider themselves definitely rooted in the soil of the Congo. Surely of the 80,000 whites residing in the Congo at the present time, no more than 6,000 or 7,000 could be called settlers in the strict sense of the term. But it is certain that their number will continue to grow as life in Europe becomes more difficult and as long as the Congo continues to offer only five inhabitants per square kilometer to compete with them.

The permanent establishment of a strong European minority will sooner or later pose the problem of integrating the two coexisting races into a homogenous political and social community. Such an integration will be difficult on the institutional level and on the psychological level, where mutual distrust arouses mutual fear. The natives fear that under the guise of an apparent generosity which would cause them to repudiate all racial discrimination in fostering their professional or other interests, the white inhabitants (whether imbued with racist ideas or not) may try to put off indefinitely representation for the native masses whose rise would place white privileges in jeopardy. On their side, the settlers fear that they will be engulfed in the overwhelming majority of natives and that they will see their labor and the capital they have invested reduced to nothing.

This problem is not of immediate importance for the colony as a whole. But it is already present in some areas such as Leopold-ville or Elizabethville, and the Colonial Council is presently study-ing a statute for towns where the presence of different races and the multiplying of interests have complicated the situation. This is especially urgent as the settlers have become extremely restive and are incessant in their demands for political rights. It is doubt-ful whether the future exercise of these rights, supposing they were granted, would allow sufficient consideration for the interests of the native population.

I think it is necessary to make one clarification which will go a long way toward explaining the apparent slowness of the Congo's political evolution towards self-government or autonomy, which astonishes some countries. Today, as it was fifty years ago, colonial legislation is worked out in Belgium and the Governor General receives his directives from the Minister of Colonies. The Govern-ment Council sitting at Leopoldville is a purely consultative body having no power of decision whatever. One might ask if this narrow political dependence of the Congo on Belgium is not in a way a survival of the unjust system of the "pacte colonial" or a new form of the now outdated "enlightened" imperialism of the last century.

Anyone who would see in this basic feature of its colonial policy

a proof that Belgium is pursuing its own interests in the Congo
to the eventual detriment of the colony's inhabitants would be
gravely mistaken. The affairs of Belgium and of the Congo have
always been completely separate and the colony's revenues benefit
the latter exclusively. No doubt it would be false to aver that
Belgium obtains no profit from its colony, but these are indirectly
acquired through the dividends that colonial companies distribute
to their share-holders. The revenues of the basic patrimony, the
product of taxes and tariffs, participation in the profits of mining,
transport, or other companies, in which the state usually holds an
important part of the stock, benefit the colony's budget exclusively.
It is well known, moreover, that the international status of the
Congo, as opposed to other colonies, does not permit Belgium to
grant itself preferential treatment. Belgian merchandise imported
into the Congo is taxed to the same degree as merchandise coming
from any other country, and when colonial opinion considers itself
in a position to denounce some measure in economic policy possibly granting an advantage to the mother country at the expense
of the colony, that opinion reacts immediately, vigorously, and
effectively. My point is that if Belgium persists in maintaining its
complete sovereignty over the Congo the reason cannot be the
substantial profits it thereby obtains.

The reason for this conservative attitude is very simple. I mentioned above the native's political incapacity. In reality, with the
exception of the Europeans and a minority of educated natives,
the great mass of the Congo's inhabitants are incapable of governing themselves. This will be so for a long time to come, because
the people are incapable of controlling their leaders or of choosing
them with any foresight. To enlarge the political rights of the
colony's inhabitants would be in reality to abandon the fate of
millions of natives to a handful of men whose interests are often
in opposition to those of the bulk of the population for whom
Belgium's guardianship is today the only protection.

If the Belgian colonial government has not been willing to enlarge the powers of colonial assemblies despite the repeated demands
of European colonists, the reason is that it has no intention of ever
abandoning to any assembly whatever the administration of the
interests of a specific area so long as it does not possess sufficient
guarantees that this assembly, by its very composition, is serving

the general good and is not in the pay of some faction. In fact, for lack of politically mature natives, a local assembly would give a fatal advantage to European or colonial interests. Now Belgium has no reason to favor one category of the population over another. It is in the Belgian Parliament, in the Colonial Council sitting in Brussels; it is with its officials trained in the mother country and ultimately responsible to the metropolitan public authorities that the 12 million natives of the Congo and the 4 million natives of Ruanda-Urundi find their protection. Belgium cannot in conscience deprive them of it as long as they have not received a political education sufficient to ensure that they can themselves protect their rights. This political education will take a long time and it will serve no purpose to wish to hasten it.

We must not forget, as King Leopold III said twenty years ago, that "the native constitutes the basis of the prosperity of any colony and that the betterment of his moral and material conditions of life is the primary task that we have to accomplish in Africa."

commentary

WILLIAM UGEUX

Editor, La Cité Quotidien

My friend Guy Malengreau has just expressed the opinion of a university professor considered in our country (Belgium) to be one of the best informed and most independent observers of our colonial problems. With good, solid documentation behind him, he has told you what is, fundamentally, the feeling of most Belgians who are interested in the Congo's problems, whether those Belgians live in Africa or in Europe.

To comment on, and weigh up Guy Malengreau's essay, the Editor, C. Grove Haines, has called upon the man in the street, someone who has neither long years of study nor exceptional documentation to enable him to do it. For I have nothing to offer but common sense and the professional solicitude of a journalist who has never thought that he could neglect any aspect whatever of the prodigious adventure in which the Belgian community in Africa has been engaged since before 1909.

One thing is an established fact: the Belgian Congo is, in 1954, a happy colony. Most of the travelers who cross Africa make the remark that both blacks and whites in the Belgian colony are active, industrious, and confident in the economic and political system in which they collaborate. But both whites and blacks, at least those of the latter who have reached a point of education enabling them to express a considered judgment, are aware that the future development of the native community, of the white community, or of the mixed community which may be born from the first two, makes some considerable changes and planning necessary.

Mr. Malengreau has told you of the very appreciable material, moral, and political progress made in the course of recent years. Before tackling the problems which, to my mind, claim our attention in the Congo, I should like to comment on one or two points in Mr. Malengreau's article.

Since World War II, said Mr. Malengreau, and partly because of the war, Belgium has been led to encourage profound changes in its African colony. These changes fall into four categories: the first concern the economic balance of the country; the second extend their effects over both the economic and the social plane; the third are purely social; and lastly we find a considerable political evolution.

Economically, we note a wise investment policy, the requisite action for raising the natives' wages, and the creation of a domestic market to compensate for the disturbance of the economic balance of the country by the jolts of the international prices of the raw materials it exports.

The picture seems to me to be perfectly correct. But I am afraid it is easy to deceive oneself regarding the upward movement of African wages. I know everything that can be said concerning the almost nonexistent productivity of most of the black workers in the Congo. I know, too, that family organization, even in centers outside of tribal law, requires that native wages be increased only to the extent that one can so organize things that this increase becomes an encouragement to productivity. It is too often a subsidy keeping a gang of idle relatives around the wage-earner. Nevertheless, one sometimes has the feeling that these weighty arguments are particularly precious to employers who are disinclined to increase their production costs. For in fact, though native wages have appreciably increased since 1940 throughout the country, there are independent observers who estimate that for the same amount of work purchasing power has slightly gone down, especially in industrial centers. In any case, very considerable efforts remain to be made by the state and by the economic powers in order to right the elements of indirect wages. As regards transport, for example, or as regards power, the situation could certainly be better. The often deplorable conditions in which the black worker lives constitute a heavy brake on the development of the domestic market, which in many respects is still in its infancy.

Recent developments in the social fields have been considerable. The experiment of the peasant body and native co-operative societies, the welfare fund, the guiding of basic teaching toward agriculture, the creation of a savings bank, and the measures intended to create skilled labor and stabilize unskilled industrial manpower are recent. None of these is immaterial. Nor have any of them developed sufficiently for us to be able to pass enlightened judgment on them. I share Mr. Malengreau's uneasiness as to present results of the native co-operative societies. Yet the experiment is being made under good conditions.

The traditional social structures of native society—if indeed one can speak of society on the one hand and consider, on the other, that the situation of one tribal group is comparable to that of another—are being broken up. The necessities of the worker, the attraction of the big centers, the results of more or less generalized education, the concern of new generations to escape from certain tribal tyrannies—all these are combining with the action of the whites to precipitate this break-up. Thus, broadly speaking, we find ourselves today with, at one and the same time:

a. aboriginals very close to their original social structure, but geographically stabilized by the strength of the whites;
b. a mass of detribalized persons, in respect of whom Mr. Malengreau has quoted the ever-increasing figures;
c. an infinitesimal minority of persons who are called "advanced," or are on the way to becoming so.

None of these three groups is conscious of its collective development. Let us speak of those who are more "advanced" or "enlightened." They are tragically isolated among the whites, as they
are among their own people. Teaching and political action have
been working too long transforming the best of the aboriginals into
Europeans with black skins without accepting either the consequences of this evolution or the means of making it frequent and
deep. The material living conditions of the advanced persons,
despite a comfortable salary (sometimes even too high in comparison with the normal scale of remuneration) , are, generally speaking,
deplorable. The centers set up outside of tribal law only very rarely
offer them the means of living in the way which their evolution
makes desirable. The creation of the system of the card of civic merit
described by Mr. Malengreau, the setting up of a university at
Leopoldville, open to the Africans, and of an interracial college
at Usumbura are evidence that the colonizing power has become
aware of this drama. But to my mind this awareness is still heavily
braked by a series of traditional prejudices and by the blackmail
exercised on both colonial administrations and metropolitan public
opinion by certain settlers' associations. As a general rule, the spirit
of these groups is retrograde and basely reactionary. While I share
Mr. Malengreau's constructive views on the inopportunity of putting the aboriginal and the white unrestrictedly on the same theoretical footing, a system which would, in fact, be disastrous for the
native and for his evolution, I am very much afraid that the Belgians
and their administrations are sometimes letting themselves be influenced far too much by these noisy manifestations of the settlers'
spirit. The evolution of the Africans, as the Belgians conceive and
push it, will be infinitely slow. Perhaps it will be wiser than many
others. The order and prosperity of the Belgian Congo give solid
support in this direction to Mr. Malengreau's optimism. For my
part, however, I have an uneasy feeling that, in this action, the
"good colonizers" of the kind hoped for by him may arrive too late.
The Belgian Congo is not isolated from the rest of Africa. Advanced
and detribalized persons are already open to propaganda which is
sometimes well-intended, sometimes directly animated by the communist spirit. The result is that in proceeding wisely with their
education, without risking any precipitate action, one runs another
risk—that of being overtaken by the irremediable deformations of

a revolutionary and destructive evolution. In Belgian Africa today there is a need for an African radio with a large listening audience, for newspapers or publications with large circulations edited by and for the Africans; there are no aboriginal political or politically interested groups worthy of the name. The Belgians are afraid—understandably so—of a too rapid evolution. To my mind, the risk must be accepted and accepted at once. If not, by the day that we are ready to create these means of education and training, or to encourage them, it may be too late. We shall find ourselves faced with already existing movements manufactured by professional agitators out of hatred for the white.

The fourth part of Mr. Malengreau's essay deals with political evolution and is extremely subtle. Broadly speaking, and with all the infidelities which a summary entails in regard to a finely-drawn conception, our writer feels that a serious effort must be made to associate the aborigines with the management of elementary political societies in order to bring them progressively to share the complex responsibilities of general administration when they are ready to do so. Actually, the very opposite is being done. To appease the claims of the advanced minority, a few natives have been taken into the government council. Eight of them have been appointed since 1951. The same thing has been done for the regional councils, the savings bank committee, the natives' welfare fund, etc.—an unfortunate system, thinks Mr. Malengreau. It puts the cart before the horse—which is perfectly true. But this system was imposed by the very method of the Belgian colonizing action. By pushing a minority of Africans toward an evolution which has brought some of them to near-university level and a large number to the qualifications of an average clerk, one is condemned to beginning at the top a political amalgam which common sense would have begun at the bottom. But what else could be done, except to generalize and precipitate the evolution—with all the risks that that entails.

I think I have, at some length, gone over the ground which Mr. Malengreau has so remarkably illuminated. I should like to renew my expression of the modesty with which I tackle this discussion, armed only with the clearsightedness and information of a man whose job is to scrutinize or enlighten public opinion. For I feel that I must, in my turn, make a few remarks about the present situation of Belgian Africa.

For half a century the Belgians have economically valorized the Congo basin. They may be reproached with having too long abandoned to private initiative (by encouraging it, incidentally) a task of education and civilization which "the powers that be" sometimes made the mistake of considering as merely one of the elements of the economic development of the country. Fortunately, a few big economic groups, on the one hand, and the missions, on the other, have considerably limited the consequences of this error. Many people even feel that involuntarily this system of education has shown itself better and closer to the aboriginal than others. The results, anyway, are largely satisfactory.

Actually, the Belgian Congo today is prosperous and peaceful. It shines by comparison with most African countries. Its operational economy succeeded in getting it over its growing pains by limiting the effects on its balance of speculative fluctuations of certain world prices. The beginnings of a very promising domestic market form the present phase of this happy evolution.

Regarding public budgets and services, sanitary arrangements, and teaching, the balance is also satisfactory. But it will no longer be so tomorrow if in Brussels and Leopoldville they do not have the courage to visualize things on a much bigger scale than heretofore. Public investments in Belgian Africa are much too small. Experience has shown that the ten-year plan conceived recently has already been exceeded in all its calculations. Here is a serious problem. It certainly seems that Belgian financial efforts can be quite appreciably increased. To my mind, they cannot be increased sufficiently or quickly enough. The future evolution of Belgian Africa must be quick enough to cut short any temptation to political adventure for the aboriginal community. However—let us get this right—that temptation exists. It is grave and precise. And I would just point out that the protection of the country, the security services, and the observation of Communist agitators are all part of the public services which I said should be vigorously enlarged.

To get back to what I was saying, the criticisms, often simplistic, of certain international bodies create a complex of fragility which in recent years has chilled the enthusiasm of many colonizers. They have become more and more convinced that the whole world takes them for exploiters and wants to put an end to their action. This situation presents a serious menace to new large-scale, long-term investments in the Belgian colony. An appeal to international capital is an inevitable prospect, unless I am very much mistaken. But as long as the formula has not been found which will render such investments compatible with a reasonable protection of the rights acquired, of the relative but real sovereignty of the colonizing power, and with the economic autonomy of the new mixed community to be created in Africa, this progress will remain in doubt. A fact is stronger than a lord mayor, and the fact here is that the Belgians will be brought to preferring the risks of a slow, less costly evolution of which they will hope to remain the masters to the risks of a rapid evolution financed and, they fear (not without some reason), politically directed against them by international circles.

I would not like to say that the white problem is socially not the most urgent. The experience of the colonial bankruptcies of Southern Asia holds lessons on this subject which link up over the decades with the lessons of the end of the colonial era on this side of the Atlantic. For a long time the whites in the Congo were close to the native. They no longer are—even in local administration; even in the missions. Improvement in their living conditions and the birth on the equator of towns that recall our own, with all their comfort, have allowed the reconstitution of the families, communities, clans, and social classes of Europeans. Two large cities, the native Leopoldville and the white Leopoldville, are separated by a security zone desired by the Europeans. They are also separated morally, more and more so, despite some generous efforts, with the result that too many whites no longer know the blacks except in terms of manpower; and too many white women see them only as cheap domestic labor.

Outside the towns the situation is hardly better. Too many missionaries who went out to take the Gospel to the blacks have become part of the clergy for the whites. Young civil servants who went out to administer an elementary territory are nothing more than bureaucratic antennas, living in a flood of forms which come and go between them and the record offices, which make up a too large part of our African activity today. The problem has its technical aspects. Perhaps the administrative territories are too large; perhaps the staff is insufficiently trained and too liberally recruited. But it has serious consequences when these whites of the base have to hold out their hands to the traditional native authority to associate the latter

in political and administrative tasks. This problem of the evolution which leads the white through the phases of conqueror, libera-
tor, creator, builder, exploiter, teacher, doctor, and educator is
general in underdeveloped countries. Is it inevitable that at the
end of this evolution parasitic, degenerated communities are created
(thank God we have not yet come to this in Belgian Africa) in
which idle whites live in domination until the day when, ruined,
brutalized, and hunted, they see the work of their fathers destroyed,
stolen, or sacked?

The black social problem is also one which is not peculiar to the
Belgian Congo, whatever those "old colonials" may think and sen-
tentiously say who consider it extremist or scandalous that anyone
but themselves should have anything to say in the matter. Stripped
down to its elements, it is a traditional social problem. It is simply
liable to be deformed and corrupted by race-inspired reactions or
in Moslem zones by religion-inspired reactions.

The privileged classes in history have not behaved differently
from many whites. And it must be recognized that, on more
than one occasion, the precipitation with which revolutions accelerated the transformation of social structures stifled certain possibilities of nonviolent improvement. In dealing with the center of
Africa, the measure of the extent to which allowance must be made
for the reservations, reticences, and counsels of prudence of wise,
far-seeing men such as Mr. Malengreau is exactly the same measure
which must be applied to the statement of this fact: in retarding
by prudence evolutions which carry risks, one has always aggravated
these risks and rarely saved the situation.

I think I may say that neither those responsible for Belgian
colonial policy nor the Congolese high administration contest the
cogency of that. But both of them have to cope with the force
of inertia of the two communities—the black, who is not, as is too
often naïvely claimed, thirsting to obtain access to the degree of
civilization of the whites; the European who inevitably stratifies
himself in the defense of privileges which have not yet ceased, for
the most part, to be highly justified.

I do not intend to make any criticisms of those wise and prudent
people who warn against forcing the two together in a single unified
cultural society. They have on their side the exceptional authority
of our greatest colonial, Governor General Ryckmans, who very

wisely said twenty years ago: "With money and machines, a sky-scraper can be built in three months. But it takes a whole summer's sunshine to ripen a simple ear of corn. The civilization of a people is not the work of a day, nor of a generation; it is a fruit which demands a long time to ripen."

But there is one thing we too often lose sight of: it is that at the present time our work of civilization has become a race against the clock. Our field is no longer virgin. The question is to know whether we shall lead black Africa to free civilization or whether it will give itself to that tyrannic system which is unacceptable to us but which to so many underdeveloped people appears, through our own defaulting, to be the road to security and distributive justice.

That is the last point I have to make. We are behaving as rivals in Africa. We are not far from finding amusement or glory in the setbacks or misfortune of our neighbors. And the idea of sharing our experiences, good or bad, seems to us a culpable weakness in regard to our "rivals." Some of the greatest human experiments have been sunk in this way. I would express the wish that the great adventure of the whites' awakening of Africa to industrial life and to Western thinking may not have to suffer this undeserved ordeal.

the impact
of the United Nations on Africa

VERNON McKAY

School of Advanced International Studies

Not long ago two of Europe's best known specialists on African problems expressed in almost identical language a striking view of the impact of the United Nations on Africa today. The essence of what they said was this: If only the United Nations did not exist, Europe and Africa might be able to iron out their differences and disagreements in a way mutually satisfactory and advantageous to the peoples of both continents and to the nations of the free world. Although this attitude may be somewhat irrelevant since the UN does exist, it nonetheless represents a view that has attracted growing sympathy as United Nations debates on African issues have widened in scope and increased in bitterness. In any event, it serves the purpose of raising the question which is the primary subject of the following analysis, namely, the nature and extent of the United Nations impact on Africa.

To answer this question many other questions must be asked, some of which are fairly obvious. For example, in what ways have the 18 million people living in the seven African trust territories been affected by the supervision of the Trusteeship Council? Does the United Nations Committee on Information from Non-Self-Governing Territories help the 90 million inhabitants of nineteen other African territories under its study? What have the three million inhabitants of the former Italian colonies gained by the decision of the General Assembly to make Libya independent, to federate Eritrea with Ethiopia, and to establish a ten-year Italian

366

trusteeship over Somaliland? And how much has Africa profited from technical assistance projects of the United Nations and its specialized agencies, particularly the World Health Organization, the Food and Agricultural Organization, the International Labor Organization, and UNESCO?

Less tangible but equally relevant, and possibly more significant in the long run, are a number of other questions. To what extent, for example, does the United Nations incite political agitation in Africa? What effect on African political behavior does the Trusteeship Council have by sending visiting missions which hear the complaints and views of Africans, by the examination of thousands of petitions and other communications, and by granting a growing number of African requests for oral hearings? Will this awakening of Africans to their opportunities and capacities for advancement serve the world well by bringing the colonial relationship to a quicker end and enabling Africa to rise to its full potentialities? Or are the unbridled attacks on the colonial powers in the United Nations playing into the hands of extremists and jeopardizing the orderly evolution toward self-government now under way? Krishna Menon, speaking for India in the Trusteeship Council on February 11, 1954, called France's colonial history "a history of violence, of the suppression of freedom, of the negation of liberty, of the integration of territory, and of the denial of self-respect." Are such onslaughts useful in jarring the colonial powers into a fuller realization of the passion generated today by the idea of colonialism? Or does the irritation they arouse tend to rigidify the attitude of those attacked? For example, has UN intervention harmed Moroccan and Tunisian nationalists by stiffening the French position, and has the UN injured the non-Europeans of South Africa by strengthening the Nationalist Party in its *apartheid* program? Or are these only short-range reactions which will be outweighed by long range benefits? Meanwhile, is the inability of the United Nations to meet the demands of African nationalists disillusioning them in the value of international organization and leading them to the conclusion (if I may reverse an old cliché) that the Europeans only understand force? And to what extent is the United Nations indirectly aiding the Communists by giving the Soviet bloc an avenue for the dissemination of propaganda in Africa, and by stimulating dissension among the nations of the free world over the colonial issue?

From the scope and variety of such questions it is evident that an analysis of the United Nations impact on Africa is full of intangibles and is difficult to organize in a meaningful way. The impact is partly political and partly technical, partly direct and partly indirect, and it varies considerably according to the geographical area concerned and the United Nations organ involved. At the outset, it is clear that millions of Africans do not even know that the United Nations exists, and many Africans who are aware of its existence have an exaggerated idea of its powers. They do not appreciate the fact that the UN, except in unusual circumstances, is limited to making recommendations which cannot be enforced. Bearing these facts in mind, let us tackle the question by first analyzing the nature and extent of UN activities affecting Africa. We will then consider what the governments concerned have done to carry out UN recommendations, and, finally, I will venture a few remarks on the effect of the United Nations on the political behavior of Africa's inhabitants.

When the Charter of the United Nations was signed at San Francisco, in 1945, many people believed that the work of the United Nations in colonial Africa would be performed largely by the Trusteeship Council. It is evident, however, that this view underestimated the depth of disagreement at San Francisco as well as the powerful emotions generated by the idea of colonialism, especially in those emerging Asian states formerly under the rule of a foreign race. The three chapters of the United Nations Charter devoted to the advancement of colonial peoples were among the most difficult and among the last on which agreement was reached. In the light of the head-on conflict that subsequently developed in the United Nations over their meaning, it appears that agreement between colonial and anticolonial powers was made possible to a considerable extent by ambiguities and loopholes in the Charter. For example, Article 77 makes provision for but does not oblige states to place any of their territories under trusteeship. As it turned out, only certain territories taken from Germany in World War I, and from Italy and Japan in World War II were placed under trusteeship. Whether the attitude of the anti-colonial group would have been appreciably modified if all colonies had been placed under trusteeship is difficult to say. Conversely, whether the colonial powers would have placed other territories under trusteeship if they had found less hostility in the United Nations is also problematical. Whatever the cause, the anticolonial group began almost from the start a more or less constant if not systematic campaign to extend the colonial activities of the United Nations throughout the whole United Nations system in a manner which went far beyond what the colonial powers thought they had agreed to in the Charter. The extent and character of this proliferation of African discussions in the many United Nations organs, councils, commissions, committees, and agencies is an important development which deserves considerable thought.

Foremost among UN organs in its concentration on African issues is, of course, the twelve-member Trusteeship Council, which annually examines conditions in Cameroons, Togoland, and Tanganyika, under British administration; Cameroons and Togoland, under French administration; Ruanda-Urundi, under Belgian administration; and Somaliland, under Italian administration. Although these seven trust territories in middle Africa represent a relatively small proportion of the continent's total area and population, they nonetheless afford the United Nations an opportunity to study and compare the general objectives and methods of these four European powers. At every session the Council makes many recommendations to the administering authorities—many more in fact than did its predecessor, the Permanent Mandates Commission. Every three years each territory is also studied on the spot by one of the four-member visiting missions sent out annually by the Council. Public interest in the United States seems to have been most attracted by the Council's consideration of thousands of petitions and other communications, particularly the oral hearing of a growing number of Africans who have come to United Nations Headquarters from British Togoland, French Togoland, French Cameroons, Tanganyika, and Italian Somaliland. The petitions work of the Council has mounted to such an extent that a Standing Committee on Petitions, which now has to meet between, as well as during Council sessions, has been created to make recommendations to the Council on the disposition of each petition. Other committees of the Council have been created to deal with problems of special interest, including higher education, rural economic development, and what are called administrative unions, that is, administrative arrangements whch provide common public services for a trust territory and an adjacent territory under the sovereignty of the same power.

The Economic and Social Council, with its numerous economic and social commissions, is a second principal organ of the United Nations which discusses many issues directly or indirectly affecting Africa. For several sessions, until 1952, certain of the noncolonial powers in the Council pressed unsuccessfully for the establishment of an economic commission for Africa to parallel the existing regional commissions for Latin America and Asia. Today the Council devotes considerable attention to the provision of technical assistance to Africa, particularly the new and struggling state of Libya. Africa also comes in for a good deal of comment in the heated discussions of the right of self-determination in the Human Rights Commission. In fact, a delegation which wants to attack Belgian, British, or French rule in Africa as a denial of the right of self-determination can make the same speech three times: first in the Human Rights Commission, which reports to the Economic and Social Council; then in ECOSOC itself; and finally in the General Assembly, where the report of ECOSOC on this item is discussed in the third committee. In a recent issue of *Foreign Affairs*, Clyde Eagleton expresses the opinion that "The speeches go far beyond anything hitherto thought of in connection with self-determination; it is not merely independence which the speakers demand, but perfect satisfaction for all human desires. Furthermore, they would limit the claims to self-determination to colonial peoples only; and thus self-determination is made the basis of combination against the colonial Powers and against the domination of the white race." [1] Since these words were written, the noncolonial powers have gone a step further by pushing through the Human Rights Commission a controversial proposal to establish still another UN organ, which would "examine any situation resulting from alleged denial or inadequate realization of the right of self-determination, which falls within the scope of Article 14 of the Charter and to which the Commission's attention is drawn by any ten Members of the United Nations." If this proposal were approved in ECOSOC and in the 1954 fall session of the General Assembly, the thirteen members of

[1] Clyde Eagleton, "Excesses of Self-Determination," *Foreign Affairs*, Vol. 31 (1952–53) , p. 593.

the Arab-Asian bloc could, for example, bring before a UN commission the Moroccan, Tunisian, or any other African question they desired, with the allegation that it was a situation likely to impair friendly relations among nations as described in Article 14.[2]

In the Security Council, African questions have not thus far been a main preoccupation, although the Council has discussed the Anglo-Egyptian Sudan and considered the possibility of taking up the Tunisian question. However, the implications of the Indonesian case for Africa should not be overlooked. Perhaps the particular combination of political forces which made the Indonesian settlement possible may not recur in Africa. Nonetheless, Indonesia's independence is proof of the fact that the United Nations can build up powerful pressures in support of its recommendations.[3]

The fourth of the major United Nations organs into which African questions have made their way is the International Court of Justice, which has given an advisory opinion on the international status of Southwest Africa and a decision in the dispute between France and the United States over the rights of the latter in Morocco. Certain of the anticolonial powers may also revive their effort to refer the question of administrative unions to the Court for an advisory opinion as to the compatibility of such unions with the Charter and the trusteeship agreements.

The role of the Secretariat, a fifth principal organ of the United Nations, should also be mentioned. Despite the fact that they walk a tightrope on the emotional colonial issue, Secretariat officers have proved themselves not only competent but indispensable in enabling the United Nations to carry on its work. The delicacy of their position is indicated by the fact that when some of them have occasionally exercised their individual initiative to assist anticolonial

[2] Since this was written ECOSOC, after a highly emotional debate, voted 9 to 6, with 3 abstentions, to ask the Human Rights Commission to reconsider its proposal.

[3] Eagleton, op. cit., p. 594, deplores what he regards as the UN's "disregard for law." He believes the Dutch were "indubitably correct" in their legal argument that the UN recommendation to "tear Indonesia away from the Netherlands" was contrary to Article 2, Paragraph 7 which forbids the UN to intervene in the domestic affairs of any Member. He regards this as a "grave precedent" and believes that the domestic-questions clause "may now be regarded as removed," since "an organ of the United Nations can do whatever it has the vote to do."

powers they have been sharply criticized by the administering authorities.

Finally, and most important of all, is the work of the General Assembly. Its African discussions and recommendations have steadily grown from year to year, until they have touched upon nearly all of the continent's main areas and problems: the disposition of the Italian colonies; the Tunisian and Moroccan questions; the Ewe and Togoland unification movement in West Africa; the eviction of Wa-Meru tribesmen from certain lands in Tanganyika; the international status of Southwest Africa; the problems of the Indians in South Africa and of racial conflict in South Africa; African economic development; Mau Mau conflict in Kenya; the Central African Federation; and many other questions.

In the General Assembly, the noncolonial powers outnumber the colonial powers 52 to 8, an overwhelming predominance of major significance for Africa because it enables the noncolonial powers to maintain constant pressure for the extension of UN activities affecting that continent. In the Assembly's fourth committee, the Trusteeship Council, whose membership is evenly divided between administering authorities and non-administering members, is sometimes attacked as a mere tool of the colonial powers. In fact, the noncolonial voting majority is responsible for a major constitutional evolution now under way in the relations between the Trusteeship Council and the General Assembly. The Assembly is taking over functions that, in the view of many observers, should be performed by the Trusteeship Council, including the granting of oral hearings to Africans from trust territories.

To get around the fact that the Charter provides no machinery to help Africans who live in colonies outside the trusteeship system, the noncolonial powers have used Article 73 (e) of the Charter as an entering wedge, and have created a Committee on Information from Non-Self-Governing Territories to examine the information transmitted to the United Nations under Article 73 (e). As a next step, the anticolonial group would like to extend the tenure and terms of reference of this Committee with a view to making it eventually into another Trusteeship Council. This, of course, is partly the result of the fact that the administering authorities have not placed any territories other than former League of Nations mandates under the international trusteeship system.

Proposals emanating from the fourth committee have also led the General Assembly to create numerous other lesser committees affecting Africa, including committees on Southwest Africa, on the problem of defining a nonself-governing territory, and on administrative unions. In addition to the fourth committee, moreover, each of the other six main committees of the Assembly, all of which are made up of the entire sixty Members of the United Nations, deal today with matters affecting Africa, and in certain instances the anticolonial group, after an unsuccessful move in one committee, has made a similar attempt in another.

From this prolific discussion of African problems, the UN has produced a multitude of recommendations. The question that now arises is whether the Africans have made tangible gains as a result. And even if the colonial powers have carried out certain recommendations, is it possible, as they sometimes contend, that the same changés would have been made if there were no UN? Answers to these questions are easier to give than to prove.

No doubt the mechanical method by which the Trusteeship Council turns out annual recommendations on each territory leaves something to be desired. Instead of concentrating on outstanding problems and giving the administering authority a limited but workable number of suggestions which hard pressed administrators could seriously consider during the year, the twelve Council Members make many suggestions on a wide variety of subjects and then appoint a drafting committee for each territory to combine these suggestions into recommendations that can win a majority vote. Almost invariably the result is a series of repetitive recommendations on each of the four general fields considered by the Council: political; economic; social; and educational. Busy officials might give Council recommendations more consideration if they were reduced to manageable proportions.

However, specific examples of action resulting either directly or indirectly from Trusteeship Council recommendations can be cited. Prominent among these are the benefits to the peoples of the two Togolands which have developed out of the Council's consideration of many oral and written petitions demanding the unification of the Ewe-speaking people or of the two Togolands.

When its investigation indicated that there was no form of unification on which a majority of Togolanders would agree, the

Council did not recommend unification. Nevertheless, as a direct result of other Council recommendations, France and the United Kingdom have taken numerous steps to facilitate freedom of movement across the frontier. More important, perhaps, are the indirect benefits to the two Togos resulting from the widespread publicity given the problem. For example, those French Togolanders who support France and oppose the unificationist party have nonetheless been encouraged by world interest in the unification movement to demand faster progress toward self-government. When the pro-French party, whose sympathies France wants to hold, thus adds its demands to already existing pressures, Paris is really under fire. Recent French steps to increase the powers of the Territorial Assembly are among a number of reforms resulting from a combination of this and other pressures.

An interesting repercussion of a still different character is Gold Coast Prime Minister Nkrumah's reaction to the Togoland unification movement. As self-government approaches, Nkrumah's Convention Peoples' Party is naturally anxious to ensure that British Togoland remains an integral part of the Gold Coast and that Togolanders vote for the CPP. This no doubt explains why Nkrumah recently promised unusually large development grants for British Togoland. Thus, although the Togolanders' demand for unification may fail, UN interest in the problem is bringing them other benefits.

The Belgian government, which reacts quite strongly against many UN views, has also modified its trust-territory policy in response, at least in part, to UN pressure. It is possible that the first visiting mission to Ruanda-Urundi and Tanganyika, whose conclusions were severely criticized by the Belgians and British, made a deeper impression than is generally acknowledged. While the Trusteeship Council has commended certain economic and social developments in Ruanda-Urundi, it has called on the Belgian government to provide higher education for Africans and to give them responsible posts in the government. Council discussions publicized the fact that, while the British and French had many Africans studying in universities overseas and working in responsible administrative posts, the Belgians did not. This publicity alone was a form of pressure on the Belgians, even if the Council had adopted no recommendations on the subject. In Belgian theory, the best way to advance Africans is to begin with social and economic development and primary education. But when the Belgians are confronted not only with criticism in the UN, but also with the example of their British and French allies, the combination is difficult to resist. It may be concluded, therefore, that the influence of the United Nations is one of the factors which has induced Belgium recently to begin the sending of Africans overseas for higher education, to accelerate the development of higher education in Africa, to bring the two native rulers of Ruanda-Urundi into the Vice Governor-General's Council, and to further develop institutions of local government.

The recommendations of the Committee on Non-Self-Governing Territories, which was set up to deal with territories outside the trusteeship system, are less effective than those of the Trusteeship Council because of constitutional limitations on the Committee's powers. The Charter designates the Trusteeship Council as one of six principal UN organs, while the Committee is technically a subsidiary organ of the General Assembly.

In contrast to the Trusteeship Council, the Committee cannot send visiting missions into Africa and cannot examine petitions from Africans. Moreover, the Committee's terms of reference limit it to general recommendations on economic, social and educational—but not political—conditions, and it cannot make a recommendation directed to a particular government on a situation in a single territory. Committee members often do refer to conditions in individual territories, however, and they sometimes cross the indefinable borderline to discuss political conditions. And in recent cases in which an administering authority has ceased to transmit information on a particular territory on the grounds that the territory had achieved self-government, the Committee has engaged in a detailed debate on the political and constitutional status of the territory.

Because of its limited terms of reference, the Committee's discussions often deal with abstract principles rather than practical situations, and it is not possible to point to any specific action, other than providing additional information, taken by the administering authorities as a result of the Committee's work.

Attempts by the anticolonial group in the assembly to extend the Committee's powers are met with determined opposition by certain administering authorities, who regard the very existence of the Committee as unconstitutional. Belgium, in fact, withdrew from the Committee in 1953, and others have threatened to do so. Similar crises have occurred when members of the fourth committee have argued over the question of whether the Assembly itself has the right to discuss political—as opposed to economic, social, and educational—conditions in nonself-governing territories outside the trusteeship system. While the anticolonial group contends that the General Assembly does have this right, a view shared by many delegations because of the Assembly's broad powers under Article 10 to discuss anything within the scope of the Charter, they have not forced the issue to a showdown, evidently because they fear certain administering authorities would cease to co-operate with the Assembly.

The nature and significance of this problem is illustrated in an interesting way by the treatment of the Central African Federation issue in the Assembly in 1953. The creation of this federation of the two Rhodesias and Nyasaland is one of the most important African developments of recent years. It was established against the wishes of a large majority of those Africans in the area who expressed their views. Some of the Africans concerned requested the Reverend Michael Scott, an Anglican clergyman, to make their opposition known to the United Nations, which he offered to do in a written communication to the chairman of the fourth committee. The committee decided to circulate the communication as an official document, and the representative of India precipitated a crisis by asking that delegations wishing to discuss the problem be given the opportunity. The issue was critical because the Central African Federation was not an item on the agenda, because certain administering authorities believed the fourth committee did not have the legal competence to discuss political conditions in nonself-governing territories, and because the communication from the Reverend Scott concerned a nonself-governing territory rather than a trust territory; and the Charter makes no provision for the consideration of petitions from nonself-governing territories. In addition to these legal objections, the United Kingdom was strongly opposed to any United Nations action which might inspire further political agitation in the three territories and weaken its efforts to make the federation a success. The British delegation, therefore, not only refused to discuss the substance of the issue but also served notice that the United Kingdom might be "unable to continue to co-operate in the work of the Committee" if the matter were made the subject of debate. The committee then adopted an Indian motion which, in effect, kept the debate open on the subject, in the event that any delegation wished to revert to it later. Evidently, the strong British opposition had its effect, however, for it was not mentioned again until the last meeting of the committee six weeks later, when the representative of India read a statement criticizing the establishment of the Federation, and referring also to the Mau Mau crisis in Kenya and the deposition of the Kabaka of Buganda. The incident was closed when the British representative replied that he had no comment to make on an episode which was, in substance, outside the scope of the committee's work. I have described the controversy at this length partly because it illustrates one of the limitations on UN action affecting Africa, and partly because it indicates that the British feared a UN discussion might have a strong impact on a critical African problem.

Let us now turn to another type of tangible impact of the United Nations on Africa, namely, the Expanded Technical Assistance Program in which, by mid-1953, more than 2000 experts from all the specialized agencies had assisted in the economic development of 82 countries and territories. The African effort under this program is small but growing. In 1950–51 it provided a total of only $444,891 for aid to Libya, Ethiopia, Liberia, and Italian Somaliland. By 1954, however, the total estimated figure had jumped to $1,429,134 (Egypt excluded), and the number of benefiting states and territories had increased from 4 to 14. Tanganyika and Tunisia appeared on the list for the first time in 1953, and Morocco and Uganda in 1954. It thus appears that the initial reluctance of some of the colonial powers to UN activities of this type is diminishing as the practical value of agricultural, health, and other UN projects is demonstrated. It is still a fact, however, that the bulk of UN aid goes to the independent states, the 1954 estimates allocating $1,109,204 out of the total $1,429,134 to Libya, Ethiopia, and Liberia.

The newly independent state of Libya provides the best example of the potentialities of UN technical assistance. Here the Food and Agriculture Organization has provided 15 specialists to implement the recommendations of a previous FAO mission, and these officers are co-operating with Libyan officials in what FAO terms in a recent report "A Skeleton Ministry of Agriculture." [4] Early in 1954, the International Labor Organization had 31 instructors on the staff of a technical and clerical training center in Tripoli who are giving instruction in metal-working, carpentry, machine shop work, and secretarial trades. In all, the 1954 Libya program provides for 99 experts from the UN itself and six of the specialized agencies, plus 94 fellowships for Libyans to receive technical training, 34 of them abroad.

UN assistance to Liberia and Ethiopia is significant but much smaller than to Libya, while elsewhere in Africa it is only a drop in the bucket in comparison with the technical assistance which metropolitan powers are providing their own territories. The representative of Belgium, for example, informed the Committee on Information from Non-Self-Governing Territories, on October 1, 1952, that, while the United Nations and its specialized agencies by the end of March, 1952, had recruited 1054 technicians for the 1½ billion people in all the underdeveloped countries, Belgium had 4673 full time European officials, most of whom were of the expert caliber sought by the UN, serving the 11½ million Africans of the Congo. While FAO had 271 experts and a budget of less than $6,000,000 for its world program on January 1, 1952, the Belgian Congo agricultural service had 633 European technicians and $14,600,000 for its 1952 program. In addition, the Belgian representative said, the Belgian Central African Institute (INEAC), of twenty years' standing, accorded technical assistance to the Congo which many another sovereign state might envy, having had, as of September 15, 1952, 273 agents in the Congo and 45 in Europe, and a 1952 budget of $6,500,000. [5]

In perspective, therefore, it is evident that the impact of the UN technical assistance program in Africa is small indeed, although the example of Libya indicates the UN potentialities, particularly as African territories emerge toward self-government.

[4] Activities of FAO under the Expanded Technical Assistance Program 1952–53 (Rome, FAO, October, 1953), p. 36; see also the Sixth Report of the Technical Assistance Board to the Technical Assistance Committee, UNOR, E/2566, April 14, 1954.

[5] UNOR, A/AC.35/SR.65, p. 7.

If the evidence thus far presented indicates that the changes in Africa resulting directly from UN recommendations and technical assistance are not of major significance, what about the more intangible realm of indirect influences? Probably the most important of these less tangible factors is the manner in which the work of the UN has affected the political behavior of Africa's peoples, Asian and European as well as African. In several important areas the UN has helped to encourage political agitation, if only by providing local leaders an additional forum and giving them moral encouragement. Whether this is good, bad, or irrelevant is a matter of individual opinion. Some observers contend that it is harmful because it upsets the orderly evolution of Africa toward self-government based on adequate economic, social, and educational foundations. Others argue that Africa can only be remade by its own people and that anything which awakens their consciousness of their capacity for advancement is therefore valuable. Still others may feel that it is irrelevant because the ferment in contemporary Africa began before the United Nations came into existence and would continue to grow even if there were no UN.

In addition to the trust territories, the main areas which might serve as case studies to test the theory of UN influence are Morocco and Tunisia and the Union of South Africa. Any of the trust territories could be cited as an example. In Italian Somaliland, despite the fact that it is far less developed than other areas, political agitation is at a high level with the formation of numerous Somali parties which have sent more petitions to the UN than those of any other territory. In the French Cameroons, the declining pro-Communist Union of Cameroons peoples found a new lease on life in its opportunities to exploit the petitions procedure. Limitations of space, however, force me to be selective, and I wish to return to the Togolands for special mention.

The inauguration of the United Nations most certainly stimulated the revival of the Ewe movement. The coming of the first visiting mission to the Ewe area, in 1949, gave local politicians a unique opportunity. In its report to the Trusteeship Council the mission has related how a Ewe propaganda barrage began even before the mission landed at Lome airport, for as their plane came down members could see at a long distance huge placards inscribed with the word "Unification" borne by a large crowd. The mission reports that it felt "it was in the presence of a rather highly organized and intelligently conducted movement not unlike movements experienced by them in their own countries." [6] As it traveled through the West African territories, the mission was met by large gatherings for whom the event was a great occasion symbolic of the new interest the world was taking in Togo affairs. If the unofficial report is correct that some of the faces seen among demonstrators in Southern Togo were seen again in Northern crowds, it appears that the Togolanders were learning fast. In any case they have certainly learned how to petition. The Trusteeship Council has received more than 800 petitions from the two Togolands, and the second visiting mission, which entered the area in 1952, was presented with 2899 communications on the unification issue. Moreover, Togoland leaders have induced their followers to produce from their limited resources many thousands of dollars to send twenty-five spokesmen to present their views orally before the Trusteeship Council and the fourth committee, eight of whom testified in New York within the past year.

The ups and downs of the numerous political parties organized to campaign for or against unification have at least taught Ewe leaders some lessons in the art of politics. UN discussion of their problem has helped them to understand its complexities and induced them to modify their tactics. The original goal of Ewe unification has been altered to Togoland unification and may more and more turn into a plea for self-government alone, leaving the unification question to be settled in the future by the Africans themselves.

Meanwhile, unfortunately, intense and bitter feelings have been aroused, particularly among French Togolanders whose disagreement has led to occasional outbursts of violence. In one incident involving the unificationists and the local police seven Africans were killed. In fact, even in the UN, thinly veiled threats of violence have been made by unificationist leaders in the hope of winning support. The disillusionment resulting from the inevitable discouragement of the unificationists seems to have strengthened the hand of younger and more radical leaders. One may also wonder whether unification is a desirable or undesirable prece-

[6] *Reports of the United Nations Visiting Mission to Trust Territories in West Africa.* UNOR, Supplement No. 2 (T/798) (New York, 1951), p. 86.

dent for similar movements in many other areas of Africa where ethnic and political boundaries do not coincide. Already demands for Cameroons unification and Somali unification have been brought to the UN, as well as a plea for a modification of the frontier between Ruanda-Urundi and Tanganyika.

Outside the trust territories, UN influences are most felt in local politics in French North Africa and the Union of South Africa, the two most highly developed areas with the largest European populations. No visiting missions can enter these areas, however, and no regular channels for petitions to the UN are open to the inhabitants except for the Southwest Africans. It is therefore more difficult for their problems to reach the United Nations. Items on the agenda of the General Assembly must be proposed by states rather than individuals and must be approved by a majority of UN Members.

Nonetheless, Algerian, Moroccan and Tunisian nationalists in North Africa have from the beginning waged a campaign for UN help. For several years, until 1951, they awakened little response because no state pressed their case. Meanwhile the Assembly decided to make neighboring and less developed Libya an independent state, thereby giving the nationalists in French territories an additional argument for their own case. Finally, in 1952, the Moroccans and Tunisians succeeded in getting their problems on the agenda at the instigation of the thirteen states of the Arab-Asian bloc. Although the nationalist leaders have never been granted an oral hearing in the Assembly, they have sent delegations frequently to lobby in the corridors. On one notable occasion, in fact, one of the Moroccan leaders turned up as a member of the Pakistan delegation!

France has contended that the Tunisian and Moroccan questions are outside the Assembly's competence and has refused to participate in first committee discussions of them. Although France has now made several moves toward accommodating Arab views, particularly in Tunisia, French anger at UN intervention may have rigidified the French position, and nationalist leaders in Morocco and Tunisia were punished with exile or jail. The presence of a large and permanent French population complicates the North African problem, and it is difficult to foresee at this time whether the UN has helped or harmed the evolution of these areas toward a satisfactory form of self-government.

In the Union of South Africa, the Bantu, colored and Indian

peoples, like the Moroccans and Tunisians, have been both encouraged and discouraged by the United Nations. For eight years the Assembly has sought to modify the Union's policy toward Southwest Africa and the Indians in South Africa, and two years ago it added a third South African item to its agenda, the problem of race conflict resulting from the *apartheid* policies of the Union government. Although the Union's response to Assembly recommendations has been generally negative, the UN impact has had a number of interesting repercussions.

Southwest Africa is the only former League of Nations mandate which has not become an independent state or a United Nations trust territory. Although South Africa maintains that it continues to administer Southwest Africa in the spirit of the mandate, it has refused either to place the territory under trusteeship or to accept the opinion of the International Court of Justice that the Union is still under the international obligations of the mandate. On two occasions when the fourth committee granted an oral hearing to the Reverend Michael Scott to speak on behalf of certain tribes in the territory, the South African delegation walked out, calling the committee's action illegal. After two years of unsuccessful effort to negotiate an agreement with the Union to implement the Court's opinion, the Assembly, in 1953, appointed a Committee on Southwest Africa to examine conditions in and petitions from the territory. Without the Union's co-operation, this Committee is now in the process of producing a first report on the territory; what its influence will be is problematical, although it is now reported that certain Europeans in Southwest Africa are voicing doubts as to the wisdom of the government's policy in boycotting the Committee. Among the interesting by-products of this UN consideration of Southwest Africa were two unique tribal consultations held by the Union government which reported to the UN that a large majority of Southwest Africans favored incorporation of their territory in the Union.

There can be no doubt that the new interest of the outside world in their problems has stimulated the non-Europeans of the Union to stiffen their resistance to their government's policies. Each year that the Assembly has discussed the treatment of the 365,000 people of Indian origin in the Union, the strong language of the Indian, Pakistan, and other delegations has given additional ammunition to the Indian press in the Union. *Indian Opinion,* edited by the son of Mahatma Gandhi, editorialized as follows on November 24, 1950:

> If the United Nations fails to save us we see dark days ahead of us and they will overwhelm the world. The third world war will be in the making, South Africa and not Korea will be responsible for it and the United Nations will have proved too weak to avoid it.

The Assembly's discussion of the item on race conflict in the Union during the past two years has aroused similar emotions. Moreover, the current efforts of certain Bantu, Indian, and colored leaders to bring their organizations into a common front may have been strengthened by the fact that the cause of the three groups has been linked in the UN.

Naturally, this outside intervention has angered the Europeans in the Union, who are confronted with perhaps the most difficult and delicate racial situation of any country in the world. Prime Minister Malan, on May 3, 1954, during a foreign-affairs debate in Parliament, acknowledged the world's need for international organization but said he was not a great friend or supporter of the United Nations, which was stirring up unrest in Africa by giving a backward people the idea that they were oppressed. In addressing a congress of his own Nationalist party followers on October 21, 1953, the Prime Minister was less restrained, labelling the UN a failure and a cancer gnawing at world peace and tranquility.

What are the consequences of UN discussion of South African affairs? It has undoubtedly intensified the pressures and tensions in the Union. Will this lead to a modification of European attitudes toward the African and a gradual development of better race relations? Or has it rigidified the lines of the race conflict and made a difficult situation more dangerous to all concerned? Ironically, Dr. Malan's critics in the UN seem to have strengthened him and his Nationalist party by providing them an effective new weapon in their campaign oratory, namely, an attack on foreign intervention. At the same time, however, the severity of the government's attacks on the UN may backfire, for the non-European's appreciation of the UN is likely to rise in direct proportion to the European's animosity toward it.

In summing up the impact of the United Nations on Africa, let me repeat that it is many-sided and often intangible. At the very least, we may conclude that the United Nations has helped Africa to push its way up from an obscure position to a position of importance in the consciousness of the world. Whether or not this will make the solution of Africa's problems easier, it is a fact that the United Nations has forced governments and peoples to recognize that the future of Africa has become of vital interest to the international community. It should not be overlooked, moreover, that the UN has performed a valuable service by its collection and publication of voluminous data on Africa, and by stimulating and assisting the serious study of African problems.

The recommendations and resolutions of United Nations organs are inevitably redundant and often ignored—a fact which stems from the very nature of international organization. Practical results nearly always take a long time. But the trust territories and, indirectly, the other territories in Africa have benefited from the fact that every year the colonial powers present their records and defend their policies before the United Nations—a continual international justification which helps them to reappraise and perfect their methods of administration.

It would be a mistake, however, to overconcentrate on the tangible results of UN recommendations. History will probably record that the manifold and sometimes conflicting pressures and tensions aroused in Africa by the UN are considerably more significant. At the same time, Africa could have a profound impact on the UN itself where heated emotions have sometimes pushed controversies to the breaking point. Already, in fact, there have been a number of withdrawals and threats of withdrawals from certain UN activities. Britain's commendable effort to broaden its white commonwealth of nations into a multiracial commonwealth may also be jeopardized by bitter disputes in the United Nations, which tend to accentuate the differences between India, Pakistan, the Gold Coast, South Africa, and the United Kingdom. One may further wonder whether the current competition of Islam and Christianity for pagan Africa will be ultimately affected by the fact that in the United Nations it is often Islamic representatives who say what Africans like to hear and Christian representatives do not. Meanwhile, the Soviet Union continues to exploit the UN to foster its aims in Africa, an aspect of the problem which I have not dealt with here.[7]

If this analysis has raised more questions than it answers, it is because the answers often lie in a future full of imponderables. It may, nonetheless, be said in conclusion that the United Nations has made its mark in Africa and that its impact will continue to grow. The extent of its influence will, of course, depend on its general effectiveness, including the willingness of its members to use and respect it in other areas. This, in turn, will depend in part on the future of race relations, that is, on the ability of white and non-white peoples to co-operate despite the racial attitudes, tensions, and suspicions that are reflected in the United Nations. In any event, the existence of the United Nations has been a significant factor in stimulating the rapid progress Africa has made since 1945, and it would indeed be a pity if the machinery which helped to make this progress possible were further undermined by an indiscriminate excess of anticolonial zeal.

Many contributors to this volume have driven home the point that Africa is a vast and diverse continent in which the political evolution of various regions will not be identical. Sweeping ideological arguments intended for uniform application to all of Africa are therefore harmful to the extent that they confuse the real issues. The aims of the Charter might be better fulfilled if UN Members took greater care to distinguish between those issues on which the UN can achieve positive results and those on which UN intervention might lead to frustration and possibly violence. If the United Nations is to make its fullest contribution to Africa, perhaps its Members should pay more attention to the old adage that politics is the art of the possible.

---

[7] See Vernon McKay, "Communist Exploitation of Anti-Colonialism and Nationalism in Africa," *The Threat of Soviet Imperialism,* ed. by C. G. Haines (Baltimore: The Johns Hopkins Press, 1954), pp. 258–74.

commentary

SHERMAN S. HAYDEN

Clark University

Dr. McKay's essay has made clear in admirable detail the character of the outside world's relation, through the United Nations, to the colonies and near-colonies of Africa. It has documented the fact that the problems of each people are the particular problems of that people alone. At the same time, this exposition has shown that these problems are specific cases of certain major and enduring difficulties in international relations. They fall into two classes: those basically administrative, though not without political complexity; and those essentially political and therefore hardest either to soften or to solve. Let us successively examine these two classes.

Dr. McKay has noted, for example, the limited role now played by the Trusteeship Council compared with what its founders foresaw or, at least, ventured in the early days to hope for—the rather wooden and uninspired topic-by-topic methods whereby it customarily examines cases and makes its recommendations, and the large number of other international agencies concerned with African life and affairs whereby a certain amount of confusion, overlapping, and inefficiency is generated. Faced with these facts, a practiced administrator will immediately look for ways in which some agencies can be consolidated, some perhaps eliminated, and the directive function centered in some single body vested with authority and prestige and manned by persons of initiative and experience commensurate with the scope of the task. If there were a Hoover Commission for the United Nations, would it not inevitably address itself to some form of reorganization along these lines? It is therefore submitted that the international supervision of African affairs is overloaded with councils, committees, and agencies concerned with the same vital and essential questions of health, education, living standards, and general welfare and that, until the relation between the Trusteeship Council, ECOSOC, and UNESCO (in particular) is clarified and restated, procedural reforms within the Trusteeship Council itself are of limited value and can take second place.

Is such a reorganization practical? I see no real reason why not, even within the framework of the Charter as it now exists. Considering the difficulties attendant upon formal amendment, it would certainly be well if this were so. Can we not assume that at least where order and efficiency are of prime concern, and political consequences are not of the essence of the outcome—which is true here if anywhere—a clear majority of national delegates will be prepared to work together on such a project, regardless of their varying political attitudes? One would expect the main resistance, apart from that offered by the Communist bloc still happily a minority, to be stirred up less by differences of ideology than by what might be called the office difficulties normally attendant upon any program of job revision and consolidation. The Charter's words of competence, under which councils and specialized agencies are alike created, seem broad enough to admit considerable elasticity in reordering the work of these agencies. I venture to hope that real progress is possible here.

But when we pass from pure administration to problems having a political character, the troubled world of international politics introduces far graver and more substantial complications into the work of the United Nations. To what extent these arise from the impact of the UN's work and programs upon Africa itself is very hard for this commentator to say. Dr. McKay has made plain that this relationship has had a marked and specific effect upon the form taken by African political movements, and he has given us extensive documentation in the particular case of Togoland—on the whole a rather encouraging example. More of the same type of study seems needed for a sound estimate of UN work and prospects.

I should like, however, to say more about the political tensions heightened by this problem among the UN Members themselves. The United Nations is much more than a complex of administrative bodies. The expression, realization, and reconciliation of political ideals constitute a major part of its reason for existence.

That these ideals differ from each other is not, in itself, anything to deplore; but when in practice differing philosophies conflict and collide, trouble always ensues. Now, in the African field outstandingly, when the interest of the metropolitan or trustee power is not obviously identical with that of the local population or with that of member nations who accept the local attitude as their own, there is just that kind of conflict. And it is the more serious because the UN, as a supervisory or administrative body, is at the same time in the dangerous position of a third party mediator between two adversaries.

This mediatory role is a difficult one at the best of times. Ideally, in the presence of a controversial situation, we would look for a mediating organ of simple structure—in the simplest case a single judge or referee—operating under well-defined rules and clearly delimited powers, and as nearly free of personal partiality and interest in the dispute as possible. But the UN as a mediator meets none of these conditions. Sixty states are represented in the General Assembly and its committees, and the membership of the two councils mainly concerned here (while in each case less than a third of that number) is still very large for anybody charged with supervision and recommendation. The Charter is quite vague as to the precise scope of the power of any of these organs, and none of them has arrived at a plain definition of its own competence, though the UN has been in operation for some eight years. Finally, the participant members of all these bodies are anything but impartial or disinterested. As Dr. McKay has reminded us, the anticolonial powers are a large and noisy majority in the Assembly, and the old metropolitan powers a stubborn and defensive minority. That this last is in some ways unfortunate seems undeniable, not least because it seriously inhibits the latter class from playing their proper role. The colonial powers, *as such,* may have had their day. They remain, however, the nations with the longest tradition of sobering responsibility and accumulated experience, both in the colonial field and in that of general world politics; and it would not be wholly absurd to suggest that the disproportionate representation of the newer states in the Assembly and the fourth committee may thus far have done more harm than good.

In the Trusteeship Council, of course, a conscious effort has been made to balance these rival forces, but the pressures of national emotion are nonetheless there, and one is led to suspect that the rather routine and prosy character of the Council's proceedings is the natural result not of knowing no better but of being unable for this reason to handle hot questions effectively. The present writer is still not wholly satisfied that the replacement of a committee of experts (the Permanent Mandates Commission) by a council of state representatives was entirely a happy step forward.

If the foregoing analysis is valid, there is no reason to assume that the present structure of the UN will, of itself, make for moderation and efficiency in the future any more than in the recent past. What then can be done about it? An obvious suggestion would be to circumscribe the powers of the General Assembly with respect to colonial or undeveloped-country questions and to concentrate them more firmly in the Trusteeship Council, with a corresponding effort to professionalize the latter body. This would follow quite naturally too, from the previous proposal to centralize the various administrative functions of the UN, in this field, under the same council and then to undertake a revision of its procedures. The picture of a reorganized Council is tempting—a Council under whose broad purview all matters affecting not only the trust territories but all countries not yet fully self-governing will be gathered, a Council staffed and supported by trained and experienced men, comparatively free of nationalistic passion and political prejudice, operating harmoniously (though the Communist Members might be a permanent exception) to the furtherance of the good life in these territories.

But I could recommend it no more than I would (if I could) abridge the role of Congress or of its investigating committees. Those of us whose paths have lain largely among scholars and administrators often incline far too much to seeking remedies for human disorder and conflict by way of well-ordered, professional, dispassionate institutions. But the world is not like that. Intelligent, qualified, and efficient administration is good, but administration protected from the voice of the world becomes deadly. While, therefore, a firmer consolidation of properly administrative functions under the Trusteeship Council is highly desirable, and a more professional and corporate spirit in the Council is to be welcomed, it should not be insulated from the General Assembly, for all the faults of that Assembly.

The plain fact is that, as everyone knows, a revolution has occurred since about 1900, has been going on for fifty years, and still continues. The colonial empires are gone or going. Some of us even believe that this upheaval—this second age of nationalism— is the greatest fact of contemporary international relations, to which even the struggle against expanding Communism will in the long run come to seem almost incidental. Some of us, too, may fairly feel that the revolution has occurred too soon and proceeded too fast for anybody's good and that the slow, progressive, and en- lightened liquidation of imperialism might have been a better major occupation of Western statesmanship than the fighting of two internecine wars, and this might have left to us a world far dif- ferent from the one we have. But all such reflections are quite aca- demic now; the lesson of Metternich's failure a century before was not learnt soon enough; and the revolution is on its way to triumph.

Can it seriously be argued that the present UN system is impos- sibly bad? Speaking generally, is it really likely that the colonial powers would come to better terms with their colonies if the poli- tical pressures of the UN system, intemperate and unwise though they may often be, were out of the picture? Would the Dutch have found a happy unassisted answer to the Indonesian case, or shall we call the disaster in Indochina a fortunate consequence of leaving French colonial affairs in French hands; and is a better fate in prospect for Tunis and Morocco? Is the outlook for the Indian minority in South Africa worse than it would be if there were no United Nations wherein India was a Member?

The special function of the Assembly I believe to be precisely the airing and expression of political views. The United Nations, like our own government, is founded upon the premise that through full and honest discussion, even though it be often acrimonious and for that matter sometimes foolish and inept, adjustments can be found and fierce conflict averted. To abridge this function of the Assembly would, I think, be tragic; for, except in this way, I see no possibility of civilizing the revolution which man cannot stop.

The problem, then, is not one of curtailment; and that is just as well, because, for this, formal amendment would certainly be neces- sary, and with the small powers in a majority it is quite inconceiv- able. If the role of the Assembly is to be effectively played, the answer lies in self-reform through patience and temperance, intelligent understanding of political issues, and appreciation of the effective limits of political possibilities. Of course the trend toward proliferation of committees is undesirable, and extravagant proposals, such as the one cited by Dr. McKay, to enforce the right of self-determination by creating yet another UN organ give ground for concern. Hardly anyone can well defend a tendency on the part of any popular assembly so to extend its supervision over administration as to make decent administration impossible. But the remedy lies within the Assembly and its member nations themselves and not in the rewriting of paper constitutions.

five   **THE ECONOMIC STATUS
AND FUTURE POSSIBILITIES
OF AFRICA**

Africa's economic potentialities

PETER ADY

St. Anne's College, Oxford University

Views upon potential development in African economies differ markedly in different parts of the world. To some, Africa appears to be a continent of vast, untapped resources, awaiting only the arrival of forceful modern enterprise to grow rich and productive. To others, it is a terrain held back by great obstacles to rapid economic development—a region of poor soil and unfavorable climate, whose peoples have been cut off from the stream of world economic progress by natural obstacles such as lack of waterways and harbors and by the barrier to white penetration offered by endemic tropical diseases. Africa, thanks to Western advances in tropical medicine, is no longer the "white man's grave"; but many other difficulties remain, and it is these which we shall have to examine more closely in making an assessment of Africa's economic potentialities.

In this assessment tropical Africa falls into a different category from either the Union of South Africa or the Mediterranean territories of the North, and it is usual now to think of Africa as separated into three broad groups. For example, the *World Economic Report* suggests "a distinction between Africa north of the Sahara and intertropical Africa which embraces the whole of Africa south of the Sahara with the exception of the Union of South Africa." [1] It points out that "North Africa, bordering on the Mediterranean, and separated from the rest of Africa by the vast wastes of the

[1] "Conditions in Africa," *World Economic Report, 1949–50*, Supplement, "Review of Economic Conditions."

395

Sahara desert, is by history and geography closely associated with southern Europe, of which in an economic sense much of it forms an integral part." On the other hand, "the Union of South Africa is economically much more highly developed than any other part of Africa south of the Sahara, which places it in many respects in a category by itself." It is tropical Africa which is of the greatest interest to us in discussing Africa's economic potentialities, since it is this area which has the most difficult problems. The extra-tropical areas of North Africa and the Union have also their economic problems, but they are more familiar in kind than those of the tropical belt. Within this belt lie most of the African colonial territories of Britain, France, Belgium, Portugal, and Spain, together with the independent Liberia and much of Egypt and Ethiopia. The total population of this area is not accurately known, but it has been estimated at about 150 millions.

There is no doubt that this area is poor. Taking the continent as a whole, nearly one-quarter of Africa is composed of desert and lakes, and about one-quarter is forest land. Most of the remainder consists of savannah or grassland, of which much is comparatively arid. The predominant form of economic organization over much of this region is that of largely self-sufficient village and tribal economies, both agricultural and pastoral. The mass of the population lives in dwellings of the most primitive type, mud-walled, palm-thatched huts, bare of furniture and of amenities. They produce food and a few simple household goods for their own immediate consumption. Clothing is scarce, if not nonexistent. The diet of these village peoples is poor, lacking in important nutrients, and malnutrition is in consequence widespread. There is a variety of endemic, debilitating diseases. Mortality rates are high. National income estimates suggest that African income per head is less than $50, while that in the Union of South Africa ranges between $200–300 per head, and in the U.S. it is over $1,000.[2]

2 Per-capita incomes in terms of U.S. dollars in contemporary prices were approximately: Belgian Congo (1949), $37; Kenya (1946), $46; Northern Rhodesia (1948), $50; Ruanda-Urundi (1948), $17; Southern Rhodesia (1949), $101; Union of South Africa (1948–49), $260; U.S. (1949), $1,400. *UN National Income Statistics, 1938–50* (United Nations Statistical Office, 1950). Such international comparisons are difficult to interpret because of problems of valuation and coverage as yet unresolved.

Causes of low productivity

The chief economic activity of this area is agriculture, well over 70 per cent of the population being engaged in farming, chiefly subsistence farming based upon shifting cultivation.

The tropics are traditionally regarded as rich and fertile, but in tropical Africa soil management, under the generally prevailing systems of soil structure and climate, presents problems of great complexity. Under the traditional system of shifting cultivation, an equilibrium had been achieved by the African peasant, but this depended upon the maintenance of a fallow period of something like ten to fifteen years, between cultivation of any forest clearing and its next recultivation. Shifting cultivation has been a relatively successful system of soil management while land was plentiful, but this equilibrium has been disturbed by Africa's contact with the world economy. In the first place, African populations are growing. The death rate has fallen because colonization has put an end to tribal warfare and because of the advances in tropical medicine which Western science has achieved. Secondly, a number of factors are tending to reduce the area available for food-crop cultivation. For example, with the spread of export crops there has been a great increase in acreage under permanent tree-crops such as cocoa and oil palms and in that devoted to other export crops such as groundnuts, cotton, and coffee. Land taken up by white settlers in East and Central Africa also reduces the total acreage available. The rise in numbers and the fall in acreage both have operated to reduce the acreage per head available for food-crop cultivation and, hence, have reduced in many areas the fallow period which any bush clearing can be allowed.

The fertility of tropical African soil under the existing system of soil management is low, and in many areas it is also falling. This is more marked in the case of food crops and others with an annual cycle than in the permanent crops where the new crop provides a good cover for the soil. Agricultural yields per acre all over Africa are low compared with similar food-crop areas elsewhere: the Food and Agriculture Organization of the UN estimates them to be less than 60 per cent of world average yields per acre. Even in the food crops most commonly grown in Africa, yields per acre are low in relation to world averages, being, for example, only 60 per cent in maize,

67 per cent in millet, 66 per cent in sweet potatoes and yams, and 60 per cent in groundnuts. The absence of specialization characteristic of subsistence production also depresses yields, since each clearing has to produce a little of each crop required by a household. Basically, the low yields are due to the complexities of African soil management, and to the many adverse factors that are tending to reduce fertility.

With the small scale of operations in shifting agriculture, output per head is lower still, being put by FAO at less than a third of world levels. Low productivity per man in agriculture is thus the main reason for the existing poverty of the people. In some areas, such as the coastal plains of the Gold Coast and Nigeria, the pressure of numbers is already showing itself in loss of fertility consequent upon a steady reduction in the fallow period of years between cultivation and recultivation of cleared forest. In other areas, such as the East African reserves, there is widespread soil erosion and overgrazing. In such areas, a further fall in living standards is to be expected as the population grows, unless new means of livelihood are found.

Subsistence agriculture has already been replaced or supplemented in some areas where mines have been opened and where export crop production has proved successful. Export-crop production has increased specialization, the peasants growing these crops for cash sale and tending more and more to buy their foodstuffs in the local market. Specialization in cocoa-farming and in palm products is virtually complete in some areas of the West African coast, though there are still many producers of these cash crops who also grow some foodstuffs for their own use. Plantation agriculture, where it has been introduced, has also fostered specialization.

Production per acre and per head is higher in these export crops, chief of which are cocoa, palm produce, cotton, sisal and hard fibres, tobacco, cloves, coffee, and tea. Yet even in these crops, yields per acre are not much above world levels and, in some cases, such as tobacco, they are actually below. Nevertheless, value productivity is higher than in subsistence food production, and the opportunity for increased specialization has benefited incomes per head in such areas, though it has reduced the amount of land available for food production. Specialization has had other disadvantages, too, notably the insecurity which characterizes monoculture in periods of price fluctuation. The inter-war years were a period of wide fluctuation in commodity prices, and these have left a pattern of peasant indebtedness, land alienation, and fragmentation of holdings which the fifteen years of steadily rising commodity prices have not yet wholly eradicated.

Mining enterprises have in general a very high productivity per man, many times that in subsistence agriculture or even in cash-crop production. Yet, as the *World Economic Report* points out, "practically all the capital upon which this production has been developed had to be imported from outside Africa and . . . this investment has had relatively little effect in generating secondary incomes and investment. Gross export receipts, in considerable proportion, are transferred as incomes abroad in the form of loan charges and dividends on invested capital." The net effect upon income per head of highly capitalized enterprises, such as mines and plantations, has therefore been relatively small, though by no means negligible.

Slow pace of economic development

Africa is sparsely populated, with an over-all density only fractionally higher than that of South America, which at fifteen persons to the square mile is the lowest in the world. This sparseness and wide scattering has hindered economic growth in many ways. It has necessitated the wasteful system of migrant labor, which has slowed down the acquiring of industrial skills. It has kept the peoples of the interior from contact with the outside world, and it has limited the development of domestic markets and handicraft industries. These obstacles to economic development have been increased by the poor communications of this continent. There are few good natural harbors. None of the major rivers has been navigable very far inland because of waterfalls and rapids, especially at the edge of the Central Plateau which is almost everywhere so near the coast. Railways, except those of Cape Province, have been developed only in the last sixty years, and then almost solely to meet the needs of some export industry. The road system, too, is export-oriented, and road surfaces are poor, suffering a rapid deterioration in the rainy season. Once off the thin network of roads, human porterage is the only method of getting goods to and from the villages of the interior. In the dry season, bicycles can be ridden along the footpaths, but heavy loads are invariably carried on foot, the load being balanced on the porter's head.

Is tropical Africa underdeveloped? Could its "national" income be increased by a better utilization of what there is? Or is Africa poor despite the fact that her resources have been exploited to the fullest extent permitted by current knowledge? What, for example, are the prospects for development in agriculture, Africa's basic form of employment? Agricultural improvement is obviously a primary necessity, and at first sight it looks a simple task to improve upon the primitive technique of cultivation which African peasants use, especially in the subsistence sector. Settled cultivation and the use of less primitive methods seem an obvious reform, as this would increase the amount of land available without increasing the labor required. Unhappily, the tsetse fly prevents mixed farming, and altogether this is less simple a change than it seems, for temperate climate farming methods cannot be transferred to tropical Africa without modification.

An important lesson of the last few decades has been the peculiarities of African soil management and water control. Whereas Europe's fields can be plowed to clear away weeds and to expose the soil to weathering, in tropical Africa a cover is needed to protect the soil from the intense effects of sun and rain. This is why African farms always seem weed-ridden by European standards, for weeds are better than no cover at all. This is also why shifting cultivation has been practiced. The soil structure is difficult to maintain without a soil cover and deep plowing does more harm than good, as it exposes more of the soil to weathering and breaks up the thin top layer of humus. There are widespread areas of mineral deficiencies, which cannot easily be offset by the use of fertilizers because these are so quickly leached out of the soil by heavy showers, even when the total annual rainfall is not high. Techniques of building up soil fertility are well-known, but the particular methods economically best suited to tropical Africa still have to be established. Pellet fertilizer technique holds out promise. American and Australian experience with dry-soil farming may also have an important contribution to make.

Yet, there are other difficulties which arise from Africa's poor

water endowment. Rainfall is a critical factor everywhere outside
the high forest. Elsewhere there is very great variability, both as
to timing and incidence of rainfall and as to its quantity. The
break of the rainy season may be early in some years, greatly delayed
in others. Annual totals show a wide variation from year to year,
whereas within any given year the incidence may show remarkable
irregularities, since the rain falls almost entirely as heavy showers.
The irregularities between one month and the next, as well as from
year to year, increase as average total fall decreases. Africa is not a
well-watered continent, and water development presents difficult
features.

Finally, widespread infestation with tsetse fly limits the possibilities of developing settled cultivation on the basis of mixed
farming. Areas free from tsetse are too arid to carry many head of
cattle, except by migrant pastoral or ranching methods.

The difficulties in the way of immediate improvements in African
agriculture are clearly very great and it is only when these have
been solved by research and experiment that agricultural progress
will become rapid. Yet nutritional standards are already deplorably
low and the demand for food increasing with numbers. An increase
in food supplies is already needed and will become still more urgent
as public expenditures on development increase cash incomes. This
is why agricultural research figures so largely in the development
plans of the colonial powers.

The failures of two large-scale British schemes of recent years
illustrate the difficulties to be overcome in the development of
African agriculture and emphasize the need for pilot experiments
based on careful research. In the first, the groundnut scheme, the
British government set itself to the reclamation, for groundnut
production, of some $3\frac{1}{4}$ million acres of almost uninhabited tropical
savannah in East Africa. The original scheme aimed at establishing
107 mechanized farm-units of 30,000 acres each, of which 150,000
acres was the target for the first year.

However, clearing operations proved slow and much more costly
than anticipated. Amongst a host of difficulties too numerous and
too technical to relate here, it seems that the exceptionally long
roots grown by trees in this arid country defied the bulldozers. Some
clearing operations were carried through despite these obstacles,
but only 30,000 acres were planted in the first season, and the crop

is said to have been less than the quantity of seeds put in. L. D. Stamp comments, "It was claimed that the rains failed and that when they did come they caused great damage by flooding, washing away of railways and roads, etc., yet it is doubtful whether the seasons experienced actually were unusual. . . ." [3] The variability of rainfall is very high, and total precipitation is small but concentrated in a few short weeks. It is no wonder that the area has been uninhabited.

The Gambia poultry farming scheme, initiated by the Colonial Development Corporation, also failed after two years. It too had been conceived on a grand scale and without preliminary pilot trials, the plan being to rear chickens, growing fodder for them locally. This scheme, which was initiated with a stock of hens, was blighted by a disease (Asiatic Newcastle) which decimated the poultry population. The London *Times* commenting on this and other development schemes in Africa said,

> The forces of nature are strong in the tropics and the conversion of bush into productive farming land is more than a task for bulldozers. The soil and its defects have to be closely studied. Usually there are good reasons why the natives have left the bush to nature. [4]

There are large-scale agricultural schemes which have been successful, for example, the Gezira cotton-growing scheme and the Gash scheme, both of the Nile Valley. Water control by irrigation, which has made possible the settled cultivation of these hitherto almost uninhabited areas, is a key to agricultural development in Africa. Even where rainfall is plentiful, there is the need for drainage and flood control. Storage and irrigation are needed where rainfall is normally moderate, both to guard against bad years and to extend the growing period. Where rainfall is low, irrigation is essential even where the total fall in most years is adequate for dry-zone crops. So much of Africa suffers from aridity that some writers go so far as to say that no rain falling on the surface of the continent should be allowed to reach the sea. Irrigation can be combined with water-power schemes as in the case of the new power dam just completed at Jinja, in Uganda. Other similar schemes such as that

[3] L. D. Stamp, *Africa: A Case-Study in Tropical Development* (London, 1954).
[4] The *Times* weekly edition (May 14, 1951).

for the Volta River in the Gold Coast and for the Kafue and Karina gorges in the Central African Federation, are being seriously studied in British territories. French, Belgian, and Portuguese plans also include large-scale water development projects.

Water control and development are also important to industry, and all sources of water supply must be tapped. In relation to the arid parts of tropical Africa the few large-scale irrigation schemes will affect only a fraction of the total agricultural area, and much could also be achieved by teaching the African peasant simpler methods of water storage and use, such as the digging of wells and tanks and the building of small dams. It is not surprising that the African peasant has not been able to evolve methods of water control, for there is little exact knowledge as yet of the water cycle in Africa. It is unfortunate also that the water table of the continent behaves irregularly because of the underlying complex of ancient rocks. Boreholes and wells are often sunk fruitlessly. The finding and tapping of underground reservoirs of water requires many surveys and the use of expensive equipment.

The importance of water development is recognized in the place it has been given alongside agricultural research as a major item in the development plans of all the colonial powers. The African territories are also receiving technical assistance for such research and development through Point Four and the UN. The development of scientific methods requires time, for Western scientists must gain practical experience of African soil and climatic conditions. As an example of what can be done, there are the successful farming ventures of the white settler population of East and Central Africa. The farming unit is relatively large, and considerable amounts of imported capital have been used for improvements, such as well-sinking and irrigation, purchase of agricultural equipment, livestock and improved seed. Attempts are being made to procure some of the economies of large-scale production for the African peasants by the promotion of group-farming enterprises in the British colonies. These are a form of agricultural extension work, planned to teach new techniques while providing common tractor services, water control and, where possible, the encouragement of good farming, such as green-manuring to procure fertility, and contour-plowing to prevent soil erosion.

Capital equipment in agriculture

Mechanization of African agriculture has been closely studied by European agricultural scientists, and it is recognized that there are a number of operations which can successfully be done by equipment, thus supplementing the existing manpower. One forceful argument against mechanization is that it will merely create a labor surplus. There are few areas (chiefly in Nigeria and Ruanda-Urundi) which one can presume to be overpopulated in the classical sense of having a continuous labor surplus. Elsewhere there is seasonal unemployment but hardly more. Labor is scarce in much of tropical Africa. This can be seen from the effects of the migrant-labor system. Labor migrating from the densely peopled palm belt of Nigeria and from Ruanda-Urundi is hardly missed at home, but elsewhere in tropical Africa the depletion of manpower through migration to the mines and towns has gone so far that agricultural production has already been handicapped.[5] The young migrant males, who often travel 100 miles or more and stay away years, are missed at peak working periods, such as clearing and harvesting, and it is at just such times that machinery can do most to help. Many of the measures recommended for better soil management are also laborious, if they are to be undertaken by hand. They can be carried through to a large extent by manual labor alone, as the Agricultural Service has demonstrated in its increasingly successful campaign against soil erosion in the East African (including Kikuyu) reserves. In India and China, manual labor is being used for land development on an extensive scale, but there is a view that the African farmer, undernourished and debilitated by disease, is not easily able to undertake the extra labor of contour ridging, well digging, and stream damming, or hoeing in green crops (green-manuring) and other laborious measures to improve the quality of his soil. Whether he is, in fact, in worse case than his Indian counterpart, there is good reason to use machinery in heavy operations where labor is depleted by migration.

On the other hand, African populations appear to be growing fast and opponents of mechanization ask what is to be done with an

[5] For example, see *Economic Survey of the Colonial Territories*, Vol. I (1951), p. 22. "There is much evidence to support the belief that too many Africans are entering employment from the point of view of the well-being of the rural areas."

increasing surplus of labor when the use of machinery will not in itself help to increase the land available for cultivation or yield per acre. The limitation upon expansion of acreage is the system of shifting cultivation which requires such a high proportion of area lying fallow. Until techniques of settled cultivation are successfully developed for the African peasant, land must be regarded as scarce.

It appears paradoxical to say that both land and labor are scarce in Africa. Yet both are true because of the techniques of resource utilization which the African has developed in its extremely difficult conditions. Africa is, above all, a problem continent, and assessment of its potentialities can only be made upon the basis of hypotheses about the probability of different trends in its development. The main hypotheses which must be set up are three. They concern the speed at which successful new techniques will be devised for agriculture, the possible development of new mining areas, and the rate at which African hopes of industrial development will be realized.

There is little that can be said upon the first two points, beyond the fact that considerable efforts are being made under both heads. The colonial powers have an increasing number of agricultural scientists at work in Africa, both in experimental stations and in extension services in the field. International technical co-operation and assistance in agriculture are developing increasingly, both through private and through government agencies. Funds are also flowing into geological survey and prospecting for minerals, for Africa's complex of ancient rocks is rich in minerals, as we already know, and new strikes may well be made.

The development of successful techniques for settled cultivation would change the African economic picture very favorably, since this would make possible the growth of a prosperous agriculture. This, with new mining enterprises, would provide a firmer basis than exists at present for further economic progress. Yet, with the present current of world opinion, especially amongst Africans themselves, it is unlikely that the development of manufacturing industry will be required to wait until agricultural progress is secure. Indeed there are industrial projects already where immigrant capital has started factory enterprises. The prospects for a rapid development of manufacturing industry in tropical Africa are too complex to analyze, and we can perhaps do no more at this stage than consider the arguments on both sides.

Factors affecting African industrial development

There are a number of factors which are not favorable to industrial development in Africa. There is virtually no African managerial skill. African labor is little used to machinery and its care and is virtually unskilled. Whereas a tradition of spinning and weaving existed in other preindustrial countries, it is a relatively recent comer to Africa. The labor force, unlike that of Japan in 1870, is undisciplined and, though well intentioned, is always described as showing inexplicable lapses of responsibility.[6] The quality of industrial output is, therefore, bound to be low in the early stages, despite the advances which have been made in the efficiency of machines in the last hundred years. African labor, as things stand at the moment, is very inefficient and, despite the extraordinarily low level of wages, it is high-cost. African manufacturers will thus be unable at present to compete in world markets.

The case for industrial development rests upon the desire to increase African productivity. With African population increasing, and with the present limitations on agricultural expansion, a fall in living standards is feared, and it is argued that this could be obviated by shifting the growing surplus of manpower from agriculture into industry. If mechanization of agriculture is introduced, the surplus of labor available for industry will be larger still. The logic of this argument rests upon the double advantage to the community, which benefits both from the new nonagricultural output and from the rise in agricultural capital (especially land) available for each worker remaining in agriculture. It is pointed out that South Africa has a well-developed manufacturing section, although its labor force is little better than that elsewhere on the continent.

There are some who see Africa standing on the threshold of an industrial revolution, faced by the same historical opportunity as nineteenth-century Japan. The twin supports of Japanese economic growth were rapid population increase, which provided an ample

6 This feature may be due to malnutrition or sickness, as the standard of health is so appallingly low.

supply of cheap industrial labor, and agricultural reform, which induced a steady rise in agricultural output per head of 1½ per cent per annum. Markets are being created by development-plan expenditure which will be the African counterpart of railway booms in nineteenth-century England and the income-generating investment which the Japanese government financed in the eighteen-eighties, chiefly in Japanese public utilities. Public investment by African governments in utilities and transport, which will increase consumer demand by wage employment of African labor, and will reduce costs by improving transport and communications, is a factor exceedingly favorable to economic development. African populations are also growing. But any prognosis of future outcome of industrial programs depends upon the hypotheses made as to agricultural reform, upon which Africa depends for increasing the supply of food, and as to new mining industries, which will provide a conflicting demand for manpower, amongst other factors. Inflationary dangers lie in the path. These will be especially critical if food supplies remain inelastic. There is no reason to suppose these dangers insuperable, given good government and proper fiscal policy, but it must be admitted that neither will be easy to maintain in the face of popular pressures for an immediate improvement in the mass standard of living. For example, it will nowadays be thought necessary, because of the change in social and ethical standards, to provide industrial labor with better urban housing, sanitation, and medical and welfare services than did the first large-scale enterprises in Africa. This will mean a higher volume of social investment in housing and amenities comparable with private investment in industry than was the case in South Africa.

It will also prove more difficult to secure a high level of voluntary personal savings. Increases in money income will tend to be spent immediately on consumption, chiefly of imported goods. Without an "Iron Curtain," as in Eastern Europe, to keep out constant comparisons with the richer countries' standards of living, the pressure for higher real consumption will be very great, a factor which will be inflationary if the scale and rate of capital formation are also maintained at a high level.

That there is as yet so little postwar industrial development in tropical Africa is partly because of these difficulties, and partly because of a deliberate omission in policy. The colonial development plans for Africa are similar to each other in their concentration upon transport, communications, water, and power, and upon agricultural research and both general and technical education. There is also an expansion of the medical and public-health services. The big gap is in investment of a more immediately productive kind, such as the establishment of raw-material-processing and other secondary industries. The logic of this omission is clear. Right or wrong, the Western democracies traditionally regard the sphere of public investment as being confined to public utilities, outside the field of manufacturing industry. They hope that private investment will promote manufacturing enterprises once the more important public services have been provided, that is, power and easy and reliable communications. Yet foreign enterprise remains reluctant to enter Africa, while native African enterprise is still, understandably, lacking. In the democracies there are also limits in the planning of demand. Russian consumer industries faced fewer problems in selling their manufactures at home, even in the early years, because competitive imports were shut out and because the pricing system and turnover tax were completely under state control. African domestic manufacturing output faces foreign competition—so far without guidance upon the possible extent of protective tariffs. While the providing of utilities will draw thousands of African peasants out of agriculture into cash employment and will therefore create a cash demand for consumer goods, it must be admitted that protected infant industries are likely to take root more easily than those facing competition from imports.

In East and Central Africa, in French North Africa, and, most prominently, in South Africa, the growing cash demand is, to some extent, being met from domestic manufacturing instead of imports. Secondary industries, financed and managed by white settlers, are already beginning to grow, and, hence, secondary incomes and employment are increasing. In West Africa, new manufacturing enterprises have begun with foreign capital. Yet these are still largely export-directed. The latest report on the British colonies says "general progress in industrialisation is illustrated by a rise in the number of persons employed in manufacture; it is estimated that in five major territories, containing nearly two-thirds of the colonial populations, employment in manufacturing industry increased by approximately 10 per cent between the end of 1950 and the end of 1952. Impetus to this process is being given by the improvement in power supplies and communications."

This rate of industrialization is still very small, when we remember that very small numbers were employed in manufacturing in 1950. The rate of progress in Africa has indeed so far been inevitably slow, even in the execution of public-policy schemes financed by foreign grants and loans. The developed countries of the world are giving funds at a greater rate than it has so far proved possible for the recipient areas to absorb capital. In 1952, even the modest sum of $500 million voted by Congress for underdeveloped areas proved difficult to place because of the shortage of technicians and limited governmental capabilities, especially in the smaller countries. Even in the British colonies, the Development and Welfare grants will not have been exhausted in the ten-year period prescribed, and they are to be extended beyond 1956. But the pace of development is increasing and it should reach much greater levels in the coming decade, other things being equal.

What remains unpredictable is the rate of growth of productive enterprises in Africa insofar as these are left to the private promoter. New institutions to encourage a greater flow of private capital to the underdeveloped countries are being studied in Europe and America. The colonial powers each have institutions through which low-interest loans are available to private investors. President Eisenhower's suggestion of an International Development Fund is paralleled by the UNESCO proposal for a special United Nations fund to make grants and low-interest loans for development. But productive investment requires not only finance but enterprise, and new institutions will need to be created also in the recipient areas if these funds are to be utilized.

That foreign private enterprise has so far been slow to investigate industrial and commercial opportunities is perhaps because of the fears of racial conflict. For, with the continued coincidence of racial with economic groupings, economic difficulties are apt to be ascribed to race differences.[7] In addition to business risks attendant

---

[7] For example, it is only to be expected that a period of rapid growth in Africa will be characterized by a sharp rise in local food prices, because of the inelasticity of domestic food supplies. Rising food prices tend to lead to industrial unrest, which will be intensified because of racial differences between master and servant in Africa.

upon new enterprises in strange markets, there are also the possible dangers of expropriation when these countries become more independent. In those parts of tropical Africa where the white population is small, industrial changes are not taking place so fast as in East and Central Africa. African incomes are too small to provide the volume of capital required if the whole industrial sector is to be privately financed, as the colonial powers desire. Few Africans have succeeded in amassing wealth, for even the domestic retail trade is dominated by non-African groups, interstitial between the giant European importing firms and the itinerant African "petty trader." Africans with managerial qualifications are few in number, for they have little experience even of commerce upon any large scale, much less of manufacturing. On the other hand, foreign capital is apprehensive toward "black Africa," as the French term it. Since the rates of return to be earned by capital in North America and Europe are nearly as high as those to be obtained abroad, foreign capital is reluctant to finance anything but the highly lucrative oil and mining enterprises in the underdeveloped countries of the world, especially Africa.

In Southeast Asia, where the problem is similar, one solution has been to supplement domestic state investment in utilities by the establishment of joint industrial enterprises, financed by a mixture of domestic public capital with foreign private investment. These enterprises enjoy foreign management and "know-how," yet they have provisions for training the nationals of the country concerned. Similar lines are being followed in the new Persian Oil Company. In Africa, and especially in British West Africa, although African private savings are small, there is domestic public capital available to finance such a share of the development program, both from budget surpluses and the considerable volume of domestic savings in the reserves of the marketing boards.

Without considerable investment, however financed, these territories may be expected to stagnate or even get poorer unless agricultural and mining development becomes rapid. The present rate of population growth is not accurately known, because of the inadequacy of demographic statistics, but all the evidence supports the view that the total number of indigenous Africans is increasing everywhere. This increase will be further stimulated by medical and public-health expenditures under the development plans. We have seen that land is becoming scarce and that fertility is falling. Unless this actual or potential population pressure can be relieved by the provision of new means of livelihood, income per head will decline.

This is the essential dilemma of Africa's economic development. The improvement in African health and education, labor-saving agricultural reforms, and the "pump-priming" effects of the public development programs are creating conditions which are favorable to economic growth and development. Yet it is only where there are white settlers that private enterprises in any numbers are being started. Where little or no foreign investment is forthcoming, it is unlikely that domestic savings, less still native enterprise, can fill the gap. It may be that agricultural progress and new mining developments will offset this, but, if not, then African poverty in non-settler areas may well increase and economic nationalism be intensified.

All the difficulties that have been enumerated can be taken as proving that African development cannot be hastened, that more research and experiment are needed in almost every field. Many people who know Africa argue, like Professor Frankel, that, "No amount of capital will buy time in Africa." Like many good epigrams, the obverse of this is also true. No amount of time will buy capital in Africa, for population growth may swallow up any small increases in income. Indeed, if the most gloomy estimates of rates of population growth are borne out, the rapid rise in numbers will even lead to a fall in income per head.

Africa has remained a poor area despite the considerable measure of economic development fostered by the various colonizing powers of the nineteenth century both through public and private invest-ment of foreign capital. With the ideas and knowledge current even in 1939, Africa had to be thought of as a continent which was still poor, although its natural resources had been developed as fully as possible upon the basis of the current knowledge of the time.

It is only since that time that there has been any general accept-ance of the view that still further development is possible. But the next stage of Africa's development depends upon the addition to her natural resources and human aptitudes of the scientific knowl-edge, the capital and equipment, and the industrial "know-how" of the more advanced countries of the world.

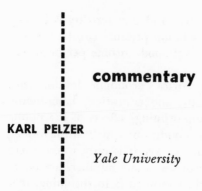

commentary

KARL PELZER

Yale University

After reading Dr. Ady's thought-provoking article "Africa's Economic Potentialities" there can scarcely be any doubt as to which of the two schools she belongs to—that of the optimists who have great hopes that the African tropics are capable of extensive development leading to greatly increased production of agricultural and mineral commodities and to the creation of an extensive network of industries processing the raw materials either for the local or the world market, or to the school of pessimists who expect little from Africa because they see physical-geographical as well as cultural obstacles to development wherever they turn. Let me state at the outset of my comments that I am considerably more optimistic than Miss Ady, although I should not go so far as do some optimists, who believe that Africa's potential is so great that economic development can easily provide a panacea for all the economic problems of Western Europe as well as provide the basis for greatly improved levels of living for the steadily increasing African population.

Dr. Ady has told you that Africa is a poor continent, nearly a quarter of which is composed of deserts and lakes and about another quarter of which is forest land. Deserts, lakes, forests, and the waste lands of the arctic tundra likewise certainly represent a very high percentage of the North American continent. And if we should also include the grasslands, which are relatively arid, we find that Africa compares favorably with North America. As we know from other parts of the world, desert regions can have fabulously rich sub-surface resources. Lakes and rivers can be the source of large quanties of protein and of hydroelectric power; they can also provide low-cost transport. Similarly, a high ratio of forest to some other type of natural vegetation does not necessarily have to be disadvantageous. I am, of course, well aware of the fact that tropical forests, on account of their heterogeneous composition, are not as valuable as the hardwood and softwood forests of the middle latitudes. But future research may very well lead to new silvicultural practices that will greatly increase the economic value of tropical forest regions.

The economic history of tropical Africa of the last fifty to seventy years includes some outstanding examples of remarkable economic growth [1] as well as some warning examples of utter failure of certain development schemes. Miss Ady has mentioned the Gezira cotton scheme of the Anglo-Egyptian Sudan; she might also have called our attention to Uganda's cotton industry, the Chagga coffee industry on the southern slopes of Mount Kilimanjaro, and to the peanut industry of northern Nigeria—where African peasants are producing more peanuts than the railroad can haul down to the coastal ports. There is the cacao industry of the Gold Coast, which owes its existence to African rather than to European initiative. On the other hand, we have the ill-fated peanut scheme of Tanganyika and the poultry scheme of Gambia, these being the two outstanding projects that failed in recent years, when the shortage of both food and foreign exchange created so much pressure and such sense of urgency that the establishment of pilot schemes was looked upon as old-fashioned—a sign of timidity. There are other smaller projects, less widely advertised, that also failed to produce the expected results. The fact that these schemes failed is, in my opinion, no reason for the pessimistic conclusion of some observers that Africa no longer has extensive areas capable of large-scale development. What has been brought out by the failures is that a great deal of preparatory research plus testing in pilot projects is required in Africa just as it is in other parts of the tropics.

Contrary to widely-held beliefs, soils of the humid tropics are usually poor, with the exception of recent alluvial and volcanic soils. It is the problem of our time to find out what kind of soil management will enable the African to produce higher yields than

1 This economic growth, measured in terms of increased production of agricultural commodities for export, particularly benefited the industrialized countries, however, while it often did not result in an improvement in the level of living for peasant producers in tropical Africa or in other tropical countries. On the contrary, in the nineteen-thirties the latter had to produce at least 50 per cent more primary commodities than in the last quarter of the nineteenth century in order to buy the same quantity of manufactured goods.

he did under the age-old system of shifting cultivation. Shifting cultivation is a sound agricultural technique only where population density is so low that each field can lie fallow long enough to regain its former fertility. However, in recent decades population growth, the development of peasant export agriculture (which increased greatly the demand for land), extensive alienation of land to individual European settlers or to plantation companies, and confinement of Africans to reservations have made it very often imperative to replace shifting cultivation by more advanced types of soil management.[2]

It is known that, prior to their contact with the European, the Africans themselves developed advanced farming techniques which permitted continuous use of the same parcel of land where local circumstances did not allow the long fallow periods necessary in most of tropical Africa. Such instances are to be found on the island of Ukara, in Lake Victoria, in southwest Sukumaland, and along the western Dinka, in the Aweil district of the Anglo-Egyptian Sudan. I mention these cases in order to bring out the fact that the African tiller did not have to wait for the Western technician before obtaining an answer to his problems.

As Dr. Ady has pointed out, the farming methods that were developed in Western Europe cannot be transferred automatically to tropical Africa or to any other part of the tropics. As a matter of fact, the agricultural techniques of Western Europe could not be applied to large parts of the United States, and the American farmer was forced, therefore, to develop agricultural techniques for the various parts of his country by the trial-and-error method. This took time. When it comes to tropical agriculture we must learn by experimenting on the spot. Recall the experiences of Lord Delamere in the Rift Valley. What is appropriate for the Kivu highlands does not necessarily suit the area around Stanleyville. Fertilizers that have proved to be extremely valuable in the middle latitudes are not necessarily suited to the tropics. The use of leguminous crops as part of the rotation turned out to be not as advantageous in the tropics as elsewhere.

[2] A valuable source of information regarding tropical soils and their utilization is, *Proceedings of the First Commonwealth Conference on Tropical and Sub-Tropical Soils, 1948.* Commonwealth Bureau of Soil Science, Technical Communication No. 46 (Harpenden, 1949).

I am not at all alarmed over the low average yields of tropical Africa, as reported by the Food and Agricultural Organization, because throughout tropical Africa we already have thousands of African farmers who have shown that even relatively poor soils are capable of yields which are two and three times higher than the average yields, provided the soils are handled properly. Poor soils can be improved, just as good soils can be ruined. We hear a great deal about destructive exploitation of soil resources in Africa, but this is by no means limited to Africans, as the recent agricultural history of European settlement in Southern Rhodesia and Kenya shows. We often read about the serious problem of overstocking of the African grasslands and the reluctance of Africans to follow recommendations of the Agricultural Extension Service. Anybody familiar with the history of the grazing lands of the United States knows that even as of this moment a considerable part of the grazing regions is seriously overstocked, despite at least half a century of efforts on the part of the U. S. Department of Agriculture and other government agencies to bring about a reduction in the number of grazing animals on the range.

The two great problems in Africa, as in other parts of the tropics, are (1) to develop farming systems which will permit higher yields per unit of land and per man-hour without adverse effects on the soil and (2) to devise effective channels of rapid transmission down to the grass roots of the lessons learned in the research stations. In the past, most tropical research stations were concerned with specific single export crops rather than with the over-all problem of better land use. In areas with European farming communities there was a tendency to devote a disproportionately large percentage of the funds to agricultural research—particularly useful to European settlers and plantations—and to neglect the problems of the African cultivator. (Since World War II, however, attempts have been made to correct this.) In the past, European farmers have been known to ask for preferential treatment in the form of sub-sidies or special freight rates, and they have requested ordinances preventing Africans from raising commercial crops in competition with Europeans. That European and African farmers can engage in the same industry and even co-operate with each other is evidenced, however, by the arrangement between the Kilimanjaro Native Co-operative Union and the Tanganyika Coffee Growers'

Association, under which the two organizations share equally in the ownership of the Tanganyika Coffee Curing Company, Ltd. at Moshi. During the years that the total coffee crop was sold to the British Ministry of Food, no effort was made to keep the coffee coming from the plantations separated from the coffee produced by these Chagga farmers.

Being a geographer, I noted with a great deal of satisfaction that Dr. Ady paid special attention to those physical-geographical aspects of Africa which offer obstacles to economic development. This awareness of the importance of the physical environment is all too often lacking among economists and other social scientists. However, when it comes to the assessment of the economic potentialities of an area, the cultural environment is just as important as the physical environment, if not more so. The culture of the people— their value system, their social structure, their attitudes toward physical labor, co-operative enterprise, individual initiative, accumulation of savings, their attitudes toward and aptitudes for such basic occupations as agriculture, livestock raising, trading or mining—these factors help to make up such a cultural environment. Many of the striking differences in the degree of economic development which one meets in Africa can be fully understood only when one examines both the cultural and the physical environment. Often it is easier to overcome physical obstacles than human opposition to change.

Dr. Ady has called our attention to the tsetse fly, which prevents the development of mixed farming in large parts of Africa. We must also remember that the tsetse fly prevented the use of the plow in these areas. The plow is an extremely dangerous agricultural implement unless it is handled properly and in combination with adequate antierosion measures. D. W. Malcolm in his recent study on Sukumaland states:

> The "go-slow" policy adopted in Nigeria and Nyasaland with regard to the introduction of ox-drawn ploughs has much to recommend it and the Sukumaland Native Authority, being alive to these dangers, has introduced local legislation for the control of ploughing. Should the use of the ox-drawn plough become general the supervision of perhaps 100,000 units to obviate soil damage would be an enormous task.[3]

[3] D. W. Malcolm, *Sukumaland: An African People and their Country* (London: Oxford University Press, 1953), p. 127.

May I also mention in passing that mixed farming involves the systematic application of manure to the land. Applications of from three to five tons of manure per acre have given yield increases of up to 300 percent in the first year. Furthermore, for as long a period as four years the residual effect of a single application was very noticeable. However, the absence of farm roads and the lack of carts make it extremely difficult to disseminate the practice of mixed farming as rapidly as desirable.

I find myself in full agreement with Dr. Ady when it comes to the importance of water development. There are extensive areas in Africa which are suitable for farming, provided the population can be supplied with adequate quantities of water for human and animal consumption. The rainfall is sufficient for the raising of a good crop, but there is no surface water available during the long dry season. The drilling of deep wells will provide water for Africans from congested areas, but locating these subterranean sources of water and sinking wells requires government assistance.

For many years the proponents of large-scale plantation agriculture expected an ultimate complete victory of the oil-palm plantations of the Belgian Congo and of Southeast Asia over the small Nigerian palm-oil producer, because, they argued, the peasant would never be able to produce large quantities of palm oil with a low free-fatty-acid content of less than 4.5 per cent. And indeed, as late as 1950 only 0.2 per cent of the Nigerian palm oil deserved the grade "special oil" on account of a free-fatty-acid content below 4.5 per cent. However, according to recent estimates, as much as 50 per cent of all palm oil purchased by the Nigerian Oil Palm Produce Marketing Board in 1953 was of the highest grade. This revolutionary change in the course of only three years seems to have been due to three factors: the system of price incentives offered by the Nigerian Oil Palm Produce Marketing Board; the introduction of hand presses; and the introduction of the so-called pioneer mills, which are power-operated and are more efficient in that they give a higher extraction rate than the hand presses. In 1952 the price differential between the highest and lowest grade of oil purchased amounted to £ 50 per ton, i.e., the difference between £ 80 and £ 30. It is quite obvious that the price incentive acted as the trigger and encouraged the acquisition of both hand and power-driven presses. The number of power-driven presses increased from 5, in

1949, to 53, in 1953, and that of hand presses from 2,700 to 5,300 in the same period.[4]

Anyone who has traveled in East Africa has heard a great many complaints about labor scarcity and the inefficiency and high turnover of labor, on the one hand, and scarcity of land, on the other hand. We are here confronted with a vicious circle. Usually the wages paid to African plantation and mine laborers are so low and housing facilities are so poor that the women and children cannot accompany the men but must stay behind and make a living by carrying on subsistence agriculture as well as they can.[5] Because they are separated from their families, the men usually return as soon as they have reached the immediate goal which led them to seek employment. A different labor policy could lead to the migration of whole families to mines and plantations. This would result on the one hand in a reduction of labor turnover and in a raising of labor efficiency, provided that a real effort were made to train the African. On the other hand, this would reduce the pressure on the land, permit an increase in the size of the farms of those who do not migrate, and would create an internal market for agricultural products. It could even lead to intensification and specialization of those African farming communities linked by road or rail with industrial areas. The Belgian labor policy in the Congo seems to have produced such results and is leading to the growth of a permanently urbanized, skilled labor force.

In conclusion, I should like to express my full agreement with Dr. Ady's observation that the development of the African tropics, like that of any other part of the world, requires a great deal of time, the one thing which those who are determined to bring about a rapid bonification of underdeveloped tropical areas are not willing to grant. Just before the groundnut scheme was started in Tanganyika, there were many persons in Great Britain and in Africa who believed that an African shifting cultivator, who heretofore

[4] *The United Africa Company, Ltd., Statistical and Economic Review,* No. 13 (March, 1954), pp. 3–14.

[5] It might be observed in this connection that this statement does not apply to the 37,000 African mineworkers employed on the Northern Rhodesian copperbelt, well over 60 per cent of whom are married and have their families living with them in housing provided by the companies.

worked mainly with the hoe, could practically overnight become a permanent cultivator, tilling the land with tractor-drawn implements. This was wished upon him in order to alleviate the food shortage in Great Britain rather than a food shortage in Africa. More intensive cultivation practices, erosion control measures, pest control, reduction of the number of livestock per unit of land, and other improvements of agriculture are necessary, but, unless the African is willing to accept the changes and is ready to co-operate, it will be extremely difficult to obtain permanent results.

Above all, the development of tropical Africa requires careful planning in order to forestall poor investment of capital. A sound knowledge, on the part of planners, of the physical and cultural setting and of the complex interrelationship between man and his environment is essential. It would be ideal to obtain the co-operation of scientists representing the natural and the social sciences. Only co-operative research of physical and social scientists concerned with the physical as well as the social and cultural problems which we meet in Africa will give us the data necessary for the planning of a sound development of the natural and human resources of Africa.

colonial development and welfare

A. CAMPBELL

Colonial Attaché, Embassy of Great Britain

Charges of "colonialism" and "imperialism" are not only made because of a particular constitutional relationship between two peoples. From time to time the United States itself is charged with these very "crimes." This is perhaps particularly irksome to the U. S. because it feels very strongly about self-government and, because of its history, is often regarded as its champion. But the fact that these charges are made does indicate that progress is indivisible and that it is dangerous to assume, as a study of American history might lead one to assume, that colonial peoples will, if they become self-governing, be able to stand on their own feet, economically as well as politically. There are in fact vast differences in population, in the incidence of disease, in geographical position, and in geological structure between the present colonial lands and the United States. It takes time and money to overcome these and to put the under-developed countries of Africa on a level with the West. The United States has found this in the Virgin Islands. Since taking them over from the Danes, in 1917, it has given over $82 million to them— a large sum of money for only 26,000 people and a rate of expenditure about 24 times that which the United Kingdom has been able to afford in a comparable period in the whole Colonial Empire. Yet the Virgin Islands are still in a territorial status. The United States could no doubt cut the painter and launch the Virgin Islands out into the world in their present unprepared state, just as the United Kingdom could with large areas of Africa, the West Indies, or the Far East. But neither thinks that that would be in the interests

420

of the inhabitants themselves or, indeed, of the world as a whole, which probably has its complement of weak, tottering components: in recent years too many relatively strong governments have fallen into the hands of the Communists, and we in the West do not want to increase the number of those who might be even easier prey.

The main reason for the development and welfare policies that the British have been pursuing must then be this: they want to assist their colonies to the utmost of their capacity and resources to establish those economic and social conditions upon which alone self-government can be soundly based.

So much for the reason. Now let us turn for a moment to the history. The British connection with most of the colonies has been short. British Africa, with its 50 millions of people has been under British influence for barely sixty years. Take Nigeria, the largest and most populous of the African dependencies. It was proclaimed a protectorate only in 1900, and it was not until 1914 that the North and South were amalgamated to form the present colony and protectorate. Uganda 1894, Kenya 1898, and so on. It is barely the lifetime of a single old man. In most of Malaya and the Pacific, British administration dates from the 1870's but reached its present extent only gradually in the course of the next 30–40 years. And when the British went to these countries, they did not find a settled community, a well-based system of government, prosperous agriculture, and a thriving export trade—they went in most cases to stop tribal wars, to combat the ravages of disease, to institute systems of government, and to develop the untapped wealth of these territories so that they could win their places in the world.

The first task of any administration was to establish law and order, to build hospitals, and to open up the country by roads and railways. In that the British were very largely successful: the death rate in Singapore, near the equator, is now no higher than that of the United Kingdom; Cyprus, where malaria was completely eradicated in 1949, has one of the lowest death rates in the world; and in Jamaica, Trinidad, and British Guiana the average length of life has increased by 15 years since 1921. In Africa there were 32 miles of railways in 1900. In 1950 there were 7,000 miles and 88,000 miles of trunk and secondary roads. The British have, I think, a good record in the provision of basic services.

All of us, I suppose, started off by being farmers or hunters. That was certainly the case in the British colonies, and the quickest way to build up the development of the colonies was to improve and expand their agricultural activities. Sometimes new crops were introduced—rubber in Malaya, cocoa in West Africa, sisal in East Africa. Where it was possible, export crops were developed, and in fact most of the colonies became, in course of time, agricultural producers, dependent—as most agricultural producers in the world are—on world prices for their produce and without very much power to influence those prices.

Colonial revenues were as a result similarly dependent, because the only source of wealth in many colonies was provided by their export crops, and in other respects the people lived in a subsistence economy. It is difficult to tax a subsistence economy: in the olden days in England the church did it with its tithes, but always had difficulty in disposing of the tithes thus paid and commuted them for cash when possible. Colonial revenues were therefore raised, by and large, in two ways. First the produce paid an export tax as it left the colony. Secondly the consumer goods which were imported to meet the needs of the people (and for which they paid with the money they got for their crop) were again taxed as they came in. You can see at once the double effect which a drop in the price of a colonial commodity could have. Take the case of the Gold Coast: its economy was (and in fact still is very largely) a one-crop economy—cocoa. After the Wall Street Stock Exchange crisis in 1929 the prices of nearly all agricultural commodities fell by as much as 50 or 60 per cent, and at the same time the demand for them fell also. So, in 1930, the Gold Coast was in double financial difficulties since its exports and therefore its export taxes fell, whilst, because less money came into the country for the purchase of cocoa, less money was available to buy imported consumer goods, and imports therefore fell off. This meant that less was collected in import duties. The effect of this can be seen by comparing the revenue figures for 1927 and 1931. In the former year government raised about $11 million but in the latter the same set of taxes plus some others only succeeded in bringing into the Gold Coast Treasury $6.5 million.[1] This placed the government in a very

[1] The author is indebted to Noel Hall, wartime Development and Welfare Adviser to West Africa, for these figures.

embarrassing position because a good deal of its expenditure, such as the salaries of officials, the interest on its loans, its contributions to sinking fund, its recurrent expenditure on schools and hospitals, could not be drastically reduced in the same way as its revenue had. The result was that all development expenditure had to be severely cut down. The Gold Coast weathered this financial crisis by living on its fat for a while, but when the crisis was over its European staff had been cut from 1200 to just over 400. This same kind of thing happened to many colonies all over the world.

Of course, in the event of a colony's going on the rocks, Britain performed salvage operations, and in fact, between 1920 and 1945, about $78 million was paid over all the colonies in such operations. But these salvage operations were not popular—on either side. For the local government could then be brought under United Kingdom Treasury control, which meant that the Treasury could, if it wished, scrutinize every single item of expenditure. It was the aim of every colonial government to avoid this if it possibly could, and this meant that they avoided also any risks in their development planning. Of course it is not always possible to plan the development of a large country without taking risks.

They were not popular either in the United Kingdom, not only because the British taxpayer disliked putting his hand in his pocket but because it was a widely held belief in the period immediately before the First World War—and for quite a long time after it— that colonies should live on their own resources and that anything which suggested permanent assistance from the United Kingdom would in the end retard their political development and pauperize them. Politically, any suggestion for a colonial subsidy was bound to run into opposition in the Houses of Parliament. Britain lived by overseas trade, but the contribution which colonial trade made to the Commonwealth was so small that the incentive to support a subsidy was lacking. This attitude is scarcely comprehensible in the light of the history of the last two decades. But it was in fact the accepted view in Britain that a dependency should have the communications, social services, and so forth, which it could afford out of its own revenues, and that economic development was properly the function of private enterprise. Some territories with good and easily accessible natural resources achieved fair progress, but this laissez faire attitude meant that in many others progress was slow.

Colonial development therefore during this period, compared with the pace that was achieved later, was an unspectacular process. Governments were, for the reasons I have given, concentrating on the establishment of basic services, and governments were also chary of taking risks in their development planning. In these circumstances the first act which provided United Kingdom funds for colonial development—the act of 1929—was somewhat of an oddity. It was passed to promote "commerce with or industry in the United Kingdom" by providing $2.8 million a year for such purposes as agricultural machinery, transport, harbors, forestry services, electicity, and public health. At this distance of time, and in view of our later record, we can afford to be charitable toward its framers, who seem to have had in mind primarily the relief of impending unemployment in the United Kingdom. Nevertheless, in eleven years about $25 million were put through this rather dubious channel into colonial development, and some good resulted. By and large, however, schemes of welfare were not included, and this measure did not involve any departure from the principle that a colony should have only those services which it could afford to maintain itself.

The 1930's, you may remember, were a period of world-wide economic distress. Its effect on the highly industrialized countries of the West was great, but its effect on the commodity producers was greater, and caused widespread disruption. Most of them were one- or two-crop economies (cocoa in Gold Coast, rubber and tin in Malaya, cotton and coffee in Uganda, palm oil and groundnuts in Nigeria). All their eggs were in one basket, and the bottom fell out of the basket. But this had a great influence in revising the ideas of Britain on how development in the colonies should be carried out. The economic distress produced a change in the attitude toward the central government's part in economic affairs, not only in Britain but also in the overseas empire, and it led eventually to the acceptance of an increased responsibility on the part of Britain for development and welfare in the colonies. The change may be stated in terms that from 1940 onwards financial assistance was made available to colonies by the United Kingdom without grant-in-aid (or Treasury) control. In fact, however, it was much wider than this, because the assistance given was increased in every way. Basically the advantage of the new Colonial Development and Welfare Acts of 1940, 1945, and 1950 was that they enabled colonies to plan their development ahead in the assurance that the plans which they had made would not be upset by temporary fluctuations in their revenues. This is what the Colonial Secretary of the day said: "If full and balanced development is to be obtained, and if colonial governments are to be placed in a position to maintain administrative, technical and social services at proper standards, some assistance from outside is necessary at this stage. Few of the colonies have the good fortune to possess substantial mineral wealth, and in comparatively few are there manufacturing industries of any magnitude. The majority are wholly, or almost wholly, dependent on the more limited resources derived from agriculture. The value of agricultural products varies widely from year to year as conditions fluctuate in the world market, with the result that colonial revenues provide an unreliable basis for a policy of steady development. In some cases the position is aggravated by a heavy burden of indebtedness. However able their government, however efficient their economic administration, many colonies cannot finance out of their own resources the research and survey work, the schemes of major capital enterprise and the expansion of administrative or technical staffs which are necessary for their full and vigorous development. Nor can they always afford, in the absence of such development, an adequate standard of health and education services."

The total sum made available in 1940 was $14 million a year for ten years plus $1,250,000 a year for research. This Act was framed under the shadow of grave events in France, and by the time the third reading was taken the situation had deteriorated to such an extent that it had to be announced that the purposes of war must have the first call on the resources of the country whether in men, material, or money. Many desirable schemes of colonial development had therefore to be abandoned unless they could be carried out with local resources of men and material and without detriment to the war effort.

The result over the five years working of the Act was that about $29 million was issued and schemes involving an additional $55 million were approved and were carried over to the subsequent Act.

In 1945 the amount for the succeeding ten years was increased to $336 million, with a limitation of $49 million in any one year. In 1950 an extra $56 million was added, and the present position is that no more than $70 million can be spent in any one year and $7 million a year on research. All of this comes out of the pocket of the United Kingdom taxpayer.

There are several things which are interesting to note about the 1945 Act. In the first place, in introducing it the Secretary of State asked colonies to review their rates of income tax so as to ensure that local revenues contributed to the maximum extent to the advancement of the territory. The introduction of income tax is itself an index of the progress that had in fact taken place in the change from a subsistence to a money economy. Secondly, funds were earmarked for individual colonies and they were told this. Allocation was a difficult matter: no single criterion was adopted for judging the requirements of one colonial territory as against another, but all the factors which were thought to be relevant were taken into account, including the size and population of the territory, its known economic resources and possibilities, the present state of development, the development schemes known to exist or to be under contemplation, and the financial resources likely to be available locally. On the whole no great injustice at the time was done, but looking at it in the retrospect of the later development of some of the colonies, it is fairly clear that the allocations meant far less to some than they did to others. And based on that allocation, colonies were asked to frame comprehensive development plans financed not only by Colonial Development and Welfare funds but also from surplus balances and loan resources.

The aftermath of war has of course radically altered the whole picture in those colonies whose products have enjoyed a series of years of very high prices. Over the whole empire the level of the exports of primary products is roughly one-third higher than it was before the war: there have been spectacular increases in the exports of bauxite, copper, petroleum, sugar, sisal, and rubber (bauxite 1936—170,000 tons, 1953—2,600,000 tons; copper 1936— 153,000 tons, 1953—388,000 tons; sugar 1936—984,000 tons, 1953— 1,505,000 tons; and so on) ; but of equal importance have been the increase by value: sugar 1936—$22.4 million, 1953—$165 million; cocoa 1936—$31 million, 1953—$238 million. This has meant that the contribution which Colonial Development and Welfare funds have made to the total development plans has assumed a less important role than was foreseen ten years ago. In fact at the first of March this year, out of a total of $1½ billion, being the total development plans for the ten-year period 1946–56, Colonial Development and Welfare contributed only $246,072,400—about 23 per cent of the whole. The balance came from loan funds and local resources. And these will no doubt be supplemented by the contributions which the autonomous marketing boards for cocoa, palm kernels, and cotton, etc., make to various development projects. In the Gold Coast where one of the most spectacular rises in revenue has taken place in the last decade the Colonial Development and Welfare contribution is only about 2.5 per cent of the whole. In other territories, however, the price of raw commodities is dropping, e.g., rubber in Malaya has been hard hit by the competition of American synthetic rubber; Hong Kong has suffered because of restrictions on exports to China; and, in Africa, Kenya is bearing the additional burden of having a local war on its hands. (Out of a budget expenditure of about $84 million, $22.4 million is emergency expenditure—over a quarter of the whole.) Here the Colonial Development and Welfare contribution will be relatively greater, but over all, whilst there are signs that the revenues of colonies are beginning to flatten out, if not to drop, the financial position seems to have changed so fundamentally that when the next Colonial Development and Welfare legislation is introduced (as has been promised soon) the 1945 pattern is bound to change. At least this must be the case if the same criteria are applied as in 1945.

What in the meantime has been achieved? Actual issues from the vote up to March 30, 1954, have been $237 million, and they include soil erosion and the development of African agriculture in Kenya, the provision of better rubber planting material to small holders in Malaya, co-operative marketing assistance in Hong Kong, inland transport in Nigeria, a series of university colleges in the Gold Coast, Nigeria, West Indies, and East Africa, harbor improvements in Freetown and Malta. In Tanganyika large sums are being spent on roads, and in fact expenditure on transport is the largest single item in the official development plans in most of the territories. The recent United Nations report on Economic Changes in Tropical Africa pin-pointed more transport and better marketing

facilities as the two chief needs in the changeover from a subsistence to an exchange economy. Varying local needs have of
course indicated varying types of projects. In some territories the
emphasis is on economic development, in others expenditure has
been mainly devoted to improving health and education. I remember well an incident that the Development Adviser for West Africa
(appointed under the 1940 Act) recounted. It was when he was
visiting the Emirate of Katsina in Northern Nigeria. After a meeting with the young Emir to discuss development plans he asked
him what was the chief need for the development of his people.
The young Emir replied: "Give my people clean water to drink
and a small amount of irrigation work." And when he was asked
"What next?" the Emir replied, "Nothing—if you give my people
clean water, it will take you and me the rest of our lives to work
out all the consequences that will follow." What he was asking to
be done was that the vicious circle should be broken. His people
have had to drink water infected with Guinea worm. Because of
Guinea worm, at the end of the dry season when they should have
been most vigorous in their fields, they were so weak that they could
not farm their lands properly. The result was that they got a smaller
crop than they should, and before the next harvest was ready, and
when the ravages of Guinea worm were at their height, they were
doubly debilitated—both hungry and diseased. Any development
plan for that area which did not attempt to break into this vicious
circle would be a waste of money.

We have necessarily become immersed in detail. If we may come
to the surface now, I think that the first thing that we should put
our eyes to is the ultimate objective. That is self-government for
the colonies, under conditions that will ensure to all their peoples
a rising standard of living and freedom from aggression from any
quarter. There is no doubt that the stimulus that the many schemes
of development and welfare have given to the colonies have made
this possible sooner and more successfully than if there had been
no colonial development and welfare. If democracy is to function
successfully in these colonies, to whom it is a Western importation,
the mass of the people must be armed with the means of controlling
their leaders—another way of saying that the gap between peasant
and intellectual must be closed. Political advancement under its
own stimuli of another war fought for democracy, of United Na-

tions influence, and of the ideology of communism had gone so far ahead that extraordinary efforts were needed to close this gap. It can only be closed by going ahead as fast as possible with education, health services, communications, and the like: and, because these create a burden in recurrent costs on any government which has them, equal attention must be given to economic development. Hence the emphasis in the Acts are development and welfare—in that order.

Striking advances have been made. In 1932 the revenues of all colonial governments were $112 million; in 1952, $1 billion. In 1948, capital formation in the colonial territories reached $532 million—in 1952, $1,120 million. In Nigeria there were 336 schools in 1920, now there are over 9,000 and so on. All of this is gratifying. But there are limitations to what can be achieved: some areas are badly underpopulated. Take British Honduras for instance: 8,000 square miles inhabited by 75,000 people—an average of about 9 per square mile. In the days of the Mayan Empire, 1,000 years ago, ten times that number were supported by that land. Other areas are overpopulated—Barbados has 1,300 to the square mile. Others are comprised of dry, barren soil like much of British Somaliland or Aden. All are in the tropical belt where water and insect-borne diseases sap human vitality. Very few are near large areas of population and highly developed communications which provide the incentive for industrial development. The rapid industrialization of the colonial empire has therefore many obstacles to overcome before it is achieved. The project at Owen Falls, Uganda, opened by the Queen on the twenty-ninth of April, 1954, will overcome one such obstacle by the provision of power in a country which formerly had wood as its only fuel. The capacity of the generating plant (at its maximum, which has not yet been reached) will be 700 million units of electricity. Consumption in Uganda has risen from 6½ million units, in 1948, to over 51 million, in 1953, but there is still a long way to go; and electricity is being supplied in bulk to Kenya. In the Gold Coast a similar scheme is however linked to an aluminum smelter; and this seems likely, by providing the Gold Coast with an entirely new and heavy industry, to give the local economy a great stimulus since growing consumption of aluminum in the world appears to be a certainty.

These two schemes (neither of them relying on Colonial Development and Welfare funds) outstrip, in their cost and their effect on local development, anything else in the colonial empire. But elsewhere where progress has been concentrated primarily on increasing agricultural productivity, there is no cause for pessimism: the farmer does not starve in a world that is gradually getting short of food. Nor does the miner in a world that is quickly finding new uses for metals which the colonies—and in particular Africa—possess: iron, manganese, cobalt, chrome, bauxite, copper, and so on. In the agricultural fields the introduction of new crops, the defeat of old pests (swollen shoot of cocoa, sudden death of cloves, etc.), the opening up of new land, the control of soil erosion, and the co-operative marketing of crops, all offer challenges of research, organization, or administration to those concerned with colonial development. And in the mineral field the completion of geological surveys, as in British Guiana, or the opening up of new communications, as in Southern Tanganyika, to mine the coal deposits, set their related problems. Besides these, such industrialization as can lessen the pressure on the land and lessen also the dependence of colonial peoples on other countries for their consumer goods—glass, cement, textiles, canned fruit come quickly to mind—is bound to have a stimulating effect on local development. There is a good basis here for progress and no cause for defeatism over the various problems I have mentioned. After all, at the close of the American Revolution the United States was not then in a class with the West Indies as a source of raw materials for Europe—and yet look at it now.

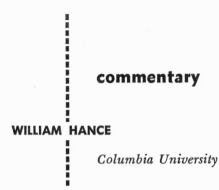

commentary

WILLIAM HANCE

Columbia University

Archibald Campbell has presented clearly the reasons for and the ultimate objectives of United Kingdom contributions to colonial development and welfare. Few of us will take exception to these basic considerations or deny that the total program has helped raise the standard of living of many colonial peoples.

We have also been reminded of the importance of historical perspective, particularly of the short period of European colonization in Africa and of the evolving attitude over the years toward colonial issues. Even if one goes back to earlier stages of conquest and exploitation and moves forward to the more recent stages of trusteeship and partnership, a relatively brief historical period is involved. The evolution away from *laissez faire* in the matter of colonial development and welfare, as Mr. Campbell points out, has been even more rapid. It has reflected, I believe, the concept increasingly accepted in the metropolitan powers that the state should be an active agent in promoting the welfare and safeguarding the economic well-being of its peoples.

Projecting this concept to the colonies, as is gradually being done, means that, in theory, a "backward" colony should receive from its controlling power the same treatment that that power would give to one of its own "depressed" or "backward" areas. In practice, this is seldom fully carried out, and it is more than doubtful that it could be. But there has been in postwar years a notable increase in the efforts to bring previously neglected areas into the stream of the modern world.

Before the war, remote areas and those poor in resources were usually neglected or given very minor roles in whatever development was taking place. Today, there are numerous examples of development and welfare programs in these less-favored areas. The southern Sudan, too distant from the seaboard to encourage commercial production, is the scene of the Zande scheme, an experiment in organized shifting agriculture designed to upgrade a tribe previously practically untouched. The northern territories of the Gold Coast have the Gonja or Damongo scheme and northwest Nigeria has the Sokoto Rice scheme, involving the mechanized plowing of seasonally flooded river-lands to provide rice for an expanded local food supply. Damongo is about 250 miles and Sokoto 130 miles from the nearest railheads.

Even the aborted groundnut scheme may have reflected, possibly unconsciously, this new philosophy. Tanganyika, which had been relatively neglected in inter-war years, was selected as its site, despite knowledge that production could more readily be expanded in existent producing areas of West Africa. This new-found concern for spreading the good rather than permitting concentration in the economically more productive regions is reflected also in France's greatly expanded interest in French Equatorial Africa and French Cameroon, previously the Cinderellas of the French Empire, to a degree in the Babua and similar schemes in the Belgian Congo, and in the development programs of such magnificently sterile areas as Somalia.

This new concern, I believe, will evolve more fully in the years ahead and will be important in future allocations of development and welfare funds.

The figures of development and welfare expenditures presented by Mr. Campbell convey, in one sense, the substantial assistance contributed by the taxpayers of the United Kingdom toward colonial development—$246 million in ten years. The *United Nations Summary of Recent Economic Development in Africa, 1952–53,* gives us additional valuable estimates of expenditures on development programs. The total proposed allotments of seventeen British African territories on ten-year development programs is $949 million; $86 million were expended in 1952 in the Belgian Congo ten-year plan; and $281 million were spent in 1952 on development in French territories south of the Sahara. Although these are assuredly considerable sums, they are less impressive when considered in relation to the size of the recipient population and the needs of the areas involved. By comparison, the New York Throughway, 1½ per cent the size of British Africa alone, will cost $500 million. I realize that it is not entirely realistic to compare expenditures in Africa with those in the United States, but my purpose is to underline the very real limitations on available governmental capital. It is far too often assumed that capital is the readiest element in development, an impression that is fostered by glowing accounts of colonial progress.

The fact that funds are restricted suggests at least two policies: one, that greater attention should be placed on formation of capital within overseas territories and on attraction of capital to them; and second, that every available pound, franc and escudo should be expended wisely.

This second point raises the question: have the sums so generously provided been well used? The summer 1954 issue of the *Times Review of British Colonies* (p. 2) states that there has been "inefficiency, mishandling, sometimes on a shocking and grotesque scale." The *Economist* (August 22, 1953, p. 489) suggests that some development funds have been "grandiosely wasted" and "fribbled away in international boondoggling."

One cannot hope in a page or two to lay down rules of what to do and what not to do with regard to expenditure on colonial development and welfare. But I should like to put forward a few considerations, based in considerable part, no doubt, on personal prejudices.

First, large scale projects should be preceded by small-scale prototypes. Tank-tractors rusting on the plains of Tanganyika, and the ghost port of Mtwara, are monumental reminders that this rule has been broken at rather substantial cost. The Sudan Gezira scheme is an example, on the other hand, of a successful project built upon considerable prior experience and experiment.

An important sub-point to this consideration is that no scheme should involve the introduction of large numbers of animals until small numbers have demonstrated their climatic adaptability and resistance to disease. So notorious is the tropical African environment in this regard that one wonders how the large-scale Gambia poultry scheme was so hopefully approved.

Second, and these considerations are presented in no order of priority, programs that call for welfare without development or that require continuing expenditure without providing any means of support should be carefully questioned. So urgent are the needs for improvement of health, housing, and education that there is temptation to commit local governments to expenditures they cannot afford. This may in turn preclude worthwhile development projects and tend, therefore, toward a static economy. The dangers of an improper approach are apparent in the case of so-called "disease eradication" programs, which must usually be financed indefinitely. Future inability to sustain a program might lead to epidemics of appalling proportions, particularly among children who had acquired no immunity to the "eradicated" disease.

Third, the per-capita and per-acre costs of development schemes of all sorts should bear some relation to the general economy of the territory involved. There have been a number of projects, both enacted and proposed, involving expenditures running to four- and five-hundred dollars an acre and several thousands of dollars per capita, both completely out of line with the value of the land or with a practical scale of personal income. Resettlement projects are perhaps the worst offenders in this regard, but available funds do not permit either the cost or the maintenance of many such colonial showplaces.

Fourth, I should like to plug for the primacy of agriculture among economic activities to be aided by colonial development funds. Conversely, expenditures on developing colonial industry should be made with exceeding care.

Fifth, I think that research could profitably be allocated more than 10 per cent of total development funds. Although there is a rapidly growing body of knowledge on African physical problems, the impressive thing is how little we really know about the tropical environment. We need studies on climate, on laterized soils, on the effects of bush-firing, on swamp control, and on a host of other basically physical problems.

We need increased research on subsistence crops. All the powers may be fairly criticized, I believe, for having given disproportionate attention in the past to research on commercial crops and for having neglected largely the basic foodstuffs, on which great improvements can undoubtedly be made. The increased inter- and intra-territorial trade in these commodities now provides economic incentive for giving attention to these crops, and the build-up of markets for internal produce is an important way of offsetting the fragility of "one-crop economies."

Research and experimentation are also needed on the *organization* of colonial development projects. The quickening pace of political development, and in some cases excessive population, create constant pressure to increase indigenous production and productivity. This cannot be accomplished simply by dissemination of oral and written advice. It requires organization, and there are a variety of organizational approaches deserving study, such as the tri-partite partnership successfully pioneered in the Gezira scheme and now being copied in a number of projects in French, Belgian, and British territories, group-farming in Kenya, and various forms of co-operatives. In eastern Nigeria, where plantations have largely been excluded in the past, interesting experiments are going forward on community-owned plantations designed to take advantage of the undoubted efficiencies of this system. Lastly, reports from several territories call for research on the organization of range and grazing control.

I may, in presenting this case for greater research and experimentation in colonial development and welfare, open myself to the criticism of suggesting delay in direct application. To such criticism I would reply, the more desperately urgent the need for development, the more important that the way be clearly charted and well selected.

U. S. technical and economic assistance to Africa

E. WILLIAM MORAN, JR.

Chief, Africa Division,
Foreign Operations Administration

Introduction

Until the last war Africa was to the U. S. truly the "dark continent." While we had study programs in our universities on most of the rest of the world and produced books and reports on such areas and their relation to the U. S., our knowledge of Africa was pretty much limited to Rider Haggard and Frank Buck. However, in the postwar period our interest in Africa has quickened—this book is just one more evidence of that. I believe this quickening of U. S. interest results at least as much from the rapidly changing condition of Africa itself as it does from any growing international interest in the U. S. I also believe our limited past knowledge and interest and our currently growing interest in Africa are points to be considered in discussing U. S. assistance to Africa.

In the last year or two, there have been an unusually large number of books published on Africa as well as an increase in the number of articles about that continent in the press and in periodic literature in the U. S. Despite the limited or popular character of most of these books and articles, much can be learned from them about the nature of the contemporary African problem and also something of the need for a U. S. concern with that problem.

This growing body of literature differs from that which has long been available on Africa, particularly in Western Europe. The publications to which I refer are not of an academic kind; they are not learned volumes on geology, anthropology, or history; they are not, for the most part, substantial works and they contain numerous inaccuracies; yet they are not either the ramblings of the returning tourist, and they all portray a continent whose peoples, though essentially still primitive, have recently been awakened from a long slumber through contact with the Western world.

The publications are concerned with people, with the political, with the politics of the present situation; with the need of the native African to participate more fully in his polity. Their titles alone are in many cases illuminating—*Before the African Storm*,[1] *Struggle for Africa*,[2] *The New West Africa*,[3] "Western Man and the African Crisis." [4] The authors of these and other books and articles agree in general on the nature of the crisis that appears to be overtaking Africa; they are in agreement that the African people are on the march, that the rising tide of political consciousness is irresistible, that the native will not much longer tolerate colonial status, that through much of Africa the indigenous peoples are not prepared for self-government, and that, by and large, self-government will have no meaning unless it raises the people out of poverty and ignorance. The tenor of all these recent writings is that unless these factors are recognized and dealt with, we and the peoples of Africa will suffer. We need them and they need outside assistance if they are to have higher standards of living, expanding economies and suitable institutions of self-government.

I recognize that in the preceding paragraphs I have been apparently more concerned with the territories than with the independent countries of Africa. I submit that the ultimate problem of territory and independent country, exclusive of South Africa and Egypt—with which I am not directly concerned in this essay—is the same. Ethiopia, Libya, and Liberia are independent countries, but there is no real participation of the mass of the people in the process of government; the standard of living in each of these countries is low, and they all lack the modern techniques and the capital which

---

1 J. Cookson, *Before the African Storm* (Indianapolis: Bobbs-Merrill, 1954).

2 V. Bartlett, *Struggle for Africa* (Toronto: Reginald Saunders & Co., 1953).

3 Basil Davidson and Adenekan Ademola (eds.), *New West Africa* (London: Allen & Univin, 1953).

4 Harold Isaacs, "Western Man and the African Crisis," *Saturday Review*, May 2, 1953, p. 10.

are basic to social and economic progress. In many ways the territories are already more advanced than the independent countries,
as they have had a European administration and what amounts to
technical assistance from Europe for many years. For the most part
they already have modern institutions of government, even though
their peoples have not ordinarily been trained for the civil services
and for the management of industrial and commercial enterprises.

The problem in Africa south of the Sahara is not an easy one to
define because of the different facets one sees in the various countries and territories. In essence, though, there is one aspect of it
which can be separated out and which is common to the whole
area. This could be stated as the growing aspirations of these
peoples who have suddenly realized they need not go hungry, sick,
and ill clothed. However, it is more than this, since they now have
the aspirations but do not as yet have the capacity even to begin
to fulfill them. It is therefore the problem of the West, if it is to
keep Africa in association with the free nations to so act in this
area as to convince the peoples that their best hope of meeting
their aspirations is to associate voluntarily with the free nations of
the West. If this is not done these peoples may flounder under
local tyrannies or succumb to the blandishments of others, including
enemies of the free nations.

I do not want to belabor the obvious, but it seems to me worthwhile to point out that the underdeveloped areas of the world are,
for the most part, regions which either were or remain colonies of
the European powers and in which Europeans have always been in
a minority. The expansion of Europe which began in the sixteenth
century witnessed the movement of the French, the English, the
Portuguese, and the Spaniards into the relatively unoccupied areas
of the world and the beginnings of the control of heavily populated
areas by the European countries. Africa was the last region seriously
to occupy the attention of the Europeans and remains the last large
area under European control. Those areas which were settled by
Europeans from the sixteenth to the nineteenth centuries have made
progress comparable to or have surpassed that of Europe. The
areas not so settled are now called the underdeveloped areas. Over
the centuries these areas did not receive the full impact of expansion in trade, commerce, agriculture, and industry that began with
the fifteenth century in Europe, which has not yet reached its con-

clusion and which has made possible the institutions and the political and economic freedom—the essence of democracy and that which we in this country enjoy beyond that which exists in most countries of the world. I believe that this expansion of European concepts is entering a further stage and that this stage is the transmitting to the backward areas of the world the techniques and ideas developed in Western Europe and the United States over the past five hundred years as a result of our continuing industrial revolution. I believe that this is essential if the world is to continue to progress economically and politically and to achieve ultimately some measure of stability. The problem facing the African territories and countries and Europe and the United States is how this can be brought about in Africa, where the concept of nationalism is already in advance of a supporting base, and to do it at such a rate as to satisfy the aspirations of the native peoples, while avoiding the tensions and conflicts that might lose Africa to the free world and end the progress of these peoples.

The U. S. interest in Africa

What is the interest of the United States in Africa? What is the importance of this area to the United States? These are the first questions that need to be asked and answered in any consideration of U. S. assistance.

I know how difficult it is to establish and define a concept of national interest, and I am aware of the apparent selfishness implicit in such a concept; however, it is, I believe, the best and perhaps only yardstick that we have for determining a course of action for the U. S. I do not for a moment discount the missionary effort, the need for the strictly humanitarian effort, or the value to the people of the United States of contributing directly or through their government to the relief of famine or other disasters in the world. I can accept that it may be in the interest of the U. S. to pursue a course of action for humanitarian reasons alone, but I believe the interest of the U. S. must be established. If we do not measure by the yardstick of national interest, not only can we very easily waste money but we can actually do more harm than good.

A well developed concept of national interest in the foreign field
has a way of clarifying many issues that otherwise remain obscure,
and it serves as a basis for establishing priorities and making
decisions.

Africa is of importance to the United States both in terms of our
direct relations with the countries and territories of Africa and of
our relations with other areas of the world, chiefly Europe, South
Asia, and the Near East, all of which have a vital concern in the
affairs of Africa. The United States' national security is now dependent upon a system of alliances which have as their twofold
purpose the restraining of the Soviet bloc in its attempt to disrupt
the Western world and pave the way for Communist domination and
the creating of opportunities for progress. Within this context,
Africa becomes of very considerable significance to the security of
the United States and its allies.

North Africa is an essential buttress to Western defense positions
in Europe, the Mediterranean, and the Middle East. The United
States, France, and the United Kingdom have located major air and
naval bases in French North Africa and Libya. Some of these territories, notably Morocco and French West Africa, are important
sources of military manpower for the French armed forces, and a
large percentage of the French troops engaged in Indochina are
Africans. The area south of the Sahara is important as it provides
an essential line of communication across Africa in the event of
war. Such areas as the port of Dakar, the mouth of the Congo, the
Gulf of Aden, and the ports of Lobito, Lourenço Marques, and
Beira are strategic areas in the event of war.

Africa is important economically to both the United States and
Western Europe inasmuch as this area is one of the most important
producers of certain scarce raw materials in the free world today.
These are materials which are now essential to the expanding
economy of the United States and of Europe and which will be of
increasing importance in the future. Africa is practically the sole
source of supply for such strategic items as industrial diamonds,
columbite, and cobalt, and is an important producer of uranium,
chrome, manganese, copper, tin, asbestos, graphite, palm oil, and
sisal. The resources of Africa have scarcely been touched, and the
development of these resources is essential to its own development
as well as to the continued expansion of the economies of the

United States and Western Europe. This expansion depends not alone upon the production of the all-important raw materials but also on the growth of bilateral and triangular trade, the development of new markets, and investment of U. S. and European money in Africa. These in turn depend upon the internal development of the economies of the various countries, territories, and regions in Africa and the maintenance of political stability in the area.

The political future of Africa is of importance to the United States, and it is in our interest to make available such assistance as is possible and necessary to assist the territories in making an orderly transition to self-government and in the growth of stable African societies. We cannot and should not attempt to define the exact form that these societies will take, for they may find it is in their interest to remain within the British Commonwealth or the French Union, to develop some new relationship with the metropolitan power, or to achieve independence. The concern of the United States is that the various areas of Africa develop into modern societies and remain in association with the West.

The independent countries of Africa are now in process of developing new political and social institutions and are evolving modern economies. The territories of the metropolitan powers are in various stages of transition from dependence to participation in government. The continued supply of raw materials to the United States and Europe, the maintenance of air and naval bases, and the investment in new production in these areas requires a high degree of political stability and friendly ties between the United States and the peoples of Africa. Should there be a failure on the part of the European countries and the United States in this period to support the peoples of this area in their effort to advance and satisfy their new-found aspirations, they may be forced to look elsewhere for leadership and direction.

In reviewing this problem of the United States and its relation to developments in Africa, it is well to bear in mind that the European countries are increasingly less able to carry the responsibility they have assumed in this area as the demands of its people increase. In the foreseeable future it is possible that they may be unable in one or another part of the area to supply assistance in such a fashion or amount as to satisfy the local peoples. Furthermore, the European countries should not carry all the load alone, for these

areas are no longer the exclusive concern of Europe but also of
the United States as leader of the free world. U. S. assistance to
Africa is therefore essential and may become more so in the future
if that continent is to acquire the technical skills and develop the
institutions requisite to maintain stable political societies in association with the West. It is of importance to the United States at
this time, when the African peoples are in this period of transition
and look to the United States for support and assistance, that we
establish with them such ties as will insure that they will continue
in a friendly association with us in the future, regardless of the
character of their political development.

Effective U. S. contribution
to African development

What effective contribution can the U. S. make to African
development? This is as important a question as that of the U. S.
interest. Americans are prone to oversimplify these problems and
consider them only in their technical phase, without sufficient
thought to the human or social aspects. We tend to forget that
technical assistance should be a two-way street, that our programs
should effect an exchange of knowledge and information, and that,
if they don't, they may fail. Ultimately what we learn may be as
important as what we teach. Unless our techniques, methods, and
ideas are sympathetically introduced to the recipient country and
adapted to the conditions of that country, they will be of little
use. The lessons we learn in that sympathetic understanding and
adapting can only improve our understanding of such a country
and our relations with it.

Africa, taken as a whole, is probably the most underdeveloped
area of the world today. It lacks information about its resources
and the means to develop them, and the levels of consumption and
production are extremely low. The population is largely engaged
in and dependent on subsistence agriculture carried on with relatively primitive techniques. Though the continent possesses great
resources of water for power, they are largely undeveloped. The
lack of rail and road transportation makes access to the interior
difficult and hinders the development of trade and commerce. There
is a maldistribution of labor throughout much of Africa, and there

is a lack of a skilled labor force. The Africans are hindered in their development by pests, diseases, malnutrition, climate, and lack of education and training. Investment in Africa in the past has been concentrated primarily on the production of raw materials for export, and practically all of the capital upon which production has been based has been imported and has had little effect on generating secondary investment. Africa, for the most part, lacks the economic and social structure within which economic growth is possible.

Perhaps the first question that should be raised in any consideration of the contribution which the U. S. can make to Africa is the form which that contribution should take. This question can only be answered in the light of a series of factors: the type of assistance which the U. S. as a government is prepared to make available; the past experience of the U. S. in making assistance available in the area; the requirements of the area and its capacity to make effective use of assistance; and relationship of the assistance to other forms of assistance already available or potentially available.

Under the existing aid program the U. S. is attempting to hold economic grants-in-aid to a minimum and limit them to defense support to back up military programs, where they are required for mutual defense, or to meet clearly defined emergencies; none of the African territories or countries would seem at this time to qualify for such assistance. On the other hand, the U. S. is prepared to make assistance in the form of technical co-operation available to underdeveloped areas such as these territories and countries.

In the field of technical co-operation, the U. S. has much to contribute to African development. The U. S., which was so recently an underdeveloped country itself, had to find solutions to many of the problems now facing Africa, particularly in the fields of transportation, agriculture, and resource development. The Europeans cannot provide all the essential skills for the territories, as many of the problems existing in Africa have never arisen in Europe, and the skills and technicians necessary to their solution have not been developed there as they have been in the United States. U. S. road-building techniques are needed in Africa, but similar techniques have not been developed in Europe. The problem of transport on the Congo River is more akin to the problem presented to us by the Ohio and Mississippi rivers than to anything in Europe.

The Europeans, while they have excellent laboratories for agricultural research, have not faced some problems common to Africa and the U. S., such as development of arid areas, nor have they developed extension and demonstration methods as has the U. S. In many cases where skills do exist, there are not a sufficient number of trained Europeans to cover the vast areas involved. The independent countries do not have the same access to European assistance, and they are almost wholly dependent on assistance from America and the United Nations. It is because of the uniqueness of the contribution which the U. S. can make that technical cooperation is of vital importance in the development of the countries and territories of Africa.

Assistance [5] has been made available under the ECA/MSA program to the dependent territories in Africa and under the Point IV program to the independent countries. The aid to the dependent territories was of four general types: (1) financing of commodity imports for the European metropoles which aided the territories either directly, because some of the commodities were imported directly into the territories, or indirectly, because it eased the financial problem of the metropole and improved its capacity to aid the territories (it is impossible to assess the amount of aid to Europe which in this way aided the African dependent territories) ; (2) direct-grant assistance to finance specific development projects and supplement the resources available in the territories and from the metropoles (this amounted to a total of $54,248,000 in fiscal years 1950 and 1951 and was broken down as follows: French territories $28,132,000; British territories $9,048,000; Belgian territories $17,073,000) ; (3) technical assistance under which 90 U. S. technicians worked for periods ranging from a few weeks to a year in the territories, and 144 participants [6] from the territories visited the U. S. to acquaint themselves with techniques and methods developed here which would be of use to them in solving their problems; (4) assistance to territorial governments or to industries in the territories to expand development of strategic or basic mate-

[5] Dollar figures in this and the following paragraph are estimates made prior to the end of the fiscal year 1953.

[6] This does not include technicians who came under European regional teams covering problems of mutual interest to the metropolitan countries and the territories.

rials; this was primarily in the form of loans which were under the strategic materials program repayable in materials for the U. S. stockpile and later under the basic materials program were repayable in the currency in which lent. Assistance under the first two categories was essentially a part of the U. S. assistance to Europe for rehabilitation and reconstruction; in effect, the U. S. was helping the European metropolitan powers meet their financial responsibilities toward their dependent territories in Africa. As the European countries have rebuilt their economic strength, such assistance is no longer required. The fourth category was for the purpose, first, under the strategic materials program, primarily of meeting stockpile requirements of the U. S. and, second, under the basic materials program, of helping to meet the raw materials requirements of the U. S. and its allies; as the raw materials position of the free world has improved, these programs have been discontinued. The third category has continued under the Foreign Operations Administration to the present and in FY 1954, was supplemented by limited amounts of economic assistance to finance jointly with the recipient countries demonstrations of the techniques and methods made available by the U. S. technicians and the training in the U. S. Such assistance in FY '54 amounted to a total of $11.3 million.

Assistance to the independent countries begun under the Point IV program and continued under FOA has been in the form of technical co-operation, i.e., U. S. technicians, training in the U. S. of nationals of the recipient country, limited amounts of essential supplies and equipment, and joint financing of demonstration of the new methods and techniques. This has amounted to a total U. S. contribution through June 30, 1954, of $4,000,000 for Liberia, $5,232,000 for Ethiopia, and $4,291,000 for Libya. This experience has clearly demonstrated that assistance in the form of technical co-operation is wanted and needed in these areas and can be effectively used; equally, it has demonstrated that the area has a limited capacity to absorb new financing unless such is carefully planned and associated with technical assistance and training.

The area as a whole is lacking in trained economists, technicians, and managerial personnel. A large part of the population is engaged in subsistence agriculture, and the small portion available as a labor supply is lacking for the most part in training and skills. Transportation and power are in most of the area barely adequate or even inadequate to meet existing requirements. The largest job to be done, if development is to proceed, is to train and educate the peoples in the skills that will be required, help them create, adapt, and staff the institutions required for such development, improve agricultural productivity while at the same time protecting the soil so that more people can be released for other productive activities, provide and or improve power and transportation facilities so that increased agricultural production can be used effectively and new productive facilities, industrial and extractive, can be developed. In most of the area large sums of external financing are not as yet required and, where they are required, can probably be secured from existing public institutions and private investors if the job of training and education is taken care of, and would be ineffective if it is not. At this point in the development of the area the U. S. can make a major contribution in the form of technical co-operation with perhaps limited amounts of economic assistance in special cases on a grant or loan basis. There will of necessity be some differences in approach as between the dependent territories and the independent countries, since the former are already receiving assistance from the metropoles, both in the form of money and technicians; that of the U. S. will be of a supplementary character, whereas the U. S. may be more of a primary source of assistance insofar as the independent countries are concerned.

Consideration must be given to the other sources of assistance: the metropoles, the U. N., voluntary agencies—both religious and secular—the International Bank, the Export-Import Bank, and private investors. Given the shortage of men and money, it is essential that every effort be made to avoid duplication of effort or competition and in a more positive way to work toward co-operation both amongst the agencies giving assistance and the countries receiving it to assure the maximum results. FOA is already making every effort to avoid duplication and, further, is taking steps to point out to the territories and countries of the area where greater co-operation between them in their attacks on common problems can result in mutual benefit. FOA has found that carefully planned technical co-operation projects can do much to lay the groundwork in such a fashion that loan financing can be secured for projects either from public institutions or from private investors. Thus, technical co-operation may at the same time help meet the financing problem of development. Here again, care must be taken not to resort to extraordinary grants-in-aid where they might compete with existing facilities which are prepared to loan funds.

Conclusion

Throughout the whole postwar period the United States has, in one way or the other, directly or indirectly, been concerned with Africa. Various kinds of assistance have been made available to the independent countries and dependent territories through Lend-Lease, UNRRA, the Export-Import Bank, the International Bank for Reconstruction and Development, DMPA, General Services Administration, ECA, MSA, and FOA. The assistance made available through these agencies, either as grants or loans or for technical assistance, has reflected both the short-term and the long-run interest of the United States in the area. Throughout this period there has evolved a programming concept which increasingly reflects the continuing interest of the United States in Africa and more effectively meets the needs of the peoples of the area. The ECA economic grant-aid program for the territories, the basic materials and strategic programs were indicative of our short-term interest in Africa and of the immediate needs of the United States and of our European allies. The evolving technical co-operation programs represent our continuing interest in Africa and our awareness of the real needs of the various areas, and they provide us with a means of participating in the development of Africa along mutually acceptable lines.

Africa will become of increasing importance to the United States. There will be a need for technical co-operation programs for many years. These programs need not require large expenditures of money. As the rate of economic expansion increases in the territories and countries, they will be in a position to make larger contributions to the programs both from indigenous resources and foreign loans. The programs must continue to be planned in the interests of the local peoples with the objective of stimulating and sustaining that rate of development which will so meet their aspirations that they will continue to associate themselves with the free world.

commentary

DAVID L. GORDON

*International Bank
for Reconstruction and Development*

It is only in very recent years, as Mr. Moran has emphasized, that the U. S. government and public have recognized any substantial national interest in Africa. Before the Second World War we were accustomed to view the entire continent, with the minor exception of Liberia, as the exclusive concern of the European nations; and while we generally deplored or denounced colonial rule in principle, we could still rely on it in practice as a pillar of international stability. The War and its aftermath have made this comfortable, if somewhat irresponsible, attitude untenable. Our national security and interests, and those of the free world as a whole, are deeply involved in the destiny of Africa, for the reasons that Mr. Moran has summarized very well. And we can no longer rely on the European colonial powers to bear the full responsibility for the continent's security and development. The colonial system, while it has unquestionably brought some very real economic and governmental benefits, is now meeting with increasing restiveness—in some cases, open violence—among the colonial peoples, and this certainly represents a weakness in the free world's position. Yet it is no solution simply to dismantle the system, so long as no satisfactory substitute is ready for the economic and governmental organization of this vast area.

Given the suddenness of the change in our relationship to Africa, and the complexity of the dilemma that it poses, it is not surprising that U. S. public policies and opinion have found it hard to make the adjustment. This difficulty is reflected in the on-again-off-again character of our economic programs in Africa over the past few years. The Economic Cooperation Act of 1948 included the dependent overseas territories of European participating countries among the areas eligible for assistance. But for the first year or so these territories figured in ECA's plans only as a one-line entry— a net surplus or deficit—in the balance-of-payments tables for the several metropoles. In 1949 Dr. Isaiah Bowman was brought in as advisor to ECA to develop a program for the African territories; and Dr. John Orchard was sent to Paris to work on the same problems with our European allies. The activation of the OEEC Committee on Overseas Territories, which became so useful a center for economic and technical studies and a meeting place for the principal economic officers of the colonial administrations, was due in large measure to Dr. Orchard's vigorous encouragement. And in 1950, ECA set aside a portion of its funds to be used directly and exclusively for development projects in the overseas territories and substantially expanded its technical assistance work in these areas.

After the Korean War broke out, however, there was a shift in priorities, and in our preoccupation with essentially military purposes the African programs (except strategic-materials projects) largely went by the board. The special Overseas Development Fund was abandoned; the overseas territories officers in the European missions of ECA/MSA were assigned to other duties, and the OEEC committee became moribund. In 1952 there was a revival of U. S. interest and activity in Africa. It survived the "riffings" and program readjustments that followed the advent of the new administration, and for the immediate future, at least, our foreign operations will include a modest effort in Africa.

In these successive changes of policy and emphasis I think our government has learned a good deal. It is my impression that the present program is more solidly based in several respects than that of the first years. But I believe also that our national purposes, and the means by which we hope to accomplish them, still need to be considerably clarified—in our own minds, and to responsible public opinion in both Europe and Africa.

A central question is how U. S. operations in Africa relate to, and what is their effect on, the colonial interests and administrations of our NATO allies. All our governmental activities in Africa should, indeed they must, be undertaken in close co-operation with these administrations and be designed in part to make them more effective; but at the same time our traditions, political principles, and long-range interests all require that we encourage real progress, as rapid as is feasible in each case, toward fully effective participation by the colonial peoples in their government, and that we use our aid and influence to promote such progress in orderly fashion.

These considerations are by no means irreconcilable, although they often seem to conflict in the short run. If the colonial administrations are effectively working to improve the position of the local population, in relative as well as absolute terms—to narrow the wide gap in wealth and status that separates the few Europeans and privileged Africans from the great mass of the people—then there is no inconsistency. A program of dynamic economic expansion and social betterment, with its benefits widely distributed, is the obvious means to ease the growing tensions in Africa and to provide the base for a corresponding extension of political power and participation. The difficulty is that in many areas colonial administrations (and this is often true also, of course, of independent governments) seem to have no clear idea how to break the vicious circle of poverty, economic stagnation, and demoralization that is the essence of "underdevelopment," nor any adequate means to do so.

The primary purpose of the U. S. programs that Mr. Moran has described is to help solve this problem and so to establish the conditions for orderly progress in Africa; and certainly we should be especially qualified in many ways to deal with it. The U. S. is the shining example of successful economic growth in a flexible, democratic social framework; much of our experience is certainly relevant; and our financial and productive resources exceed those of all the rest of the free world combined. But—and this is the crux and conclusion of my comments—I wonder whether we have yet devised an approach to this problem of promoting development that is anywhere near adequate, in conception and scale, to do the job that needs to be done in Africa. This question, of course, applies to other areas as well; but in Africa, perhaps because of our ambivalence toward the colonial system, we seem to be proceeding even more cautiously than elsewhere.

We are relying essentially on three elements for the promotion of development: technical assistance, private investment, and limited loans through the International and Export-Import Banks. All three are unquestionably valuable. But technical assistance alone, without substantial investment of capital, can produce only limited results. And I fail to see any early prospect that private foreign investment will be sufficient to meet the need, outside of mining and other production of raw materials for export, in a large part of Africa. I trust that private investment will meet a progressively increasing share of the capital needs in underdeveloped countries, but such investment is attracted mainly to countries where development is already relatively advanced, where buying-power exists, and especially where a large amount of public investment in power, transport, sanitation, and other basic facilities has already taken place. Thus private funds are no substitute for such public investment, in which large parts of Africa are notably deficient.

Some of the African territories probably have substantial public borrowing capacity, in the metropoles or from the International or Export-Import Banks, but the public revenues and foreign exchange earnings of a number of others—French West and Equatorial Africa, Nyasaland, Bechuanaland, Angola, etc.—are quite limited for the foreseeable future; and the capital resources of the respective metropoles are already stretched thin.

I shall not try, in the scope of this brief commentary, to suggest any definite answers to this problem, which involves enormously complex issues of public policy. I do not think personally that a further massive program of U. S. grants is either politically acceptable or desirable, although limited grant aid for certain areas and purposes would doubtless be a necessary part of any adequate solution. I believe that the foreign lending policies of the U. S. government—the objects and terms of loans, the conditions and forms of repayment—could be made considerably more varied and flexible without becoming "fuzzy"; and that we could usefully adapt to international investment, both public and private, some of the devices used in our own country and in Europe to promote development along desirable lines.

Certainly, also, a good deal could be done to increase the effectiveness of the capital already available, through better planning of public investments and development policies, better organization of local financial resources, and their better co-ordination with technical assistance programs and the prospects for private investment from abroad. Technical assistance programs—both those of the U. S. government and of the United Nations agencies—have mostly dealt with specific economic sectors or technical problems and have rather neglected the central function of the organization and management of balanced economic growth. It is a much more difficult and touchy undertaking, to be sure, to advise and attempt to influence another country on its basic national plans and policies than on such essentially technical matters as how to kill mosquitoes or what fertilizer to use on a given type of soil; and the difficulties are compounded where we are dealing with a dependent territory. But it seems to me that a more intimate, responsible participation in the over-all planning and execution of national development programs not only would increase the effectiveness of U. S. technical and financial assistance to economic progress in the African territories but also would afford valuable opportunities to keep in contact with, and perhaps to influence constructively, their political and social development.

These comments and questions are in no sense a criticism of the work of Mr. Moran and his associates, who are responsible for the FOA programs in Africa. Quite the contrary—in my view they have done a really outstanding job of gaining acceptance for these programs and making them as effective as possible within the limits of our present national policies; and they are as much aware as anyone of the more fundamental problems that remain to be solved. I would only stress my belief that the solutions are not yet clear and my hope that the present preoccupation with the problem may help in finding them.

private enterprise in Africa

BERNARD BLANKENHEIMER

*Chief, African Section, Near Eastern and African
Division, Bureau of Foreign Commerce,
Department of Commerce*

Misconceptions regarding Africa, its people, and its resources are legion. Loose references are often made to the "boundless" natural wealth of Africa and the immense potentialities
existent for further development of those resources. The presence
of so many natural resources is further linked to promising prospects
for establishing local industries, the success of which is contingent
solely on the obtaining of sufficient capital. Talk of Africa's vast
area and population, of untapped mineral deposits and rich tropical
lands conjure visions in many people's minds of glittering prospects
for private investment and private initiative. But what are the
facts? And what are the prospects for private enterprise in Africa?
These are the main questions which this article proposes to deal
with.

There are few generalizations which apply with equal validity to
the continent as a whole. Indeed, wide variations are encountered
regionally and even within given territories with respect to political,
social, and economic resource conditions. Territories north of the
Sahara are economically linked by virtue of their geographic position to Mediterranean Europe and socially are closely oriented to the
Near East. That vast area south of the Sahara exhibits a bewildering complexity of different population strains, topographic features,
economic resources, and political conditions. West Africa, for example, is essentially a tropical economy based on subsistence agri-

453

culture and the production for export of a few principal mineral, agricultural, and forest products. Small landholdings are the rule, and climatic considerations effectively rule out large-scale permanent white settlement. East and South Africa (exclusive of the Union of South Africa) on the other hand, though predominantly agricultural and mineral, contain large areas of extensive white settlement; and, in elevated areas, subtropical and temperate crops are grown, such as cotton, coffee, tobacco, and wheat, on a large-scale plantation basis.

The Union of South Africa is in a special class representing by far the most economically advanced country, certainly, south of the Sahara and, by many standards, the continent as a whole. Not only are mineral and agricultural resources well developed, but it has also made significant strides towards attainment of a diversified industrial economy. At the present time, the country has, in terms of plants already constructed or now in process, a steel industry with an annual output of 1.2 million ingot tons, a cement industry capable of 2.3 million tons per year, a highly developed explosives and chemical industry now undertaking the synthesis of oil from coal, an advanced electric-power industry, and a consumer-goods industry producing textiles, shoes, clothing, and a variety of other items.

Africa is an important world source of supply for a formidable array of mineral, agricultural, and pastoral raw materials. The United States depends heavily on Africa for such mineral products as diamonds, manganese, tin, copper, cobalt, chrome, asbestos, lead, and mica, and of course, uranium; for such vegetable or animal products as cocoa, rubber, palm oil, sisal, mahogany, and hides and skins.

Impressive as is the list of African resources, it is unfortunately the case that these resources are unevenly distributed and, paradoxically enough, are often a cause of internal economic instability in given territories whose prosperity, like that of Northern Rhodesia or the Gold Coast, is dependent on the exportation of a single raw material. It is also true that natural resources are often found in remote and sparsely populated interior regions, requiring importation of labor and heavy capital expenditure on basic facilities such as housing and roads, in addition to plants and equipment. Areas blessed with rich mineral resources may be seriously deficient in other resources—often essential to the exploitation of the mineral. An example is the Northern Rhodesian copper belt, which depends on imported coal from Southern Rhodesia to mine and process the copper. Food production likewise is often a problem both regionally and interregionally, since soils are poor over vast areas and subject to erosion and leaching. In so rich a country as the Union of South Africa, for example, it is estimated that only about 15 per cent of the land area is arable, and there agriculture is often a marginal enterprise.

Although encompassing about a fourth of the world's land area, the continent as a whole contains an estimated 8 per cent of the world's population; of this population (198,000,000 in 1950, according to a United Nations estimate),[1] only some 5,000,000 are of European origin, and half of these are settled in the Union of South Africa. The bulk of the remainder is concentrated in North African coastal regions, with some 320,000 in East and Central Africa and some 80,000 in West Africa.

For the most part, exclusive of the Union of South Africa, the bulk of the indigenous population south of the Sahara is still illiterate and, despite the inroads of Mohammedanism and Christianity, largely pagan.

A primary distinguishing feature of the African society is the tribal organization, which remains very largely directed to subsistence activities. With the accelerated development of Africa in the past two decades, more of the indigenous population has been drawn into the money economy; cash crops produced by the tribe and migratory labor offered for wages in mines and plantations are becoming more important. A significant trend toward urbanization of the natives has become evident in virtually every part of Africa, notably in the Union of South Africa, where employment opportunities in manufacturing industries have been a significant attraction. Yet by and large, it must be recognized that a large part of the indigenous population in Africa engages in agricultural and pastoral production for subsistence and that, in consequence, commercial and economic activities remain largely directed to production for export which, in turn, has depended upon foreign capital investments.

[1] *Review of Economic Conditions in Africa*, United Nations, Department of Economic Affairs, March 1951.

The growth of export industries has, to a significant extent in some African areas, created a permanent native laboring force, broadened the internal market for goods and services, and has made possible the gradual accumulation of local savings. Nevertheless it remains unfortunately true that the great part of the indigenous native laboring population in Africa is migratory and unstable, untrained and unskilled, and receives a wage level which hardly permits the satisfaction of any but simple wants.

It has been estimated that, for tropical Africa as a whole, the average per capita income is not over $50 per annum. In the Union of South Africa, Southern Rhodesia, and other areas of extensive white settlement, there is a very wide gap in income and purchasing power between the various racial components. Diversified consumption expenditures, consequently, are to all intents and purposes restricted to the minority European or white population which enjoys a relatively high standard of living. In the Union of South Africa, although native wage rates are relatively high in comparison with tropical Africa, Europeans receive five to six times the wage paid to the native, who is generally relegated to unskilled work. Native wage rates here average about £8½ per month in contrast to about £50 for the average European industrial worker. Official data on the distribution of South Africa's national income, as between racial groups, are not available, but the evidence is that the European segment of the population (comprising only one-fifth of the total population) accounts for the great bulk of the country's total national income.[2]

The import of these general observations on prospects for continued expansion of private enterprise in Africa becomes readily apparent. On the one hand, they indicate that, in the light of the limited internal capital formation capabilities in Africa, with the possible exception of the Union, expansion of private enterprise must depend on reinvestment of earnings of existing private inter-

---

[2] For example, the Department of Economics of the University of Natal, in a study using 1936 census data, calculated that the European population segment in the Union accounted for 74.5 per cent of the country's national income in that year. See *Handbook on Race Relations in South Africa* (Oxford University Press, 1949) , Chap. XIV. A study for the period 1939–40 by South African economists Frankel and Herzefeld reached similar conclusions. Details of this study were published in the *South African Journal of Economics* (June, 1943) .

ests and/or on the attraction of new private investments from abroad. On the other hand, they indicate that the diversification of economic activities and of private investment enterprises in Africa will depend greatly on governmental efforts to remove current deficiencies in basic facilities, such as water resources, transportation, power, and communications; to increase productivity through agricultural research, soil conservation, etc.; and to raise living standards generally through improvement of public services in such fields as health, education, and social welfare.

Colonial governments and independent nations alike in Africa have long recognized the validity of these basic propositions, but it is only recently that interregional co-operation has been displayed and extensive public investment embarked upon to expand basic services and facilities.

Prior to World War II, the various European nations administering African dependencies adhered to a general policy that the economic development of the respective areas was the responsibility of the area itself. It was assumed that each colony should be economically and financially self-supporting and that each colony should be left to care for its development needs as best it could. Colonial policies, however, underwent a radical metamorphosis in the postwar period, and the various metropoles now adopted the principle of extending direct grant as well as loan aid to the colonies and of instituting extensive centralized public economic planning in the colonies. Wartime dislocation of markets and sources of supply, postwar raw material shortages, balance-of-payments problems, and recognition of the political necessity to modify traditional colonial concepts and to broaden the economic base of colonial areas are among factors which have prompted Britain, France, Belgium, and Portugal in putting into effect in their respective African dependencies broad long-term programs of economic and social development which, if carried out as planned, will involve an estimated public investment of some $5 billion.[3] These public programs are discussed elsewhere in a separate article, but

3 Of this figure, $3.7 billion in public investment have been earmarked under ten-year plans; the remaining $1.3 billion represents public and semipublic investment not covered by ten-year plans. See *Investments in Overseas Territories in Africa, South of the Sahara* (Organization for European Economic Co-operation, Paris, 1951).

suffice it here to say that, to the extent that these development programs carry out their objectives, environmental deterrents to new private investments will be considerably reduced and, undoubtedly, avenues for new enterprises pointed up. On the other hand, certain features of current colonial-development policies and programs in Africa can be regarded as a "mixed blessing" for private enterprise.

On the assumption that certain operations would be unattractive to private enterprise or involve too great a capital expenditure, colonial governments have shown a distinct tendency not merely to extend public enterprise and activity to fields regarded as properly within the public sector (which in most African areas have now come to include such fields as transportation, communication, and utilities) but also to direct productive enterprises in agriculture, mining, and industry. Thus, for example, in the British Cameroons, banana plantations are operated by a public corporation, coal mining is a government monopoly in Nigeria, and in various French African territories public capital engages in peanut production, forestry, and saw-milling, among other activities. In many instances, semipublic or "mixed" organizations have emerged in which private enterprise has been encouraged to participate. Yet, even here the tendency has been for government to assume an increasing degree of regulatory and managerial authority. Such a pattern of government intervention, while somewhat new to French and British African areas, has long been established in Portuguese and Belgian Africa.

Indeed the general trend toward extension of governmental activities in economic fields is not exclusively confined to colonial territories in Africa. It has also been manifest in the Union of South Africa, where the government of late has gone into the synthetic production of oil from coal, the production of DDT, and the mining of natural phosphates.

In support of such policies, government authorities have been at pains to stress that these involve no deliberate design on private enterprise as such and that they are intended to "supplement private enterprise and not supplant it." It is asserted that certain enterprises are not sufficiently attractive to private capital or require too large a capital expenditure, and that activities by public and semipublic bodies in productive fields should open new opportunities for private investment, either independently or in conjunction with public financing. There is, of course, much validity to this general view. Yet, experience unquestionably demonstrates that, once government is established in given fields, it becomes quite difficult for government to disengage itself. It is also questionable whether governments in all instances have exhausted all possibilities of private capital sponsorship before undertaking the enterprise. The criteria of "national interest" also has played a role in shaping governmental decisions to undertake and participate in development of mineral and other raw-material resources. Carried to the extreme, obviously such criteria would leave little scope for private enterprise in Africa. Certainly this eventuality would not be intended by any of the governments concerned, since all recognize the fundamental importance to Africa's future development of a continued expansion of private activity. Yet it is not always clear that these governments have been alive to the dangers inherent to private enterprise in extending the scope of public activity in Africa.

It has been noted previously that expansion of private enterprise in Africa is basically contingent on an increased inflow of private capital from abroad. It follows then that such expansion requires, both on the part of established private interests and government bodies in Africa, a vigorous policy of encouragement of private foreign capital.

Colonial governments in Africa are acutely conscious of the need for additional private capital investments in support of over-all efforts to develop and diversify colonial resources; yet for the most part the various metropolitan countries have not developed an active program for soliciting such capital beyond their own borders.

Dating back to the early "chartered" company period, close economic and commercial ties have been maintained between the various colonial areas and the metropolitan country, with many raw materials traditionally being channeled through the metropole for processing and subsequent reexportation. Preferential tariff arrangements and, in recent years, absence of trade and exchange restrictions within currency areas also have facilitated strengthening of trade patterns with the metropole. Such close trade ties naturally have contributed to the predominant position of metropolitan country private capital investments in the African dependencies. It must also be recognized, however, that in many instances metropolitan country policies, regulations, and administrative practices have been more conducive to private capital investments from the metropole than from other sources.

In recent years, it has become evident both to private interests and colonial governments in Africa that new foreign sources of private capital must be tapped in order to meet private investment needs. The evidence is that while private capital has increased substantially in colonial territories, much of it has involved reinvestment of profits earned by existing firms rather than fresh capital from abroad; also, that a substantial part of such new investment has been used for the maintenance and replacement of existing equipment rather than expansion of activity.[4] In these circumstances colonial governments, conscious of the shortage of private capital in the metropole, are looking to new sources, and notably to the United States, for fresh private capital.

In various statements, the metropolitan countries have affirmed their conviction in the mutual benefits deriving from private foreign investment, both to the host country and the recipient country. All have expressed a desire for expanded capital inflow, particularly from the United States. Yet such policy statements, while desirable and helpful, will not produce results unless they are followed up by an active program of encouragement and promotion of foreign investment. Such programs necessitate not only an examination of legislative requirements and administrative procedures, with a view toward removal of those regarded as impediments to investment, but also the offering of inducements to such investment. Finally, if it is American capital that is desired, it needs to be more generally recognized by African countries that investment opportunities in Africa must compete on favorable terms not only with investment opportunities in other underdeveloped areas but in the United States as well.

Obviously, while it is a basic economic policy of the United States to encourage and facilitate private investment in underdeveloped areas of the world, the actual movement of private capital abroad is, after all, the responsibility and the decision of the private investor himself.

Estimates of the U. S. Department of Commerce place the total book value of American direct investment in Africa, exclusive of

[4] See *Investments in Overseas Territories in Africa, South of the Sahara,* p. 52 ff.

Egypt, at $458 million as at the end of 1952 (latest year available).
By comparison, in 1950 the comparable figures stood at $312 mil-
lion, and in 1943, $113 million. As Table 1 indicates, both new
capital and reinvested earnings have been important factors contributing to the rise in such direct investments.

As of 1950, some 52 per cent of the total value of U. S. direct
investment was confined to the petroleum industry, mainly in marketing and distribution. Mining accounted for 20.5 per cent and
manufacturing 15 per cent (Table 2).

On the basis of country distribution as of 1952 (Table 3), almost
three-fourths of the total of U. S. direct investments in Africa,
excluding Egypt, was concentrated in two independent countries,
Liberia and the Union of South Africa. A total of $66 million, or
15 per cent of the total, was invested in British Africa; and direct
investments in French African territories amounted to $36 million,
or 8 per cent of the total. It is interesting to note that of the latter
figure only some $12 million was invested in French Africa, south
of the Sahara, and mainly in petroleum marketing. In the Belgian
Congo and Ruanda-Urundi, U. S. direct investments in 1952
amounted to some $9 million, while only about $5 million was
invested in the Portuguese and Spanish dependencies combined.

Outside of the Union of South Africa, most of the American
direct private capital is invested in extractive activities and petroleum distribution. Agricultural enterprises, except in Liberia, are
relatively minor. U. S. investment in manufacturing is almost entirely confined to the Union of South Africa, where in 1952 such
activities accounted for $55 million, or 28 per cent of our total
direct investment in that country. American capital here has played
an important part in development of the country's automobile-
assembly and rubber-tire industries among others, and more recently, some $20 million has been invested in South Africa's first
oil refinery.

Although these figures point to a total private investment by the
United States which is not inconsiderable, there is little doubt that
the volume of U. S. private capital in Africa could be further
augmented. Likewise the regional distribution of U. S. private
capital could be further diversified.

In this connection, it is encouraging that members of the OEEC
in Paris have sponsored several meetings to determine ways and

means of attracting foreign private investments from the United States and elsewhere to African dependent territories.   Several colonial governments have enacted specific regulations offering tax and other concessions to new investments. In 1952, the Southern Rhodesian government published a brochure for distribution in the United States calling attention to investment opportunities there. The Member for Commerce and Industries of the Kenya government, Mr. A. Hope-Jones, recently traveled to the United States in an attempt to arouse interest in Kenya among specific U. S. firms. The Belgian government for the first time has assigned an attaché for Belgian Congo Affairs to its Embassy in Washington. These are sound and constructive measures in the right direction, but they represent only a bare beginning.

A recent study [5] issued by the U. S. Department of Commerce, which surveyed investment impediments in various countries or areas in Africa and other continents, concluded for nearly every African area surveyed that a major factor accounting for the paucity of American investment in the area was the lack of publicity in the United States given to investment opportunities. Another basic factor impeding the flow of American private investment funds to Africa—particularly to colonial territories—the study concludes, is the absence of clear-cut firm statements of government policy outlining the conditions, regulations, and requirements under which American private capital investments are to be made. Let us examine these conclusions in more specific terms.

At the present time it is unfortunate that information disseminated in the United States by the respective foreign missions representing African dependencies or countries bears little on economic and commercial matters of interest to prospective investors. For example, several of the governments administering African territories maintain information offices in the United States which pour out large quantities of printed matter—often expensively prepared with colorful illustrations. For the most part, however, the contents of these publications appear to be directed more to tourists, students, and study groups than to the practical businessman and potential investor. Indeed what appear to be sadly lacking in current efforts to attract American private capital to Africa are cen-

[5] *Factors Limiting U. S. Investment Abroad*, Part I, "Survey of Factors in Foreign Countries" (U. S. Government Printing Office, Washington, D. C.).

tralized facilities maintained by the foreign governments concerned, both in their countries and in the United States, for the promotion and servicing of foreign investments.

Quite apart from the fact that insufficient information is currently made available to the American investment community concerning specific opportunities for investment in the various African areas, a common problem encountered by prospective American investors is that they do not have generally available to them a centralized office maintained by the foreign government which can answer their questions promptly and authoritatively. By way of illustrating this problem, let us take a case of an American firm interested in a given investment enterprise in one of the colonial territories. Before even a preliminary investment decision is possible, the firm may require answers to a wide variety of questions, including laws and regulations, government policies, labor conditions, transportation and power facilities, etc. The firm communicates with the respective embassy in Washington and receives some general material; such information as is available in the United States Department of Commerce is provided in response to a visit or correspondence; yet the firm still does not have all the information it desires. An on-the-spot investigation becomes necessary, and the firm sends a representative to the African area. Here it develops that many important answers cannot be given except by the colonial office in the metropolitan country. A further trip to the metropolitan country is then undertaken whereupon the answers are finally provided after a series of referrals from one government unit to another with an accompanying delay of perhaps weeks or months.

Associated with impediments to American private investments resulting from inadequate informational and service facilities are those stemming from the absence or inadequate nature of public statements clarifying all aspects of government policies in connection with such American private investments. This is particularly pertinent for countries administering African territories, but in greater or less degree it has applicability to all African areas or countries.

With respect to African dependent territories, it has been the experience of a number of American investors that the lack of clear-cut firm metropolitan government statements of policy outlining conditions, regulations, and administrative requirements governing the entry and operation of American private investments, has given rise to uncertainties and local administrative decisions and practices which are often at variance with each other.

Rightly or wrongly, many American investors have the conception that colonial territories in Africa are often treated as reserves for metropolitan country capital and that American private investments are opposed or simply tolerated rather than warmly received and encouraged.

The U. S. investor needs to know general limitations or restrictions concerning fields of economic activity open to private investment: whether the foreign government will permit majority-share ownership by the American investor, or in what instances private metropolitan capital or government majority participation is to be required; he needs to know what restriction, if any, would be placed on American management and technical labor to operate the enterprise; he needs assurances on government policies relative to remittances of earnings and repatriation of capital investments, on nationalization, on access to basic facilities and needed raw material, and a host of other pertinent topics.

Summing up the foregoing, what seems to be required, therefore, in carrying forward a positive program to expand American private investments in Africa, both on the part of foreign governments and private groups, is essentially "selling" the American businessman on Africa as a field for investment. Such a selling job requires an active effort to publicize specific opportunities, to dispel popular misconceptions by pronouncements of firm, comprehensive official policy statements, centralization and co-ordination of governmental machinery responsible for screening and reviewing foreign investment applications.

Throughout Africa there are numerous activities worthy of investigation as possible investment enterprises. I cite a few at random.

Ethiopia, emerging gradually from centuries of isolation, offers possibilities for foreign investments in plantation agriculture, including coffee; in cattle ranching and meat-packing (enormous quantities of livestock are slaughtered each year primarily for the hides) ; and in mining.

Off the Angolan coast, the Atlantic Ocean abounds in tuna and a variety of other fish, yet here the fisheries industry is still in its infancy. Mozambique's mineral resources are still largely unknown, and the present construction of a rail line from Lourenço Marques to Pafuri on the Southern Rhodesian border (connecting with the Rhodesian rail system) will open up a practically virgin stretch of territory in southern Mozambique to settlement and resource development opportunities.

In Liberia, coffee cultivation, once a flourishing activity, has been allowed to dwindle almost to extinction until recent years when attempts have been made by the Government to increase plantings and re-establish the industry as an important activity. The country is climatically suitable for coffee culture on a plantation basis and presents itself as offering prospects for American investment.

The new Federation of the Rhodesias and Nyasaland—particularly Southern Rhodesia—also offers investment prospects in base minerals, agriculture, and, significantly, in manufacturing industry which already has made striking progress.

Important mineral finds, such as the manganese strike in French Equatorial Africa, and iron ore and copper in French West Africa, indicate that possibilities for further development in extractive activities are continuing there.

Hydroelectric power and dam projects in Uganda, the Gold Coast, and elsewhere will open new vistas for the local processing of raw materials.

There is little question that, given a favorable investment climate and an active promotional program, additional interest in possible investment in Africa could be stimulated among the American investing community. It must be stressed, however, that publicity efforts and a favorable investment climate in themselves provide no guarantee that increased private capital will flow from the United States.

As a general proposition, the very poverty of Africa represents a basic deterrent to the expansion and diversification of private enterprise and private investment. Experience has demonstrated that economic and social progress in Africa is a slow, gradual, and costly process.

Nevertheless, it is equally valid to assert that little social and economic progress in Africa can be expected without foreign private investments. It is one of the paradoxes of underdeveloped economies that private enterprise and private investment which are themselves impeded by the poverty of the area constitute at the

Table 1

United States direct private investments in Africa*... capital movements and undistributed subsidiary earnings, by country or area group, 1949–52

(In millions of dollars)

Country or Area Group	Value end of 1949	Changes 1950			Changes 1951			Changes 1952		
		Net capital out-flows	Undistri-buted subsidi-ary earnings	Value end of 1950	Net capital out-flows	Undistri-buted subsidi-ary earnings	Value end of 1951	Net capital out-flows	Undistri-buted subsidi-ary earnings	Value end of 1952
All Areas Total	269	63	20	352	15	43	410	32	62	504
Colonial Africa										
British Territories (including Federation of Rhodesia and Nyasaland)	37	3	1	41	6	7	54	6	6	66
French Territories (including French North Africa)	27	2	2	31	(1)†	1	32	-1††	5	36
Other European Territories (including Belgian, Portuguese and Spanish Africa)	10	2	(1)	12	(1)	(1)	12	1	1	14
Independent Africa										
Egypt	38	-1	2	39	2	3	44	(1)	2	46
Liberia	47	32	3	82	(1)	22	104	(1)	36	140
Union of South Africa (including South West Africa)	105	23	12	140	7	10	157	25	12	194
Other Independent Countries (e. g. Libya, Ethiopia)	5	2	(1)	7	(1)	(1)	7	1	(1)	8

SOURCE: U. S. Department of Commerce, Office of Business Economics. Extracted from data published in "Survey of Current Business," January, 1954. *American direct investments abroad are those enterprises in which the American investor has a controlling interest; in general, these enterprises are either wholly owned branches or foreign incorporated enterprises in which the American investor owns at least 25% of the voting stock.
†(1) Less than $500,000.   ††Reduction of investment.

Table 2

U. S. direct private investments in Africa (excluding Egypt)
for the years 1943, 1950, and 1952

(In millions of dollars)

Type of business	1943*	Per cent of total	1950†	Per cent of total	1952†
Mining	23	20.4	64	20.5	not available
Petroleum	37	32.7	162	51.9	not available
Manufacturing	11	9.7	47	15.1	not available
Utilities	1	.9	3	.9	not available
Trade	18	15.9	21	6.7	not available
Agriculture and finance	20	17.7	13	4.3	not available
Miscellaneous	3	2.7	2	.6	not available
Total	113	100.0	312	100.0	458

Source: U. S. Treasury census of American-owned assets in foreign countries, 1947.
†Source:* U. S. Department of Commerce, Office of Business Economics.

Table 3

U. S. direct private investments in Africa, south of the Sahara . . .
1952

(In millions of dollars)

Area or country	Type of business						
	Total	Trade	Mining	Manfg.	Petroleum	Agriculture	Miscellaneous
British areas	66	*	35	*	26	*	*
French areas	12	*	*	—	9	*	—
Portuguese and Spanish areas	5	*	*	—	*	*	—
Belgian Congo (with Ruanda-Urundi)	9	*	*	*	*	*	—
Liberia	140	*	*	—	106†	*	*
Union of South Africa and South West Africa	194	19	47	55	67	—	*

Included in total.   SOURCE: U. S. Department of Commerce, Office of Business Economics.
†Includes oil tankers registered under Liberian Flag but owned by U. S. controlled companies.

same time the most expedient and effective weapon of attacking this poverty. Indeed the degree of economic and social advancement attained in some African areas, as contrasted with the slow gains achieved in others, tend to reflect in large measure the extent to which private foreign investments have or have not been developed.

American private investments in Africa, despite the fact that they constitute to date only a small proportion of the total foreign private capital investment represented in that continent, have contributed significantly to African development. They offer a striking illustration of the fact that newly developing areas stand to gain important benefits from projects freely undertaken by private investment capital.

commentary

W. CLIFFORD SHIELDS

Vice President, Farrell Lines, Inc.

One realizes that the vastness and variety of the problems of free enterprise in Africa call for imaginative thinking and initiative on the part of those who would propose or actually participate in the solution. This commentary will amplify and emphasize certain aspects of the problems discussed by Mr. Blankenheimer; notably, what can and should be done to increase the participation of private (American) capital in the development of the African economies. The mere statement of certain difficulties, e.g., "a common problem encountered by prospective investors is that they do not generally have available to them a centralized office maintained by the foreign government which can answer their questions promptly and authoritatively," suggests the proper approach to those difficulties.

It is customary to speak of Africa as if it were one place, a homogeneous whole. To do this is inconsonant with the facts. As Mr.

Blankenheimer has pointed out, "wide variations are encountered regionally and even within given territories." The five principal areas of Africa—North, West, Central, East, and South Africa—not only differ greatly from one another but there are wide divergencies and disparities within each area. Paradoxically, North Africa is so non-African that often it is not included in discussions of African affairs. This exclusion of North Africa is indicated by such a restrictive designation as "Africa south of the Sahara." The reference to "tropical Africa" excludes South Africa as well as North Africa.

The vastness of the continent of Africa must at all times be borne in mind. Africa south of the Sahara alone encompasses some 9 million square miles and is therefore three times the size of the continental United States.

Throughout Africa today, as Mr. Blankenheimer has outlined, there are "long-term programs of economic and social development which if carried out will involve a public investment of some $5 billion . . . which can be regarded as a mixed blessing for private enterprise." Government ownership of railroads and harbor facilities, air and (in instances) road transport services, telephone, telegraph, and radio communications, iron- and steel-making, engineering, and the production and distribution of electricity, as well as ownership of other undertakings in Africa, is more in the European tradition of socialism and nationalized industry than in the American tradition of free enterprise. However, government has considered it necessary to undertake some projects, which would make fuller use of the country's natural resources, because private capital has been unwilling to take the risks involved. The hydrogenation of coal in the Union of South Africa by the South African Coal, Oil and Gas Corporation, known colloquially as "Sasol," a government-financed undertaking, might be cited as an example of such a project.

Private enterprise is desirable because through taxes it contributes to the revenue of the government; through wages and salaries it improves the domestic market; through exports (if some of its products are exported) it betters the country's foreign exchange position; and through savings it creates domestic private investment (and reinvestment) capital. If a country's economy and its legislation are such as to cause and to encourage the investment and reinvestment of domestic private capital, there is created a climate attractive to foreign private capital. All countries in the process of development and industrialization—such as the countries in Africa—have a need for foreign private investment capital; whereas highly industrialized countries—such as the United States—have reserves of private capital available for investment in profitable opportunities at home and abroad.

This need for a climate attractive to foreign capital is brought out by Mr. Blankenheimer when he states that "if it is American capital that is desired, it needs to be more generally recognized by African countries that investment opportunities in Africa must compete on favorable terms not only with the investment opportunities in other undeveloped areas but in the United States as well."

When the United States was a comparatively young country, expanding westward with its rail lines and its industries, it was materially aided by investments of foreign private capital. Forty years ago, at the beginning of World War I, foreign portfolio investments in United States securities amounted to $5.4 billion of which nearly $3.8 billion was in railroad stocks and bonds.

American portfolio investment is limited to the financing of certain African enterprises, in whole or in part, by a few American banking houses and fewer American individual investors, and to those Americans who purchase stocks in African companies available on our stock exchanges or in over-the-counter dealings. The number of these stocks available in the United States to the American investor can be counted on the fingers of one hand. Yet the Johannesburg Stock Exchange is an active market for the stocks of a great number of African industries, and the London Stock Exchange is an active market for a great number of African stocks, collectively known as "Kaffirs." It would seem reasonable to believe that American private capital might find its way into African enterprises if the stocks of these enterprises were listed on American stock exchanges so that they might be readily purchased for American portfolios.

Although there is little American portfolio investment in Africa, and American direct investment in African private enterprise is relatively small, direct investment is increasing. Between 1949 and 1952, private investment in Liberia increased from $47 million to $140 million; in South Africa, from $105 million to $194 million; and in the rest of Africa, excluding Egypt, from $79 million to $124 million. These private investments are primarily direct investments by American companies in such enterprises as distributive facilities for petroleum products, an oil refinery, a rubber plantation, a cocoa plantation, automobile assembly plants, tire factories, a sawmill and plywood factory, a hosiery-making factory, a coast-wise shipping service, a hotel, and a cold-storage warehouse. A number of American companies have branch offices with resident American representatives in Africa. One American shipping company, for example, has branch offices at Cape Town, Johannesburg, Nairobi, Monrovia, and Takoradi with fourteen resident representatives and their local staffs.

The foregoing list of American activities shows that there is variety in interest, but, as pointed out earlier, American investment in African private enterprise is small in relation to the needs of emergent Africa and to the financially attractive opportunities awaiting recognition. Governments can—and sometimes must—undertake projects that require the outlay of a large amount of capital. When it is necessary for government to do so, government acquires an interest-bearing debt in place of a tax-producing industry; and funds (or credit) are diverted from the building of schools, roads, and other nonprofit public works which only government will undertake.

To find American private investment funds for major projects and to convince African governments that their funds (or credit) might be required for the ordinary purposes of government will take a certain amount of imaginative thinking.

Datelined June 23, 1954, at Salisbury, Southern Rhodesia, a special article to the *New York Times* was headlined "Rhodesia-Nyasaland Federation seeks loans to develop power. $100 million needed to start two of world's largest hydro-electric plants." These two projects have been conceived as public works and will be constructed for and operated by "public authorities" with the necessary monies borrowed by the government of the Federation of Rhodesia and Nyasaland.

These two projects, the Kafue River Project and the Kariba Gorge Project, might be cited as examples of excellent opportunities for attracting—or, at least, attempting to attract—private capital so as to conserve the funds and the credit of a newly-formed African government. The basic elements necessary for an undertaking by private capital are present, viz., an ample supply of raw materials (water power) and an ample and expanding market for its product (electricity) . There is an urgent requirement for this electric power by the mines in the copper belt of Northern Rhodesia which are now in operation and by those mines which will come into production within the next few years. There is an equal need for electric power by the steel industry of Southern Rhodesia, as well as generally for the domestic and industrial requirements within the Federation. If these hydro-electric-power projects were undertaken by private capital, certain agreements would have to be reached with the government of the Federation outlining the obligations and guaranteeing the rights of all parties, including the rights of the consumers to electricity at a reasonable price. With our acceptance today of the regulatory policing and administrative powers of government, such agreements should impose no insuperable obstacle on the part of the interested parties. Would American companies singly or in groups—those companies whose business is engineering and construction in supplying the necessary equipment, in operating such utilities and distributing the electricity produced—be interested in investing in such an undertaking? Would American banking houses and the American public be interested if stock in such an undertaking were made available? The answers may be uncertain but, if determined, would be interesting. The private capital that might be invested need not be limited to sources in the United States but should include similar sources in the Federation of Rhodesia and Nyasaland, the Union of South Africa, and Great Britain.

If opportunities in African ventures, such as in these two new power projects or in established industry, are either unavailable or uninteresting to American private capital for portfolio investment, then we may expect a continuance of the present pattern of direct investment by American interests for the procurement of raw materials and for obtaining markets in Africa for the products of American industries.

six THE UNITED STATES AND AFRICA

the United States and Africa: an American view

PAUL H. NITZE

President, Foreign Service Educational Foundation;
Former Director, Policy Planning Staff,
Department of State

Most of the articles and commentaries in this book have been directed toward helping us to a better understanding of the complex and interrelated questions and challenges which contemporary Africa presents. Rarely have I participated in a series of discussions which have given me a greater sense of the deep seriousness and dynamic interaction of living cultural, political, and economic forces.

Any policy worth its salt must start from understanding. We in the United States must confess to only a dim and partial understanding of Africa, but I believe that understanding is growing and will continue to grow. A policy worth its salt, however, also implies choice and decision, perhaps tentative, perhaps subject to future modifications and amplifications, but nevertheless decision. And finally, it implies action. Action can consist in part in the use of words or even the non-use of words, but in general, more than mere words are required if policy is to be effective.

I take it that the central issue presenting a choice to the United States with respect to Africa is the issue of colonialism. Perhaps colonialism is the wrong word. Certainly the South African problem is not that of the relations of a metropolitan power to a dependent territory, nor does it involve any other external restraint upon the sovereignty of a nation. It is rather an internal problem of the

475

adjustment of cultural differences symbolized by race differences and the attendant problems of the internal allocation of political power and responsibility and of the direction of its interest. Even though this problem is internal in origin, it has implications and concerns for all of us to whom Africa is important.

Perhaps there is some more meaningful and precise word to describe the central issue presenting itself in Africa than colonialism. But whatever the word, the question is what alternatives present themselves to United States policy. One alternative would be to support holding fast to things as they now are in the dependencies of Africa. This would mean that we would encourage the metropolitan powers to "hold on the lid" in areas of their responsibility, which would signify our willingness to see the legitimate aspirations of both Moslem and tropical Africa sacrificed to a short-term interest in order and administrative coherence.

I do not need to dwell on the fact that such a course would be abhorrent to American sensibilities and would fly in the face of our traditional sympathy for the underdog and for the ideals of self-government and self-determination. But even if such an attitude were psychologically tolerable, we should certainly be compelled to examine its effects on the strategic interests of Africa and of the United States in Africa.

I need not cite examples of the fate which overtakes nations that misconstrue stagnation for stability. A repressive colonialism, even one tempered by fatherly benevolence, will only increase the force of the ultimate explosion and create the conditions of a nationalism fanatical and sterile in form. We have already seen too many examples of this type of development.

A second course would perhaps offer greater psychological satisfaction for the average American but would, I think, be equally fatal to the long-term interest of Africa. We would simply swim with the current and decide that, since there is no resisting the tide of nationalism, we may as well move with it without restraint and give it our full inspiration and support. If we would adopt such a course we might earn a short-term popularity among some of the inhabitants of the continent. We would, however, also be encouraging within the dependent areas divisive tendencies whose existence are today masked and controlled by the presence of the protecting and administering power. We should risk setting Berbers against Arabs, Bantus, Indians, and Europeans, one against another, and fanning the fires of dissension between Islam, Christianity, and tribal religions. We would also gravely endanger that solidarity of the Atlantic community, which is necessary to the defense of Africa against a new and more permanent colonialism from without.

The consequence would be weakness in all those things in which the United States would like to see Africa strong: weakness in protecting human rights; weakness in maintaining order; weakness in the bases from which social and economic justice can grow; weakness in safeguarding that external security within which independence can develop. The results of unthinking encouragement of extremism in Africa could be as harmful to the interest of Africa as the results of unthinking acquiescence to old-style colonialism.

The United States does not dispose with respect to Africa. Our relations with colonial Africa are in large measure through those European countries that do have responsibilities and commitments in the area. This is not to discount our relations with the dependent peoples nor our interest in their welfare and advancement. We have never had any colonial commitments in Africa and have no intention whatever of undertaking any. Nevertheless, the historic development of world forces has placed the U. S. in a position where it must, somewhat against its tradition and prior disposition, assume responsibilities or share the responsibilities formerly assumed by others. This is not an enviable position, for it requires of us, if we are to fulfill the role of protecting ourselves and the non-Soviet world generally, that we enlist and secure the co-operation of those who aspire to greater freedom while, at the same time, maintaining the co-operation of our European friends. On the practical side, it is quite clear that in conducting our day-to-day business with colonial Africa we must deal in the first instance with our European friends who now administer those areas.

Some are troubled by the fact that the United States today has two concurrent lines of interest. One springs from its anticolonial tradition; the other springs from its strategic interest in dependable bases and safe lines of communication necessary to the support of the strategic responsibilities it has been forced to assume. The fact that there are two lines of United States interest does put on us a far greater responsibility for careful and well-considered choice and action than was ours when we could follow sentiment alone. In large measure, however, the two lines converge toward a common line, a third course, which is neither the course of "keeping on the lid" nor the course of unthinking inspiration of conflict and revolt. This is the course of throwing our weight behind the acceleration of self-determination for all peoples, under conditions which will see preserved these precious freedoms once attained. As in most things in life really worthwhile, success in this course is not easy. It does not lend itself to catchy propaganda slogans easy for those whose policy seeks to destroy rather than to build. It does not seek to raise illusory hopes. It seeks instead to build, step by step, the solid foundations of independence coupled with that voluntary interdependence necessary to an association of viable self-governing states in a free world.

Fortunately, with few exceptions, this is the course being followed by our friends both in Europe and in Africa. If they are to succeed, they may need wise and sympathetic help from the United States. Perhaps together new ways can be found, not simply to accelerate the process but also to achieve a broader common understanding of our mutual interest in seeing that this process develops along constructive lines. Everyone, including the Africans, would stand to suffer from an exacerbation of conflict.

Some argue that such a third course is tantamount to avoiding a decision one way or another. I do not believe this to be so. In relations between contending friends it is unseemly if not also unwise to take the initiative in seeking a solution, yet the very absence of an initiative combined with friendly counsel and an inconspicuous display of one's views may represent a decisive action of the highest importance. In this sense the third course, as I have called it, seems to me to have involved already decisions of great consequence in the cases of Iran and Egypt.

Some have argued that the British-Egyptian agreement with respect to Suez was a debacle. I can remember only too clearly the brick-bats that were hurled at us for urging restraint in contemplating the use of force in Iran and for arguing instead for patient negotiation. Just as the Iranian settlement now gives hope for a return to progress and the patient steps of cumulative economic and political development, so the Suez agreement may well be the foundation on which the mutual interests of one of the countries of Africa and of the West can be developed.

I am not suggesting that the United States has been all wise in its judgments on the crucial issues of the relations of one nation to another or of one group to another within nations. As has been brought out in this book, there are deep philosophical problems, as well as practical and theoretical issues, on which we may have much to learn from Africa as well as to give. In large measure, it is this willingness both to give and to learn which sustains our hope and our confidence.

the United States and Africa: an African view

KOFI A. BUSIA

University College of the Gold Coast

The increasing interest which the United States is taking in our continent fills us with hope for the future. As Mr. Nitze has said, the essays and commentaries in this book have revealed how extremely complex are the problems which face us in Africa today. Even the most optimistic may well ask if we have any reasonable cause for hope.

I think we have cause for hope. My confidence is based on the belief that the potentiality of Africa, which will ultimately shape her future, does not lie in her material resources but in the unpredictable mystery of her human resources. This unpredictable but determining factor of man himself is often ignored in our analyses.

There have been two strands in man's quest for knowledge and truth. The first was predominant in the heyday of Greece; and for a long time after was the quest for the understanding of man himself: his nature; his society; his goals; and the meaning of his earthly existence. The second strand is the one with which Europe and America have been largely preoccupied for the last two hundred years or so: the search for the understanding and conquest of nature.

In my view, there are two challenges that face mankind in the twentieth century. There is the challenge presented by the atom bomb, the latest symbol of man's ever-widening conquest of nature, which nevertheless threatens mankind with annihilation.

The second challenge of the twentieth century derives from the

480

quest for the understanding of man himself. That challenge does not offer the possibility of annihilation but of survival. The discovery made from the long and arduous quest along tortuous paths of learning for the understanding of the nature of man and society does not appear to be startling or revolutionary. It is merely the apparently commonplace discovery that mankind is one species and that we all share a common humanity; or as John Masefield would put it: We are "Brothers akin . . . /Guesting awhile in the rooms of a beautiful inn."

Commonplace as this may seem, it does really present the nobler challenge of our time. We are apt to divide men into primitive and civilized, superior and inferior, and so find justification for injustice, or selfish greed, or the exercise of power, or benevolent paternalism. But the stark fact is that the earth is inhabited by man. There is no primitive man or civilized man. Some men live in primitive conditions and others in civilized conditions, but there is only one species of man on the earth.

I think this both important and relevant to the problems discussed in this book. The conditions of life in Africa are harsh and primitive; but the inhabitants of Africa have the intelligence, the spirit, and the capabilities of contemporary man. Therein lies our ground for optimism.

Why must America take an interest in Africa? Various good reasons have been given: self-preservation; the interest of peace; to secure strategic bases; the interchange of goods and services; to secure Africa against Communism; to help raise the standards of living of the African. Laudable as these reasons are, they stem from either a negative or materialistic approach to the problem.

I think international questions might be approached by focussing much greater attention on man himself than on the conditions of his life. I would plead with you in America and Europe to help us in Africa first of all by expressing your faith in us as belonging like yourselves to the "old proud pageant of man." Show by your actions toward us, whether in the New World or the Old, that you accept and believe in the fact that we all share a common humanity. We in Africa can and will respond to the outstretched hand, our hearts can beat in tune to the warmth of friendship, our hands can turn to new skills, our minds are open to new ideas. This human approach does indeed involve practical tasks; but they will be rightly directed toward the achievement of a true and positive goal.

I believe that the positive goal we must aim at is the creation of a world community of free men, bound by ties of friendship and mutual respect, united by fundamental agreement in the democratic way of life, and by faith in the equality and dignity of man, freely co-operating for the enrichment of human life by the unhindered interchange of our diverse gifts.

To aid in this common purpose we in Africa offer our richest potential—the unpredictable mystery of our manhood and womanhood.

> Full many a gem of purest ray serene,
> The dark unfathom'd caves of ocean bear,
> Full many a flower is born to blush unseen,
> And waste its sweetness on the desert air.

We ask you to help us through the communication of ideas and skills and the interchange of goods and services, on the basis of our common humanity, to develop our human potential; we shall then together solve not only the problems of Africa; but also, through the links of friendship—indeed of brotherhood—that we shall thus forge, we may discover a new way of creating a world society in which Homo Sapiens may live a richer, fuller life, free from war and from the haunting fear of annihilation.

We in Africa contemplate the future with hope, because we believe mankind will rise to the challenge of our time by recognizing our common humanity and by shouldering the responsibilities that that recognition entails. We are happy to have evidence that America— this great nation that has won for herself the leadership of the world—intends to play a leading role in this the heroic adventure of building a world community of free men freely associated for the realization of man's highest aspirations.

appendix   **MAU MAU**

Mau Mau

*The following appendix is an abridgment of a
lengthy press conference held with
Sir Philip Mitchell, former Governor of Kenya,
on the subject of Mau Mau.*

Probably the underlying grievance of the Kikuyu people toward the European in Kenya stems from the tremendous propaganda among the Kikuyu themselves to the effect that the Europeans have stolen their land. The facts are that, of 6,000 square miles which are now recognized as, and which were in the past, Kikuyu tribal land in the very early days of settlement (around 1906), about 106¾ square miles were inadvertently allotted to new settlers—land which did, in fact, belong to one particular family group of Kikuyu, the group of the old chief called Koinangi.

When this was discovered, as a result of the appointment of the Carter Land Commission to inquire into the land question after many years of protest and agitation by the Kikuyu, restitution was made in money and by the addition of more land—not only 106¾ square miles but a substantially larger area, although much inferior land.

For the Kikuyu, like many other African tribes, the only cure for the shortage of land is to fell more forests, as had been the case with the early settlers in the United States.

But there comes a time, of course, when anywhere in the world you reach the end of available forests to fell. There came a time—it came twenty years ago—when the Kikuyu began to find it difficult to find new forests to fell, because above them farther up the mountains, in their own interests and in the interests of the colony as a whole, the forests had been protected for conservation; and lower

485

down the slopes they ran into the fences of the settlers' property. They naturally came to the conclusion that they were being prevented from clearing more land by the Europeans, and from that it is a very short jump for them to believe and to say that the Europeans have stolen their land.

Actually, the Kikuyu were not the first occupants of the land. In the country, in the forests, there were people called the Ndorobo, who were primitive bush-dwellers, very small in number. The Kikuyu themselves say, in petitions to the Governor of Kenya, for example, "my grandfather bought this land from Ndorobo so-and-so for seven goats and so many pots of beer." Around 1909, the Kikuyu scarcely extended further south, along the east side of the Aberdare Mountains, than the Maragua River, which was the southern and southwestern boundary, from the forest reserve down into the plains. The Kikuyu were on the north side of that and on Mount Kenya but were already infiltrating farther south and west and were numerous in an area called Dagoretti, west of Nairobi. When they were in the Fort Hall region, many of them, including Koinangi's family, penetrated across the river and made contacts with the Ndorobo whom they met, "buying" the land in the sense that they bought the right to cultivate the land. There was no conception of conveyancing in the European sense of buying the land and acquiring absolute ownership.

In 1899–1900 the British government, with coolie labor from India, built a railroad from Mombasa to Lake Victoria in an attempt to break up the slave-trade at its source on the Great Lakes. At that time the British found the land in the highlands of Kenya virtually uninhabited, so settlement was encouraged on the part of the Europeans in order to utilize the land and help the railroad, so as to make it pay for itself. Actually the country was not as empty as the British then thought. There were more people than, in fact, anybody imagined—although even so not in great numbers. Many tribes had been compelled to hide in these forests because of the fierce Masai, who slaughtered them if they found them outside. However, this is another story, which does not bear on the Kikuyu land-claims, which, as you can see, are tenuous when advanced on behalf of the tribe as a whole.

Nevertheless, to the Kikuyu, who have virtually no written history, these land-claims seem justified, especially when the people are agitated and propagandized by a shrewd leader such as Jomo Kenyatta.

It is a rather curious and almost sardonic commentary on the Kikuyu problem that around 1910 a district commissioner in Kenya wrote a book called *The Vanishing Tribes of Kenya*. Actually, the major problem that Kenya now has is the fantastic fertility of the tribes, who are multiplying out of all proportions. Before European settlement and the building of the Uganda railroad, indeed, even as late as 1912, when I first came out as a very young man to Nyasaland, the tribes had always been thinned out by famines, plagues, and intertribal wars. But when transportation stopped famine, and when medicine stopped plagues, and when the colonial governments stopped intertribal wars, the population grew with unimaginable acceleration. It was inevitable, then, that the available land would not support the people, and they would feel that they must look for more land—hence these tenuous claims were fabricated, based, as a matter of fact, only on the injustice I mentioned previously of misappropriating 106¾ square miles.

There is no doubt that, after the Second World War, tribal unrest was blowing up, stimulated by war and the large numbers of returned soldiers—Kikuyu who went abroad mostly as drivers and clerks, what you might call the skilled labor part of the army. They came back from the Middle East, Burma, and all over the world with pockets full of money and nothing very obviously appropriate to do. It is important to realize that the Kikuyu had prospered as practically no tribe had prospered, I should think, in the history of Africa, except perhaps in the Gold Coast. They are transportation contractors and own buses and trucks; they own real property in Nairobi; they own shops and eating houses; they are in the civil service as medical officers, police inspectors, clerks, and a host of other things. In terms of wealth in Africa they are prosperous.

In this muddled postwar situation there appeared this extraordinary personality, Jomo Kenyatta, who had left Africa in the twenties as a largely self-appointed emissary to lay the grievances of the Kikuyu before the Secretary of State and Parliament, in England. He got, from his point of view, very little satisfaction in that. I think it probable that a wiser approach to the problem then, on the part of the British government at home and the colonial government, in Kenya, might have turned Kenyatta into different ways. When I first met him, in Geneva in 1931 at the League of Nations, and every time I have met him since, I have felt the force of this extraordinary personality. He is a big, burly, bearded man, and he has the most piercing eyes I have ever seen in any man.

Well, he came back, having achieved nothing very much in his particular mission, although he had remained away from Kenya from about 1922. In London he had got in touch with the intellectual left wing, and from there he drifted to Moscow, where he spent considerable time and was, I suppose, thoroughly indoctrinated by the then Bolshevik government, and I think taught a great deal of revolutionary technique.

At some stage he became deeply impressed with Ghandi. I have talked to him about it, and I have little doubt, myself, that Kenyatta's objective for what we now know as the conspiracy he was organizing—the Mau Mau—was a nonviolent Ghandi-like refusal of all participation in the economic life of Kenya and co-operation with the Europeans. I believe—I cannot prove it from evidence—that his conception was that, at a given date when he was ready, he would, so to speak, blow the whistle, and every black man from Mombasa to Lake Victoria would stop working for Europeans.

Kenyatta and his close associates are now serving long prison sentences for complicity in organizing and managing Mau Mau, having unsuccessfully appealed to the Court of Appeals for East Africa and to the Judicial Committee of the Privy Council in London. It has been announced by the Governor that they will never be permitted to return to the Kikuyu districts but will be required to live in a remote part of the northern frontier.

Kenyatta himself is a type of the fanatical revolutionary, animated, I believe, by a lust for personal power and the gratification of his physical appetites more than anything else. Such people invariably hold themselves out as patriots, idealists, liberators; and the world today is sadly familiar with them. All ordinary restraint, all sense of proportion and of pity are soon corroded by the evil will to have and use power. I have said that I believe that Kenyatta's immediate objective was nonviolent, but I have no doubt that that was not because he had any abhorrence of violence but simply because he thought it might pay best, until he had seized despotic power over all Africans in Kenya if possible, but if not, at least over the Kikuyu. He was certainly sufficiently intelligent to realize that his plans must bring ruin to thousands of prosperous Kikuyu, but I doubt if that caused him the slightest remorse.

How he established the extraordinary hold he had over the Kikuyu while absent in Europe is one of those mysteries of the human mind and spirit for which no satisfactory explanation has been given. How did a man like Hitler get power? It is simple enough, by his methods or Kenyatta's, to keep it: but how is it got at first over masses of people by whom the self-appointed Fuehrer is unknown and unseen? If you can answer that, you can answer the riddle of Lenin, Hitler, Kenyatta, and many others of their kind; I have not a clue.

However, his plan did not work out the way he thought it would. The first obstacle he came across was that the other tribes would have nothing to do with him. The Kikuyu are, as a rule, cordially detested by nearly all the other tribes in Kenya. They often settle in little groups in other tribal territories, and they always repudiate the local tribal authority and refuse to obey it. A governor of Kenya on tour may go, say, to the west of the colony, to the Kisii district, and he will at once receive a petition from the local Kisii chiefs to remove the Kikuyu from their country. On the other hand, the Kikuyu have, in the course of fifty years of the colony's life, shown themselves not only incomparably the most able and enterprising but also the most efficient people. Whether it is as laborers on European farms, or in their own businesses, they are the most efficient people.

Well, this unrest I mentioned was blowing up after the war, and there is no doubt that Kenyatta was aware of it and that he intended to make use of it for his own purposes—he and a few associates. I personally doubt that he had intentions of creating violence, anyhow at first; and I say that with all the more conviction because, in fact, when he was arrested with his five immediate associates on October 22, 1952 (and almost immediately afterwards), his second-rate followers took to violent steps with what I could only call extraordinary incompetence; there was no general massacre.

It is generally accepted for fact in many countries, including perhaps the United States, that the Mau Mau is an anti-European uprising, which brings me to the main point of the thing. If they had intended an anti-European rising and the slaughter of Europeans, well, they could have killed five hundred or two thousand or more of them on the first night.

In the autumn of 1952, in England, I was shown a newspaper which had banner headlines across the front page: NIGHT OF LONG KNIVES IN KENYA. I got a shock and thought there had been a general massacre, but, in fact, one man had been killed; and that is how it has gone on all the time. The greatest massacre—the Lari massacre—that the Mau Mau perpetrated was not of Europeans at all. It was of the Kikuyu themselves. In the early days of 1953, because the then gang leaders—but this is speculation and not a known fact—were becoming alarmed that things seemed to be going flat, they conceived the lunatic idea of a massacre of their own people. It was organized with considerable skill and great secrecy. They fell upon an area called Lari, which is about twenty-five to thirty miles from Nairobi, and with the most frightful atrocities they massacred men, women, and children—Kikuyu men, women, and children—including an old retired chief and his family. On the final count there were close to a hundred dead bodies recovered, but so many houses were burnt that many bodies must simply have been incinerated with nothing left at all. And there were as many very grievously wounded as there were killed. Pregnant women were seized and sliced open and the foetus was dragged out of each woman and bitten and eaten by some of the people. Many of the atrocities are simply too horrible to go into here, but they were much worse than this.

About this time, also, another Mau Mau gang broke into a European farm, mutilated and hamstrung the cattle, and left them to die a lingering death. In other words, the object was not to kill beef and eat it but to inflict suffering. The object apparently was not even to inflict loss on the European; it is difficult to say really what their object was. It all fits into a pattern of a people who have gone maniac.

When you consider some of the Mau Mau oaths, you can see that this movement is an advanced form of group insanity. Here I should explain the importance of oaths to the Kikuyu. The ordinary way of settling a serious dispute between two Kikuyu people is for the accuser to call upon the defendant to take an oath. The oath has to be taken voluntarily; it has to be taken publicly and in daylight; and it has to be taken in the presence of reputable witnesses, with the consent of the family. It is seated deeply in the customs of the tribe, and the belief is that the one who breaks an oath may be killed by that oath. For example, the first oath in the Mau Mau, when the movement was not yet violent, reads as follows:

    (a) If ever I reveal the secrets of this organisation, may this oath kill me.
    (b) If ever I sell or dispose of any Kikuyu land to a foreigner, may this oath kill me.
    (c) If ever I fail to follow our great leader, Kenyatta, may this oath kill me.
    (d) If ever I inform against any member of this organisation or against any member who steals from the European, may this oath kill me.
    (e) If ever I fail to pay the fees of this organisation, may this oath kill me.

Almost any political underground organization anywhere in the world might have an oath similar to this. But the Mau Mau take a succession of oaths, each more horribly obscene than the last. After one particularly revolting and sickening ritual, the oath administrator gives to the inductee the following commandments:

> You are eating the Batuni Oath.
> This is a man's oath.
> You are to destroy everything.
> You will be sent to do anything we wish you to do by day or night, at any time or in any weather.
> If you are told to get a man's head or steal cattle, or any other thing, you will obey.
> When you have killed a man you will eat his flesh, you cannot refuse.
> If your Father, Mother, Brother or Sister refuses the Mau Mau in any way, you will kill them.
> You will obey all Batuni orders.

It is the degradation of human beings until they have reached a stage of having neither will nor resistance nor sense of decency. It is the Black Mass all over again. This is partly the result of the method used in administering oaths. The fee for having an oath administered used to be fifty shillings, and originally the people who took these oaths must have been very carefully selected individuals who wanted to join the movement. But after Kenyatta had been arrested, it became more and more the practice simply to round up gangs of terrorized peasantry and administer compulsorily the oath to them; and, therefore, oath administrators sprang up all over the place, for much the same reason that mock preachers often spring up during an evangelical movement, for the sake of the offertory. In addition to that, the movement attracted an increasing number of the underworld from towns like Nairobi. It soon became a racket for the forcible administration of the oath to Kikuyu at fifty shillings.

Soon the gangs began to break into warehouses and steal property and trucks to carry it away in, sometimes murdering Kikuyu who resisted. Also as a means of terror, they would murder Kikuyu who were Christian ministers, teachers, government servants, or tribal chiefs who in any way opposed their methods.

There has never been any perceptible pattern in this movement which would enable you to say that this, that, or the other objective was the main purpose. There was no attempt to disorganize the railways, although the main line and two branches run through the heart of the disturbed districts. Except for a very occasional piece of iron on the line, there has been nothing resembling sabotage. They derailed a couple of trains in two years by sticking stones on the line.

The whole of the water supply of Nairobi is derived from two big dams in the Kikuyu district. The pipes run right through the heart of the Kikuyu district, yet no attempt has been made to break the pipes or pollute the water. We know they have had high explosives, because sticks of dynamite have on occasion been thrown at policemen. They have never cut the telegraph or telephone wires, except when raiding some particular house or store, nor have they ever seriously interfered with the suburban population of Nairobi, which stretches about twenty miles out into the country and commutes daily to and from its places of business.

The confession of one of these men—and confessions are getting more and more frequent today—goes like this:

> Our gang was staying in the forest near the Fort Hall reserve, we lived in a kraal, we had one shotgun, one pistol, simis (short swords), and pangas (cutlasses). These weapons were seized by the government.
> We murdered six men during the night with simis and pangas. Each of the victims was murdered in his own hut.
> We used to send one of our gang who knew the man, to get him to open his hut. We murdered him, put his body inside the hut, and set it alight.

The victims cry out when they are killed, but their neighbors cannot come to their rescue because they are Mau Mau.

Mwangi s/o Minua, Kiiru s/o Karienye, and myself murdered Gathua s/o Kariru. We put his blood in a tin, it was about half a gallon. We drank some of his blood, then dug a hole and poured the rest into it.

We took with us goats from his house. We did not use the gun as we were afraid of being heard. We slaughtered the six goats and then hid them in thick bush in the Reserve.

During the months of May and June we wandered about in the Reserve, hiding in the bush.

It is impossible to relate this kind of action to any political motive, to any rebellion, to any "liberation movement," or to any of the catch phrases of our day.

The Lari massacre, which I described above, was the decisive moment, because it disgusted, infuriated, and horrified the Kikuyu themselves, so that the resistance movement, which had been confined previously to small numbers of devoted and courageous people, rapidly began to gain strength until today the fight against Mau Mau is conducted, in the main, in the Kikuyu districts by the Kikuyu Home Guard, which is between 25,000 and 30,000 strong and growing rapidly. The astonishing thing is the way the Kikuyu Christians, with extraordinary courage—not only the clergy and the schoolteachers, but just ordinary men and women living in their houses—have resisted Mau Mau with the faith of martyrs. It is this Christian attitude, in my opinion, which will kill the Mau Mau; it is this faith that has already broken it, in fact.

There are certainly social ills, grievances, and hardships, and to ensure that they are understood and, as far as possible, remedied so that this sort of thing may have no encouragement to break out here again or in any other place in British East Africa, a Royal Commission has been appointed to look into the social conditions and economic problems of these peoples. No doubt the problem of replacing the shocking slums and the housing situation in general will be one of the major investigations that this commission will conduct. This should be of great value, given a steady spread of education and the development of a strong, I hope, Christian, local African civilization.

INDEX

index

Date Due

MAY 9 '58	JAN 27		
JAN 2 3 '59			
MAR 2 0 '59			
APR 1 0 '59			
MAY 8 '59			
MAY 1 5 '59			
AUG 2 6 '59			
MAY 2 7 '60			
OCT 2 9 '60			
DEC 2 '60			
APR 2 8 '61			
MAY 2 6 '61			
NOV 16 '62			
FEB 20 '67			
DEC 8 1972			
ⓖ	PRINTED	IN U. S. A.	